Retrofitting Cities

Developing an up-to-date critical framework for analysing urban retrofit, this is the first book to examine urban re-engineering for sustainability in a socio-technical context. *Retrofitting Cities* examines why retrofit is emerging as an important strategic issue for urban authorities and untangles the mix of economic, competitive, ecological and social drivers that influence any transition towards a more sustainable urban environment.

Retrofitting Cities comparatively explores how urban scale retrofitting can be conceptualised as a socio-technical transition; how to critically compare and contrast different national styles of response in cities of the north and global south; and, how to develop new research and policy agendas on future development of progressive retrofitting. Bringing together a group of researchers from a variety of disciplinary backgrounds that reflect the complexity of the research challenge, *Retrofitting Cities* looks across different infrastructures and types of built environment, dealing with diverse urban contexts and examining formal as well as community responses. This is a uniquely practical book for urban planning and policy professionals as well as for researchers in urban studies and urban design.

Mike Hodson joined Manchester University as Research Fellow in April 2014. He is based jointly in the Sustainable Consumption Institute (SCI) and the Manchester Institute of Innovation Research (MIoIR), and he primarily works on a comparative EU Framework 7 project, PATHWAYS assessing transition pathways across electricity, mobility, land-use and agro-food sectors, comparatively across national contexts. Mike was previously Senior Research Fellow at Salford University, where he spent a decade in the Centre for Sustainable Urban and Regional Futures (SURF) working in the area of urban and regional governance and transitions. He has published and presented widely on this research agenda. His developing research interests are at the interface of systemic transitions and territorial transitions.

Simon Marvin is a Professor and Director of the Urban Institute at the University of Sheffield. His research interests focus on the changing relations between cities and infrastructure networks. To date, he has played major roles within urban research towards addressing important questions surrounding telecommunications, infrastructure and mobility, sustainability, smart meters, interdisciplinary urban research, and, most recently, cities, systemic transitions, climate change, ecological security and smart cities.

Retrofitting Cities

Priorities, governance and experimentation

Edited by Mike Hodson and Simon Marvin

LONDON AND NEW YORK

First published 2016
by Routledge
2 Park Square, Milton Park, Abingdon, Oxon OX14 4RN

and by Routledge
711 Third Avenue, New York, NY 10017

Routledge is an imprint of the Taylor & Francis Group, an informa business

British Library Cataloguing-in-Publication Data

A catalogue record for this book is available from the British Library

Library of Congress Cataloging-in-Publication Data
Retrofitting cities : priorities, governance and experimentation /
edited by Mike Hodson and Simon Marvin.
pages cm
ISBN 978-1-138-77587-9 (hardback) -- ISBN 978-1-138-77588-6 (pbk.)
-- ISBN 978-1-315-67823-8 (ebook) 1. City planning--Environmental
aspects. 2. Sustainable urban development. 3. Urban policy. 4. Regional
planning--Environmental aspects. I. Hodson, Mike, editor. II. Marvin, Simon,
1963- editor.
HT166.R445 2016
307.1'216--dc23
2015024478

ISBN: 978-1-138-77587-9 (hbk)
ISBN: 978-1-138-77588-6 (pbk)
ISBN: 978-1-315-67823-8 (ebk)

Typeset in Sabon
by Fish Books Ltd.

Printed and bound by CPI Group (UK) Ltd, Croydon, CR0 4YY

Contents

Figures

Tables

Acknowledgements

Re-making the built environment, infrastructure systems and material flows at the level of the city is a key challenge of our time. Yet, there are many ways of re-making the city in what is a deeply political struggle. From the challenges posed by climate change and energy security, struggles about what shape economic activity in cities should take and the politics and governing of who decides. This book engages with the diversity of retrofitting responses.

The book is structured to illustrate a range of responses. It organizes these in terms of the ways in which the retrofit problem is understood, the organization of governing responses and the very tangible ways in which retrofitting is demonstrated and experimented with. This acknowledges the city as a site of retrofitting activity. It also recognizes the diverse social, technological, political and citizen interests involved in retrofitting and the variety of ways in which they come together, how this takes place and emergent effects of these processes.

The book contains chapters from both established and early career researchers. They contribute to a collection which addresses retrofit as a socio-technical problem, that is organized as both top-down and bottom-up responses and which are illustrated through developments in the global north and south. We would like to thank all these researchers for their contributions and for the spirit in which this has been undertaken.

The book is the culmination of a process that began with early versions of these chapters being presented at an International Comparative Urban Retrofit workshop held in Salford in September 2012. We would like to express our thanks to the UK EPSRC-funded Retrofit 2050 project, the Mistra Urban Futures Greater Manchester Local Interaction Platform and the UK ESRC Sustainable Practices Research Group for their support of the workshop.

We are also grateful for the support of colleagues in the Sustainable Consumption Institute and the Manchester Institute of Innovation Research at the University of Manchester and the Department of Geography at Durham University.

Manchester and Durham, October 2015

Contributors

Mike Hodson joined Manchester University as Research Fellow in April 2014. He is based jointly in the Sustainable Consumption Institute (SCI) and the Manchester Institute of Innovation Research (MIoIR), and he primarily works on a comparative EU Framework 7 project, PATHWAYS assessing transition pathways across electricity, mobility, land-use and agro-food sectors, comparatively across national contexts. Mike was previously Senior Research Fellow at Salford University, where he spent a decade in the Centre for Sustainable Urban and Regional Futures (SURF) working in the area of urban and regional governance and transitions. He has published and presented widely on this research agenda. His developing research interests are at the interface of systemic transitions and territorial transitions.

Simon Marvin is a Professor and Director of the Urban Institute at the University of Sheffield. His research interests focus on the changing relations between cities and infrastructure networks. To date, he has played major roles within urban research towards addressing important questions surrounding telecommunications, infrastructure and mobility, sustainability, smart meters, interdisciplinary urban research and, most recently, cities, systemic transitions, climate change, ecological security and smart cities.

Michele Acuto is currently Research Director and Senior Lecturer in Global Networks and Diplomacy at STEaPP, UCL. Michele is also a Fellow of the Institute for Science, Innovation and Society (InSIS) at the University of Oxford. He is currently principal investigator for the ESRC project Urban Connections and the Director of City Leadership Initiative, which aim at engaging urban practitioners and at assessing the role of city leadership and city strategies in responding to global challenges. Michele's research also focuses on the role of STS thinking in international relations and on the changing landscapes of diplomacy. Michele is the author of *The Urban Link* (Routledge), editor of

Negotiating Relief (Hurst), co-editor of *Global City Challenges* (with Wendy Steele) and *Reassembling International Theory* (with Simon Curtis) and of the series *Cities and the Global Politics of the Environment* (with Sofie Bouteligier) all for Palgrave Macmillan.

Bipasha Baruah is an Associate Professor, Department of Women's Studies and Feminist Research, Western University. Bipasha's research identifies the social, economic, legal, cultural, political and institutional factors that influence women's ability to own property; and develops theories, methodologies and analytical frameworks for conducting interdisciplinary research on gender and property ownership. She also conducts research on women's participation in the green economy and explores the opportunities and constraints that low-income women face in securing equitable, healthy and decent jobs and entrepreneurial opportunities in low-carbon economies focused on renewable energy and resource efficiency in different world regional contexts. Findings from Bipasha's research enables governments, non-governmental organizations (NGOs) and other stakeholders to formulate appropriate policy responses to women's needs for land, housing and sustainable livelihoods.

Emily Boyd was appointed Professor in Resilience Geography at Reading University in 2013 specializing in climate change, development and resilience. Emily is currently a Steering Board member of the Governmental Strategic Research Programme at Stockholm University Ekoklim and Resilience Programme Leader at the Centre for Food Security (CFS). She is on the Editorial board of Climate Risk Management and Editorial Associate for the *Journal of Ecology and Society*. She has been a reviewer for *The Intergovernmental Panel on Climate Change* (IPCC) FAR WGII and Guest Editor for *Antipode, Geographical Journal and Development Policy Review*. She is a senior Research Associate of the Stockholm Resilience Centre and an Associate of the Walker Institute for Climate Systems Research.

Halina Szejnwald Brown is a Professor of Environmental Science and Policy as well as the Programme Director of the Environmental Science Undergraduate Major Department of Environmental Science and Policy Department of International Development, Community and Environment, Clark University, Worcester. During the past several years, Halina has concentrated on research in three areas. The first area concerns the role of small scale experiments as the means for affecting a transition to more sustainable large scale socio-technical systems. Her primary focus has been on the built environment, which she views as a complex socio-technical system. The second research area concerns the process of institutionalization of voluntary reporting on environmental and social performance as an instrument for holding corporations accountable to society. The third research area concerns sustainable consumption.

Harriet Bulkeley is a Professor in the Department of Geography, Durham University. Her research focuses on the processes and politics of environmental governance. Her recent books include *Cities and Climate Change* (Routledge 2013), *Governing Climate Change* (Routledge 2010), Cities and *Low Carbon Transitions* (ed. Routledge, 2011), *Governing the Climate: new approaches to rationality, power and politics* (ed. CUP 2014) *Transnational Climate Governance* (CUP, 2014), and *An Urban Politics of Climate Change* (Routledge 2014). She is currently involved in researching the politics and practice of smart grids in the UK, low carbon transitions in southern Africa, and continuing work on urban responses to climate change through the JPI Urban and ESRC project Governing Urban Sustainability Transitions (GUST 2014–2017). Harriet has undertaken commissioned research for the Joseph Rowntree Foundation, Friends of the Earth, UN-Habitat and the World Bank. In 2014, she was awarded the King Carl XVI Gustaf's Professorship in Environmental Science and a Visiting Professorship at Lund University, Sweden.

Vanesa Castán Broto joined the Bartlett Development Planning Unit in January 2011, with the aim to contribute to achieve socially and environmentally just development in cities in the global south. Vanessa contributes to this objective through doing research relevant to planning on topics such as: the dynamics of social learning following infrastructure crises and natural disasters; participatory methodologies for the implementation of mitigation and adaptation strategies in cities in developing countries; and the political consequences of urban innovation for climate change. Vanessa believes that achieving social and environmental justice depends on engaging with multi-dimensional and complex issues. Vanesa has an interdisciplinary background in natural resources engineering and environmental sociology, having completed postgraduate degrees in Spain (Universidad Politécnica de Madrid) and the Netherlands (Wageningen University) and an engineering doctorate in the UK (University of Surrey). Prior to joining the DPU, she was involved in post-doctoral research at Durham University which examined the processes of social and technological innovation within the city in response to climate change.

Tony Dalton is a Professor in the RMIT Australian Housing and Urban Research Institute Research Centre. He contributes to the program of urban housing research in this research centre and teaches in the areas of research strategies and urban studies. The focus of Tony's research has been on changing housing markets, distributional outcomes in a period of social and economic restructuring. More recently he has developed a research interest in the issues that climate change poses for urban housing provision. This has led to research projects focusing on reinvestment in housing through renovation and the housing industry. Throughout his research, he has maintained a focus on the institutional context for the making of housing policy. His research interests are connected to his long involvement in non-government sector policy work and advocacy through Shelter, ACOSS, Hanover Welfare and Housing Justice Roundtable.

Carla De Laurentis is currently completing an EPSRC doctorate study. She has worked as a researcher for Cardiff University since 2002. Since joining the Welsh School of Architecture in April 2011, she has worked on the EPSRC project Re-Engineering the City 2020–2050 Urban Foresight and Transition Management, investigating sustainability transitions at city-region level. During her research career she has gained extensive knowledge and expertise in innovation, local and regional development and clustering dynamics in high technology sectors (particularly renewable energy, ICT and new media). Her current research interests lie within the study of innovation, energy policy, renewable energy and sustainability transitions. She has contributed to a number of publications exploring the role of regions in the dynamics of innovation and transformation of the energy sector towards sustainability.

Robyn Dowling's research research focuses on the governance and patterns of everyday life in cities, especially suburbs. In collaboration with Pauline McGuirk (University of Newcastle) and Harriet Bulkeley (Durham University) an ARC-funded project investigating how carbon is being managed in Australia's cities. It focuses on the roles and partnerships of government, private sector, non-profit agencies and activist groups in reducing Australian's reliance on carbon. Her current research explores technologically and socially disruptive forms of mobility as well as transitions to low carbon futures in commercial spaces.

Jonathon Ensor is currently at the Stockholm Environment Institute, York. He is a Social Scientist with research interests in participatory and 'bottom-up' development processes. As a Development Practitioner (with the NGO Practical Action, up to 2012) his work centered on research for programme and policy influencing in relation to community-based adaptation and food and agriculture. Recently, his focus has been on the potential of participatory planning and social learning processes in adaptation and as a means of accounting for power and social justice in resilience thinking and adaptive governance. His work is informed by an interest in human rights-based and social movement framings of development.

James Evans is a Professor in Human Geography in the School of Environment, Education and Development at the University of Manchester. He has an abiding interest in the role science plays in transforming urban space, particularly the ways in which environmental knowledge is produced and used in decision-making. He is currently leading projects exploring these issues in relation to smart sustainable cities and living laboratories and is a Formas Visiting Researcher at the International Institute of Industrial and Environmental Economics at the University of Lund, Sweden.

Ralph Horne is the Deputy PVC, Research and Innovation for the College of Design and Social Context at RMIT University. Ralph is interested in social and policy change for environmentally sustainable design and development, has extensive experience of environmental techniques and sustainability appraisal, and has a specific research interest in relations between housing quality and benefits for households. He combines research leadership and participation in research projects concerning the environmental, social and policy context of production and consumption in the urban environment.

Sirkku Juhola is an Assistant Professor in urban environmental policy at the Department of Environmental Sciences, University of Helsinki. She is also a Visiting Scholar at the Department of Real Estate, Planning and Geoinformatics at Aalto University and an Adjunct Professor of Social and Public Policy at the University of Jyväskylä. Sirkku is the Deputy Chief Scientist of the Nordic Centre for Excellence on Nordic Strategic Adaptation (NORD-STAR) and a Member of Finland's Climate Panel that was set up in 2011 to advice the Finnish Government on climate policy. Sirkku's current projects focus on environmental issues in cities

Andrés Luque-Ayala is a Lecturer in the Department of Geography, at Durham University (UK). His research focuses on the socio-political dimensions of emerging infrastructural configurations and narratives in cities in the global South. As part of this, his work critically examines the emergence of a local governance of energy and the interface between urban digital technologies, ecological security and development modes.

Pauline McGuirk is the Professor of Human Geography and Director of the Centre for Urban and Regional Studies at the University of Newcastle, NSW. She is an urban political geographer whose recent work focuses on two key themes. First is the role of urban-based actors in the governance of carbon and energy transition. This research (with Robyn Dowling (Macquarie University) and Harriet Bulkeley (Durham University)) explores the evolution of the urban governance of carbon in Australian cities, across an array of state and non-state actors, and teases out its modes and political implications. We understand the city in this work as a key strategic arena in the response to climate change and a critical site in the politics of climate governance. The second theme is the regeneration of cities. Here, informed by assemblage thinking as a critical yet generative framing, her recent work (with Kristian Ruming and Kathy Mee) explores the multiple ways in which urban regeneration occurs across formal and informal, strategic and everyday actions.

Susie Moloney is a Senior Research Fellow within the Centre for Urban Research in the School of Global, Urban and Social Studies, RMIT. Her recent research has focused around urban sustainability and the interconnections between the social, technical and governance changes required to improve our urban environments and social practices. Susie was appointed as a Post-doctoral Research Fellow at the Centre for Design, RMIT to work on a three year ARC Linkage project 'Carbon Neutral Communities: Making the Transition' (2007–2010) which focused on the role of local governments and community in transitioning. She has worked as a lecturer and tutor in RMIT's Environment and Planning programs on courses including Strategies for Sustainability and Managing Contemporary Planning Issues.

Stephanie Pincetl is the Director and Professor-in-Residence at the California Center for Sustainable Communities at UCLA, UCLA Institute of the Environment and Sustainability. She has published extensively on issues of environmental policies and regulation. The content of her research is land use, land use change, with a focus on urban environments and the transformation of their natural environments. The theoretical core of her research is environmental politics, policies and governance and specifically, the ways that rules and rule-making impact the participants in decision-making and the content of decisions. Rules can be formal or informal, hard or soft, but they form the boundaries of what is perceived of as possible. Stephanie has studied land use, infrastructure, and environmental preservation or services. She teaches courses on land use and the environment, environmental policies and politics in the US, and sustainable cities.

Benjamin Sims is a sociologist with the Statistical Sciences Group at Los Alamos National Laboratory with broad interests in qualitative and quantitative social science. He has a PhD in Sociology and Science Studies from the University of California, San Diego. Ben's dissertation research was on the development of earthquake engineering knowledge and methods for reinforcing bridges in California. His publications have addressed a variety of topics, including the development of earthquake engineering knowledge, safety in laboratory work, the impacts of Hurricane Katrina, and post-Cold War developments in the U.S. nuclear weapons complex. Ben's current research focuses on the sociology of infrastructure and repair and retrofit of sociotechnical systems. His broader interests include the organization of scientific and professional work, tacit knowledge and expertise, and safety and risk in socio-technical systems.

Bas J.M. Van Vliet is an Environmental Sociologist and Associate Professor at the Environmental Policy Group of Wageningen University. He studies and publishes on urban infrastructures for electricity, water supply, sanitation and waste management services in Europe and Africa and their dynamics concerning consumer-provider relations, social practices and the environment. He was a Co-Editor of *Social Perspectives on the Sanitation Challenge* (Springer) and Co-Author of *Infrastructures of Consumption: Environmental Innovation in the Utility Industries* (Earthscan).

Philip J. Vergragt is a Professor of Technology Assessment of Delft University of Technology; a Senior Research Scientist for the George Perkins Marsh Institute at Clark University, Worcester, MA and a Fellow at the Tellus Institute, Boston. His research interests include technological innovation for sustainability; sustainable consumption; housing and community development; backcasting; and technology assessment of emerging technologies. He has widely published in academic journals and book chapters, and co-authored three books. He is a Founding Member of the Worcester Housing, Energy, and Community (WoHEC) group; a Founding Member of the Advisory Board of the Greening of Industry network; a Founding Member of the Executive Committee of the Sustainable Consumption Research and Action Initiative (SCORAI); and a Co-Founder of the Global Research Forum on Sustainable Consumption and Production.

Janette Webb is a Professor of Sociology of Organisations, Institute of Governance, School of Social and Political Science, University of Edinburgh. Jan's research is about the sociology of energy, and local engagement in energy systems. Her main project, Heat and the City, is funded by the RC-UK Energy Programme. It focuses on urban energy governance and business organisation, in the context of globalising energy markets. Associated research funded by the Energy Technologies Institute and UK Energy Research Centre is analysing and modelling local engagement in energy developments. Jan was a member of the research team funded by UK Government to examine prospects for deployment of heat networks as a means of affordable, low carbon and economic energy provision. Its report is used in the 2013 UK Government Heat Strategy. Together with colleagues in Informatics and Geography Jan is also studying the interaction of households with sensors designed to give personalised feedback on energy use. This work, funded by EPSRC, will allow us to understand household energy practices across a large number of homes.

Jana Wendler is a Post Graduate Researcher from the University of Manchester is exploring the idea of experimental spaces in cities – spaces that allow urban inhabitants to re-imagine and physically re-shape their environment as an alternative to dominant urban conceptions. Such spaces, which are often connected to autonomous or pioneer projects, are highly unique. At the same time there are certain processes that cut across initiatives and localities, connecting them as experiments in urban living. Tracing these different dynamics, and their potential in reconfiguring the city from the bottom up, is the central aim of Jana's research.

Chapter 1

Introduction

Mike Hodson and Simon Marvin

The critical challenge for contemporary urbanism is how cities develop the knowledge and capability to systemically re-engineer their built environment and urban infrastructure in response to climate change and resource constraints (Hodson and Marvin, 2009, 2014). In the UK and elsewhere cities are increasingly confronted with, or have voluntarily adopted, challenging targets for increasing renewable and decentralised energy, carbon reduction, water savings and waste reduction (Bulkeley *et al.* 2011, 2012; Flint and Raco, 2012; Hodson and Marvin, 2013; While *et al.* 2010). Looking forward to 2020 and beyond as current ecological challenges, economic pressures and policy drivers begin to bite, we need to envisage a systemic transition in our existing built environment, not just to zero carbon but across the entire ecological footprint of our cities and the regions within which they are embedded, whilst simultaneously promoting economic security, social health and resilience (Hodson *et al.* 2012; May *et al.* 2013).

Responding to this challenge in a purposive and managed way requires those claiming to represent cities to bring together two strongly disconnected issues: 'what' is to be done to the city (technical knowledge, targets, technological options, costs, etc.) and 'how' will it be implemented (institutions, publics, governance) (Perry *et al.* 2013). We start from the perspective that the processes of urbanisation that underpin the development of cities are complex, and that urban environments can best be understood as complex socio-technical systems (Graham and Marvin, 2001). Cities become 'locked in' to particular patterns of energy and resource use – constrained by existing infrastructural investments, sunk costs, institutional rigidities and vested interests (Graham and Thrift, 2007). Understanding how to better 're-engineer' our cities and urban infrastructure, to overcome 'lock in' and facilitate systems change, will be critical to achieving sustainability (Kelly, 2009; Lomas, 2009; Lowe, 2009).

The core aims of this book are to comparatively explore how urban scale retrofitting can be conceptualised as a socio-technical transition; to critically compare and contrast different styles of response in cities of the north and global south; and, to contribute new research and policy agendas on future development of progressive retrofitting. The book looks across different infrastructures, different types of built environment, deals with very different urban contexts – world cities, cities of the global south, small cities and towns – and examines formalised corporate and policy responses as well as more informal bottom up and community responses. Whilst energy efficiency and carbon reduction inevitably dominate much of the debate over urban retrofitting, we also examine broader sustainability concerns such as those relating to water and waste.

The book is organised as a threefold critical framework for analysing urban retrofit given the dominance of more normatively focused techno-economic approaches (Hodson and Marvin, 2012; Hodson *et al.* 2012, 2013). This has three objectives. First we need to examine why retrofit is emerging as an important strategic issue for urban authorities and untangle the mix of economic, competitive, ecological and social pressures and drivers. Second we need to understand how retrofit capacity and capability is currently being organised with what inclusions and exclusions. And third we seek to assess the implications of differential capacity distributed within and between cities and what the social and material implications are of this.

In responding to these objectives the book seeks to address three gaps. First to review what is missing from current techno-economic approaches – power, difference, contested logics, social interests etc. Second, to develop an alternative framework that recognises that retrofit is a social and cultural process and is closely related to existing context, governance capacity and existing drivers. Third, to examine the ways in which retrofit is contested and disrupted in practice and how learning takes place about the limits and opportunities for retrofit under different assumptions and conditions.

The book brings together a carefully selected group of researchers from a variety of disciplinary backgrounds that reflects the complexity of the research challenge. We were particularly keen to engage with researchers who conceptualise retrofitting in both social and technical terms – rather than as a narrow techno-economic problem. There are three cross-cutting themes:

THE PROBLEMATIC OF URBAN RETROFIT AND ITS DYNAMICS

Generically, the term urban retrofit refers to re-shaping the built environment, the networks and resources that flow through them and the physical fabric of the city. This has often been understood at the level of buildings and neighbourhoods. It has also frequently been the domain of engineers and construction interests. This view primarily sees retrofit as repair and maintenance and as ongoing activity in replenishing the built environment (Graham and Thrift, 2007). Retrofit is not new in this sense. Yet a new set of ecological, economic, social and political pressures are being exerted at the level of cities that create a set of conditions for re-shaping the built environment of cities and the networks and resources that flow through them (Bulkeley *et al.* 2011; Hodson and Marvin, 2009). Engaging with this and developing effective responses requires not only up-scaling understanding of retrofit to the scale of the city but also expanding the conceptual and empirical frame of urban retrofit from the domain of engineering and construction to encompass places, policymakers, finance, systems, natures, users and other interests and issues (Kelly, 2009). It means setting out and engaging with the ways in which different configurations of these issues and interests and their dynamics present multiple framings of the problematic of urban retrofit (Hodson and Marvin, 2012). The critical question in setting out the problematic is: what are the different ways of framing urban retrofit?

Governing and organising urban retrofit

What follows from different framings of urban retrofit is a need to understand the governing interests that produce multiple framings and that also seek to translate visions of urban retrofit into tangible examples (Braun, 2014; Gabrys, 2014). This means developing appreciation of the multiple issues, motivations and interests involved and excluded from urban retrofit and how governing and organisation is mediated through different economic, ecological and social justice rationalities (Hodson and Marvin, 2012). Urban retrofit, for example, may promote green economic growth. As a response to economic and financial crises this raises the issue of whether cities become sites for the development of responses that promote green forms of growth and eco-competition (Harvey, 2012). Urban retrofit may be concerned with the social organisation of resource flows and access to (decarbonised or lower carbon) energy flows that have become increasingly salient issues in securing the social, economic and ecological security of places (Hodson *et al.* 2012). Yet these pressures provide the basis for a struggle to gain control over the social organisation of resource flows. Urban retrofit can also focus on questions of affordability and fuel poverty where issues of decarbonisation, green growth and the social organisation of resource flows are wrapped up with social justice, affordability and warmth (Hou, 2010). The questions that follow from this are: what are the different governing and organisational forms that promote urban retrofit? What rationalities are they promoting, what forms of socio-technical interests do they mediate and with what effects?

Experiments, demonstration and practices

What this means is that urban retrofit and efforts and aspirations for radical decarbonisation meet multi-level governing frameworks through which transition in the built environment and in energy systems can be achieved. There is, though, no single, effective template for how these multi-level governing frameworks are reconfigured to enact urban retrofit. A critical issue is how governing capacity and frameworks are constructed to develop retrofit responses in cities (Hodson *et al.* 2013). That being so, the challenge of developing effective governing for urban retrofit, particularly in an era of multiple ecological, economic and political crises, is a matter of ongoing experimentation, formal and informal demonstrations and also bottom-up shaping of retrofit through users and practices (Castán Broto and Bulkeley, 2012). An important issue here is in learning from experiments, demonstrations and initiatives and building mechanisms for capturing learning at three levels: within substantive initiatives, about an initiative and also between initiatives (Hodson and Marvin, 2013). The key questions are: what does the landscape of urban retrofit experiments, demonstrations and user practices look like? And what lessons can be learned from these initiatives for the problematic, governance and organisation of urban retrofit?

The insights and examples that populate this threefold structure to the book also provide a framework for the book's conclusion. The conclusion uses the book's material to address the following questions: First, in responding to contemporary ecological, economic and political pressures, what does retrofit at the scale of a city, rather than at the level of a building or neighbourhood, look like? Second, as a response to these pressures, is urban retrofit mobilised as a means of transforming the city? Or does it work to use the language of retrofit to maintain the governing status quo and their rationalities for governing? Third, what alternatives and forms of urban retrofit experimentation are being developed and with what implications?

STRUCTURE OF THE BOOK

The chapters in the book are organised in the threefold structure – the problematic of retrofit; governing and organisation of urban retrofit; experiments, learning and urban retrofit – through which significant aspects of our understanding of urban retrofit are developed. There are overspills across these themes but in each theme the chapters highlights distinctive parts of the overall retrofit argument.

Part one: the problematic of urban retrofit and its dynamics

Part one of the book focuses primarily upon the issue of why retrofit emerges as a critical issue in a variety of different contexts, focusing on the pressures and drivers at a number of different sites and scales – globally, professionally, within urban contexts and through different urban networks. Together these chapters develop an understanding of retrofit as a socio-technical process that means retrofitting must engage both with socio-cultural and different material–technological contexts. This then raises a broader issue of how governance capacity is constituted to manage such complex social and material relationships.

In the first chapter in this section, Ben Sims develops the concept of socio-technical repair. More specifically, he highlights the processual nature of repair that is driven by the relationship between a normative view of the adequacy of artefacts in relation to standards, codes and social needs and a substantive view based on beliefs of the material condition of artefacts. He addresses the relationship between these two issues in terms of breakdown and obsolescence and what this means for retrofit responses.

In the following chapter, Carla De Laurentis, Mike Hodson and Simon Marvin address urban retrofitting – as the systematic reconfiguration of socio-technologies of energy in the existing built environment and infrastructure – through examining urban retrofit responses in two UK city-regions: Greater Manchester and Cardiff. The chapter addresses who is constructing city-regional retrofit responses and also why they are being constructed. It does this to address the question: is it to transform the city-region and, if so, in what ways?

The book then focuses on district heating and cooling networks in a UK context. Jan Webb sets out the very limited uptake of district heating and cooling in the UK but also highlights a new policy promotion of the technology as a contributor to low carbon futures. The chapter illustrates the tensions on the one hand between the privatised energy markets and finance capitalism that have developed in recent decades – with associated efforts to reduce risk and delocalize investment decisions – and the local and contingent emphasis of district heating and cooling, with its high upfront investment costs, long-term payback and risks on the other. The chapter highlights the need to bridge this gap through the development of governance capacity and the introduction of supportive regulatory measures.

The book then moves on to expand on dominant conceptions of retrofit to include efforts to contribute to ecological sustainability through biogenic retrofitting. Stephanie Pincetl makes the argument that as a response to the challenges posed by climate change, resource use and the generation of pollution, that cities are developing strategies to respond to these challenges through enhancing biogenic infrastructure to address environmental impacts. The chapter illustrates this through the case of Los Angeles' efforts to plant a million trees. It details the complex, multi-layered and messy processes of governance but cautions that more critical analysis in this area is required.

In the last chapter in this section, Bas J.M. Van Vliet sets out the importance of the role of users and consumers in retrofit. Within a wider context of the shift to privatization and liberalization, the emergence of multiple network providers and differentiation in technologies, products and services, he examines what the implications of this are for the role of end-users and also the emergence of new relationships between users and providers. Using examples from drinking water supply, waste water management and electricity supply in the Netherlands the chapter identifies differentiation of consumer roles towards provision and use of water and energy services in various ways.

Part two: governing and organising urban retrofit

Part two primarily focuses upon the issues involved in the development of capacity and knowledge for the governance and organization of retrofit. All the chapters address the what, when, where, who and how of urban retrofitting in different comparative contexts. These are primarily exemplified through different intermediaries that work between a particular urban context and other networks (such as the C40 network of cities), between different scales of retrofitting activity (from networks of cities to a slum dwelling), between cities of the global north and south (from UK to India), between different sorts of capacity, finance and expertise and the intersection of all these issues. Collectively these chapters help us develop three sets of critical insights; first, to understand how it is that organizations constitute the capacity and knowledge for retrofit activities; second, to assess the different forms of intermediaries and styles of intermediation and to establish their effects; and third, to illustrate the differential material and social implications of these changes in terms of the extent to which these are transformative or business as usual and systemic or piecemeal in orientation.

Michele Acuto opens, this section, with a chapter focusing on the C40 network of global cities. He sets out the interconnectedness of leading, world cities and other international actors, such as the World Bank. This politics of an interconnected network is important in the way in which the C40 has defined an urban agenda around retrofitting, financing and climate policy measurement. The development of such a 'vision' is intended to reshape not only the cities involved but also the global governance of the environment in general.

The following chapter provides a contrast to the scale of inter-city networks by addressing the role of homeowners as community members within a socio-cultural context. The chapter focuses on housing retrofit in Worcester, Massachusetts as a bounded, sociotechnical experiment. Philip J. Vergragt and Halina Szejnwald Brown detail a sociotechnical experiment to upgrade the existing housing stock in a Worcester neighbourhood; one in great need of economic development and poverty reduction. They set out the processes, actors, dynamics and framing of this experiment over a period of years. In doing this they illustrate the ways in which the City of Worcester, the university community and several grassroots and local economic development organizations negotiated and framed high performance buildings as reducing environmental impacts but also as contributing to economic development, job creation and sustainable community development.

Ralph Horne and his co-authors set out a chapter that addresses private rental housing in the Australian context – specifically focusing on private landlords in Melbourne. They assess how landlords maintain their properties and what their responses are to the challenges posed by climate change and the opportunities for retrofit. They address the assumption in much literature that a 'split incentive' dis-incentivises eco-retrofit niche development through semi-structured interviews with landlords and intermediaries and a large scale survey examining private rental housing asset maintenance, dwelling upgrades and tenant management. They illustrate the diversity of the private rental system and the need for policy to recognize a flexible range of local experiments.

From Australia, the book moves on to India. Bipasha Baruah highlights the meanings of urban retrofit in relation to informal settlements and water supply and electrification. Building cases of two NGOs based in India – the Self-Employed Women's Association (SEWA) and Saath – the chapter focuses on a multiple-stakeholder pro-poor electrification program. Drawing on a range of methods – from academic literature on urban infrastructure provision, project reports and evaluations, pricing surveys and interviews with electricity utility and NGO staff – the chapter makes the argument that NGOs can be very effective as intermediaries between utilities, municipalities and urban poor communities. It cautions, however, that this requires strong state involvement in developing a policy framework to facilitate NGO participation in the design and implementation of pro-poor electrification activities, and in the energy reform process in general.

Andrés Luque-Ayala's chapter addresses Sao Paulo in Brazil. Through focusing on Sao Paulo's favelas, the chapter details both irregular and precarious service provision and responses to develop more regularized electricity supply networks. The chapter sets out the way in which this is not only a story of access but also of configuring the urban poor as clients in a process of marketisation. The chapter illustrates the process, negotiations and elements of this through combinations of social and technical interventions. In doing this the chapter illustrates how urban retrofit and energy transitions in action become integrated with issues of poverty alleviation, community wellbeing and citizenship.

Part three: experimenting with and learning from retrofit

Part three of the book focuses on learning about the future development of retrofit through careful analysis of retrofit demonstrations, niches and practices. These take place in quite different contexts of the laboratory, urban retrofit experiments in the global north and south, squatter communities and the global development of new energy cooling technologies. Within each of these cases the chapters examine who is experimenting and then seek to examine what can be learnt about the limits and potential of up-scaled retrofit from these different contexts. Critical here is the development of understanding of what the limits are on retrofit, how experiments help understand obduracy and spaces in existing sociotechnical configuration and the difficult issues of what needs to be changed to up-scale and replicate small scale experiments. This in turn helps develop lessons for the governing and organization of retrofit.

James Evans's chapter raises a critical issue for retrofitting: given that there are so few precursors on which to base retrofit action, what are the approaches and methodologies that should be mobilized? This chapter responds to this challenge through highlighting one response in particular – 'living laboratories' – and their role in learning to retrofit. Living laboratories are designated spaces for real world experiments in built design and sustainable technologies from which learning about retrofit, which informs future action in context, can be gleaned. The proponents of living laboratories claim that experiments may produce knowledge, technologies and responses that have wider applicability and transferability beyond the confines of the laboratory. The chapter assesses these claims, their construction and the ways in which they inform particular retrofit pathways and the up-scaling of urban experiments.

Robyn Dowling and her colleagues address the Australian context. They question the prevalence of city-wide discourses and practices of retrofitting in the Australian context but highlight the role of local governments, businesses and 'third sector' organizations in retrofitting projects at 'sub' urban scales. They present both a survey of initiatives and actors across Australian cities and also develop case studies of urban retrofitting in Sydney. The chapter assesses projects in terms of retrofitting and demonstration, the politics and participation of their development and the mechanisms and relationships through which they are connected to the existing carbon governance regime. The chapter reflects on the transformative potentials of the examples it raises at both local and city-wide scales.

In the following chapter, Vanesa Castán Broto and her colleagues address the notion of partnership in the provision of urban services and infrastructure provision. The chapter sets out how this is informed by new models of governance. It draws on the case of Maputo, Mozambique. Maputo is the focus of plans to extend partnership working – where it used in managing waste collection services in the city – to deliver a climate change plan for the city. This is the focus of a pilot action-research project. The chapter uses the case to ask: what is the potential of partnerships to deliver transformative urban change with socially and environmentally progressive outcomes? To address this, the chapter asks what are partnerships; who intervenes in them; why; and with what impact. It sets out how in practice, multiple forms of agency intervene in shaping partnerships limiting the opportunities for direct appropriation but opening spaces for integrating dominant rationalities of economic development and climate resilience.

In the final chapter in this section, Jana Wendler and James Evans bring together 'squatting' with a conception of retrofitting. The idea of 'squat-tech' involves existing features, recycled materials and improvisation to re-build structures and functioning systems in buildings occupied by 'squatters'. The chapter draws on case studies from squats in Barcelona and Copenhagen. It highlights the sociotechnical processes through which often cheap, ad hoc, communal and less resource intensive solutions are developed. The chapter identifies that underlying these responses is a strong current of creativity that pervades both individual projects and the wider approach to alternative forms of urban living.

Following these 14 chapters, Mike Hodson and Simon Marvin present a conclusion to the work. The conclusion is divided into three parts. First, the main argument of the book is summarised. Second, the three main themes developed in the book are reviewed and conclusions and synthesis looking across the book is presented. Third, the future research and policy challenges of this agenda are identified.

References

Braun, B.P. (2014) A new urban dispositif? Governing life in an age of climate change. *Environment and Planning D: Society and Space* 32:1, 49–64.

Bugliarello, G. (2011) Critical new bio-socio-technological challenges in urban sustainability, *Journal of Urban Technology*, 18:3, 3–23.

Bulkeley, H., Castán-Broto, V., Hodson, M. and Marvin, S. (2011) (eds), *Cities and Low Carbon Transitions*.First Edition. Routledge: London.

Bulkeley, H., Hodson, M. and Marvin, S. (2012) 'Emerging strategies of urban reproduction and the pursuit of low carbon cities'. In Flint, J. and Raco, M. (eds) *The Future of Sustainable Cities*. Policy Press: Bristol.

Castán Broto, V. and Bulkeley, H.A. (2012) A survey of urban climate change experiments in 100 cities, *Global Environmental Change*, 23:1, 92–102.

Coaffee J., Murakami, Wood, D. and Rogers, P. (2009) *The Everyday Resilience of the Cty: How Cities Respond to Terrorism and Disaster*. Palgrave MacMillian: New York.

Collier, S.J., and Lakoff, A. (2014) Vital systems security: reflexive biopolitics and the government of emergency. *Theory, Culture and Society*, 32:2, 19–51.

Flint, J. and Raco, M. (2012) (eds), *The Future of Sustainable Cities*. First Edition. Policy Press: Bristol.

Gabrys, J. (2014) Programming environments: environmentality and citizen sensing in the smart city. *Environment and Planning D: Society and Space,* 32:1, 30–48.

Gossop, C. (2011) Low carbon cities: An introduction to the special issue. *Cities* 28:6, 495–497.

Graham, S. and Marvin, S. (2001) *Splintering Urbanism: Networked Infrastructures, Technological Mobilities and the Urban Condition*. Routledge: London.

Graham, S. and Thrift, N. (2007) Out of order: understanding repair and maintenance. *Theory, Culture and Society*, 24:3, 1–25.

Harvey, D. (2012) *Rebel Cities: From the Right to the City to the Urban Revolution*. Verso: London.

Hodson, M. and Marvin, S. (2009) 'Urban ecological security' A new urban paradigm? *International Journal of Urban and Regional Research*, 33:1, 193–215.

Hodson, M. and Marvin, S. (2010) *World Cities and Climate change – Producing Urban Ecological Security*. Open University Press: Maidenhead.

Hodson, M. and Marvin, S. (2012) Mediating low-carbon urban transitions? Forms of organisation, knowledge and action. *European Planning Studies*, 20: 3, 421–39.

Hodson, M. and Marvin, S. (2013) *Low Carbon Nation?* Earthscan: London.

Hodson, M. and Marvin, S. (2014) (eds), *After Sustainable Cities?* Routledge: London.

Hodson, M., Marvin, S. and Bulkeley, H. (2013) The intermediary organisation of low carbon cities: a comparative analysis of transitions in Greater London and Greater Manchester. *Urban Studies*, 50:7, 1403–1422.

Hodson, M., Marvin, S., Robinson, B. and Swilling, M. (2012) Reshaping urban infrastructure: material flow analysis and transitions analysis in an urban context. *Journal of Industrial Ecology*, 16:6, 789–800.

Hou, J. (ed.), (2010) *Insurgent Public Space: Guerrilla Urbanism and the Remaking of Contemporary Cities*. Routledge: Abingdon.

Huber (2009) Energizing historical materialism: fossil fuels, space, and the capitalist mode of production. *Geoforum*, 40:1, 105–115.

Jonas, A.E.G., Gibbs, D. and While, A. (2011) The new urban politics as a politics of carbon control. *Urban Studies*, 48:12, 2537–2554.

Kelly, M. (2009) Retrofitting the existing UK building stock. *Building Research and Information*, 37:2, 196–200.

Leigh-Star, S. (1999) The ethnography of infrastructure. *American Behavioral Scientist*, 43:3, 377–391.

Lomas, K. (2009) Decarbonising national housing stocks: barriers and measurement. *Building Research and Information*, 37:2, 187–191.

Lowe R. (2009) Policy and strategy challenges for climate change and building stocks. *Building Research and Information*, 37:2, 206–212.

May, T., Hodson, M., Marvin, S. and Perry, B. (2013) 'Achieving systemic urban retrofit: a framework for action'. In Swan, W. and Brown, P. (eds), *Retrofitting the Built Environment*, Wiley: Chichester, pp.7–19.

Perry, B., May, T., Marvin, S. and Hodson, M. (2013) 'Re-thinking sustainable knowledge-based urbanism through active intermediation'. In Anderson, H.T. and Atkinson, R. (eds), *The Production and Use of Urban Knowledge: European Experiences*. Springer: Dordrecht.

While, A., Jonas, A.G. and Gibbs, D. (2010) From sustainable development to carbon control: eco-state restructuring and the politics of urban and regional development. *Transactions of The Institute of British Geographers*, 35:1, 76–93.

Part I

The problematic of urban retrofit and its dynamics

Priorities, places, finance, systems, natures and users

Chapter 2

Seismic shifts and retrofits

Scale and complexity in the seismic retrofit of California bridges

Benjamin Sims

INTRODUCTION

Infrastructure systems play a crucial role in the relationship between humans and the natural world, in part because they are the only human technological systems built on a large enough scale to have geophysical relevance (Edwards 2003). Many of the chapters in this book focus on infrastructure retrofit as a means to reduce human impact on the environment. This chapter instead focuses on retrofit to protect human beings from their environment: specifically, seismic retrofit of bridges to prevent them from collapsing in earthquakes. Although the impetus for retrofit may differ, the program discussed here raises many issues that are likely to be relevant for any kind of large-scale retrofit program that impacts urban settings. In particular, it provides examples of the complexities that arise in implementing a systemic retrofit program (May *et al.* 2013). This kind of systemic effort can be particularly complex because of the tension between global and local aspects of retrofit. At a global level, such a program must attend to the factors that sustain a systemic effort, such as engineering standards, funding sources, and political support. At a local level, each individual retrofit project has the potential to become entangled in localized contingencies of communities and the built environment. This chapter examines the characteristics of infrastructure that play into this global-local tension, the processes by which changes in sociotechnical systems become mobilized as worrisome problems, and the resulting practices of infrastructure repair, of which retrofit is one variety.

INFRASTRUCTURE RETROFIT

This chapter is primarily about retrofit of infrastructure technologies, in particular those that are locally massive and difficult to change, such as buildings, roads, and bridges. Compared to other technologies, infrastructures are unique in the fact that they are *globally embedded*: they have broad, global reach but are simultaneously deeply embedded within local practices and systems, to the point where they can become almost invisible if they are working properly (Star and Ruhleder 1996, Bowker and Star 1999: 35). This tension between local and global scales accounts for much of the complexity involved in both developing and retrofitting infrastructure systems. Bridges and overpasses, for example, must function as part of a larger road system that is built to certain universal standards, such as minimum lane widths, allowable vehicle weights, and road surface characteristics. At the same time, however, each structure has to be designed to accommodate the unique form and characteristics of the land beneath it (hence the specialty of geotechnical engineering), and to integrate into other local infrastructure configurations – for example, an overpass might have to be built without impacting local sewer lines, or may be required to carry gas lines or electrical cables. After structures are built, they tend to become increasingly integrated with other local systems and practices (Hommels 2005, Sims 2007a, 2007b, 2009), which, in some ways, makes retrofitting infrastructure components more complex than building them in the first place.

In a more general sense, we can understand infrastructures as networks that manifest themselves in different ways at different scales across a range of locales and social worlds (Edwards 2003). Although many infrastructures are widely understood to be networks in a material or logical sense, they also exist in the context of heterogeneous sociotechnical networks of people, things, ideas, documents, etc. – what Bruno Latour and others call 'actor networks' (Latour 1987, 1996). At a global administrative level, for example, bridges and overpasses are embedded in a network that includes regulations and standards (for example, those associated with the interstate highway system), government budgets and elected officials, and broad public interests, such as those of commuters. At an engineering level, they are associated with networks that include engineers from a variety of professional specialties (structural engineering, traffic engineering, landscape engineering, etc.), managers and organizations, design methods, building practices, and computer codes and software. At a geographically local level, they are part of networks that include other infrastructure components; local communities that may have opinions about things like traffic, bike lanes, and aesthetic impact; and environmental conditions like soil settlement and runoff from nearby surfaces.

A key problem for any systemic retrofit program is managing the tension between the global and local networks it interfaces with (Law and Callon 1992). To explore how this works in practice, I use the example of the California Department of Transportation ('Caltrans') seismic retrofit programs of the 1970s, '80s and '90s (Sims 1999, 2000).[1] This retrofit process was driven by a series of earthquakes that damaged bridges in ways not anticipated by Caltrans bridge engineers, which coincided with rapid changes in engineering knowledge about how structures respond to dynamic forces like earthquakes, making many existing bridges appear dangerously obsolete. This led to efforts to retrofit bridges, which culminated in a massive state-wide retrofit program following the 1989 Loma Prieta earthquake, a major temblor which caused extensive damage to freeway structures in the San Francisco Bay Area.

To better explain how retrofit programs interact with global networks, the first Caltrans case study below covers changes in general engineering practice at Caltrans from the 1970s through the 1990s, and its relationship to broader political and professional networks. The second Caltrans case study focuses on the sociotechnical network surrounding one particular project, the seismic retrofit of the Coronado Bridge in San Diego, which illustrates the complexities that can attend local implementation of a systemic retrofit program.

SOCIOTECHNICAL REPAIR

Retrofit can be understood within a larger context of 'sociotechnical repair', as articulated by Henke and Sims (Henke 2000, 2007, 2008, Sims and Henke 2012; see also Graham and Thrift 2007 and Jackson 2014). We conceptualize repair as an ongoing sociotechnical process that is essential to maintaining the perceived stability of sociotechnical systems.[2] Both social and technological aspects of repair are important to consider because they often happen concurrently. For example, a chemical company that has experienced an accident may work to fix the technological systems and organizational processes that led to the accident, while simultaneously using these repair efforts as part of a discursive effort to repair the company's public image. For simplicity, for the remainder of the chapter I will refer primarily to technological systems, with the understanding that humans generally are part of these systems in one way or another.

Technological systems are not inherently stable entities. Instead, they can best be viewed as dynamic processes in which system functionality, internal coherence, and boundaries are accomplishments that, once attained, are in constant danger of being lost in the ongoing interplay of social and technological forces. Repair practices are fundamental and ubiquitous because they are the key to stabilizing technological systems. Paradoxically, they also play a major role in technological change, because vast numbers of relatively small repair efforts can, in aggregate, lead to significant historical trends.

SLIPPAGE, REPAIR AND RETROFIT

Sociotechnical repair is often motivated in terms of a kind of 'slippage', over time, between beliefs about a technological system's current state, and ideas about how it ought to be functioning. The first are often presented in objective terms, based on studies, measurements, or observations; the second are usually presented in more normative terms, prescribing an idealized system state.

In the context of infrastructure, the current condition of a system might be described in terms of structural integrity, network redundancy, usage patterns, or interfaces with other infrastructure systems and the natural environment. These are often expressed in terms of measurements against a given scale. The normative view of system functionality might take the form of specifications and margins expressed in these same measurement scales, which themselves are often embodied in complex technical standards and building codes. It may also be expressed in more overtly moralistic terms, in terms of aspirations, goals, redress of grievances, and judgments about the societal role of infrastructure and its designers and builders.

Slippage is a useful way to analyse breakdown and repair because these processes are typically framed in terms of change from some pre-existing equilibrium – either a return to an equilibrium that has been disrupted, or adjustment of an equilibrium in anticipation of future threats to stability of a system. There are two ideal types of slippage: degradation and obsolescence. Degradation is when normative expectations remain stable, but objective conditions are seen as having changed, or being in danger of changing: for example, a building has sustained earthquake damage, a bridge's paint has a five year life span, or call volumes on a mobile phone network are expected to increase. Repair, in cases of degradation, is usually described in terms of maintenance, restoration, or what we might call 'simple' repair of something that is broken: fixing earthquake damage, initiating a preventive maintenance schedule, adding cellular communication towers.

The other ideal type of slippage, obsolescence, is when objective conditions are perceived as stable, but normative expectations have changed: for example, engineering standards and building codes have been updated, there is a movement to add bike lanes to existing bridges, broadcasters want to transmit high definition television signals. Existing technology comes to be seen as outdated or not responsive to social needs.

In most cases, particularly in the global North, obsolete technological artefacts are simply destroyed or thrown away, and replaced with something that meets current standards. The less common alternative is to retrofit existing artefacts. This possibility generally comes into play only when, for whatever reason, the destruction or disposal of existing technological artefacts is perceived to be costly or otherwise undesirable. In the global North, the cost of replacement has generally been an insurmountable issue only with fixed, massive infrastructure components like buildings and bridges. However, particularly in the context of energy efficiency, the environmental cost of complete replacement of existing artefacts has become more recognizable, which in many cases shifts the balance in favour of retrofit. Retrofit may also be preferred in situations where the problematic technological artefact has historic or aesthetic significance.

In the broader context of sociotechnical repair, then, retrofit is a specific kind of repair that generally occurs when normative standards for technology change under conditions that limit our ability to replace existing technological artefacts. In these cases, we are no longer just fixing something that is broken, we are essentially going back and rewriting history by altering past technology to fit current technical standards and social needs: tying down old houses to their foundations more securely to meet current seismic safety standards, making bridges wider to accommodate bike lanes, changing broadcasting systems and receivers to support digital television.

PROBLEMATIZING OBSOLESENCE AT CALTRANS

The history of seismic design and retrofit of bridges at Caltrans provides useful insight into the complexities of problematizing a technology as obsolete and in need of retrofit. In particular, it illustrates the complex interplay between 1) actors, 2) objects and events, and 3) knowledge during periods of significant change in a sociotechnical network. During the time period discussed here, the sociotechnical networks surrounding bridge design both expanded and experienced significant changes in their composition. As engineers' understanding of seismic performance of bridges changed, specific elements of these structures emerged as 'risk objects' within the network (Hilgartner 1992). (In Caltrans parlance, 'bridges' refers to a range of objects, from small overpasses to large toll bridges like the Coronado Bridge and the Golden Gate Bridge. In this portion of the case study, 'bridges' refers mainly to reinforced concrete overpasses, freeway ramps, and elevated road structures.)

In the Caltrans case, there appear to have been three key conditions that led to decisions to retrofit, which may be generalizable to other infrastructure retrofit decisions. First, there was slippage away from the knowledge, practices, and norms that were in play within the relevant networks when the technology was created. Next, based on this slippage, a specific set of technological artefacts or systems was identified as obsolete. Finally, the obsolescence was articulated as a risk or problem in a public arena that included relevant decision makers and stakeholders, enabling negotiation of access to sufficient resources to carry out a retrofit program.

It is useful to think in terms of three broad eras in the articulation of earthquake risk to bridges within Caltrans networks. First, prior to 1971, earthquake risk was acknowledged, but played a relatively small role in the design and construction of bridges. There was little understanding of how bridges might respond dynamically to earthquakes, design standards generally required little reinforcement beyond that needed for a bridge to support traffic, and engineers had had little or no opportunity to observe earthquake impacts on bridge structures. In 1971, a major earthquake in the San Fernando Valley, near Los Angeles, damaged bridges in a freeway interchange under construction, revealing unexpected weaknesses. This ushered in a second era of risk definition, in which certain specific design details were recognized as problematic, the dynamic response of bridges to earthquakes became better understood, and a minimal retrofit program was undertaken. The third era of risk definition followed the Loma Prieta earthquake that caused extensive damage in the San Francisco Bay Area in 1989. This included the collapse of the Cypress Viaduct freeway structure, which killed 41 people and finally associated obsolete bridges with danger to the general public (Governor's Board of Inquiry 1990: 27). This brought political decision-makers, the media, and dramatically increased financial resources into the Caltrans bridge engineering network, which led to an era of massive change at Caltrans, in which the network expanded to include members of the earthquake engineering research community, new design methods and tools, and a massive retrofit program for state bridges.

THE NETWORK PRIOR TO 1971

Prior to 1971, the significant actors in the Caltrans bridge engineering network were primarily Caltrans engineers themselves; there was little interaction with engineering researchers, and very little useful research had been conducted on earthquake impacts to reinforced concrete structures. In addition, there had been very little systematic observation of how actual earthquakes damaged structures, so earthquakes and earthquake damage were not significant objects within the risk network. The state of the art in seismic design practice was to calculate whether a bridge could stand up to a static horizontal force equal to some percentage of its own weight, depending on the nature of the bridge footings and underlying soil (Governor's Board of Inquiry 1990: 122). In most cases, bridges that were designed properly for the weight of traffic would have already met seismic design criteria (Governor's Board of Inquiry 1990: 123). This slowly began to change in the late 1960s, when it was discovered that taller, more slender structures, with longer natural periods of vibration, were less susceptible to earthquake damage (Governor's Board of Inquiry 1990: 122–123). This enabled engineers to reduce the horizontal force requirements for most bridges. At the same time, early computational tools made engineers more confident in designing bridges with lower margins of safety. As a result, bridges became more aesthetically interesting, but in retrospect actually less able to resist earthquakes (Sims 2000: 42). None of these changes called into question the safety of older bridges, so Caltrans engineers did not view older structures as posing any special risk. Up until 1971, no notable earthquake damage had been observed in modern concrete bridges in any case, and there appears to have been little or no public interest in the seismic design of bridges.

1971–1989

In 1971, a 6.6 magnitude earthquake shook the San Fernando Valley, then a rapidly-developing suburb of Los Angeles. At the time, Caltrans was in the process of building two major freeway interchanges in the area, and large portions of several finished (but not yet in service) structures collapsed in very dramatic fashion. The extent of damage caught Caltrans engineers by surprise. The bridges were new, designed to the latest standards, and were expected to be able to withstand an earthquake of this magnitude. This led to an internal investigation and the beginnings of a major rethinking of seismic design standards (Sims 2000: 43).

The most obvious change in the bridge engineering network in this era was the inclusion of specific instances of earthquake damage to bridges (Sims 2000: 52–57). Caltrans created formal procedures for investigating damage to bridges after earthquakes; at the same time, earthquakes began to impact bridges more frequently, mainly due to the massive expansion of the California freeway system in the 1960s. Investigations into the San Fernando earthquake, and subsequent events, changed the knowledge and practices of Caltrans engineers in significant ways. Engineers observed two damage mechanisms in the San Fernando event. First, they noticed that the roadways had come apart at joints between segments of the bridges, allowing sections to fall. Second, they saw that the steel reinforcement ('rebar') in the concrete columns had ruptured, leading to collapse of columns (Sims 2000: 44–45).

The first observation led Caltrans engineers to think about ways of preventing roadway joints from separating, and an inexpensive solution was quickly devised: drill holes in the ends of the bridge segments and tie them together with steel cables. This led to the first Caltrans retrofit program, a low-cost, low-priority effort to install 'hinge restrainers' that continued slowly through the 1980s (Sims 2000: 48–51). This effort was small enough that it could be carried out without expanding the bridge engineering network to include actors with access to resources outside Caltrans.

Ductility is the ability of a material or structure to deform beyond the level where it springs back elastically without losing strength. For example, a paper clip can be bent into many different shapes without losing its integrity because it is made out of steel, a very ductile material. In the 1960s and '70s, engineers were just beginning to understand the importance of ductility in earthquake resistance. New research showed that the key to ductility in concrete structures was not just reinforcing them with sufficient steel rebar, but the specific configuration of the steel. In particular, it was recognized that concrete itself could behave in a more ductile manner if it were tightly confined within a cage of rebar, and that the continuity of horizontal reinforcing hoops was crucial to this ability (Sims 2000: 46–47).

As a result of the San Fernando earthquake, Caltrans engineers retooled their design standards based on this new research. The new standards required a continuous spiral of horizontal reinforcement for the entire height of a bridge column, which corresponded to a 5- to 8-fold increase in horizontal reinforcement, as well as improved continuity in vertical reinforcement. These changes were all at the level of what engineers call 'design details'; Caltrans engineers still did not understand how to incorporate ductility into design in a comprehensive way (Sims 2000: 47–48).

At this point, it was recognized that existing bridge columns did pose a potential risk, but there was no immediate column retrofit solution available, little funding available beyond what was being spent on the more urgent joint retrofits and still little public interest in the earthquake resistance of bridges.

Toward the end of this era, in the mid-1980s, the actors represented in the Caltrans risk network began to change in small but important ways. Specifically, Caltrans began to fund research at California universities. In 1984, they funded a University of California, Los Angeles researcher to test hinge retrofit designs (Sims 2000: 73). More significantly, the University of California, San Diego (UCSD) hired Nigel Priestley, a world-renowned researcher in earthquake resistance of concrete structures from New Zealand. Caltrans engineers were already aware of Priestley's work and were eager to collaborate with him. Of particular interest was research Priestley had done on reinforcing bridge piles with steel jackets. Steel jackets rapidly emerged as a leading possibility for retrofitting existing bridge columns: the jackets could be put in place around the columns, and the intervening space filled with concrete, increasing the confinement of the concrete and the ductility of the columns (Figure 2.1). Caltrans obtained a small grant to begin research on this technology, but had just begun thinking about a retrofit program when the Loma Prieta quake hit in 1989 (Sims 2000: 61–63).

This era, then, introduced several significant new objects into the Caltrans bridge engineering network, most notably earthquakes themselves and their impact on actual bridges, with joints and columns as key locations of risk. This led to increased understanding of the importance of ductility, and changes in design practice, albeit primary at the detail level. Most importantly, Caltrans engineers recognized a slippage between their new design standards and existing structures, identified the older structures as obsolete in significant ways, and associated that obsolescence with a risk of bridge collapse. This led to the hinge restrainer retrofit effort, inquiries into

Figure 2.1 Seismic retrofit in progress, State Route 52 overpass at Genesee Avenue, San Diego. Steel shells have been placed around a column, and will subsequently be welded together and filled with concrete grout to complete the retrofit. The column footing is also being reinforced. Photograph by the author, approximately 1997

column retrofit, and expanded relationships with university researchers. But the risk of earthquake damage to bridges in California was still very much a local problem, understood by Caltrans engineers and a few others, but not much discussed in wider professional or public arenas.

AFTER 1989

The 6.9-magnitude Loma Prieta earthquake struck on October 17, 1989. The majority of deaths that occurred in the quake were the result of the collapse of the Cypress Viaduct, a reinforced concrete structure that carried a portion of Interstate 880 in Oakland. For the first time, this tied seismic design of bridges to the real possibility of bodily harm, in the eyes of the public, and briefly led to intense media scrutiny of Caltrans design practices. Governor George Deukmejian and other political figures claimed that they had been told that all freeways in the state could withstand an earthquake of this magnitude (Sims 2000: 97). These political figures, and the media, initially tried to frame the Cypress Viaduct collapse as a 'moral disorder' story – a story in which disaster was tied to human errors or misjudgements, and where blame was to be apportioned accordingly (Sims 2000: 93–97). Initially, it appeared that Caltrans might take the blame. Fortunately for Caltrans engineers, they were able to develop contacts in the media, and their work on retrofit in the 1970s and '80s provided a useful alternative narrative, one in which Caltrans had developed the knowledge and techniques needed to make bridges safe, only to be stymied by lack of money and political interest. This ended up being the dominant frame for the story, and as a result political actors hastened to provide Caltrans with a large amount of money to undertake a comprehensive, state-wide seismic retrofit program (Sims 2000 99–105). The Governor also appointed a Board of Inquiry, which was made up largely of engineers and ended up being primarily an intra-professional effort, focusing on engineering explanations for the failures rather than apportioning blame (Sims 2000: 105–124).

The effect of these developments was to provide political and media validation of the bridge engineering network and risk objects that Caltrans bridge engineers had developed in the 1970s and '80s. In fact, Caltrans engineers felt they had learned nothing new from the collapse of the Cypress Viaduct, whose inadequacies were readily understood. The bridge engineering network grew by adding political and media actors to the mix, but no new objects or practices were introduced. At least, this was the case initially. The actual retrofit effort led to dramatic changes in these aspects of the network.

One key change was a dramatic expansion of the number of actors in the bridge engineering network, to include practicing engineers and academic researchers throughout (mainly) the state of California. Caltrans employed peer review panels to validate their retrofit plans for specific structures. For several important structures, these peer review panels acted less as independent reviewers and more as collaborators in the design process. They began to insist that Caltrans use more sophisticated design methods that more precisely incorporated ductility into the design process, which they then helped implement (Sims 2000: 132–165). Nigel Priestley, of UCSD, played a particular prominent role, and his work served as a touchstone for the retrofit program, to the extent that an internal Caltrans memo reported that 'designers feel they are to do what Nigel Priestley recommends because they feel management is behind his opinion' (Sims 2000: 187). At the same time, Caltrans started funding research on earthquake engineering at a number of universities, including UCSD and UC Berkeley, bringing researchers into the risk network in yet another way (Sims 2000: 74).

The new design methodologies had two elements. First, Priestley and another professor at UCSD, Frieder Seible, introduced Caltrans to a method called 'displacement ductility analysis'. Without getting into technical details, this approach enabled engineers to design structures with controlled areas of deformation that could be built with the required ductility to remain intact during an earthquake. This approach finally enabled Caltrans engineers to incorporate ductility into the design process in a systematic way. At the same time, Caltrans engineers began using more sophisticated models of entire structures that incorporated the displacement ductility approach (Sims 2000: 174–178).

These new methodologies required Caltrans engineers to work in new ways. In particular, new computational tools were required. One younger Caltrans engineer, who had recently completed his PhD, began developing tools for displacement ductility analysis, but initially had to do so on his own time because bridge engineers were forbidden from writing their own computer code. This situation was soon resolved, and by the mid-1990s, most of the bridge engineers were using his codes as part of their design process (Sims 2000: 179–181). Up until the mid-1990s, even as the retrofit program was in full swing, the new design methodologies were surprisingly informal, spreading across the organization primarily through the circulation of memos, unofficial guidelines, and computer software, and gaining legitimacy primarily through peer review. They were gradually moulded into increasingly formal documents and eventually into official design standards by the end of the 1990s. This formalism defined a new, relatively stable state of the art (Sims 2000: 181–197).

Caltrans' funding of academic researchers also introduced significant new objects into the risk network, in the form of laboratories and test specimens. Many of the new design and retrofit approaches were validated directly through testing of models of Caltrans structures in the laboratory, in many cases at a scale close to that of the actual structures. These large test specimens had to be built by technicians with actual concrete building experience, designed to correspond to actual or proposed Caltrans designs, and manipulated with very large hydraulic jacks and 'shake tables'. This helped ground the new design methods very concretely in structures that were representative of what Caltrans actually employed in the field, freeing engineers from having to wait for actual earthquakes to test their designs (Sims 1999, 2000: 202–247).

The history of seismic retrofit at Caltrans shows how changes in the makeup of sociotechnical networks can introduce destabilizing elements that leave parts of the network in tension with others. In the hinge restrainer retrofit program of the 1970s and '80s, the tension that emerged was between new engineering understanding of what an earthquake-safe bridge looked like, and already-constructed bridges that could not easily be rebuilt. This tension was articulated as a problem internally at Caltrans, and retrofit was inexpensive enough to be carried out with available resources. After the Loma Prieta earthquake in 1989, a new tension emerged between public expectations of how bridges would perform in earthquakes, and the reality of how existing bridges actually performed in a large quake. This new tension shifted the slippage into a public and political realm, where a case could be made for committing more significant resources to a retrofit program to solve the problem. The public controversy phase was, however, very brief and never evolved to include a wide range of interest groups. This may have been because the existing bridge engineering network was so thoroughly dominated by Caltrans engineers, and already provided a coherent narrative to explain events. Ultimately, no other actors came forward with the resources to challenge that narrative. This appears to be a common pattern in professional involvement in public controversies (Gusfield 1981: 10–15, Abbott 1988: 59–85).

The large changes in the Caltrans bridge engineering network after 1989, however, raise an interesting point: Retrofit is not necessarily the end of a process of slippage and realignment in networks. Instead, in this case, retrofit actually opened up the network to additional changes, such that reaching closure on the retrofit process involved a complex convergence between the form of bridges and evolving technical norms, rather that retrofitting bridges to meet a clearly defined set of criteria.

NEGOTIATING URBAN RETROFIT: CHICANO PARK AND THE CORONADO BRIDGE

The changes to the Caltrans bridge engineering network that have been discussed to this point in the chapter mainly relate to the interface of that network with more global networks, in particular California state politics, the engineering research community, and a variety of earthquake impacts on bridges. The actual implementation of individual retrofits, however, required extension of the network into localized environments, often in infrastructurally dense urban settings. This required a very different problem-solving approach from what was required to come up with general engineering approaches to retrofit, including extensive review of 'as-built' plans (if they were even available), inspection and measurement of the existing structure, identification of possible co-located utilities, coordination with relevant state and local agencies, assessment of potential environmental and cultural impacts, and ultimately design of retrofit systems customized to the form of the bridge in question. This was a particularly complex process in the case of large, architecturally significant structures like San Diego's Coronado Bridge (Suchman 2000).

The initial design and later retrofit of the San Diego-Coronado Bridge exemplifies the many ways infrastructure projects, and retrofits in particular, can become complexly entangled in localized social and technological arrangements. This bridge is a major structure connecting the city of San Diego to the 'island' of Coronado, across San Diego Bay. Coronado, which is actually attached to the mainland by a thin strand south of San Diego, hosts several military facilities and is home to many military personnel, and also features a number of resort hotels. The bridge was built in the 1960s with the support of Governor Edmund G. Brown, a champion of bridge-building as a tool of economic development. Various local groups were opposed to building a bridge, including Coronado residents who protested the bridge because they feared it would destroy the small-town character of the island. In addition, the Navy initially opposed a bridge because it might interfere with ship movement in and out of San Diego Harbor. They later softened their opposition, but insisted on at least 200 feet clearance over the main shipping lane. In order to accommodate this height without making the bridge too steep, engineers designed the bridge with a 90 degree curve in the middle to increase its length (Fisher 1996: 2–3, Sims 2000: 265–266).

One major interest group was not accommodated in the design process, however: the community of Barrio Logan, a largely Hispanic neighbourhood at the San Diego end of the bridge. Because shipping lanes were closer to the San Diego side, the highest portion of the bridge was built on the San Diego side. In addition, the bridge had to connect to Interstate 5, a quarter of a mile inland, which also required construction of a large complex of ramps and overpasses connecting the freeway to the bridge. For various reasons, it was decided that the bridge should come ashore at Barrio Logan, and a wide swathe of the neighbourhood was levelled to build the interchange. In contemporary accounts, however, this is never mentioned; Barrio Logan was invisible to decision-makers and the media. One of the architects of the bridge later explained that the area was simply seen as a 'path of least resistance', with low property values and little potential for political mobilization (Sims 2000: 266).

By the late 1960s, however, Chicano political activism was on the rise nationally, and was becoming particularly important in California. The

Barrio Logan community, which had already suffered through numerous policy and infrastructure projects that threatened its integrity, was in the midst of a political awakening. The pivotal moment came when the state announced plans to build an enormous California Highway Patrol station on the already desolate land under the bridge and approach ramps. The community, which had had an unhappy relationship with police, was finally pushed over the threshold into dramatic political mobilization. A group of several hundred residents occupied the construction site for twelve days, preventing construction from proceeding and demanding that a community park be built instead. The state backed down, and entered into negotiations with the city of San Diego that eventually resulted in the establishment of what became known as 'Chicano Park' under the bridge interchange (Coffelt 1973, Brookman and Gomez-Pena 1986, Fisher 1996: 13–14, Sims 2000: 269).

The park became a focal point of community activity, but remained a noisy and sometimes gloomy place, dominated by the grey concrete of the bridge structure. Partly to combat this gloominess, a loose coalition of local artists conceived the idea of painting murals on the approach ramp columns in the park. Over next thirty years, at least 40 brightly-coloured, symbolically-dense murals were painted on the columns by artists from San Diego and throughout the Southwest (Figure 2.2) (Fisher 1996: 17–19).

The design and construction of Chicano Park, and the painting of its murals, was itself an urban retrofit project, taking a grim, unloved space and reclaiming it as a meaningful centre of community activity and political awareness. The community identified a slippage between the actual form of the bridge and their ideals of how a community ought to be considered in infrastructure decisions, identified it with clear harm to the community, and through civil disobedience, forced the city and state to incorporate the wishes of the Barrio Logan community into future decisions about the bridge. Here, the constraint that led to retrofit, rather than replacement, was that the community did not have anywhere near the political power to effect the actual removal of the bridge, so instead focused on improving the existing artefact in ways that mitigated its terrible impact on the community. The fact that the improvements were largely aesthetic in nature in no way diminishes the significance of this retrofit. Thirty years later, this retrofit would come into conflict with the larger, systemic, technical, state supported Caltrans seismic retrofit program.

When the Coronado bridge finally came up for retrofit in the mid-1990s, Caltrans officials and engineers, as well as the San Diego-based engineering firms designing the retrofit, were aware that the murals could pose a problem, but do not appear to have been aware of the depth of the community's commitment to the artwork and the degree of political difficulty that could attend any disruption of the park. In order to get ahead of the issue, Caltrans held public meetings early in the

Figure 2.2 Three of what are now 79 murals painted on the San Diego approach ramps to the Coronado Bridge. From left to right: *Coatlicue*, Susan Yamagata and Michael Schnorr, 1978; *Virgen De Guadalupe*, Mario Torero and the Lomas Youth Crew, 1978; and *Muralistas Mexicanos: 'Los Grandes'*, Rupert Garcia, Victor Ochoa, and Barrio Renovation Team, 1978. Photograph by the author, 1996

design process, at which they presented a range of possible retrofit measures, most of which would have had a significant impact on the murals – including completely replacing the columns, encasing them with steel jackets, and thickening the existing columns in the lateral direction. Decades of community mistrust of Caltrans came to the surface immediately, and community activists began to dig in their heels for a fight. Some questioned whether the bridge really needed to be retrofitted at all. An artists' group sent out a newsletter demanding 'no retrofit, not now, not ever!' A mural was painted in Chicano Park with the prominent message 'No Retrofitting'. In sharp contrast to the invisibility of the Barrio Logan community during the building of the bridge, local politicians and newspapers soon took up the cause of preserving the murals (Sims 2000: 270–272). The message of slippage between existing bridges and evolving design standards, and its associated risk to human life, that had worked so well at the state political level began to lose its power amid the local contingencies surrounding Chicano Park and the bridge interchange.

Seeing that discussions were not going well, San Diego-based Caltrans environmental planners, who saw themselves as having a better grasp on local politics and concerns about the retrofitting, began to take a much more aggressive role in courting community leaders, holding numerous additional public meetings throughout the course of the retrofit development. At the same time, Caltrans historians and archaeologists who developed the required environmental impact documentation for the project had come to the conclusion that the murals probably qualified for inclusion in the U.S. National Register of Historic Places, further complicating matters. Indeed, laws like the U.S. National Environmental Policy Act (NEPA) are one reason why the political processes surrounding infrastructure have changed so significantly since the time when the Coronado Bridge was initially built, and are a key point of leverage for communities like Barrio Logan.

The turning point in the retrofit struggle came from the engineering research community. Frieder Seible, one of the UCSD engineers who played a major role in Caltrans research and peer review panels, was on the peer review panel for the Coronado Bridge retrofit. Realizing that their relationship with the community was on shaky ground, local Caltrans officials approached Seible to discuss the technical issues with community leaders. Seible brought the activists to UCSD to tour the structural engineering laboratory there, where he explained the reasons for the retrofit and showed them large-scale test specimens of bridge columns that had been put through simulated earthquakes. This apparently made a significant impression on community leaders, and convinced many of the sceptics present that retrofit was actually needed (Sims 2000: 272).

Seible worked both sides of the problem, however. Using his position on the peer review panel, he pushed Caltrans to require a more detailed analysis of the overpass columns in the design process, including testing sample columns at the UCSD lab. When this analysis was completed, and with new data on soils at the site, the designers concluded that retrofitting work could be limited to only the footings of the columns. In other words, almost all the work could be done below the existing ground level, sparing the murals (Sims 2000: 272–273).

The events surrounding the Coronado bridge retrofit created a local extension of the Caltrans bridge engineering network that included columns as risk objects in two ways: as structures that could collapse in earthquakes, and as structures bearing murals that were at risk of damage in the retrofit process. Key actors, practices, and objects from the larger, systemic Caltrans retrofit program were redeployed within this local network, most notably university researchers, with their technical knowledge and status as experts, and the laboratories and test specimens they controlled. In addition, a host of local actors became involved, including community groups, politicians, and locally-based Caltrans environmental planners. The result was a localized network that was more closely adapted to local circumstances surrounding one particular retrofit project. This ultimately enabled that local project to proceed, contributing in a small way to the larger, systemic retrofit effort.

The story of Chicano Park and the Coronado Bridge retrofit also shows that urban retrofit projects can involve much more in the way of conflict and adversarial power relations than the comparatively consensus-driven process that characterized the Caltrans retrofit program at a systemic level. Actors who lack political voice may be marginalized and made invisible. Slippage may be driven not by gradual drift in technical standards over time, but by new actors forcibly inserting themselves into existing networks of power and vehemently disagreeing with the status quo. These highly charged political and cultural meanings can invest sociotechnical networks with yet another localized layer of complexity that engineers and planners must account for in the retrofit design process.

CONCLUSION

The Caltrans seismic retrofit program is a story of heterogeneous engineering (Law 1987), in which a group of engineers put together a network of ever-increasing complexity that enabled them to sustain a retrofit program amid a variety of local and global contingencies with the potential to destabilize it. To do so, they articulated key slippages between bridge structures as they existed, and bridge structures as they ought to be to prevent loss of life in earthquakes, according to changing engineering standards. In doing so, they positioned themselves as retrofit experts and maintained control over their engineering practices through a period of rapid technological change. However, the Coronado bridge case also drives home the fact that it is not only engineers who engage in heterogeneous engineering and retrofit; activists and community groups can push their own agendas for urban renewal, which intersect and play off of engineers' efforts in interesting and complex ways. The overall view that emerges is that retrofit, like other infrastructural projects, involves construction of networks of people, things, and practices that span a wide range of scales and locales. Retrofit is especially complex and difficult because new networks must integrate particularly closely with already established networks, greatly constraining what can be done. Resolution of these tensions and constraints is what makes a successful retrofit program possible.

Non-systemic retrofit is a ubiquitous feature of urban environments: governments, property owners, and communities are constantly repairing, remodelling, expanding, and adapting elements of the built environment to fit evolving local and global needs. Over time, these changes may create a local equilibrium that reflects the negotiation and settlement of a variety of political, economic, and cultural interests. Systemic retrofit programs often reflect the agendas of global professional, business, and political groups, and are usually planned at a regional or national level where it is difficult to take these myriad localized settlements into account. This was certainly the case with the Caltrans seismic retrofit program, which initially took shape through a complex series of interactions between engineers, legislators, the governor, and state and national media. As a result, at the point of local implementation, these programs may threaten to disrupt established power relations, possibly putting groups included in existing settlements on the defensive, or providing an opening for previously excluded groups to assert their interests.

This can create a delicate balancing act for local retrofit planners and engineers, who must weigh technical and cost requirements against the potential for antagonizing political and economic interests. As a result of more inclusive urban development policies since the 1960s, they may also be constrained by laws and ethical standards that require sensitivity to the interests of relevant local stakeholders, including those who have been excluded in the past. In the Coronado Bridge retrofit case, managing these issues required the involvement of Caltrans historians and bridge engineers at the state level, local Caltrans engineers and environmental planners, academic researchers, and political and community leaders, all of whom had different degrees of engineering knowledge, scope of understanding of local needs and interests, and levels of credibility within Caltrans and the local community.

Of course, there are many retrofit programs that will not encounter this kind of local complexity so acutely, possibly because the proposed retrofits are less visible, have less impact on culturally meaningful structures, or simply don't mobilize any local opposition. Alternatively, cultural and political complexities may be ignored or discounted because a decision has been made at the systemic level that the need for retrofit of a certain form out-weighs local concerns. Even though it may not be representative of all systemic retrofit programs, the Caltrans seismic retrofit program provides useful illustrations of the possible complexities that may emerge in less dramatic form even in more routine retrofit projects.

Systemic retrofit, like any kind of infrastructure engineering, is a thoroughly sociotechnical problem, requiring adaptation to both global and localized cultural and material constraints. In urban environments, balancing these constraints becomes particularly complex due to the dense local layerings and interpenetrations of social, cultural, and technological networks. Retrofit can open up latent tensions within and between local networks, generating controversy and conflict that can threaten to derail the engineering process. Systemic retrofit programs are typically developed within a larger global network, where they may be shaped by very different sets of constraints than are encountered at the local level. As a result, they may initially be insensitive to local contingencies. Where these tensions become acute, managing them is critical to maintaining a sustainable and socially responsive systemic retrofit program.

Notes

1   Elements of this chapter are drawn from the author's PhD dissertation, *On Shifting Ground: Earthquakes, Retrofit, and Engineering Culture in California* (Sims 2000). Many of the specific details regarding Caltrans activities are drawn from interviews with engineering researchers and Caltrans engineers, planners and consultants conducted between 1996 and 1998, and from documents in Caltrans internal archives. Detailed notes regarding sources for specific observations and events can be found in the referenced pages of the dissertation.

2   Our definition of repair draws on both its colloquial meaning of fixing broken machinery, and its use in the field of ethnomethodology, where it describes how people restore conversational order and meaning following breakdowns or misunderstandings (Schegloff *et al.* 1977). We expand these uses of repair to encompass larger-scale efforts to restore order at a systemic level.

References

Abbott, A., 1988. *The System of Professions: An Essay on the Division of Expert Labor*. Chicago, IL: University of Chicago Press.

Bowker, G.C. and Star, S.L., 1999. *Sorting Things Out: Classification and its Consequences*. Cambridge, MA: MIT Press.

Brookman, P. and Gomez-Pena, G. (eds), 1986. *Made in Aztlan: Centro Cultural de la Raza Fifteenth Anniversary*. San Diego: Tolteca Publications.

Coffelt, B., 1973. No Man's Land: A Transformation – Chicano Art, Chicano Power, a Park and a Bridge. *San Diego Magazine*, 26 (2), 84–115.

Edwards, P.N., 2003. Infrastructure and Modernity: Force, Time, and Social Organization in the History of Sociotechnical Systems. In T.J. Misa, P. Brey and A. Feenberg, (eds) *Modernity and Technology*. Cambridge, MA: MIT Press, 185–225.

Fisher, J., 1996. *Historic Resource Evaluation Report for the San Diego-Coronado Bay Bridge [#57–857], Chicano Park and the Chicano Park Murals, San Diego County*. Sacramento, CA: California Department of Transportation, Environmental Analysis Branch B.

Governor's Board of Inquiry on the 1989 Loma Prieta Earthquake, 1990. *Competing Against Time: Report to Governor George Deukmejian from the Governor's Board of Inquiry on the 1989 Loma Prieta Earthquake*. Sacramento, CA: State of California, Office of Planning and Research.

Graham, S. and Thrift, N., 2007. Out of Order: Understanding Repair and Maintenance. *Theory, Culture and Society*, 24 (3), 1–25.

Gusfield, J.R., 1981. *The Culture of Public Problems: Drinking-Driving and the Symbolic Order*. Chicago, IL: University of Chicago Press.

Henke, C., 2000. The Mechanics of Workplace Order: Toward a Sociology of Repair. *Berkeley Journal of Sociology*, 44, 55–81.

Henke, C.R., 2007. Situation Normal? Repairing a Risky Ecology. *Social Studies of Science*, 37 (1), 135–142.

Henke, C.R., 2008. *Cultivating Science, Harvesting Power: Science and Industrial Agriculture in California*. Cambridge, MA: MIT Press.

Hilgartner, S., 1992. The Social Construction of Risk Objects: Or, How to Pry Open Networks of Risk. In *Organizations, Uncertainties, and Risk*. Boulder, CO: Westview Press, 39–53.

Hommels, A., 2005. *Unbuilding Cities: Obduracy in Urban Socio-Technical Change*. Cambridge, MA: The MIT Press.

Jackson, S.J., 2014. Rethinking Repair. In T. Gillespie, P. Boczkowski and K. Foot, (eds). *Media Technologies: Essays on Communication, Materiality and Society*. Cambridge, MA: MIT Press.

Latour, B., 1987. *Science In Action: How to Follow Scientists and Engineers Through Society*. Cambridge, MA: Harvard University Press.

Latour, B., 1996. *Aramis, Or the Love of Technology*. Cambridge, MA: Harvard University Press.

Law, J. and Callon, M., 1992. The Life and Death of an Aircraft: A Network Analysis of Technical Change. In W.E. Bijker and J. Law, (eds). *Shaping Technology/Building Society*. Cambridge, MA: MIT Press, 21–52.

May, T., Hodson, M., Marvin, S. and Perry, B., 2013. Achieving 'Systemic' Urban Retrofit: A Framework for Action. In W. Swan and P. Brown, (eds). *Retrofitting the Built Environment* (pp. 7–19). Chichester: John Wiley and Sons.

Schegloff, E.A., Jefferson, G. and Sacks, H., 1977. The Preference for Self-Correction in the Organization of Repair for Conversation. *Language*, 53 (2), 361–382.

Sims, B., 1999. Concrete Practices: Testing in an Earthquake-Engineering Laboratory. *Social Studies of Science*, 29 (4), 483–518.

Sims, B., 2000. On Shifting Ground: Earthquakes, Retrofit and Engineering Culture in California. PhD thesis, University of California, San Diego. Available from http://public.lanl.gov/bsims/pdf/thesis.pdf, accessed January 3, 2014.

Sims, B., 2007a. 'The Day After the Hurricane': Infrastructure, Order, and the New Orleans Police Department's Response to Hurricane Katrina. *Social Studies of Science*, 37 (1), 111–118.

Sims, B., 2007b. Things Fall Apart: Disaster, Infrastructure, and Risk. *Social Studies of Science*, 37 (1), 93–95.

Sims, B., 2009. Disoriented City: Infrastructure, Social Order, and the Police Response to Hurricane Katrina. In S. Graham, (ed.). *Disrupted Cities: When Infrastructure Fails*. Abingdon, Oxon, UK and New York: Routledge, 39–51.

Sims, B. and Henke, C.R., 2012. Repairing Credibility: Repositioning Nuclear Weapons Knowledge after the Cold War. *Social Studies of Science*, 42 (3), 324–347.

Star, S.L. and Ruhleder, K., 1996. Steps Toward an Ecology of Infrastructure: Design and Access for Large Information Spaces. *Information Systems Research*, 7 (1), 111–134.

Suchman, L., 2000. Organizing Alignment: A Case of Bridge-Building. *Organization*, 7 (2), 311–328.

Chapter 3

Retrofit in Greater Manchester and Cardiff

Governing to transform or to ungovern?

Carla De Laurentis, Mike Hodson and Simon Marvin

INTRODUCTION

Increasing attention has been directed towards understanding the role that the built environment can play in achieving ambitious carbon reduction targets and wider sustainability goals (Lomas, 2009; Lowe, 2009; Kelly, 2009). The built environment in Europe accounts for an average of one-third of energy consumption and research has shown that interventions in the existing building stock and improvements on the energy performance of buildings can provide both short and long term opportunities to reduce carbon emissions. The need to decarbonise the built environment has often been understood at the level of buildings and neighbourhoods and has been primarily the domain of engineers, architects and construction interests. The repair, maintenance and renewal of the built environment and infra-structures as an on-going activity in replenishing the built environment are not a new concept (Graham and Thrift, 2007). However, the compelling pressures of climate change and resource constraints put renewed emphasis on the need to retrofit or re-engineer the built environment and its existing building stock at scale to meet new and more demanding environmental and energy priorities (Hodson and Marvin, 2009).

Up-scaling retrofit from a largely ad-hoc and piecemeal activity into strat-egic and systemic programmes that transform the built environment has gained increased prominence within research and policy arenas (Hodson and Marvin, 2013; May *et al.* 2013). As the implementation of carbon mitigation options at scale is associated with a wide range of ancillary benefits (e.g. Urge-Vorsatz *et al.* 2007), narratives for retrofit at national, regional and city-regional scales have therefore been developed in response to a complex set of pressures, political priorities and economic drivers ranging from climate change, energy security, green growth, social equity and fuel poverty. Changing political priorities, pressures and economic drivers are experienced, interpreted and acted-upon in different ways across different scales and places (While *et al.* 2010). This chapter, in particular, focuses upon the manner in which changing UK policies and priorities touch down and are reconstituted in two UK city-regions: Greater Manchester and Cardiff city-region.[1] In particular it focuses on the dynamics of urban retrofit in two city-regions, Greater Manchester and Cardiff/SE Wales. This work is primarily based on an extensive literature review of policy documents and strategies and over seventy in-depth interviews. These were conducted with relevant experts and stakeholders at national, regional and local levels, involving representatives from national, regional and local governments, housing association (HA) managers and groups and organisations involved in energy efficiency in the two city-regions. Each interview focussed on issues such as: guiding vision(s) and priorities; policy drivers and pressures for change; capacities and capabilities; energy efficiency technology and skills; and, the learning and scaling up opportunities of current and prospective retrofit initiatives in the city regions.

This chapter is structured as follows. First, we briefly consider how national priorities and pressures for retrofitting the built environment are framed within the UK government context. Second, we then identify the key drivers and pressures for city regional retrofit responses. Third, we provide an overview of the city-regional retrofit responses in the two case study city regions: Greater Manchester and Cardiff/ South East Wales. This focuses on which social interests are constructing city-regional retrofit responses, how these are framed and in whose interests and for what purpose they are constituted. Fourth we then compare the styles of retrofit responses emerging in the two case study contexts. Finally we present the conclusions and issues for further research.

NATIONAL RETROFIT STRATEGIES

The UK government has set a legally binding commitment to decarboni-sation, enshrined in targets of 80 per cent reductions in greenhouse gas emissions by 2050 and 34 per cent by 2020. These have put renewed focus on the impact of the built environment on carbon emissions, considering that emissions from buildings and industry accounts for more than two thirds of total Green House Gas (GHG) emissions in the UK (Committee for Climate Change, 2010). Consequently, retrofitting the built environment constitutes a very significant challenge in meeting the UK's carbon emission reductions targets. Since the onset of the financial crisis in 2007, retrofit has been promoted across a range of UK national government bodies in different ways. Post-2007 until 2010 the retrofit agenda was seen, on the one hand, as providing a focus for the creation of new 'green' markets and, on the other hand, retrofit was understood as a means to potentially provide a basis for newly constituted interventionist regional, low carbon industrial policy. A set of UK national government policies, priorities and programmes exemplify this struggle: from the Decent Homes programme, to Building Schools for the Future (BSF), the Community Energy Saving

Programme (CESP), the Carbon Emissions Reduction Target (CERT), Feed-in-Tariffs (FITs) for incentivizing the uptake of renewable generation, the creation of Low Carbon Economic Areas (LCEA), and the government's Green Deal initiative (Hodson *et al.* 2012).

Since the UK general election of 2010, however, the 'market makers' have been in the ascendancy. A number of existing responses had ended or were cancelled by the new coalition Government while others such as LCEAs are much less prominent in times of austerity governance than they were prior to 2010. New policy developments established by the coalition Government are shaping responses within city-regions across the UK. Central to this is the Green Deal, run from the Department of Energy and Climate Change, and described as a flagship policy for delivering energy efficiency to homes and building in the UK. The Green Deal, in its simplest term, establishes 'a framework to enable private firms to offer consumer energy efficiency improvements to their homes, community spaces and business at no upfront costs, and recoup payments through a charge in instalments on the energy bill' (DECC, 2010: 5). Under the Green Deal, retrofit is understood in primarily economic terms as a market making process. As such, city-regions are seen as sites for experimenting that will provide lessons for a wider scale building of markets for retrofit and the sorts of necessary governance frameworks that would facilitate this process. The translation of this top-down economic framing at city-regional scale is however not quite so straightforward. As this chapter shows, different governance contexts and social interests are at play in revealing different framings of the retrofit agenda that often can move away from the predominant economic framing established at national level.

PRESSURES FOR AND ON CITY-REGIONAL RESPONSES

Whilst cities are seen as being the source of many environmental and resource depletion problems, the increased concentration of population in cities offers great opportunities for scaling up the deployment of techno-logical responses to climate change and for the provision of infrastructure and services that can offset environmental impact. A new set of pressures are being exerted at the level of cities that create a set of conditions for a re-shaping of the built environment of cities and the networks and resources that flow through them. As concern over climate change and resource con-straints grow, many cities and city-regions across the world are trying to achieve a low carbon transition, developing expectations, targets and strat-egies that will lead to a more sustainable pattern of resource use (Hodson *et al.* 2013; Hodson and Marvin, 2013).

Many urban governments have started to realise that the economic and financial down-turn experienced in recent years provides both an opportunity and an incentive to promote a greener model of economic growth and development (While *et al.* 2010). The need to invest in low-carbon infrastructure, the requirement to manage low carbon budgets and carbon regulation coupled with the opportunities for growth offered by low carbon markets place renewed emphasis on to sub-national territorial units and their ability to better manage energy consumption and accelerate the development of low carbon transitions in energy production, consumption and mediation through the built environment.

In the UK, a key issue in contributing to the shape of decarbonisation responses are frequent changes in the organisation of sub-national governing frameworks (Hodson and Marvin, 2013). This has meant re-organisation and, in some cases, abolition of regional, city-regional and local authority tiers of governing since the 1970s. It has also seen 'innovation' involving the construction of new governing frameworks, notably in terms of devolution for Scotland and Wales, the construction and abolition of regional frameworks of governing in England and experimental attempts to create statutory city-regional governing arrangements in Greater Manchester and Leeds from the second half of the 2000s onwards. What this means is that efforts and aspirations for carbon emission reductions meet frequently changing governing frameworks through which transition in energy systems and their relationships with the built environment can be achieved. A strategic approach to planning and targets for renewables at the city regional level has translated into the emergence of a new city regional level governance for renewable energy. Nevertheless, the recent re-organisation of governance frameworks – the abolition of the regional tier of government and the new localism agenda – in addition to an austerity agenda and the promotion of cuts has also meant reduction of capacity and institutions, raising important questions regarding how governing capacity and frameworks are constructed to develop retrofit responses in these city-regions.

Indeed retrofitting, by its very nature, does not occur on a blank slate and will occur in existing social, governance and physical structures and existing systems of infrastructure organised (politically, technically, production/consumption, regulatory) in a particular way. It is important to acknowledge this, and understand how economic, social, political and demographic structures might influence how retrofit is constructed, embedded and/or adapted to address priorities and a shared vision of the many different social interests at city-regional scale. Questions around urban retrofit therefore are not just about the technical issues, but also about widening the framing of infrastructure to involve the concerns but also the potential offered by a wide variety of social interests – utilities, regulators, developers, residents, citizens, environmental groups, business (Borup *et al.* 2006). Issues of decarbonising at a city-regional scale will involve social interests and material structures across different scales of activity. How this looks will depend on the nature of the governing formations – the organisation of interrelationships of social interests – producing responses and the relative weight of different interests in being able to influence the shape of city-regional responses.

CITY-REGIONAL RETROFIT RESPONSES IN GREATER MANCHESTER AND CARDIFF

In responding to these pressures the remainder of the chapter seeks to understand how retrofit in the UK is mobilised as a means of transforming the city-region and to examine the role of different governing frameworks shaping the responses. We answer these questions by providing two examples of retrofitting responses in Greater Manchester and Cardiff/ South East Wales city-regions. We structure our understanding of retrofit responses in terms of four sets of issues:

1   An analysis of the city-regional governance frameworks within which each of the retrofit responses is constructed;
2   The ways in which these governance frameworks are mediating and interpreting wider sets of global pressures at city-regional scale and which of these – economic, ecological, governing, social justice etc – pressures are more and less prioritised;
3   The responses – i.e. retrofit visions and strategies – that are being constructed in each of the city-regions, what they look like and set out to achieve;
4   The set of key issues that follow from these responses and developing a comparative understanding of them.

Greater Manchester: retrofitting ON and IN

Governance and Retrofit in Greater Manchester: Greater Manchester is a metropolitan county of around 2.6 million people, encompassing 10 local authorities. Greater Manchester was established in 1974 and operated on the basis of two-tier governing arrangements where the strategic level, Greater Manchester County Council, shared power with the 10 metropolitan boroughs that constituted it. The Greater Manchester County Council was abolished in 1986 and subsequently many powers were devolved back to the 10 boroughs while others powers – including transport and emergency services – operated at the metropolitan level through the Association of Greater Manchester Authorities (AGMA) and associated agencies. We have written elsewhere and in detail about the political and governing context of Greater Manchester (Hodson and Marvin, 2012).

There has been a further step-change in the second half of the 2000s with Greater Manchester, along with Leeds city-region, being designated Statutory City-Regional Pilots in the 2009 UK Budget. The result of this has been the emergence of a new metropolitan governance but one where the embedded capacity to act is limited, where national priorities remain an important shaper of metropolitan priorities and where the financial crisis post-2007 has created the conditions for an era of austerity within which efforts to constitute the capacity to shape retrofitting strategies needs to be understood.

In terms of the low carbon agenda generally and retrofit specifically these dynamics are visible in the development of the dominant representation of retrofit in Greater Manchester where these agendas are concerned with positioning the city-region externally. What this means is that Greater Manchester is presented and discussed as a low carbon first mover to attract inward investment and where the function of governance is to promote Greater Manchester in this way and to provide business support in relation to this agenda. Underpinning this is the logic of the low carbon agenda being one that extends the economic development agenda of post-1986 governing into low carbon 'entrepreneurialism' and the opportunities this affords. The narrative headline that supports this is that this will help avoid the economic costs of inaction on climate change and allow the city-region to move rapidly to accrue the economic opportunities and benefits (Deloitte, 2008). In one estimate, effectively addressing climate change in the city-region over the five year period of Greater Manchester being a Low Carbon Economic Area will contribute to saving 6m tons of CO2, 34,800 jobs and be a demonstrable exemplar for the wider region and the UK (GMLCHRS, 2011).

This broad view is promoted by a number of plans and strategy documents from the Mini-Stern to the Sustainable Energy Action Plan and the Low Carbon Economic Area (LCEA) for the Built Environment. These are often plans being promoted by a small number of interests and often doing so as a test-bed for national targets. The LCEA designation for Greater Manchester in 2009 required Greater Manchester governing commissions working with national government departments (Department for Business Innovation and Skills, Department for Energy and Climate Change), national agencies (Carbon Trust, Energy Savings Trust) and the regional development agency (NWDA). Yet with this five year programme there was no specific government funding despite it being the basis for experimenting with how to create and shape markets and low carbon goods and services and to address national targets and programmes in doing so.

Pressures facing Governing in Greater Manchester

As is the case with many city-regions, Greater Manchester has to achieve significant carbon emissions reductions. It needs to do this in the context of contributing to national emissions reduction targets and also as part of an emerging world of ecological competition between city-regions to have secure access to the 'cleaner' energy resources necessary to literally fuel economic activity. In Greater Manchester a framework for doing so has been set out to achieve targets for delivering domestic carbon reductions of 55 per cent by 2022 as part of wider targets of 48 per cent carbon emissions reductions by 2020. The Greater Manchester low carbon housing retrofit strategy sets out what needs to be done so that the retrofitting of nearly 1.2 million homes contributes to those targets (GMLCHRS, 2011).

Additionally, the developing context nationally is one of 'austerity' governance. The dominant political priority is one of post-financial crash deficit reduction. This means cuts in public spending. Alongside this the UK coalition government, in office since May 2010, has worked to strip out significant aspects of existing sub-national governing architecture – particularly regional development agencies (RDAs), but also other national agencies with responsibilities for urban areas. The coalition has replaced RDAs with local enterprise partnerships (LEPs) which are an effort to intensify the economic development remit of the abolished RDAs. Significantly, there are many more LEPs (38 announced by January 2012) than RDAs (9 in England) and there has been a reduction in funding from the annual RDA budget around £1.4 billion a year in 2010 to a new regional growth fund originally around £1.4 billion over 2 years when it was announced in 2010 which was increased to around £2.4 billion in 2011. This means there are more spatial units competing for less funding. The issue here is one of austerity and sub-national restructuring underpinning the intensification of geographical competition.

Greater Manchester responses – retrofitting IN and ON

There are a wide range of retrofit activities in Greater Manchester which we characterise as two emergent pathways for urban retrofit (see Hodson et al. 2015).

The first of these is a dominant national/city-regional policy and business led view of the relationship between Greater Manchester and retrofit which is 'top down' and can be characterised as retrofitting ON Greater Manchester. The broad governance history of the development of the retrofit agenda in Greater Manchester, through the LCEA and going back even further has been set out above. Within this context the current state of Greater Manchester plans for a retrofitting agenda can be seen in the draft Greater Manchester Low Carbon Housing Retrofit Strategy published in October 2011 (GMLCHRS, 2011). The historical politics of Greater Manchester over the last three decades or so can be seen in the ways in which the retrofit agenda is seen as: reducing emissions in relation to Greater -

Manchester's carbon reduction emissions targets in a broader national context positioning Greater Manchester as a test-bed for national retrofit programmes; also as a way of achieving 'first mover' economic status and positioning Greater Manchester as leader in an emerging UK retrofit market. In doing so the development of a retrofit agenda is seen as a way to attract private investment to the city-region where the dominant message of retrofit in Greater Manchester is that it is about the making of new markets. That is it is about governing Greater Manchester to make it amenable to the market opportunities afforded by retrofit. Retrofit is also seen as being able to address fuel poverty and improve wellbeing, to improve existing homes, streets and neighbourhoods and the effectiveness and efficiency of the existing building stock, to create attractive places to live.

A second set of responses are a range of community and embedded activities within Greater Manchester which are 'bottom up' and which can be characterised as retrofitting IN Greater Manchester. By 'bottom up' we are talking about initiatives that primarily emerge from and are developed in particular neighbourhoods, organizations or places to meet, or at least try to address, the motivations of groups of local interests and people. They are in some sense motivations that emerge from local contexts and that seek to reconfigure in local contexts. In contrast to the retrofitting ON approach, there are a wide range of projects, initiatives, schemes around 'retrofit' in Greater Manchester. A fuller discussion of these examples can be found elsewhere (Burrai, 2014; Hodson, 2014). Many of these rather than being part of top down schemes or programmes emanate within communities. That is not to say that there is no policy involvement – as there may be through, for example, national or city-regional funding schemes – but it is to say that these initiatives are largely developed by neighbourhood or place-based groups, organisations, businesses and collections of individuals. Given this the motivations for involvement in embedded retrofit activities in Greater Manchester range from those that seek to: promote economic development through carbon reduction; reduce the carbon footprint of a town, and promote 'sustainability'; use the retrofit agenda as vehicle for education, outreach and building refurbishment; as part of wider processes of building community engagement. Motivations for embedded retrofit and community engagement are manifold. What is clear is that the concept of community cannot be understood in its singularity. Within and across places communities interact and interrelate.

The dominant characterisation of retrofit in Greater Manchester is the top down retrofitting ON Greater Manchester. There is significant retrofitting IN Greater Manchester, although this is less prevalent in wider public debates. Table 3.1 summarises the key aspects of retrofitting ON and IN.

Table 3.1 Greater Manchester – retrofitting ON and IN

Retrofitting ON		Retrofitting IN
'Top down'	**Approach**	'Bottom up'
Primarily economic development and positioning	**Motivations**	Manifold – economy, community engagement, security, voice
National priorities and local capacity and priorities in asymmetric relation	**Negotiation**	Small numbers of disposed individuals or groups in each initiative – working to accrete capacity
Making retrofit markets – demonstrating national priorities	**Aim**	Building embedded capacity – achieving local values
Translating into embedded capacity	**Critical challenge**	Connecting to other communities, funding and forms of capacity
Narrowly constituted elite governance	**Governance**	Multiple, fragmented initiatives

Cardiff: retrofitting as an alternative to national strategy

City-regional governance frameworks

Since 1997 there has been a progressive process of devolution and the development of a regional government in Wales. The Government of Wales Act (1998) provided two statutory obligations for the Welsh Government (WG): an emphasis on inclusive governance and equal opportunities and a requirement to pursue sustainable development. The approach to decision making embraces, therefore, the long-term, encouraging joined-up thinking and active participation at all levels (people, communities, businesses, the third sector, and the public sector). The WG's vision is one that reinforces, therefore, a collaborative rather than a competitive approach towards public service provision and improvement among its delivery arm, the local authorities.

Although the concept of a Cardiff city-region is a nebulous one without the clear geographic boundaries of city-regions like Greater Manchester, the interdependencies between Cardiff and its surrounding areas are clear both historically and in the contemporary region, showing very different characteristics: the coastal area is relatively prosperous, housing the cities of Cardiff and Newport while the Heads of the Valleys area is in need of regeneration. As such, a question mark remains as to how a more unified city-region would function. For our purposes the conceptual city-region of South East Wales has been extended to include the local authorities of Neath Port Talbot and Swansea to the west, as represented in Figure 3.1. This is intended to capture the strong economic connections between the three urban regions along the south coast (Newport, Cardiff and Swansea) which differ significantly from the neighbouring rural regions of West and Mid Wales. Cardiff city-region is home to 1,831,915 people, 60 per cent of Wales' population despite spanning only 17 per cent of its area; indeed, the three urban centres of Swansea, Cardiff and Newport account for 24 per cent of the Welsh population. The region continues to suffer pockets of social and economic deprivation, with gross value added (GVA) standing at 80 per cent of the UK average in 2009 and average gross weekly income at 86 per cent of the UK figure in 2011 (Stats Wales, 2011; 2011a).

The historical development of the region (for a review see Hunt, 2011) coupled with the economic and population growth experienced in the 1800s has had an important role in shaping the built environment (both in terms of infrastructure and the housing stock) in the city-region. Mass immigration in the South Wales Valleys put several pressures on the housing stock and in order to accommodate its swelling population (Minchinton, 1969) a number of houses were quickly built to low standards. The issue of poor quality housing stock is closely related to the issue of fuel poverty as, in Wales, 332,000 households were estimated to suffer fuel poverty in 2008, an increase of 15 per cent since 2004.

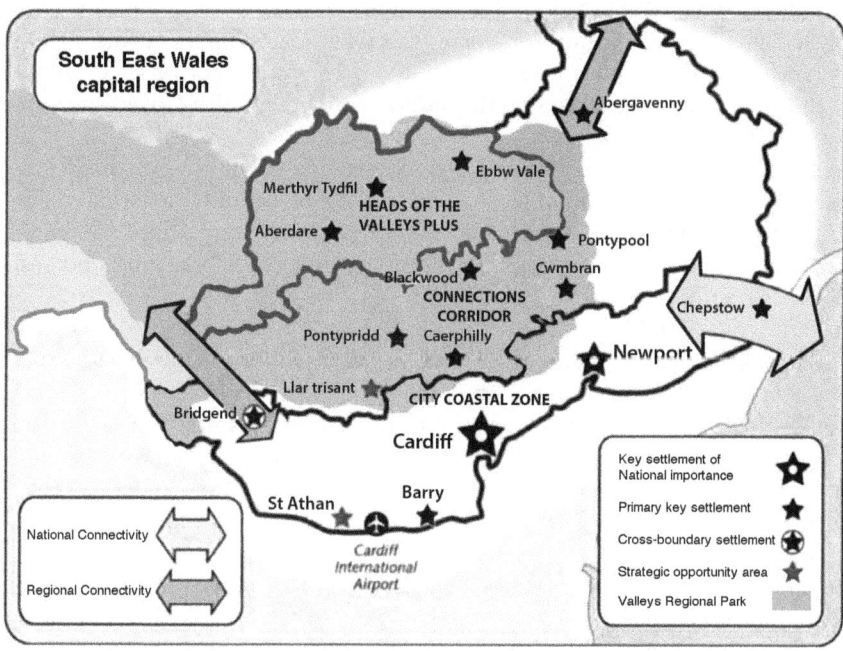

Figure 3.1 Cardiff South East Wales Conceptual city region
Source: Authors re-elaboration following WAG, 2008. Contains National Statistics data © Crown
    copyright 2012

Mediating global pressures at city-regional scale

The statutory duty to promote sustainable development has been translated in recognising sustainable development as the central organising principle of all policies and programmes, across all Ministerial portfolios. This meant that, on the one hand, the WG has set an aspiration to become an exemplar organisation in the way it mainstreams sustainable development and demonstrates leadership, encouraging and enabling others to embrace sustainable development. On the other hand, the key expected outcomes are that, firstly, sustainable development considerations are put at the core of the evaluation and development of WG policies and new and existing investment proposals. Sustainable development in Wales firmly focuses on improving and sustaining people's quality of life, the wellbeing of people and communities, embedding social justice and equality for all.

Sustainable development is seen therefore as a cross-cutting theme that informs individual strategies, policies and initiatives that are put in place to respond to the several pressures that impact upon the environment, resource use, the economy and the wellbeing of people. Although, the WG has shown strong political and organisational leadership in relation to sustainable development, however the challenge remains how to apply sustainable development aspirations and interpret specific actions and outcomes in practice (PWC, 2011). Neither the legal duty to have a sustainable development scheme nor a duty to make sustainable development the central organising principle have been passed onto other public bodies such as local authorities raising challenges on the influence that the Welsh Government has over its delivery agents.

The WG, through a series of policy documents and strategies, has established a vision for sustainable, low carbon Wales detailing a series of new and existing initiatives designed to reduce emissions and adapt to change across a range of policy areas, including among others housing and residential energy, agriculture and land management and waste (see for instance WG, 2010).

Through the One Wales agreement in 2007, the WG committed to a 3 per cent annual reduction in carbon emissions in areas of devolved responsibility from 2011. Reducing energy and resource consumption, increasing energy and resource efficiency in the domestic, public, business and industrial sectors, through behaviour change initiatives, financial incentives, regulation and standards are key areas in which the WG plans to act.

The compelling issues and challenges posed by climate change are seen as an opportunity to make progress on a range of other policy objectives including: generating green jobs (the Green Jobs Strategy for Wales, Capturing the Potential (2009)); supporting the energy, environment and construction sectors; promoting renewable energy production and diffusion (The Low Carbon Revolution, the Energy Policy Statement for Wales (2010));

promoting energy efficiency in order to secure benefits for the people, businesses and the environment in Wales (The National Energy Efficiency and Savings Plan- NEESP (2011)). The WG has also renewed its focus on tackling fuel poverty which is defined as having to spend more than 10 per cent of income (including housing benefit) on all household fuel use to maintain a satisfactory heating regime. Where expenditure on all household fuel exceeds 20 per cent of income, households are defined as being in severe fuel poverty. The new Fuel Poverty Strategy (2010) represents a further attempt to demonstrate how sustainable development is at the core of the Welsh Government's actions. It is stressed that fuel poverty and its impact are a cross cutting theme in many different areas of the WG's policy, and the strategy is well suited in delivering social, environmental and economic benefits.

These policy objectives, set at regional level, often, get translated and re-aligned with local interests in the local context. The vision of sustainable development with its complementary visions of energy efficiency, fuel poverty, economic development and regeneration, at local authority level, is often re-oriented towards more doable, preferable and credible pathways such as tackling fuel poverty.

The responses

While retrofit is not framed formally as a policy area within the Welsh Government, it is slowly emerging as a potential delivery mechanism (solution) for addressing and implementing different policy priorities stemming from the sustainable development agenda. A narrative for retrofit is constituted around the challenges of climate change (adaptation and mitigation), a wider low carbon economy goal, which includes the creation of green jobs, maximising the opportunities offered by the deployment of renewable energy sources and fuel poverty. Most of the retrofit initiatives in the city-region have been undertaken under:

1   the area-based ARBED, Strategic Energy Performance Investment Programme, Phase I which improved the energy efficiency of over 6,000 homes in Wales (nearly 4,500 homes in the city-region);
2   ARBED, Phase II which aims at improving the energy efficiency of over 5,000 homes in Wales in a three year period;
3   the demand-led Home Energy Efficiency Scheme (2001–2010) that has improved energy efficiency in 124,000 households since being set-up (the scheme has now been replaced by the NEST scheme);
4   the WHQS, with 75 per cent of LAs and 82 per cent of housing associations homes reaching SAP 65 in 2011/2012 (WAG, 2011, Social Landlords' Performance in Achieving the Welsh Housing Quality Standard);

5   the Heads of the Valleys (HoVP) Low Carbon Zone Programme which aimed at installing up to 40,000 micro generation technologies, assessing 65,000 homes for energy efficiency and implementing 39,000 energy reduction measures in social housing.

Many local authorities in the city-region are also taking forward smaller-scale retrofit projects. These include often a few measures at a time (such as external wall insutation (EWI)), loft and cavity insulations and energy efficiency measures), a small number of properties adopting a street-based approach (e.g. RCT Borough 'community approach') or type of property approach (Cardiff Council 'bungalows project'), in order to retrofit some of their housing stock but also encompassing privately owned homes. What is evident is that the areas chosen are often selected by 'targeting the right areas first'. These are either deprived areas in fuel poverty, with elderly occupants and houses that represents the 'worst performing stocks'. This area-based approach, very common in regeneration activities, has also been utilised in the delivery of Arbed Phase I and Phase II. The properties targeted were located primarily in the strategic regeneration areas (SRAs) of Wales characterised by particularly low household incomes (the lowest 15 per cent income domain of the Welsh index of multiple deprivation), targeting both areas in need of regeneration and households in fuel poverty.

   To summarise, retrofit is an emerging process within the city-region that ranges from planned and responsive maintenance programmes to targeted energy efficiency improvements and major refurbishment programmes. There is a move towards a more 'scaled up approach' to increase impact and above all, deliver the ambitious targets that the WG and LAs are aiming to achieve. Most of the activities are driven by public funding which targets mainly social housing, excluding the private rented and private housing sector. It is important to highlight that most of the projects reviewed focussed on regeneration areas and aimed at reducing fuel poverty and establishing a demand for greener technologies that will create local jobs. Since the outset of the flagship refurbishment programmes Arbed, it was realised that 'the full potential of energy efficiency schemes can be realised if these schemes are embedded into Wales' broader economic development and regeneration agenda' (WAG 2010). As stressed, this focus on regeneration and community renewal has offered a more inclusive approach to retrofit.

GREATER MANCHESTER AND CARDIFF CITY-REGION IN COMPARISON

In setting out retrofit responses in Greater Manchester and Cardiff our aim has been to comparatively understand whether these are attempts to transform the city-region and, if so, in what ways? (see Table 3.2) Within

Greater Manchester there is an overarching emphasis in the dominant retrofit response to position the city-region as an economic first mover, an attractor of inward investment and a test-bed for national priorities. While the response at a Cardiff city-region scale emphasises social justice and fuel poverty elements of retrofit within a longer-term governance framework oriented to sustainable development. Since the process of devolution in Wales began in 1997 there has been much more emphasis on promoting inclusive governance and sustainable development. Although the duty to sustainable development has not been passed onto local authorities or other public bodies, there is an effort to promote sustainable development at all governance levels. In its effort to retrofit the built environment the WG provides an example of 'governance by government', that appears quite inclusive.

Both housing associations/RSLs and local authorities are participating and are fully engaged with the WG in delivering the sustainable development and retrofit agendas. While there is an extensive reliance on public funding channelled through the WG, housing associations/ RSLs have been very receptive to energy efficiency and carbon emission reduction and have interpreted their role in a wider sense, encompassing strategic development, economic development and reducing climate change. LAs have also been able to play an important role in mobilising and engaging with communities, tenants and private sector households. It is worth emphasising, however, that most of the retrofit initiatives are still targeting social housing and have had a limited impact on the private sector (both privately owned and privately rented households). New incumbent actors are, however, playing an important role. They are often organised as community interest companies and they provide stronger links with the communities and existing organisations within these communities.

Contrariwise, in Greater Manchester the two different responses to retrofit highlights a lack of coordination between the spaces where the narrative of retrofit is constituted (at metropolitan level) and where retrofit is taking place (at neighbourhood level). The emergent metropolitan governance at Greater Manchester scale is perceived as top-down, pursued by an 'eliterian/ elitist' group of businesses, agencies and politicians and deeply shaped by national priorities. The grassroots approach, conversely, consists of 'a range of community and embedded activities', often led by communities, neighbourhood or place-based groups and organisations that seek to tackle issues that are specific to the local context. In this sense, retrofit is seen as a means to 'making communities relevant again', 'giving voice to community and empowering them'. However, the lack of coordination signifies that projects are piecemeal and isolated.

Finally, the two different approaches to retrofit have wider implications for the Green Deal. While the Greater Manchester region's response reproduces and aligns with the national narrative that informs the Green Deal, the Welsh approach differs from the Green Deal in many ways. In the

Cardiff city-region the choice of retrofit delivery is through an area-based approach that ensures that deprived areas and most disadvantaged households are prioritised. The ways in which the two responses to retrofit differ in the two case study regions are set out in the comparative table below.

CONCLUSION

The case studies analysed show that different governance contexts and different social interests are at play in revealing different framings of the retrofit agenda that often move away from the predominant economic framing established at national level.

Table 3.2 Comparing retrofit in Greater Manchester and Cardiff city-region: transformation and market-making

Understanding retrofit	Greater Manchester	Cardiff city-region
Drivers and Pressures	A means to position the city-region externally to attract investments • 'retrofit markets'	A means to deliver SD • Economic, environmental and social benefits
Governance and cultural context	Emergent metropolitan governance at GM scale: • top down up and less inclusive • limited capacity to act and shaped by national priority • mainly *aspirational* Grassroots approach: • a range of communities and embedded activities • tackle issues that are specific to the local context • can be piecemeal and isolated	Inclusive governance and partnership • SD organising principle • Governance by government • HAs/ RSLs/ LAs /private sector
Social organisation of responses	Ambitious targets and plan to retrofit at scale Driven by businesses and elite politicians • hierarchy of responses • dominant technological approach • raise funding from private and public sector 'cherry picking' Little coordination between the two styles of governance	Area-based approach: Focus is on vulnerable communities and households • 'targeting the right area first' • 'Worst performing stock' Alignment of interests Establishing links with community groups and existing organisations

Retrofitting, by its very nature, occurs in existing social, governance and physical structures and these influence the way changing political priorities, pressures and economic drivers are experienced, interpreted and acted-upon. Although the nation-state is still important so also, increasingly, are various other levels and scales of governance which are related often in complex and different ways in various contexts (Hodson *et al.* 2015). There is a need to increasingly acknowledge the role of city and regional scales in shaping technological transitions as part of a wider devolution of responsibility, but not necessarily powers, to reshape the technological and economic competitiveness of places.

The case studies discussed stress that the dynamics of innovation, transformation and co-evolution of retrofitting cities towards sustainability are better understood by considering the importance of spatial heterogeneity. Our argument is that transitions take place in particular places and that places are differentially positioned in terms of their ability to inform transitions. In doing this, the chapter has examined the visions that have been developed for retrofitting at scale and the negotiations of these visions: including the social actors involved and the expectations from different positions embodied in them. It can be concluded that, in some instances, cities can be conceived as 'receiving' national transition that are then implemented in the local context. However, cities can also develop further capacity and capability to envision and enact their own locally developed transition. Whether, these transition initiatives are taken up by the national context and incorporated in new national transitions (see Hodson and Marvin, 2009), is a matter to be analysed by further research.

Note

1   This chapter presents some results of research conducted under the UK EPSRC-funded project, Retrofit 2050, that has sought to engage with UK city-regions in terms of shaping retrofit transitions pathways. See www.retrofit2050.org.uk

References

Borup, M., Brown, N., Konrad, K. and Van Lente, H. (2006) The sociology of expectations in science and technology, *Technology Analysis and Strategic Management*, 18:3–4, 285–298.

Bulkeley, H., Hodson, M. and Marvin, S. (2012) 'Emerging strategies of urban reproduction and the pursuit of low carbon cities'. In Flint, J. and Raco, M. (eds) *The Future of Sustainable Cities*, Policy Press: Bristol.

Burrai, E. (2014) Retrofit alternatives in Greater Manchester, Working Paper EPSRC Retrofit 2050 project. Available from www.retrofit2050.org.uk/sites/default/files/resources/workingpaperEB_FINAL_29012014.pdf, accessed 17 August 2015.

Committee on Climate Change (2010) The Fourth Carbon Budget, Reducing Emissions through the 2020s, London, Available from www.theccc.org.uk/archive/aws2/4th%20Budget/CCC-4th-Budget-Book_with-hypers.pdf, accessed 17 August 2015.

DECC, (2010) The Green Deal, A summary of the Government's proposals, Department of Energy and Climate change, London, Available from www.gov.uk/government/uploads/system/uploads/attachment_data/file/47978/1010-green-deal-summary-proposals.pdf, accessed 17 August 2015,

Graham, S. and Thrift, N. (2007) Out of order: understanding repair and maintenance. *Theory, Culture and Society*, 24:3, 1–25.

Hodson, M. (2014) Remaking the material fabric of the City? Why it matters, how it is being done, and what this tells us. Report for the Greater Manchester Local Interaction Platform of Mistra Urban Futures.

Hodson, M. and Marvin, S. (2009) 'Urban ecological security' A new urban paradigm? *International Journal of Urban and Regional Research*, inaugural article Urban Worlds section.

Hodson, M. and Marvin, S. (2012) Mediating low-carbon urban transitions? Forms of organisation, knowledge and action. *European Planning Studies*, 20:3, 421–39.

Hodson, M. and Marvin, S. (2013) *Low Carbon Nation?* Earthscan: London.

Hodson, M. Marvin, S. and Bulkeley, H. (2013) The intermediary organisation of low carbon cities: a comparative analysis of transitions in Greater London and Greater Manchester. *Urban Studies*, 50:7, 1403–1422.

Hodson, M., Marvin, S. and Späth, P. (2015) 'Subnational, inter-scalar dynamics: the differentiated geographies of governing low carbon transitions – with examples from the UK'. In Günter Brauch, H., Oswald Spring, U., Grin, J. and Scheffran, J. (eds), *Handbook on Sustainability Transition and Sustainable Peace* (STSP), Hexagon Series on Human and Environmental Security and Peace 10, Heidelburg/New York/Dordrecht/London: Springer-Verlag.

Hodson, M., Marvin, S. and Thompson, M. (2012) Retrofit and Greater Manchester: landscape, governing and practice. Unpublished paper.

Hou, J. (ed.) (2010) *Insurgent Public Space: Guerrilla Urbanism and the Remaking of Contemporary Cities*, Routledge: Abingdon.

Hunt, M. (2011) Cardiff and South East Wales: Social, Economic and Sustainability Context. Retrofit 2050 Working Paper, Cardiff University, Cardiff. Available from www.retrofit2050.org.uk/sites/default/files/resources/WP20112.pdf, accessed 17 August 2015.

Kelly, M. (2009) Retrofitting the existing UK building stock. *Building Research and Information*, 37:2, 196–200.

Lomas, K. (2009) Decarbonising national housing stocks: barriers and measurement. *Building Research and Information*, 37:2, 187–191.

Lowe, R. (2009) Policy and strategy challenges for climate change and building stocks. *Building Research and Information*, 37:2, 206–212.

May, T., Hodson, M., Marvin, S. and Perry, B. (2013) 'Achieving systemic urban retrofit: a framework for action'. In Swan, W. and Brown, P. (eds) *Retrofitting the Built Environment*, Wiley: Chichester, pp.7–19.

Minchinton, W. (1969) 'Industrial South Wales, 1750–1914'. In Minchinton, W. (ed.) *Industrial South Wales 1750–1914: Essays in Welsh Economic History*, Routledge, Abingdon.

Perry, B., May, T., Marvin, S. and Hodson, M. (2013) Re-thinking sustainable knowledge-based urbanism through active intermediation. In Anderson, H.T. and Atkinson, R. (eds). *The production and use of urban knowledge: European experiences.* Dordrecht: Springer, pp. 157–167.

PWC, (2011) Effectiveness Review of the Sustainable Development Scheme: A report to Welsh Government. PricewaterhouseCoopers, Cardiff. Available from www.assembly.wales/Laid%20Documents/GEN-LD8769%20-%20 Effectiveness%20Review%20of%20the%20Sustainable%20Development%20S cheme%20A%20Report%20to%20the%20Welsh%20Government-23012012-229674/gen-ld8769-e-English.pdf, accessed 17 August 2015.

Stats Wales (2011) Sub-regional Gross Value Added (GVA) by Welsh Economic Region. Stats Wales, Cardiff.

Stats Wales (2011a) Average Gross Weekly Earnings by Welsh Local Authority. Stats Wales, Cardiff.

Ürge-Vorsatz D., Harvey L., Mirasgedis S. and Levine, M. (2007) Mitigating CO_2 emissions from energy use in the world's buildings. *Building Research and Information,* 35:4, 379–398.

WAG, (2010) A Low Carbon Revolution – The Welsh Assembly Government Energy Policy Statement March 2010. Welsh Government, Cardiff. Available from www.mng.org.uk/gh/resources/100315energystatementen.pdf, accessed 17 August 2015.

While, A., Jonas, A.E.G. and Gibbs, D. (2010) From sustainable development to carbon control: Eco-state restructuring and the politics of urban and regional development. *Transactions of the Institute of British Geographers,* 35:1, 76–93.

Chapter 4

Socio-technical innovation in heat networks

Challenges of financing new systems in UK cities

Janette Webb

> ...our goal is to make sure that investable projects across our priority
> sectors can obtain finance in the market place.
> (UK Government Officer, Low Carbon Investments [LCI])

INTRODUCTION

A plethora of low carbon transition policies and scenarios project an urban
future founded on low energy consumption in a sustainable socio-technical
system. Behind the aspirations however lie highly contested, and uncertain,
models for how any such transformation may be brought about, by whom,
using what resources and with what implications for shares of costs and
benefits. Some of the major unanswered questions concern the retrofitting
of established urban centres, which are the embodiment of the finance-
oriented materialism constitutive of modern societies. As a site of early
industrialisation and urbanisation, the UK is a potent case study for
questions relating to the financing of such retrofit, which in the current neoliberal political-economic settlement, looks for answers derived from
market-oriented provision.

This paper explores one element of retrofitting, that of decentralised energy
generation and supply. In high density areas of towns and cities, energy
generated close to its point of use, at the meso scale,[1] has recognised social,
economic and environmental value in relation to energy and carbon saving,
affordable heating and urban regeneration, and has potential to re-localise
inter-relations of use, ownership and control (Kelly and Pollitt, 2010; see also
http://chp.decc.gov.uk/cms/chp-benefits/). In the past, the acknowledged
benefits have not however resulted in significant UK provision. District energy
technologies serving heat networks are well-established in Europe, but
provide only around 2 per cent of UK space and water heating (Pöyry, 2009).
Current energy policy developments focus largely on devising market-based
incentives to stimulate investment by transnational utilities in centralised
renewable or low carbon electricity generation.

Recent policy discussion has however begun to engage with questions about the future of heat supply to existing buildings and the complex cost benefit equation of converting such supply to electricity. One result of this is renewed interest in the potential for decentralised energy provision, using urban heat networks, to contribute to a more resilient, affordable and low carbon energy system. Such networks are regarded as justified by urban density and diversity of heating requirements, and the likely availability of a variety of low cost heat sources (DECC, 2012; 2013). The evaluation of feasibility of heat networks is however framed within a neo-liberal policy model which assumes that an efficient market will work to allocate resources to such energy technologies, because their value can be captured in financial returns to investors in a for-profit economic model. In its idealised form, this model, which has been actively developed in the UK under both Conservative and Labour governments since the 1980s, asserts that macro-economic planning of integrated infrastructure by the state leads to inefficiencies and rigidities. These can be avoided by reliance on market competition to format provision, with the role of government restricted to enabling the removal of market barriers through information and incentives (Mitchell, 2008). The social and political dimensions of such innovation processes, and questions of what non-financialised public value might be placed on different forms of, and routes to, sustainable energy for urban settings, remain obscured.

Retrofitting of urban heat networks requires skills and capacities not just in project development, engineering and management, but also in relation to infrastructure finance. There are well-known sources of difficulty in such financing, the most challenging of which is the relatively high upfront capital cost of network infrastructure, combined with the lag between initial capital expenditure and revenues. The financing principles generally used in configuring such projects are illustrated in the box below.

The illustration shows how the development of local energy generation and supply infrastructure is typically financed *de novo*. This means that it is at a cost disadvantage, relative to 'sunk investment' in established gas and electricity networks where the costs of extensions and upgrades are shared across the existing large-scale customer population; the UK-regulated asset base model for gas and electricity network operators also ensures predictable and secure returns to investors. Energy policy instruments and regulation are at present oriented to the centralised gas and electricity systems which comprise the majority of generation and supply, and the responsibilities of the UK energy regulator OFGEM (the Office of Gas and Electricity Markets) do not extend to regulation of heat. Consequently the UK lacks established supply chains, skills, and business models, and the unfamiliarity of supply from heat network systems militates against easy demonstration of reliability and affordability, and means that there is no ready-made user base for generation of revenues. All of these factors mean that configuring finance for urban retrofitting of heat infrastructure is highly challenging, but what is less publicly debated, and indeed is frequently 'naturalised', is why, when the wider value of district energy is accepted, the measured financial value is low. This question concerns the framing of financial assessments in the context of three factors: first, political pre-commitment to the attributed efficiency of market mechanisms over other public and community models for energy provision; second, the interests of incumbents in maintaining profitability of sunk investments in centralised carbon-intensive energy networks; and third, the logics of globalising energy and financial markets.

A sociological approach to understanding financial innovation for urban energy infrastructure

Much contemporary academic debate about development of a sustainable energy system is formulated in terms of a multi-level socio-technical systems perspective (MLP), which aims to identify pathways for change in technological regimes (Geels, 2010; Geels and Schot, 2007). The MLP has proved to be a valuable heuristic model for the analysis of technological systems innovation, but has paid relatively limited attention to the implications of

---

▶   Financing made up of Debt, Equity, or a combination.

▶   Debt is traditionally cheaper, so idea is to include as much as possible, traditionally project financed waste or social infrastructure projects made up of c. 80% debt, c. 20% equity, based on project risk profile.

▶   Equity normally provided by shareholders in equal proportions to shareholding. Public sector needs to fund its equity requirement, from reserves, PWLB, grants etc. Drivers may be more than financial returns, so social and economic outcomes.

▶   Financial model takes account of funding approach and costs, project revenues need to support cost inputs – IRR (return requirement) will decide the funding route taken.

▶   Private sector return requirements (10%+) higher than public sector (5–6%).

▶   Reducing risk will increase IRR – robust electricity and heat off takes, easier with electricity, heat often seen as not bankable.[1]

Source: Ernst and Young, Extract from Presentation to Financing District Heating Workshop, London, April 2012.

---

1 There is ambiguity in the final point of the extract, which states that reducing risk will increase IRR (or the rate of return required on project lending). Reducing risk should reduce costs of lending. The point is that secure long-term heat and electricity supply contracts improve cash flow and business revenues, reducing risk of investment in CHP/DH.

Figure 4.1 Financing principles – urban heat networks

innovations in 'soft' technologies, such as those characteristic of recent financial engineering in deregulated markets. In much social science analysis of socio-technical change, finance is often background rather than foreground, but the contemporary political-economic commitment to market mechanisms shapes the field of possibilities, situating financial devices as a significant dimension of innovation in urban infrastructure. The powerful neo-liberal discourse of the last 30 years has asserted that financial innovation, particularly derivatives used to accelerate the recycling of capital, is a major contributor to risk management for socio-technical development and economic prosperity (Engelen et al. 2010). In this model markets are defined as rational-instrumental means of resource allocation, which generate economic value by allocating capital efficiently according to its calculated productivity. Problems of raising private finance for project development are conceived as amenable to engineering solutions, defined as a means of 'de-risking' investment. The underlying epistemology informing such evaluation instruments, and what is included or excluded as relevant factors in investment decisions, generally remains outside the frame and is largely unexamined.

Financial markets and associated engineering devices can instead be studied as a problem in the sociology of knowledge, where knowledge is understood as shared belief, which may or may not be justified in practice (Callon, 1998; MacKenzie, 2009). This work has been stimulated by critical appraisals of the 'financialisation' of advanced economies (Erturk, et al. 2008), indicated by the centrality of financial value as the core indicator of corporate success, and the widespread legitimacy of discourses of shareholder value (Crouch, 2012; Preda, 2009). Questions about authority, power relations, and knowledge are the subject of renewed sociological focus through the analysis of practices of *evaluation* as a means of understanding the social production of material value (Beckert, 2009), and of different 'orders of worth' (Boltanski and Thevenot, 2007), which are central to the coordinated production and functioning of markets. Actor network theory treats the economy not as an independent object, but as a social phenomenon itself constituted by economic theory and practice (Latour, 2005). The boundaries, differential qualities, and the relative value of resources to be transacted all have to be negotiated in order to constitute a market. Structured power relations are amenable to analysis through study of interaction processes and outcomes. Knowledge formations, and their embodiment in 'soft' as well as 'hard' technologies, are conceptualised as the, at least partial, fixing of outcomes of struggles for power. Economic models and devices in these terms are not derived from empirical observation of a fixed economic reality, but contribute to bringing the attributed phenomena of a particular market rationality into being (Callon, 1998; MacKenzie, 2006). In the context of energy markets, the aims of a sociology of knowledge framework are to gain insight into the processes of evaluation and judgements which produce knowledge, and shape decisions, about finance for future energy systems. The following discussion is an exploratory account of some implications for urban energy retrofit of the current forms of knowledge at work in financial markets, and their standardising, delocalising assessments of value.

Developing a sociological perspective on financial evaluation of urban energy infrastructure

In order to understand financial markets and their implications for meso-scale district energy retrofit projects, the sociological perspective seeks insights from market actors' context-bound accounts of their experiences, their use of formal techniques for evaluation of investment options, and their views on the consequences of these for decision-making. The aim is to gain insight into the actor's perspective, while seeking to avoid assumptions about the pre-given, normal or taken for granted qualities of the processes being explored. The arguments advanced in this chapter are hence derived from discussions with financial and energy market experts, participation in specialist cross-sector workshops concerned with solutions for district energy finance, interaction with government policy makers, and with district energy suppliers and developers through the UK Combine Heat and Power Association. The material is described in more detail in a note at the end of the chapter.[2]

Interpreting the evaluation of urban energy retrofit in the UK

The conundrum posed by the dominant frame: 'Constrained public finances' and a centralised energy market

> ...and we all recognise that there's a finite pool of public funding out there. So if we are limited to that sort of funding to invest in the green space, that is going to severely constrain the base investment.
>
> (UK Government Officer, LCI)

Two interlocking narratives stemming from the neo-liberal political-economic consensus provide the dominant frame for evaluating the viability of urban energy developments. In the above comment, the absence of public finance for development of low carbon public utility infrastructure is presented by the government representative as a commonly understood matter of fact, rather than of political pre-commitment to the value of private finance for public infrastructure on the one hand, combined with innovation in a deregulated financial market on the other. This commitment has not been radically destabilised, despite the current global economic crisis associated with some forms of financial innovation designed to accelerate recycling of debt (Crouch, 2012).

UK energy generation and supply was subject to privatisation, and liberalised regulation, in the 1990s, with the result that business has been progressively redirected away from the financial logics of national systems of energy production to those of internationalising capital markets, technology and fuel supply chains (Winskel, 2002). Relatively rapid consolidation of smaller regional utilities into transnational ownership has given much of the initiative in energy provision to large corporations with 'a strong lobbying ability with government' (Asset Management Consultant). In a market context structured by private corporations whose performance is measured by shareholder value, capital investment decisions are made according to the most financially attractive rates of return available; this has typically resulted in emphasis on short-term investment horizons and on marginal efficiency improvements in network operation, at the cost of long term planned infrastructure upgrading (Besley et al. 2013). Such corporations have typically had strong balance sheets and were considered able to manage new infrastructure investment by virtue of the available 'deep pools of capital for utility type risk' (Officer of UK Government Green Investment Team). Strong balance sheets, established procurement models and, more recently, a regulatory framework intended to incentivise low carbon and renewable electricity have created favourable investment conditions: the large scale utilities 'know exactly what they're building; they know exactly how to do it... The actual projects themselves are large scale, economically viable, generation schemes' (Asset Management Consultant). External investors similarly focus on replicable investment opportunities, producing reliable returns, measured by standardised risk assessment instruments:

> If you're a bank ... you want the lowest risk, the best return that can be churned out like a sausage machine.
>
> (Environmental Finance Specialist A)

> And it's systematised; they've done it before and they'll carry on doing it again... Cookie cutter.
>
> (Environmental Finance Specialist B)

> It was. That's a good phrase: cookie cutter. This [district energy] is exactly the opposite of that.
>
> (Environmental Finance Specialist A)

For low carbon electricity infrastructure, the UK government regulatory framework guarantees predictable returns on large-scale investment. Using established procurement models:

...the utilities satisfy their investors on the basis that they can provide predictable returns, because [it is] through a regulatory environment...
(Officer of UK Government Green Investment Team)

In standardising the evaluation of investment options according to maximisation of predictable financial returns, such instruments and templates also decontextualise and delocalise decisions. Although this is in principle constituted as technology neutral, in practice it means that the economics of locally customised small scale combined heat and power (CHP) and urban heat networks reliant on new infrastructure are constituted as riskier and marginal (Kelly & Pollit, 2010). The uncertainties associated with particularities of place, upfront investment ahead of revenues, necessity for secure contracts for supply of heat, and long-term and often relatively low rates of return, result in increasing costs of debt finance, limiting the financial viability of projects:

...go and talk to Drax and they'll say 'we're very happy to talk about... replacing a big power station, but what on earth would we want to go and invest what would be ten times the amount of staff to do probably a hundred times as many, little, individual CHP schemes dotted around. Where on earth is the economics behind that?'... And you compare everything there is opposite to CHP: small scale relatively, ad-hoc procurement, disparate interested parties. They've got to get through all the planning bureaucracies of doing development in the middle of big cities; regulatory risk; policy uncertainty; lack of clarity over revenue risks and who is taking which risks; promoted by small industry players, who, you know, you can't blame them for trying, but they just don't have the same lobbying ear that the big six have. And that's really the conundrum isn't it?
(Asset Management Consultant)

The problem of urban energy retrofit for decentralised heat networks and power generation is construed therefore as a problem of securing private finance for investment in public infrastructure, using standardised, universalised risk assessment tools which are unresponsive to particularistic non-financial indicators of public value. In relation to heat networks:

...finance is not the issue. The issue is risk, perceived risk.
(Finance Investment Consultant)

...the big challenge is how do you de-risk them [heat networks] in such a way that you can attract the pools of low cost finance.
(Officer of UK Government Green Investment Team)

...unfortunately with heat, the key risk and the key downside is... you haven't got a heat grid. So you come back to, again and again, [to] the bankability of that heat and the credit worthiness of the heat off-takers.

(Environmental Finance Specialist B)

In the conventions of the private finance model, the risks of construction, operation and maintenance remain with private investors; in exchange government/public finances guarantee profitable returns. In practice however market actors do not necessarily regard such technical risk allocation models as absolutes. Private sector contributors to this research considered the state, rather than business, to be responsible for 'the investment fundamentals' of stable, secure and predictable cash flows, the:

private sector won't invest speculatively... Large industrial players ... will invest once policy certainty and detail are established... CHP requires industrial and political sponsors.

(Asset Management Consultant)

The constitution of electricity market reform, including guaranteed strike prices for low carbon electricity, has for example entailed considerable negotiation between government and utilities in relation to a proposed new generation of nuclear power stations. Before the final decision about a strike price for new nuclear electricity supply, public debate concerned the necessity to ensure that private investors accepted the risks of construction and electricity generation:

They're saying that they'll only be funded if the power companies are prepared to actually take the risks of producing and generating the electricity off them. But that is disingenuous, because the disposal of the nuclear waste, they're saying 'don't worry about that, we'll sort that out.' Well hang on a minute, you know, the infrastructure involved in disposing of nuclear waste is going to be enormous, not just in terms of engineering, but in terms of cost... But... there are very strong backers within government for nuclear power.

(Asset Management Consultant).

This comment suggests that risk and its distribution are less precise matters in practice than they are presented as being in the abstract, with their parameters shaped by politically dominant understandings of what constitutes relevant costs and benefits. The UK government decision late in 2013 to guarantee a minimum price of £92.50 per megawatt hour, for 35 years, for electricity from a new nuclear power station in England remains contentious, and EU regulators have commenced an investigation into the compatibility between this significant public subsidy and rules on state aid.[3] (Barker *et al.* 2014). The main 'risk' in investment in local energy systems therefore seems to stem not so much from its 'price' *per se* as from its lack of fit with the established high value placed on centralised electricity markets, and large-scale, decontextualised technology, structured around publicly guaranteed rates of return on capital.

Making the market work for low carbon investment?

> The holy grail is this model which enables both to be done in an intelligent manner, combining both public and private finance.
>
> (DB, UK LCI)

A powerful theme in the narrative is that the role of government is to address 'market failure' in areas where private investment is lacking, such as those concerned with energy saving and cleaner energy infrastructure. Government policy is managed by the quasi-autonomous agency the UK Green Investment Bank, which is charged with 'crowding' private finance into clean energy projects in targeted sectors, without providing start-up or low cost capital. Rather than 'rethinking the problem, and doing it a different way' (Finance Investment Consultant), the current model relies on the use of a fixed amount of public finance to invest on commercial market terms, which is intended to incentivise rapid recycling of capital through securitisation of assets in order to increase 'deal flow':

> We have to focus on commercially viable investments and we're about leveraging private capital into the market... Additionality and leverage is really important to our mission... If we can demonstrate to the market that you can make good money in these sectors, then private capital will follow in large volumes.
>
> (Officer of UK Government Green Investment Team).

Addressing the problem of constituting a market where investors perceive little or no financial value is not however resolvable through standardised technical means. Matters of legitimacy and cultural acceptability are noted as significant, making visible the social investment in creating and sustaining shared belief that financial returns can be reliably achieved in currently disregarded sectors. The legitimacy of UK Green Investments is consciously built through the selection of officers who 'understand how the City works' (Finance Investment Consultant). In turn they must not only select fund manager partners with a track record for efficiency and reliability in allocating and managing funds and project portfolios, but such partners must also pass 'the reputation smell-test... we call it the

Sunday Mail test' (Officer of UK Government Green Investment Team), indicating that cultural dimensions of evaluation practices are expected to be a significant factor in making low carbon energy and energy efficiency markets work. The UK GIB is hence positioned as a significant market intermediary channelling information about the trustworthiness of trading partners through social networks; the resulting reputational capital, anchored in shared beliefs about reliability, cultural capital and social status, is expected to resolve uncertainties over the financial value of the products traded (Granovetter, 1985; Podolny, 2001; White, 2002).

The stance taken by the UK Government is however subject to question by other finance experts:

> And one of the problems... rather than moving commercial debt to prudential rates, which is the French model, UKGI [UK Green Investments] is saying 'well we're going to move prudential rates on to commercial levels, because we're not prepared to lend unless the banks do... because it's not on market terms.
>
> (Asset Management Consultant)

One of the perverse consequences of the present centralised energy market and private finance regimes therefore, is to make project finance for local energy infrastructure potentially more expensive, by prior political decision to reject the use of public finance to provide low cost loans or equity to lower the total cost.

The risk to public interests

> It's very much sort of only the gold plated, de-risked projects that are actually going forward, with private sector funding in them.
>
> B (FAC)

Dominant modes of financial evaluation hence tend to work against locally-customised urban energy retrofit, unless profitability for private investors is pre-given by factors such as the anticipated reputational value of investments. In relation to district energy utility Cofely's investment in the Olympic Park Development for example,

> I think they're [Cofely] banking on the fact that it's probably the highest profile development site in the country, and if it turns into a white elephant it'll be a national embarrassment.
>
> (Environmental Finance Specialist B)

While contracts governing such projects are positive in demonstrating the potential structures for, and flexibility of, private public partnerships, and access to private finance, the private sector also has control over their future direction, which may mean limited long-term public benefit:

> Effectively the public sector needs to package something up, hand it over and keep their fingers crossed that they will be able to somehow influence the private sector going forward.
>
> (Environmental Finance Specialist B)

Most urban areas however lack 'that sort of brand' (Environmental Finance Specialist A) associated with public investment in developments such as the Olympic Park 'where we know it's going to happen' (Environmental Finance Specialist A). Hence to attract investment at sufficiently low cost of capital for a project to proceed,

> Somebody within that circle has got to absorb a higher degree of risk. Now in the deals that we've done to date that has ... been pre-dominantly the public sector end user that, because of lack of capital, has commercially taken the view that they'll accept that risk provision.
>
> (Corporate Banking Investment Manager)

The higher risk, and its cost, then remains with the public sector, even when the majority of capital investment and associated risk is formally allocated to the private sector partner. This may mean that many towns and cities risk use as experimental sites for market testing a privately-financed 'green development' model, where the future substantive risks to the locality of their contribution to guaranteeing private returns are not captured by standard risk instruments. Wider public value may prove tenuous; private finance is legally accountable to shareholders, and local accountability and wider public value may prove difficult to secure.

Bricolage and alternative hierarchies of value

When technical devices such as those of financial economics are established as authoritative in evaluating energy investment options, then interpretive flexibility has been restricted, and the value of some technological trajec-tories has been given relatively fixed, durable meaning (Clegg, 1989). Such configurations of power are not however monolithic. During periods of major political economic uncertainty, as at present, the concept of a singular stable and self-perpetuating energy market regime under-recognises the tensions within and among regime institutions, or the potential for a plurality of 'partial' regimes to be in operation, with different goals and assumptions. Such tensions are manifest in the current UK energy system;

the major utilities are stepping back from large scale electricity generation investments, as the profitability of such assets has fallen, and the closure of older, and high carbon, electricity generating stations means that one fifth of current plant is scheduled to close by 2020. These structural fault lines may work as catalysts to innovation and change, as suggested by sociological analyses of the productivity of intra- and inter-organisational dissonance, and discrepancy in assumptions and understandings between different groups (Boltanski and Thevenot, 2007; Stark, 2009). Indeed the practitioners cited here, and the discussions and presentations at district energy finance events which have formed part of this research, provide evidence of such dissonances and of the recognised need for new variants of situated financial innovation. This is innovation of an improvisatory kind, characteristic of the bricolage responses of financial actors to changing circumstances (Beunza and Stark, 2003), but guided by a continuing dominant theory (MacKenzie, 2003) of the laws of private finance:

> I guess what you have to try and do is work with what you have inside the system, and then tweak it rather than require a fundamental new idea to introduce, because the more dramatic the change, then the longer it's going to take, the more painful it's going to be for it to happen.
>
> (Officer of UK Government Green Investment Team)

Such bricolage, Engelen *et al.* (2010) argue, may work to reformat markets by turning the 'nodal possibility into a profitable position by using whatever instruments are to hand to create a business model' (p. 56). This does not however recognise that bricolage also embodies subordinated knowledge of alternative social and cultural hierarchies of value which could be brought into play:

> It would be interesting if someone carved out three or four hundred million, and they said 'okay, London, with parts of Birmingham, Manchester, Glasgow, Edinburgh, here we go, thirty/forty million pounds each; go and develop your scheme.' But that's very much going back to the nineteen thirties; it's New Deal, it goes against the culture of where we are... and I don't see that happening.
>
> (Environmental Finance Specialist B)

JW (interviewer): 'Do you think that will be forthcoming though?'

> Probably not, because ... it's not in the ethos or the culture of how the government wants to deal with energy. It doesn't really want to step in and be a big planner.

Yes, you could float the argument really: leaving it all to the market, actually, what are you doing? You're really just abdicating your responsibilities and side-stepping.

(Environmental Finance Specialist B)

Conclusion

We keep using the phrase 'the best is the enemy of the good', and you've got to go out there and make some of it happen, because if nothing happens because we're all paranoid about doing something, then that's the worst outcome of all I think.

(Officer of UK Government Green Investment Team)

Attempts to reconfigure financial evaluations of locally-organised energy infrastructure represent a moment where large-scale energy and financial market interests encounter questions about their future trajectory, and the future qualities, costs and control of urban energy retrofitting. What is observable in the interviews, policy meetings and industry forums discussed here are the attempts of actors to uncover some potential solutions, while securing relative socio-economic advantage from such improvised means. The current neo-liberal orthodoxy about markets structures decision-making to rule in, and rule out, options. While expert practitioners engage in the critical deconstruction of such orthodoxies, they are simultaneously resistant to the implications of radically different models. The 'sunk investment' in professionalised knowledge and expertise, as well as in material infrastructure, the lobbying power of corporations, and the disempowerment of local levels of government in the UK mean that the search for solutions centres on minor adaptations to the dominant private finance model, referred to by one practitioner as 'son of PFI'. (Perhaps an unintentionally apt attribution of masculinity to the technicalities of financial engineering).

At the level of localities, bridging the gap between rationalised finance and local political and economic interests in urban energy retrofit requires considerable capacity, and has significant transaction costs for local authorities with limited resources. There is nevertheless a high level of interest among local project teams, as evidenced by the 31 local authorities in England and Wales alone, representing 54 heat network projects, applying for the first round of small scale feasibility funding from the UK Department of Energy and Climate Change Heat Networks Delivery Unit. The Scottish Government is also supporting local authorities in identifying feasible projects, and has proposed targets for development. In the current political-economic settlement, and facing declining budgets, urban authority politicians and finance directors however struggle to identify benefits from the demands of retrofitting localised sustainable energy.

Significant urban leadership requires supportive regulatory measures designed to value the long-term social and environmental benefits at urban scale. While such measures would need careful negotiation between local and central governments, some of the basic principles can be derived from the analysis in this chapter. First, although it is routinely acknowledged in heat policies that local authorities are key intermediaries, they lack the necessary direct mandate from their respective central governments. This would support the development of low carbon heat and cooling networks in densely populated areas, where this can be shown by project teams to be the most sustainable long term solution when dispassionate assessments of social, environmental and economic risks are all factored in to the decision. Such a mandate would of course require new local authority finance to provide dedicated capacity for clean energy project development and management. This could come from UK Treasury funds, or from more devolution of powers to local government to raise a higher proportion of income for localised energy from local taxes and revenues, and from exemptions of non-profit district energy retrofit from business rates. Development of a local heat map, and identification of sources of waste heat and heat network anchor loads, would need to be mandatory as part of localised energy and carbon planning measures to create district heating priority areas. Much heat mapping work has already been done, but strategic use of maps for directed planning has been limited. Having identi-fied the key areas of high density heat demand, and assessed feasibility, large building owners would need to be under an obligation to connect to local heat (and cooling) networks, and producers of waste heat would need to be obliged to find means to supply the heat to the network. Such an obligation is needed in order to maximise carbon savings while supplying heat and hot water cost effectively, and in turn provides secure revenues for project developers. With stronger government mandates, public buildings and owners of multi-storey housing (predominantly housing associations and councils) could be required to connect to heat and cooling networks in line with renovation and boiler or electric heating replacement schedules. Commercial building users required to register for the UK energy efficiency tax, the CRC (originally known as the Carbon Reduction Commitment), already have financial incentives to connect, because heat supplied via heat networks is rated as zero carbon. A general tax on energy use could be used to incentivise all commercial building owners in the target area to connect to localised low carbon heat and cooling. While these measures would support revenues for heat and cooling network operators, they would need to be balanced with a system for licencing and regulation to ensure that there is no abuse of long-term monopoly supply contracts. The Danish Energy Regulatory Authority (DERA) for example regulates electricity, natural gas and district heating markets. For district heating, both production and network companies are regulated as non-profit undertakings. DERA monitors prices and delivery terms, and takes action if these are not in line with the non-profit model or if they are in any other way unfair.

In addition, the EU Energy Efficiency Directive provides the opportunity for UK and Scottish Governments to create a strong legal framework for locating all new power stations closer to urban heat loads, and requiring operation in combined heat and power mode. Beyond this, a stable, secure and straightforward source of low cost finance is required for local investment in district energy infrastructure, where this is a non-profit enterprise. The lowest cost route is likely to be public borrowing, but this remains off the political agenda in the current UK Treasury fiscal austerity regime. Even without direct public finance, the risk-reduction measures discussed above would reduce the cost of capital, making more projects economically feasible. Where heat and cooling are provided from local CHP systems, the electricity exported could also be granted the same status as large scale nuclear or offshore wind, under the new 'contracts for difference' strike prices for low carbon electricity supply. Operators would then have a risk underwriting mechanism which would reduce the cost of capital. This is however a form of regressive taxation, because it operates as a levy on all energy bills. The same is true of current energy company obligations (ECO) to provide finance for carbon and energy saving projects; ECO, and its predecessors, have contributed to urban heat network retrofit projects, but have been complex and subject to inconsistent carbon pricing. Recent reductions in the scale of funding to be made available under such obligations have also stalled planned projects. Such levies could instead be funded more fairly, and their resources deployed more speedily and consistently, through general taxation.

The measures outlined above require development of alternative low carbon heat and cooling pathways, which displace techno-economic assessments of value with assessments of substantive risk and value in relation to public goods of ecology, economy and society. It may be that financial innovation through the mainstream of structured asset classes and de-risked investable projects is indeed the eventual trajectory for urban retrofit, but the resulting projects can also be managed through a variety of governance and ownership structures, some providing more public accountability, transparency and checks on unearned private profits than others. There is also potential for a more differentiated energy system, with large scale centralised generation complemented and balanced by distributed, locally-embedded generation and supply, which is expected to improve resilience and reduce the total financial costs of the transition to low carbon supply. Such localised systems could provide better opportunity for a wider variety of ownership structures, including greater local democratic control. An alternative to the privatised financial market model is for example a non-profit model, with energy provision governed by community interest companies, or mutual enterprises:

> The not for profit model is more suited for where there is in effect a demand guarantee, which was the Aberdeen context... because the projects have got to be developed anyway. So there wasn't this risk problem to be solved. So retrofit ... the, sort of, community interest company approach does fit that very well.
>
> (Finance Investment Consultant)

Around one third of UK municipal authorities are developing localised energy projects which test a variety of forms of ownership and control (Hawkey *et al.* 2014), but in the current political-economic settlement, the local heat and cooling projects are typically developed through the determination of 'wilful individuals' (Local Authority Officer) who continue to believe that local government has a broadly specified responsibility for public welfare. If there is a genuine democratic commitment to evaluation of options for a future sustainable urbanism, then such options need to be explicitly and actively maintained on the public agenda.

Notes

1   'Meso scale' heat energy systems are defined here as ranging from a Combined Heat and Power (CHP) engine, or heat-only boiler, supplying a small number of buildings, such as a housing estate &/or public and commercial buildings, up to a number of boilers, thermal stores, heat recovery devices and CHP engines at different locations connected by a network of pipes to supply heat, hot water and cooling to buildings across the city.

2   The materials used in the chapter are drawn from a wider data set developed through the RC-UK *Heat and the City* research project. The analysis is based on:

*   In-depth semi-structured interviews with seven financial market experts
*   Interaction with senior managers and Non-Executive Chair of a 'Big 6' utility through their Environmental Forum meeting about the concept of Smart Cities.
*   Presentations and discussions at two workshops on financing district energy, organised jointly by the Heat and the City research team and a community energy practitioner. Approximately 60 delegates attended each workshop, representing local authority officers, government policy-makers and a mix of finance experts, consulting engineers and district energy businesses.
*   Interaction with the UK government Dept of Energy and Climate Change including: analysis of heat policy documents; attendance at a workshop on government-planned research on district heating, and membership of the consortium responsible for subsequent research on UK barriers to heat network deployment carried out as a component of government Heat Policy formation.

- Interaction with the UK Combined Heat and Power trade association (CHPA), to gain insight into their articulation of a strategic position on urban heat network policy instruments.

Extracts from interviews and discussions cited in the chapter are derived from the following contributors:

- Finance Investment Consultant - former civil service economist with responsibility for UK government privatisation policies; former Director of a firm of Consulting Engineers; currently independent.
- Officer of UK government green investment team and former Director of a firm of Consulting Engineers.
- Environmental Finance Specialist A, Transnational Finance and Accounting Corporation.
- Environmental Finance Specialist B, Transnational Finance and Accounting Corporation.
- Asset Management Consultant and former consulting engineer, construction industry specialist, former director of private equity fund in a major bank, currently independent.
- Corporate Banking Investment Manager, responsible for investments in energy efficiency in the built environment, including district energy infrastructure.
- Utility Senior Manager, energy networks - professional engineer with leadership and operational expertise in gas and electricity infrastructure. International experience of energy market restructuring.
- Local Authority Officer – team leader in sustainable development and energy in an English Borough Council; developer of a financial model to analyse options for local energy investments, and participant in the UK District Energy Vanguards network.

3   The initial statement from the EU Regulator is available at http://ec.europa.eu/ competition/state_aid/cases/251157/251157_1507977_35_2.pdf

References

Beckert, J. (2009) 'The social order of markets', *Theoretical Sociology*, 38(3): 245–269.

Besley, T. Coelho, M. and Van Reenen, T. (2013) 'Investing for prosperity: skills, infrastructure and innovation', *National Institute Economic Review* No. 224. www.lse.ac.uk/researchAndExpertise/units/growthCommission/documents/pdf/GCReportSummary.pdf (Accessed 5/13).

Beunza, D. and Stark, D. (2003) 'The organization of responsiveness: innovation and recovery in the trading rooms of lower Manhattan', *Socio-Economic Review* 7(1): 135–64.

Boltanski, L. and Thevenot, L. (2007) *On Justification: Economies of Worth.* Princeton, NJ: Princeton University Press.

Callon, M. (ed.) (1998) *The Laws of the Markets.* Oxford: Blackwell.

Clegg, S. (1989) *Frameworks of Power.* London: Sage.

Crouch, C. (2011) *The Strange Non-Death of Neo-Liberalism.* Cambridge: Polity.

Engelen, E., Erturk, I., Froud, J., Leaver, A. and Williams, K. (2010) 'Reconceptualizing financial innovation: frame, conjuncture and bricolage', *Economy and Society*, 39(1): 33–63.

Erturk, I., Froud, J., Johal, S., Leaver, A. and Williams, K. (eds) (2008) *Financialisation at Work: Key Texts and Commentary*, London: Routledge.

Geels, F. (2010) 'Ontologies, socio-technical transitions (to sustainability) and the multi-level perspective', Research Policy 39, 495–510 .

Geels, F. and Schot, J. (2007) Typology of sociotechnical transition pathways. *Research Policy*, 36, 399–417.

Granovetter, M. (1985) 'Economic action, social structure and embeddedness', *American Journal of Sociology*, 91(3): 481–510.

Hawkey, D., Webb, J. and Winskel, M. (2013) 'Organisation and governance of urban energy systems: district heating and cooling in the UK', *Journal of Cleaner Production*, 50 (1): 22–31.

Kelly and Pollitt (2010) 'An assessment of the present and future opportunities for combined heat and power with district heating in the UK', *Energy Policy* 38(11): 6936–6945. Available at: http://dx.doi.org/10.1016/j.enpol.2010.07.010 (Accessed 11/08/2015)

Latour, B. (2005) *Reassembling the Social: An Introduction to Actor Network Theory*. Oxford: Oxford University Press.

MacKenzie, D. (2006) *An Engine Not a Camera: How Financial Models Shape Markets*, Cambridge, MA: MIT Press.

MacKenzie, D. (2009) *Material Markets: How Economic Agents are Constructed* Oxford: Oxford University Press.

Mitchell, C. (2008) *The Political Economy of Sustainable Energy* Basingstoke: Palgrave Macmillan.

Podolny, J. (2001) 'Networks as pipes and prisms of the market', *American Journal of Sociology* 107(1): 33–60.

Pöyry Energy (2009) 'The potential and costs of district heating networks', (Oxford: Poyry, Faber Maunsell, AECOM). Report to the UK Government Department of Energy and Climate Change, www.poyry.co.uk/news/potential-and-costs-district-heating-networks-report-decc-poyry-energy-consulting-and-faber-maunsell-aecom (Accessed 01/05/2015).

Preda, A. (2007) 'The sociological approach to financial markets', *Journal of Economic Surveys*, 21(3): 506–533.

Stark, D. (2009) 'The sense of dissonance: accounts of worth in economic life', Princeton, NJ: Princeton University Press.

UK DECC (2012) *The Future of Heating: A Strategic Framework for Low Carbon Heat in the UK*. Available at www.gov.uk/government/uploads/system/uploads/attachment_data/file/48574/4805-future-heating-strategic-framework.pdf (Accessed 11/08/2015).

UK Government DECC (2013) 'The future of heating: meeting the challenge', www.gov.uk/government/publications/the-future-of-heating-meeting-the-challenge (Accessed 30/06/14).

White, H. (2002) *Markets from Networks: Socio-Economic Models of Production*. Princeton, NJ: Princeton University Press.

Winskel, M. (2002) 'When systems are overthrown: the "dash for gas" in the British electricity supply industry', *Social Studies of Science* 32:4, 565–599.

Chapter 5

Retrofitting biogenic urban infrastructure

Stephanie Pincetl

INTRODUCTION

Cities concentrate human activities, and this includes resource use and the generation of pollution. With increasing concern about climate change, attention has turned towards cities for their capacity to enhance and use biogenic infrastructure – nature's services – to remediate some of their own environmental impacts (Alberti and Susskind 1996, Rees and Wackernagel 1996, Alberti, 2008). Biogenic infrastructure encompasses urban tree planting, watershed restoration and green streets programmes to capture storm water and dry weather runoff through techniques such as bioswales and water infiltration zones. Yet little thought has been given to what this new approach may imply for the ways in which cities are managed and funded, including the organisation of existing departments and agencies, urban morphology and land use, public interest and potential unanticipated consequences.

Mayor Villaraigosa of the city of Los Angeles made an ambitious campaign promise: to make Los Angeles the greenest city in the USA. To do so, among other initiatives, he promised to plant a million new trees. Mayor Villaraigosa is not alone. Mayor Bloomberg of New York also promised to plant a million more trees in New York, and cities across the country are embarking on campaigns to add to their existing tree canopy to improve the environment. These initiatives could be written off as campaign promises, but their popularity, and the emerging science quantifying the benefits of urban trees, suggests there is more going on.[1] For example, McPherson *et al.* (2008), estimated that a million more trees in Los Angeles could, per tree, intercept from 102 gallons annually to a high of 1481 gallons a year, based on the tree size, rainfall amount, and foliation period. Over the 35-year life span of the million-tree project, there could by a reduction of runoff by 13.5–21.3 billion gallons. Energy use reduction was projected to range from 718,671 to 1.1 million MWh and atmospheric carbon dioxide reduction could range from 764,000 to 1.27 million tons over the same 35-year period. A million more trees in Los Angeles could also improve human

health and environmental quality through the interception of small part-
iculate matter (1,846 to 2,886 tons from power plants), the uptake of ozone
(2430–3813 tons) and nitrogen dioxide (1949–3039 tons) (McPherson *et
al.* 2008: 5–6). Such ecological services situated in the city itself, are seen to
help mitigate the negative environmental impacts generated in that place.

Using the example of the million tree-planting initiative the chapter raises
a set of issues about the retrofitting of green infrastructure that go beyond
Los Angeles. The chapter shows that urban environmental management in
the USA has a set of institutional contexts, and a path dependency that
shapes current debates, expectations, and patterns. Nature's services infrastructure therefore finds itself nested in a whole set of political and
economic shifts towards governance, a secular shift in state-market-society
relations that implies that important new economic and social conditions
and attendant problems have emerged which cannot be managed or
resolved readily (Jessop 1998: 32). The chapter identifies the tensions they
create with current city organisational structure for democratic accountability and participation and for equity.

The creation of the modern city

By the end of the nineteenth century, the impacts of rapid industrialisation
and population growth on cities were harmful to human health and well
being, and for local environments. Now classic works, starting with Engels'
Condition of the Working Class in England (1844) to Jacob Riis' *How the
Other Half Lives* (1890) and Upton Sinclair's novels, drew attention to the
egregious circumstances of working people's daily lives, corruption and
lack of regulation. Excesses fostered an age of reform that lasted nearly 30
years: the Progressive Era (Hays 1959, Weibe 1967, Pincetl, 1999). The
edifice of modern city management was constructed during this period. In
1899 in the USA, the National Municipal League promulgated a model city
charter, including expanded home rule, a stronger mayor and council,
trained administrators and an emphasis on qualified personnel selected by
civil service, bringing many classes of 'experts' into municipal government
(Scott 1969: 41–42). Governmental budgeting and accounting practices
were changed so that costs could be clearly associated with specific
activities of government; allocation and accountability performance
measures were introduced, making reports comparable between
communities among other budgeting reforms (Williams 2002: 458). Civil
service procedures were adopted by municipal governments by 1935
(Tolbert and Zucker 1983) resulting in professional civil service cadre of
trained professionals becoming the norm in city bureaucracies. These
included planners, civil engineers, traffic engineers, and sanitation
specialists of many types. Bacteriology and civil engineering were applied to
the urban fabric, bringing citywide distribution of fresh water after being

treated in purification plants, sewage systems were built to take waste-water out of neighbourhoods to treatment plants (Melosi 2000: 69). By 1935, the transformation of a city government from a politically based system to a science-based, bureaucratic-based system was well underway (Hays 1972: 9).

The sanitary city was constructed over a century into the modern net-worked city. Standardised roads, water systems, waste removal and treatment, energy provision and communications as single, integrated and standardised systems covering municipalities, cities, regions, and even nations were part of the modern idea of progress (Graham and Marvin 2001: 41). In fact, the dominant characteristic of the modern city is its networked character. These technological networks of water, gas, electricity, information, are the mediators through which the perpetual process of the transformation of nature into city takes place (Kaika and Swyngedouw 2000: 1, in Graham and Marvin 2001: 10). Further, infrastructural networks have traditionally been central to the normative aspirations of planners, reformers and social activists to define their notion of the good city (Friedmann 2000, in Graham and Marvin 2001: 12). The modern networked city had a universalising discourse, in which all spaces were to be integrated by ubiquitous, democratically accessible and homo-geneous infrastructure grids, usually under public ownership, even if violated in practice. The networks were quasi-public, goods to be consumed by all, at similar generalised tariffs, guided by the principles of non-exclud-ability and non-ejectability (Graham and Marvin 2001: 102, 80).

The city services we are concerned about – water supply, sewage sanitation, street maintenance, and so forth – are now provided by trained professionals whose professional societies, such as the American Society of Civil Engineers or the National Water Quality Association, play important roles in developing standards and certifying their members. Each of these specialties – sanitation, street services, planning – works in a bounded realm informed by specialised competences siloed into departments and agencies. They operate from a general framework of rational comprehensive planning of large-scale infrastructure. The Progressive Era established the foundation of legitimacy for state-led solutions in infrastructure provision and governmental authority and this approach was carried out through the 1960s–1970s, driven by public funding and commitment to creating efficient and sanitary cities.

Disillusionment with the modernist project has grown as it has not been able to keep up with increasing population growth, infrastructure demand and the complexity of technology and the economy. Tax revolts of the late twentieth century in the USA and especially in California, skepticism about the role and ability of government to plan have led to more of a project-by-project approach and a pragmatic attempt to address perceived local problems rather than a utopian or visionary framework for re-engineering metropolitan areas (Graham and Marvin 2001: 103). Fragmentation, or unbundling, of networks has also occurred. Undermined by critiques from both the left and economic liberals, overtaken by the rapidity of techno-logical change, especially in information technologies, the traditional systems of government-led infrastructure provision have faltered, though still lye within the mission statements and responsibilities of most local public agencies. The competent delivery of these systems also remains in the expectations of urban residents – cities should deliver clean water, elec-tricity, access to open space, healthy neighbourhoods, sewage treatment, and other infrastructure amenities of modern living. Municipalities are also often legally required to provide the service as well. Thus, in the early twenty-first century, local municipalities still carry the burden of performance of the modernist era, but without the capacity – whether monetary, or of legitimacy.

Environmentalism of the past quarter century then drew attention to the quality of the environment: air pollution, water pollution, toxic substances, and now greenhouse gas emissions. The problems had changed from cholera and polio, to particulates, volatile organic compounds, and other kinds of chemical pollution concentrated in urban environments, affecting people and health of the ecosystem. Many of these pollutants are highly concentrated in cities that are among the most profoundly altered and managed ecosystems on the planet (Collins *et al.* 2000). Not only are humans for the first time ever predominantly urban dwellers, but also it is increasingly evident that urban areas are the biggest generators of global environmental pollution and greenhouse gases, grave threats to life as we know it. Environmental rules and regulations were added to the responsi-bilities (and costs) of governments, and of localities. Sustainability has been one of the responses, adding to the pollution control technology regulatory strategy. While the core meaning of sustainable development remains messy (Jordon 2008: 28) at an urban scale there are strategies that are generally recognised as sustainable. Nature's services fall under that definition, in addition to green building, renewable energy and so forth.

The integration of nature's services in city departments

Nature's services, following the Millennium Ecosystem Assessment (2005) definition, are the benefits to humans provided by ecosystems. They provide provisioning services such as food and water, regulating services such as climate, floods and water quality, cultural services such as recreation and aesthetic enjoyment, and supporting services such as soil formation, pollination, and nutrient cycling (ibid.: 39). Natural processes persist in our anthropomorphic urban environments, but since the advent of the industrial sanitary city and population growth they are highly manipulated and often impaired. With the understanding of the importance of cities as the new home of human kind, the ecological role of urban areas is now seen as potentially transformative. An aspect of this potential involves how and where urban areas can remedy their own negative externalities through nature's services-based integrated infrastructure.

Daily (1997) and Robert Costanza's pioneering work on the value of nature's services have inspired a consideration of the importance of nature's processes for human survival (Costanza 2006, 2008, among many articles and books). Earlier ecologists and urbanists had also drawn attention to nature in the city and the powerful ways it could be worked with, rather than ignored or hidden, but the historical time was not propitious for the integration of their observations (McHarg 1971, Spirn 1984, Hough 1995). More recently, the rise of the concept of nature's services has resulted in studies estimating of the value of services such as trees in the city for human benefit. However, to institute such nature's services infrastructure is challenging as biogenic infrastructure must be designed correctly to provide the desired services. Nature's services infrastructure needs to be placed at optimal locations, properly sized, and not too diffuse in geographical extent to make a difference.

Nature's services infrastructure requires coordination and cooperation among traditionally separate departments such as planning, transportation, sanitation and other utility providers, and new biological knowledge about soils and microbes and their pollution filtration potential, which trees are the most appropriate for bioregion, climate, and desired function. Unlike grey infrastructure that is generally hidden underground, in pipes, or else made inaccessible in concentrated facilities, nature's services infrastructure is in plain sight, it takes up real physical space, and if it is not regularly maintained (gardened), it will look unattractive, may not work and/or it will die. This implies a different knowledge and maintenance regime from the networked modern city to one more akin to parks. As nature's services infrastructure will need to be geographically distributed throughout the city, at low but extensive intensities. It is likely to be an expensive proposition for cities themselves to maintain with traditional means, including siloed civil service employees and rules.

To implement nature's services infrastructure in a different way, for example, in an interdisciplinary/interdepartmental way, would require quite a few fundamental changes in city personnel, budgeting, administrative organisation, and land use. To date, many cities have contracted with non-profit organisations to implement this infrastructure sprinkling nature's services onto the existing urban landscape where opportunities arise, and opposition is low through tree planting, stream daylighting, or watershed restoration – a far cry from the implementation of an integrated ecosystem services infrastructure.

Nature's services infrastructure butts up against the epistemological structuring of disciplines reflected in city agencies that is based on divergent and exclusive framings of each subject and distinctive methods of inquiry and problem solving: meeting stormwater runoff requirements, for example, is an entirely separate function from providing clean drinking water, though they could be united under a common agency that ensures that stormwater is not wasted and becomes integrated into water supply (Petts *et al.* 2008). Nature's services infrastructure also has multiple distributed benefits. Urban forests, for example, are alleged to cool the urban environment (reducing energy use), encourage walking (improving public health), mitigate storm water (relieving flooding and storm water purification costs), and more. Yet in today's hierarchically and vertically organised city, one department will be responsible for the forest and incur all the costs. There is no way to account for the multiple benefits, nor any cost sharing among agencies that might obtain a benefit through avoided costs (such as less hospital visits, providing less electricity for cooling in the summer months) (Pincetl 2007). Finally, nature's services infrastructure impact residents – tree limbs may fall on parked vehicles or roots may infiltrate sewer pipes, trees drop their leaves and need to be picked up, and trees need irrigation in drier climates. All of these costs are borne by the individual residents.

MILLION TREES LOS ANGELES

Over the course of almost three years, researchers interviewed about 20 people involved in the Million Trees Initiative. Researchers also monitored local press reports, conducted literature surveys, participated in tree give-away and planting events associated with the programme and collected information about tree-planting programmes across the country. In addition, we studied water use by trees in the city and the effect of trees on the city's urban heat island over 30 years. Results from these investigations point to complexities not only in implementing such an ambitious pro-gramme, but also in the environmental impacts of trees in the urban environment. While trees have been found generally to reduce the urban heat island effect, they have also use a great deal of water, do not consis-tently improve property values, and are not uniformly embraced. Planting an additional infrastructure is multi-faceted. The implementation of the programme is our focus here, though it touches on all the other issues as it is being implemented in the belief that trees have positive multiple environ-mental and social benefits.

Mayoral candidate Villaraigosa's 2004 campaign promise to plant a million trees was one of several programmes he put forward to make Los Angeles the greenest big city in the USA. One of his close political advisors explained that it was proposed to Villaraigosa by a campaign advisor and it seemed like a great idea at the time (Swiller 2007). The implementation was seen as relatively straight-forward and unproblematic (Swiller 2007, Freeman 2009).

Strategic interest in the potential role of biogenic infrastructure has happened in a period in which there has been a shift in confidence away from government and by a reduction of funding for many levels of state government. Tax cuts, exemplified by California's Proposition 13 slashing property taxes and requirements for second or third majority votes for new local taxes, both passed through ballot initiatives, have reduced the margin of manoeuvre of the government. At the state level, the annual state budget must also be approved by a two-thirds majority vote. The result for Los Angeles, for example, has been a budget decline of an average of 4.73 per cent per capita since 1968 for Urban Forestry despite an increase in population of about a million people (Los Angeles Almanac 2000). The budget of Department of Recreation and Parks over the same period increased a little over 1 per cent per capita (Chief Legislative Analyst Budgets). Urban Forestry, despite the Million Tree programme has had no additional funds to plant more trees (Gonzales 2007). Such budget limitations affect the ability of city departments to expand services. The current Los Angeles budget has been reduced from this period. The Bureau of Street Services where Urban Forestry lies has received a 13.6 per cent cut, the Environmental Affairs Department a 13.0 per cent cut, the Planning Department a 22.4 per cent cut (http://budget.lacity.org/). In the best of times, to achieve the goal of planting more trees, the city would have to cobble together many sources of funding and enlist non-governmental actors, including homeowners and non-profit organisations, to co-produce the urban forest.

First located in the Department of Public Works, the programme had a rocky start. The Public Works Commissioner put in charge launched an ambitious planning effort for the programme, bringing together the main tree-planting non-profit organisations of the city, city departments from planning to urban forestry, consultants and academics (the author was among the group). A plan was established, many issues were discussed from climate appropriate tree selection, working with the nursery industry to increase the availability of such trees, interagency collaborations and more. The Commissioner jawboned the non-profits to agree to plant trees in assigned council districts (one non-profit refused and its participation is limited to planting trees in parks exclusively) and the programme was launched (Daniels 2007). With no funds available from the city's budget for the city to plant the trees itself, non-profit organisations assumed the major responsibility for planting the trees with assurances – as each of the consecutive Million Tree Programme Directors confirmed – they would be recompensed through funds raised by the Mayor from the private sector (Daniels 2007, Morris 2007, Sarno 2007).

Nine months later the Mayor had raised no money for the programme, tree planting non- profits had participated in several Million Tree Initiative launch events, incurred staff costs, and were beginning to express their unhappiness with the programme; they had not been paid, and the

Commissioner was in an awkward position since she had depended on the Mayor to follow through on his promise to raise the necessary funds (Daniels 2007). There were other problems too. Trees being offered to the public included spindly one-gallon seedlings and rumours abounded about these trees ending up on people's balconies but counting toward the million mark, all of which provided fodder for critical articles that began appearing in the press. The Mayor's office, sensitive to negative press, acted swiftly and shifted the programme out of the Public Works Department out from under the Commissioner and gave it to another person, whose status was ambiguous. She was in Public Works, but under contract and also in the Mayor's office, given even less resources and direction, and lasted only a couple of months (Morris 2007). It was then sequestered in the Mayor's office where a trusted political operative of the Mayor was put in charge of the programme, where it still is as of this writing. Much of the initial planning work was set aside, work on tree species and targeting locations was shelved, and the new Director of the programme engaged each tree planting non-profit individually about their participation, holding no coordinating meetings, nor developing an alternative implementation plan. Additional tree plantings, outside the Council Districts farmed out to the non-profits, were targeted on an opportunistic basis, for example, in planting strips near schools in areas of the city with low canopy cover (Sarno 2008).

Today there is no plan guiding the tree planting, and there is little public information available about the programme, including the budget and sources of funding, numbers of trees planted, locations, and species of trees chosen. Many of the links on the city's Million Tree Los Angeles website are inactive (www.milliontreesla.org).

Million Trees Los Angeles (MTLA) engages five different NGOs to plant trees. Four of the NGOs area assigned Council Districts within which they are to plant. Tree sizes, species and the tree itself are determined by MTLA. MTLA's Director fundraises for the programme and the local utility – the Department of Water and Power – provides the trees, but the NGOs must also raise their own funds for the programme from state, federal and Foundation sources. It is a highly competitive terrain among the NGOs, for funds are scarce. Characteristically, employees are paid NGO wages and there is no job security. Questions of organisational capacity, funding, staffing often outpace the political power or organisational capacity of any single NGO (Bullard 1990, in Bure 2007, Romano 2007, Svendsen and Campbell 2008).

Management of the tree planting NGOs by the city is done behind closed doors and often organisation-by-organisation, so there is little or no transparency relative to the delegation of tasks, or funding, and dialogue among the NGOs is rare and often contentious (Bure 2007, Romano 2007, Smith 2007). Further, since there is no public plan for the Million Tree Program there is no ability for residents to know what is being envisaged relative to this new infrastructure. Million Trees is opaque and mysterious with its decentralised implementation to multiple public–private partnerships and the city can only exercise 'loose leverage' (Kettl 1993).

The non-profit tree planting organisations in Los Angeles – hired to bring greater nature's services to communities that have less trees than more affluent areas – find real resistance. Residents in areas of high crime in the city often do not want street trees planted in front of their properties, or more trees at all since they fear that criminals will be able to hide in the trees (Bartlett 2007, Bure 2007, Sarno 2008).

Furthermore, not only do some residents consider trees a potential crime danger, but there are residents who do not like trees, nor do they do not wish to assume the additional water costs for irrigation, and potentially end up paying if the tree roots damage sewage lines (the NGOs must have a resident's accord to plant a tree in the planting strip in front of a house or apartment building and that agreement comes with an obligation to maintain the tree for 3 years). They may also not want the shading effect of trees on their existing landscaping. These concerns illustrate the ways in which a nature's services approach can affect residents. While grey infrastructure is also costly, it is generally invisible and does not require maintenance by city residents. Contrary to the modern city, the sustainable city will be far messier and less sanitised. Vegetation will be climate appropriate, so in places like southern California, this may mean summer dormancy – in other words brown untidy plants rather than clean green lawns. The land uses of horizontal suburban cities, to accomplish the ends of a nature's services infrastructure, will have to devolve away from impermeable hard surfaces devoted to the automobile to shared spaces for plants, insects and microbiota; an evolution into a very different looking landscape, and a different management regime.

Yet the governance aspect of this new use of the public commons for ecosystem services for urban infrastructure is both part of and different from the modernist paradigm. It fundamentally believes that good science and information will yield better results – a modern, progressive view – and at the same time it questions the dominant structure of knowledge and organisational form of cities.

The underside of urban biogenic governance

Non-profit organisations have become nature's services amenity providers as the fiscal ability to provide infrastructure, including parks and the new green infrastructure, has shrunk in many cities as a result of the decline of revenues (Pincetl 2003, Svendson and Campbell 2008). These civil society organisations themselves may or may not genuinely reflect, or engage with, grassroots civil society power, but are often the de facto interface with state power. As Swyngedouw (2005) and others have pointed out (Jessop 2003,

Hajer 2003) public private partnerships that involve governance arrangements seem to offer the promise of greater democracy and grassroots empowerment, but they may also exhibit a series of contradictory tendencies (Swyngedouw 2005). They reflect a state government that has had to reorganise and to mobilise a new set of 'technologies of governing' to respond to changing socio-economic and cultural conditions (Swyngedouw 2005) with. '[N]o clear rules and norms according to which politics is to be conducted and policy measures are to be agreed upon' (Hajer 2003, in Swyngedouw 2005: 1992).

Further nature's services infrastructure is a physical thing, it takes space in neighbourhoods and changes and impacts existing land uses. Nature's services infrastructure impacts people's daily lives and property. Its health and maintenance of this infrastructure requires a new approach to urban land use and zoning in which public space is appropriated for ecosystem services (rather than the car), including shared streets with increased room for plants, bios- wales and water filtration, greened alleyways, greater room for street trees narrowing streets, and dedicated storm water infiltration areas' grey water treatment areas. It may also include new rules about private land use too in order to enlist as much of the city's unbuilt spaces as possible to provide the services of ecosystems. Ecosystem services infrastructure are land intensive and the services do not stop at the line between private and public property.

All of this does suggest a new management model for the city in which the role of the state is more coordinative utilising a fusion of public and private resources and individual property owners (Evans 1997, and Payne 2000, in Pierre and Peters 2000: 25). Nature's services draws on more communitarian views of the organisation of society wherein not only do ecosystem services in urban areas help mitigate the impacts of cities broadly, but the place-specific addition of these services improve people's quality-of-life and health – street trees encourage pedestrian activity, reducing obesity while also serving to cool the urban heat island effect, mitigate storm water flows and so forth. Hence, there is a kind of assumption that nature's services infrastructure is a public good that the public, from the bottom up, will assist in implementing, including through NGOs. As the Million Trees Initiative in Los Angeles shows, the implementation of this new approach is not so smooth with unintended complexities and contradictions of implementing nature's services. The shift to governance – public–private partnerships, co- production and management of services, coordinated by government – comes about as a reaction to the perceived failures of the Keynesian state (Kettl 2000 p. 494). At the same time, there is a shift from formal to informal techniques of government and the appearance of new actors on the scene of government (e.g., NGOs), (Lemke 2002: 50, in Swyngedouw 2005: 1997). The displacement focuses attention on the service provider – the NGO – and not the city itself that is piloting the programme behind the scenes. Bakker (2002) aptly describes this as a process of re-regulation characterised by an emergent new form of governance and of resource allocation.

In the Los Angeles instance, power is concentrated in the Mayor's office, and there is little or no transparency about the goals, ends and plans of the programme for either the non-profit partners or the target communities. Rather, the city directs the programme according to its own internal logic, but through the NGOs. In contrast, if the programme had been implemented by the Urban Forestry Division of the Bureau of Street Services, public consultation would have been obligatory due to administrative rules guiding city procedures. If the city had implemented the programme it would have fallen within the rules of the modernist city of public disclosure of a plan, comments on the plan, and possible modifications of the plan. Instead, the programme is relying on an opaque mixture of public and private funds funneled to an unaccountable non-profit organisation for the programme.

The use of NGOs to implement programmes in cities that urban government cannot afford to implement themselves is a form of outsourcing and allows the avoidance of public involvement and scrutiny that would be required under entirely, city-funded and implemented planning and implementation. The gradual substitution of the use of non-profit organisations to provide services (Wolch 1990, Kodras 1997, Lake 1997, Trudeau 2008) requires theory that can appreciate the variegated interactions that take place between state and non-state actors to form hybrid public/private relationships that have multiple facets. One thing is for sure; there is no going back to the modernist city where the state is wholly responsible for service and infrastructure provision. Trudeau (2008) observes that NGOs have multiple and diverse roles in places – there is a continuum of possible relationships that they can form with government and that NGOs too have multiple constituencies to whom they are accountable. Still the use and integration of NGOs in service provision, the forms of governance and co-production programmes take, are both emergent and require greater understanding. For the implementation of nature's services ecosystems that affect people's properties the relationship of the city, the NGO and the property owner is particularly tricky.

Thus, the implementation of a decentralised green infrastructure – if indeed this is one of the key elements for greater urban sustainability – remains unproblematised. With the Sanitary modern City come the city-provided services. With the hollowing out of the state have come governance and the contracting out of services to non-profit organisations. For ecosystem services-based sustainability, there is yet no well-articulated management architecture, but a great deal of faith in the approach. Unlike the modernist city's infrastructure of water purification and delivery systems, of sewage sanitation plants, roads and freeways, and communications networks, the sustainable city's green alternative is largely one built on sentiment and common sense, but little scientific knowledge and even less engagement with how the organisational constraints of current land use and urban governmental structure, funding, rules, regulations and mandates may need to be changed. Moreover, as an article of faith, implemented outside of traditional processes of hearings and plans, there is no place for communities to comment about the changes.

Shifts in the implementation of service delivery of public goods (like nature's services- based infrastructure) to semi-public and private governance – contracting out tree planting to several autonomous non-profit organisations – alters established systems of accountability that people understand and know. Networked approaches make it less easy to locate loci of power, to identify where decisions are being taken and who is responsible. Important questions emerging from governance arrangements, as Van Kersbergen and Van Waarden (2004) point out, are those of governability, accountability, and legitimacy. Governance, as Hirst (2000) points out, has a post-political thrust that evades the issues of democracy and political conflict (ibid. 33).

CONCLUSION

The transition from the progressive era sanitary city to the sustainable city is complex, multi-layered and messy. While the environmental benefits of nature's services in cities have started to be quantified by biophysical scientists, little critical analysis has yet been conducted on the implementation of this new and different type of infrastructure. Human's relationships to nature are deeply and subtly shaped by culture, including technology, science, history, and economy. In the aftermath of the disillusionment with the modernist city, the rise of the environmental movement and the understanding that Earth systems are being altered by human activity, it is almost paradoxical that cities have been discovered by biophysical scientists and others for their role as sources of air and water pollution and as potential sites of remediation. Doing so through using nature itself has become a popular notion, inspiring programmes such as planting the urban forest. This approach represents a sea change relative to the city that has been seen as a place to escape from in order to experience nature. Little by little there is recognition that nature exists in cities too, and that there is potential for naturalisation of the urban fabric for multiple benefits. Care should be taken to understand the origins of this shift and its assumptions about the benefits of nature in order to be able to thoughtfully and successfully create the sustainable city. Attention should also be paid to the new ideas of nature that underlie this new approach. Urban nature is a humanly determined nature, a garden, but perhaps not an Eden.

Note

1   See USDA, Northern Research Station 2008 for extensive bibliographies on tree benefit research www.nrs.fs.fed.us/pubs/

References

Alberti, M. 2008. *Advances in Urban Ecology, Integrating Humans and Ecological Processes in Urban Ecosystems*. New York, NY: Springer.

Alberti, M. and Susskind, L. 1996. Managing urban sustainability: an introduction to the special issue. *Environmental Impact Assessment Review*, 16 (4), 213–221.

Bakker, K. 2002. From state to market? water mercantilizacion in Spain. *Environment and Planning A*, 34 (5), 767–790.

Bartlett, M. 2007. Environmental Affairs Department, City of Los Angeles Department of the Environment. Personal Interview, August 18.

Beatley, T. 2000. *Green Urbanism: Learning from European Cities*. Washington, DC: Island Press.

Birch, E.L. and Wachter, S.M. (eds) 2008. Growing greener cities, urban sustainability in the twenty-first century. Philadelphia, PA: University of Pennsylvania.

Bulkeley, H. and Betsill, M.M. 2005. Rethinking sustainable cities: multilevel governance and the urban politics of climate change. *Environmental Politics*, 14 (1), 42–63.

Bure, D. 2007. Korean Youth Community Center, Personal Interview, August 1.

Collins, J.P. *et al.* 2000. A new urban ecology. *American Scientist*, 88 (5), 416.

Costanza, R. 2006. Thinking broadly about costs and benefits in ecological management. *Integrated Environmental Assessment and Management*, 2 (2), 166–173.

Costanza, R. 2008. Ecosystem services: multiple classification systems are needed. *Biological Conservation*, 141 (2), 350–352.

Daily, G. (ed.) 1997. *Nature's Services: Societal Dependence on Natural Ecosystems*. Washington, DC: Island Press.

Daniels, P. 2007. Public Works Commissioner, City of Los Angeles, 16 March.

Evans, J.P. 1997. Wildlife Corridors, Local Environment, 12: 129–152

Fiorino, D.J. 2006. *The New Environmental Regulation*. Cambridge, MA: The MIT Press.

Freeman, D. 2009. Deputy Mayor for the Environment, General Manager Los Angeles Department of Water and Power. Personal Interview, 9 August.

Graham, S. and Marvin, S. 2001. *Splintering Urbanism*. London: Routledge.

Gonzales, G. 2007. Director, Urban Forestry, Director Street Tree Services, City of Los Angeles. Personal interview, 16 June.

Hajer, M. 2003. Policy without polity? Policy analysis and the institutional void. *Policy Sciences*, 26 (2), 175–195.

Hays, S. 1959. *Conservation and the Gospel of Efficiency, the Progressive Conservation Movement 1890–1920*. Cambridge, MA: Harvard University Press.

Hays, S. 1972. The new organizational society. In Israel, J. (ed.) *Building the Organizational Society. Associational Tendencies in Early Twentieth Century America*. New York, NY: Free Press, 1–9.

Henderson, W.O. and Chaloner, W.H. (trans and eds) 1968. The condition of the working class in England/Engels; Stanford, CA: Stanford University Press, 1968.

Hirst, P. 2000. Democracy and governance. In Pierre, J. (ed.) *Debating Governance, Authority, Steering, and Democracy.* London: Oxford University Press, 13–33.

Hough, M. 1995. *Cities and Natural Processes.* New York, NY: Routledge.

How the other half lives: a Jacob Riis classic (including photography). Jacob A. Riis. Published/Distributed:[San Bernardino, CA]: ReadaClassic.com, [2012]

Haughton, G. and Hunter, C. 2003. *Sustainable Cities.* London: Routledge.

Jessop, B. 1998. The rise of governance and the risks of failure: the case of economic development. *International Social Science Journal*, 50 (155), 29–45.

Jessop, B. 2003. *The Future of the Capitalist State.* Oxford: Blackwell.

Jordon, A. 2008. The governance of sustainable development: taking stock and looking forwards. *Environment and Planning C: Government and Policy*, 26 (1), 17–33.

Jordon, A., Wurzel, R.K. and Zito, A. 2005. The rise of 'new' policy instruments in comparative perspective: Has governance eclipsed government? *Political Studies*, 53 (3), 477–496.

Kaika, M. and Swyngedouw, E. 2000. Fetishising the modern city: the phantas-magoria of urban technological networks. *International Journal of Urban and Regional Research*, 24 (1), 122–148.

Kettl, D.F. 1993. *Sharing Power: Public Governance and Private Markets.* Washington, DC: Brookings Institution.

Kettl, D.F. 2000. The transformation of governance: globalization, devolution and the role of government. *Public Administration Review*, 60 (6), 488–497.

Kodras, J. 1997. Restructuring the state: devolution, privatization and the geo-graphic redistribution of power and capacity in governance. In Staeheli, L. Kodras, J. and Flint, C. (eds) *State Devolution in America.* Thousand Oaks, CA: Sage Publications, 79–98.

Krueger, R. and Gibbs, D. (eds) 2007. *The Sustainable Development Paradox, Urban Political Economy in the United States and Europe.* New York: The Guilford Press.

Lake, R. 1997. State restructuring, political opportunism, and capital mobility. In Staeheli, L., Kodras, J. and Flint, C. (eds) *State Devolution in America.* Thousand Oaks, CA: Sage Publications, 3–20.

Lemke, T. 2002. Foucault, governmentality, and critique. *Rethinking Marxism*, 14 (3), 49–64.

Los Angeles Almanac 2000. Population by City, 1960–2000 [online]. Available from: www.laalmanac.com/population/po27.htm [Accessed 8 August 2008].

McHarg, I. 1971. *Design with Nature.* Garden City, NY: Published for the American Museum of Natural History.

McPherson, G.E. *et al.* 2008. *Los Angeles 1-million Tree Canopy Cover Assessment.* Albany, CA: U.S. Department of Agriculture, Forest Service, Pacific Southwest Research Station, p. 52, Gen. Tech. Rep. PSW-GTR-207.

Melosi, M.V. 2000. *The Sanitary City, Urban Infrastructure in America from Colonial Times to the Present.* Baltimore, MD: Johns Hopkins University Press.

Millennium Ecosystem Assessment, 2005. *Ecosystems and Human Well-being: Synthesis.* Washington, DC: Island Press.

Mouffe, C. 2005. *On the Political.* London: Routledge.

North, D.C. 1990. *Institutions, Institutional Change and Economic Performance.* New York, NY: Cambridge University Press.

Nowak, D.J., Hoehn, R.E. III, Crane, D.E., Stevens, J.C. and Walton, J.T. 2006a. Assessing urban forest effects and values, Washington, DC's urban forest. Assessing urban forest effects and values, Washington, DC's urban forestry, *Resources Bulletin NRS-1.* Newtown Square, PA: U.S. Department of Agriculture, Forest Service, Northern Research Station, p. 24.

Nowak, D.J., *et al.* 2006b. Assessing urban forest effects and values, Casper's urban forest. Resources Bulletin NRS-4. Newtown Square, PA: U.S. Department of Agriculture, Forest Service, Northern Research Station, p. 20.

Payne, J. 2000. Globalization and modes of regionalist governance. In Pierre, J. (ed.) Debating governance. Published/Distributed: Oxford, U.K.; New York: Oxford University Press, 2000. pp. 201–218.

Petts, J., Owens, S. and Bulkeley, H. 2008. Crossing boundaries: interdisciplinarity in the context of urban environments. *Geoforum*, 39 (2), 593–601.

Pierre, J. and Peters, B.G. 2000. *Governance, Politics and the State.* London: Macmillan Press Ltd.

Pincetl, S. 1999. *Transforming California, a Political History of Land Use in the State.* Baltimore, MD: Johns Hopkins University Press.

Pincetl, S. 2003. Nonprofits and park provision in Los Angeles: an exploration of the rise of governance approaches to the provision of local services. *Social Science Quarterly*, 84 (4), 979–1001.

Pincetl, S. 2007. Accounting for environmental services in cities: the new frontier for sustainability. *Social and Environmental Accounting Journal*, 27 (1), 3–8.

Pincetl, S. Implementing municipal tree planting: Los Angeles Million-Tree initiative. Submitted.

Platt, R.H., *et al.* 2008. Urban stream restoration: recovering ecological services in degraded water-sheds. In Birch, E.L. and Wachter, S.M. (eds) *Growing Greener Cities, Urban Sustainability in the Twenty-First Century.* Philadelphia, PA: University of Pennsylvania. pp. 127–151.

Portney, K.E. 2003. *Taking Sustainable Cities Seriously, Economic Development the Environment, and Quality of Life in American Cities.* Cambridge, MA: The MIT Press.

Ravetz, J. 2000. *City-region 2020: Integrated Planning for a Sustainable Environment.* London: Earthscan.

Rees, W. and Wackernagel, M. 1996. Urban ecological footprints: why cities cannot be sustainable – and why they are a key to sustainability. *Environmental Impact Review*, 16 (16), 223–248.

Rhodes, R.A.W. 1996. The new governance: governing without government. *Political Studies*, XLIV (4), 662–667.

Romano, S. 2007. Executive Director, Hollywood Beautification Team, 7 August.

Salamon, L.M. (ed.) 2002. *The Tools of Government, a Guide to the New Governance.* Oxford: Oxford University Press.

Sarno, L. 2007. Director Million Trees Los Angeles, Personal Interview, 11 August.

Sarno, L. 2008. Director Million Trees Los Angeles, Personal Interview, 8 August.

Satterthwaite, D. (ed.) 2001. *The Earthscan Reader in Sustainable Cities.* London: Earthscan Publications Ltd.

Scott, M. 1969. *American City Planning since 1890*. Berkeley, CA: University of California Press.

Smith, L. 2007. Former Director, NorthEast Trees (resigned), 11 June.

Spirn, A.W. 1984. *The Granite Garden: Urban Nature and Human Design*. New York, NY: Basic Books.

Stoker, G. 1994. Local governance in Britain, Glasgow, Department of Government, University of Strathelyde, mimeo, November, p. 6. In Wilson, D.J., Game, C., Leach, S. and Stoker, G. (eds) (1994) *Local Government in the United Kingdom*, London, UK, Macmillan, p. 400.

Svendsen, E. and Campell, L.K. 2008. Urban ecological stewardship: understanding the structure, function and network of community-based urban land management. *Cities and the Environment* [online], 1. Available from: http://escholarship. bc.edu/cate/vol1iss1/5 [Accessed 27 August 2009].

Swiller, A. 2007. Political advisor to Mayor Villaraigosa, personal interview, 12 November.

Swyngedouw, E. 2005. Governance innovation and the citizen: the Janus face of governance-beyond-the-state. *Urban Studies*, 42 (11), 1991–2006.

Tolbert, P.S. and Zucker, L.G. 1983. Institutional sources of change in the formal structure of organizations: the diffusion of civil service reform, 1880–1935. *Administrative Science Quarterly*, 28 (1), 22–39.

Trudeau, D. 2008. Towards a relational view of the shadow state. *Political Geography*, 27 (6), 669–690.

USDA, Northern Research Station, 2008. *Publications and products* [online]. Available from: www. nrs.fs.fed.us/pubs/ [Accessed 13 January 2009].

VanKersbergen, K. and Van Waarden, F. 2004. 'Governance' as a bridge between disciplines: cross-disciplinary inspiration regarding shifts in governance and problems of governability, accountability and legitimacy. *European Journal of Political Research*, 43 (2), 143–171.

Weibe, R.H. 1967. *The Search for Order, 1877–1920*. New York, NY: Hill and Wang.

White, R. 1995. *The Organic Machine: the Remaking of the Columbia River*. New York, NY: Hill and Wang.

Wiland, H. and Bell, D. 2006. *Edens Lost and Found: How Ordinary Citizens are Restoring our Great American Cities*. White River Junction, VT: Chelsea Green.

Williams, D.W. 2002. Before performance measurement. *Administrative Theory and Praxis*, 24 (3), 457–486.

Wolch, J. 1990. *The Shadow State: Government and Voluntary Sector in Transition*. New York, NY: The Foundation Center.

Chapter 6

Innovation in urban networks

Co-evolving consumer roles

Bas J.M. Van Vliet

INTRODUCTION

Urban retrofitting refers to the reshaping of the built environment, including the urban networks and energy and water flows that run through them. This chapter has its emphasis on the latter.[1] In most of the literature and in practice, urban retrofitting has been the domain of engineering, using material flows analysis as a common ground to understand the empirical dynamics of resource flows through cities (Hodson, *et al.* 2012). Material flow analyses identify flows conducted through cities and supported by urban infrastructures, ending up as stocks or moving through production-consumption cycles and transforming them into wastes, goods and services. Retrofitting in these terms is then to redesign urban infrastructures to increase resource efficiency or productivity (Hodson, *et al.* 2012: 792). This chapter's socio-technical analysis of urban retrofitting includes the governance of infrastructures and flows, and the actors and institutions involved in the processing of flows and their passage through the city.

It has been widely acknowledged that the consumers' connections to and their use of urban networks like electricity grids, water supply and sewer works encompass a significant share of their total natural resource use. Most of the literature on this, either from the angle of consumer studies, science and technology studies, or environmental engineering discusses consumption of network-bound services from the perspective of a particular system. So it is either the consumption of water supply services (Chappells and Medd, 2008; Hegger *et al.* 2011; Marks, 2006; Medd and Marvin, 2008) or electricity supply services (Hughes, 1983; Sauter and Watson, 2007; Wuestenhagen *et al.* 2007) or sanitation (Hegger, 2007; Melosi, 2000; Van Vliet *et al.* 2010; Zeeman, 2009) that is the focal point in most of the literature. The similarities and differences between consumer connections and uses of various urban networks, or the dynamics therein have rarely been taken up, with the exception of work on environmental consumption and urban networks (Van Vliet, Chappells and Shove, 2005; Southerton *et al.* 2004; Spaargaren and Van

Vliet, 2000). Yet, urban networks providing environmentally relevant services to consumers have a lot in common.

First, they roughly share historical patterns and phases of development from private provision in the late nineteenth century via universal service provision by public utilities towards the 1980s to a splintered provision from the late twentieth century on (Graham and Marvin, 1995; Guy and Marvin, 1998; Guy et al. 2001; Van Vliet et al. 2005).

Second, they can be characterized as Large Technical Systems (Hughes, 1983; Summerton, 1994) as they consist of huge material infrastructures, sunk costs and vested interests among governmental and corporate entities. The change of Large Technical Systems therefore is considered to take the shape of a socio-technical transition (Geels, 2002; Kemp et al. 2001), an approach for transformative system change involving multiple levels and multiple actors and a long term.

Finally, the three systems of water supply, waste water management and electricity supply have been subject to market liberalization, private party participation, and environmental renewal with various outcomes. Striking, however, is that the envisioned and actual roles of consumers in service delivery and consumption in general and in environmental innovation in particular has been altered considerably due to these developments. Rather than delving into the three urban networks on a *systemic* level, this chapter therefore focuses on the dynamics at the *consumption side* of the three urban networks.

It is worth exploring these new roles for consumers in urban network innovation and the wider urban retrofitting, as consumer roles in utility services were until recently non-descript, or labelled as the 'demand side' or as 'connections'. And second, whereas the three systems may be distinguishable in terms of their physical lay-out, or their legal and policy frameworks, at the consumption level, they come together. It is therefore relevant to explore how consumers combine the use of infrastructures in their daily lives. A combined understanding of changing consumer–provider relations and social practices, and the socio-technical, socio-environmental dynamics that are at stake in urban networks would equip us with the means to understand the instruments for the governance of environmental innovation in urban networks.

This chapter aims to answer the question of how environmental innovation in urban networks can be understood if we take it from a consumers' perspective. It draws on studies in three urban networks: water supply; waste water management and electricity supply in the Netherlands. As for water supply, a research project was executed on consumer market opportunities for water supply companies, based on an inventory of recent innovations in the sector, 3 focus group discussions and a survey among 3452 water consumers (Hegger et al. 2010). Innovation in sanitation was studied in diverse projects over the last decade (Van Vliet and Stein, 2004;

Van Vliet *et al.* 2010) all with a focus on consumer perspectives on innovation. Finally, for electricity a literature study supported with expert and consumer interviews was executed on smart grids, smart meters and smart behaviour (Naus *et al.* 2014).

DIFFERENTIATIONS IN URBAN NETWORKS AND THE RE-INVOLVEMENT OF THE CONSUMER

Differentiation in urban networks takes shape on multiple levels: differentiation in resources, providers, consumers, and in technology and infrastructure. At the level of resources, one could think of a shift from drawing on a single resource towards using multiple resources. In most cases, this will also imply a shift from centralized provision by single units (power plants, pumping stations) towards decentralized provision or distributed generation (EC, 2006; Estache, 1995; Guy and Marvin, 1998; Hammons, 2008; Kok *et al.* 2009; Wuestenhagen *et al.* 2007). A differentiation of resources may be accompanied with a differentiation in providers of services with utility companies no longer operating in a monopoly but experiencing competition from other service providers. New providers may be of similar size and levels of provision, but not necessarily so. With forms of distributed generation and small-scale provision, local providers emerge on the scene. There is also differentiation at the level of consumption. Here, I refer to the roles of consumers towards service provision that can transform from being a 'captive consumer' which refers to obliged consumption of urban network services provided by a monopolist provider, to consumer roles that can evolve into three categories: (i) a customer, (ii) a citizen-consumer and (iii) a co-provider (Chappells, 2003; Sauter and Watson, 2007; Van Vliet *et al.* 2005). The role-types reflect the role of end-users in service provision and consumption and the kind of relationship between providers and consumers. A *customer* role is defined by a commercial relationship in which providers compete for consumers who have a choice between providers and/or between services. The citizen-consumer role is defined by a relationship coloured by a concern about societal or environmental impacts of energy or water provision and consumption. Lastly, a co-provider role refers to a relationship where consumers participate in the provision of electricity or water services to themselves and/or to other consumers.

Finally, technologies and infrastructures that form the material backbone of urban networks may differentiate from uniform and standardized systems (such as generation units, pipes and cables, taps and sockets) towards a range of new technologies and standards such as those for solar energy, biogas, grey water and the like. The process of differentiation of centralized, monopolist utility services into differentiated decentralized co-provision of utility services is schematically summarized in Figure 6.1.

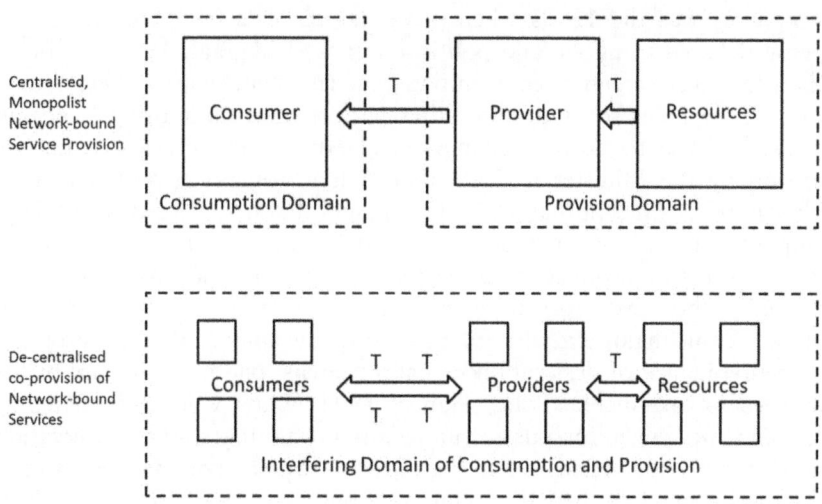

Figure 6.1 Differentiation of utility services in terms of resources (Rs), technologies (T), providers (Ps) and consumer roles (Cs)

Source: Van Vliet (2012)

Given these socio-technical dynamics in water supply, waste water and electricity supply systems, the question is what they mean for (i) the relations between providers and consumers; (ii) the role of consumers in providing the services in general and (iii) more specifically for retrofitting with respect to urban networks. Apart from possible similarities between water supply, electricity supply and waste water services, the differences between them need to be analysed, focusing on the specific differentiation of consumer roles that can be observed in the three urban networks under study here. In the following sections, it is analysed how this role division emerges in innovation projects of water supply, waste water management and electricity supply, respectively.

SOCIO-TECHNICAL CHANGES IN WATER SUPPLY, SANITATION AND ELECTRICITY SUPPLY SYSTEMS

Water supply

Water supply in the Netherlands has been a public affair since the beginning of the twentieth century. From the highest number of 229 mostly municipal-owned Water Companies before WW-II, due to mergers the number dropped to 100 in 1980 (VEWIN, 2008) and to only 10 in 2010. A crucial period determining the current position of Dutch Water

Companies was the 1990s when privatization of Water Companies was openly debated in public and political arenas (Dijkgraaf, 1997); amongst others leading to a water sector-initiated internal benchmark system among Water Companies so as to show that performance monitoring is not an exclusive feature to a privatized market. The discussion was closed after the decision by the Minister in 2003 that Water Companies will remain in public hands.[2] It meant that Water Companies that had merged with energy companies in multi-utilities before had to be split off again as electricity distribution and production activities were to be sold from local and regional authorities to private companies. At the same time, Water Companies became major executers of a national environmental policy program on the avoidance of desiccation of natural areas, one of the pillars of the National Environmental Policy Plan of 1994. Water Companies acted as the main messenger for public campaigns promoting water conservation and they actively participated in the diffusion water-saving technologies in households (such as dual flush toilets, water-saving showers) (Van Vliet, 1995, 2002). Water Companies presented themselves as 'environmental companies' to their customers, while at the same time exploring possibilities for product and services differentiation and for creating new markets, pending the then on-going discussion on liberalization of the water sector.

One of the most visible outcomes of this position of Water Companies in the 1990s was a series of household water projects emerging in new residential areas. Household water is a lower quality of water, derived from local surface water or rain water and delivered through a second piped water system to households, with connections to the toilet, the washing machine and the outdoor taps. The assumed environmental benefit of delivering a second water quality for purposes not needing drinking water quality (flushing, washing, gardening etc.) is that precious groundwater can be saved for nature. But household water projects were also a good opportunity for Water Companies to present themselves as customer-oriented (answering the commonly raised customer remark that flushing toilets with drinking water is a waste), being innovative, modern and environmentally concerned (Van Vliet, 2003). Eventually, the experiments came to a halt, after misconnections were made between the two piped systems in a huge project in Utrecht. For the sake of public health, the Minister of Environment in 2003 stopped the experiments and put a ban on new ones in the future.

In the years after the decision not to privatize Water Companies, the emphasis in service delivery turned to 'excellent trustworthy service provision including comfort and convenience services'. Water saving has disappeared from Water Companies' agendas, while household water has become an issue better not to be brought up again in consumer surveys.[3]

The main challenge Water Companies are facing nowadays is the lack of opportunities to respond to a number of competitive activities in the water market. Although water delivery is restricted by law to Water Companies alone, increasing competition at the fringes of water service delivery can be observed: from selling bottled water in supermarkets and schools, to providing hot tap water by Energy Companies and rain water devices by third parties. Water Companies' responses to these challenges vary. Some are pushing the limits set by their public monopolist position to reclaim their market share. These companies are now exploring possibilities to enter markets of bottled mineral water; water suspension machines at schools; advisory or certifying activities. Others keep concentrating on their core business of water supply only. For some Water Companies, finding new markets is a necessity in the longer term, as demand for water supply will decrease due to a shrinking population in the region they serve (Hegger *et al.* 2009).

New roles for water consumers

With the decision not to privatize the water supply sector, domestic water consumers remain 'captive': Water Companies hold a monopoly in water supply in the region and consumers do not have a choice between water providers. However, our research findings (Hegger *et al.* 2010) on new market opportunities for the water sector suggest that client contacts and communication are high on the Water Companies' agenda. Water Companies are keen to make their consumers feel like customers, citizens and co-providers of water services. The customer role is visible in the sense that client communication has gained importance: regular monitoring of client contacts, satisfaction and complaint handling is done to improve services and as input for an indicator in the sector wide tri-annual benchmark (VEWIN, 2007). The role of citizen–consumers emerges when clients are invited to participate in development projects their Water Company is involved in, like the assistance Water Companies offer in water and sanitation projects in the South. The co-provision role can be observed in cases where water users install rainwater or grey water recycling systems for certain water uses in and around their homes.

Such picture of consumer roles towards Water Companies is however rather one-sided as it only sketches a provider point of view concerning consumer roles. In two subsequent research projects, it was identified how water consumers view their Water Companies' and their own roles in terms of water provision and innovation. The first project aimed at qualitative assessments by experts and consumer focus groups of environmental innovations and consumer expectations on innovations and roles of Water Companies therein (Hegger *et al.* 2009). The conclusion is that a general shift can be observed from supply-side thinking towards more consumer-inclusive innovation strategies in the Dutch water supply sector. Water Companies are investigating and experimenting with new roles to complement their classical role of being an upstream operating (public) provider of water. Water managers are now considering several innovation routes also at the downstream end of the water chain and are starting to think beyond the core business of piped drinking water supply. The new provider roles identified vary from being 'supplier of other than merely plain water flows', 'consultant/advisor', 'certifier', 'provider of services', 'provider of products', to a role as 'company with an active consumer orientation'. These different roles can be said to represent different degrees of orientation on consumers' water practices, different forms of envisaged inter-provider competition and different levels of environmental ambition. Both our qualitative (focus groups) and quantitative (survey) assessments show that consumers associate Water Companies with efforts for the environment, high water quality and public health. Much less obvious for consumers is the potential commitment of their providers with 'luxury' and 'wellness' products and services. Consumers do envisage new services and new roles for the water industry, but only as long as they build upon and are in line with the classical view of Water Companies as public organizations that act responsibly and do not engage in risky, commercial services (Hegger *et al.* 2010). In terms of consumer roles, this points to a preference of consumers not to be treated as market actors (customers) but as citizen–consumers of a trustworthy, and societal and environmentally sound public service.

Wastewater and sanitation

The Netherlands is one of the most densely sewered countries in the world, with 111,000 km of sewer pipes and 99.6 per cent of households being connected to them (Rioned, 2009). For historical reasons, there has been a separation between responsibilities for water supply (by public companies), sewerage services (mostly by municipalities) and sewerage treatment (by regional Water Boards) (Juuti and Katko, 2005). The provision of sewerage and waste water services to consumers has been the most public as well as the most 'invisible' service provision of the three services discussed. All domestic consumers pay one of the two fixed rates for wastewater treatment, either for a single or for a multiple person household. Through municipal taxes they pay for sewerage operation and maintenance. Efforts to integrate tariffs for water supply and sewerage never materialized, at least not to the full, due to disagreements on cost recovery of services between Water Companies and Water Boards. Also the integration of Water Supply Companies and Water Boards has been proposed several times but has not been followed up, except for the city of Amsterdam, where the municipal Water Supply Company and parts of the Regional Water Board have been brought under one public company called Waternet.

Similar to the drinking water supply sector, the past decades have seen a process of up-scaling and merging of Water Boards. Nowadays, there are 23 Water Boards left, geographically designated according to water sheds, and institutionally positioned between provinces and municipalities. Water Boards constitute the fourth governmental level next to local, provincial and national governments. While formerly the general board consisted of representatives of stakeholders like farmers and Water Companies, since 1992 General Board members are elected by all constituents in the region, including (urban) consumers. The turnout of domestic consumers at Water Board elections held so far are however notoriously low (i.e. 23 per cent in 2004 and 45 per cent in 2015, as a result of combining elections for the Water Boards with those for Provincial Parliaments).[4] With 47 per cent of all sewer pipes being built before 1980 (Rioned, 2009), huge replacement investments are needed in the near future. Also the replacement of mixed sewers by separated sewer systems for storm water and waste water requires huge investments. Sewer charges are therefore expected to double in the years to come. Emerging challenges for the current sewer and treatment systems are the persistence of medicine residues in waste water treatment effluent and the emission of Phosphorus and Nitrogen to surface waters (Waste water treatment plants count for 41 per cent and 25 per cent of total emissions of P and N, respectively (Rioned, 2009)).

Although the central sewer system and waste water treatment plants are the dominating technologies for waste water collection and treatment, there is a growing number of projects aiming at research, development and implementation of decentralized collection, treatment and reuse of domestic waste water flows (Hegger, 2007; Zeeman, 2009). Such projects are typically niche developments, in new built areas and initiated by various consortia consisting of Water Boards, researchers, municipalities, housing corporations and citizen groups. Decentralized systems have been designed for urine separation and reuse; nutrient (P, N) recovery from black water; water saving and biogas production. They are implemented as alternatives to the central sewer and treatment systems that are validated as being over-dimensioned and spilling water, nutrients, materials and energy (Lens et al. 2001).

New consumer roles in waste water management

Traditionally, the most anonymous and captive consumers are to be found at the entry points of waste water networks. The production of waste water is not metered, nor individually monitored, while connecting to a sewer system is an obligation for all households. Other consumer roles emerge at the margins of the bigger waste water systems, notably in the experiments with various kinds of new – decentralized – sanitation. Hegger (2007) has investigated many of such projects in Western Europe and categorized them in either expert-led or consumer-driven projects. An example of the first are two new sanitation projects in Sneek (Lemmerweg Oost and Waterschoon in Noorderhoek), where 32 houses (Lemmerweg Oost) and 32 apartments and a retirement home (Noorderhoek) are connected to vacuum sewer systems that lead toilet waste to an anaerobic digester tank within the same neighbourhood. Similar to other expert-driven new sanitation projects, the consortium of a housing corporation, the regional Water Board, and a production company was eager not to bother householders in the design or management of the system. The only aspect householders found different is the shape of the toilet, the vacuum flush method and the different sound it makes. Our interviews in Noorderhoek (Naus and Van Vliet, 2012) were focussed on the skills and meanings of the social practice of toilet use. The skills of using a toilet are roughly the same as with conventional toilets. The flushing itself is different from normal flush toilets. Flushing means pressing a button which opens the valve with a short and loud 'bang' that resonates throughout the building. Because of this noise (up to 96 dB, Telkamp *et al.* 2008) people developed different strategies to avoid the nuisance. For instance, refraining flushing during the night, or not flushing at all after only peeing. We found that respondents were proud to be pioneers of a new environmentally sound system. In terms of environmental soundness mostly water conservation was mentioned, rather than producing energy or recovering nutrients. The toilet is considered modern, high-tech and hygienic and takes the principle of 'flush and forget' to the extreme.

Interviews with householders in both expert-driven projects show that more involvement from their side in the design, management and display of the system to the outside world would have been preferred (Hegger, 2007). Providers rightly assume that consumers would like to be kept away from waste water management, but when treatment systems become decentralized to a neighbourhood level this cannot always be sustained. In case of toilet systems like urine separation or composting toilets that do need behavioural change (like men having to sit down on urine separation toilets, or managing the composting conditions and emptying the tank), it would be necessary to involve end-users as co-providers of sanitation services. In so-called consumer-driven sanitation projects where residents initiated and co-designed their own sustainable housing estate (Van Vliet, 2006) the role of consumers is obviously much more visible. Householders see themselves here as co-providers of decentralized sanitation systems and organize the modes of management and maintenance of the grey water treatment systems among themselves and other providers of waste water services. Consumer roles become an object of negotiation rather than being fixed, especially in the planning phase and during the initial years of living in the project (Cuijpers, 2006; Hegger, 2007). Overall, the dominant role of users in waste water systems, including most of the innovative pilot projects, is still being a captive consumer, while only in a few citizen-driven innovation projects, roles of citizen–consumer and co-provider come to the surface.

Electricity supply

Over the last decades, the electricity sector in the Netherlands has been the most dynamic of the three urban networks discussed. After a series of mergers between regional electricity production and distribution companies, the assets and services of electricity production, transmission, network management and distribution have been split up since 2007 into public grid operators and private energy supply companies. The Electricity Act of 1998 was a major step away from regional monopolies and 'captive consumers', which specified that domestic consumers may choose which energy company they wish to buy their electricity from. Since 2000, many new intermediary companies without production facilities or distribution networks have entered the market, passing electricity produced from various national or foreign production facilities to consumers in packages of green, grey or cheap electricity over existing distribution networks managed by public grid operators. In 2006, with reference to upcoming EU legislation and at the cost of huge opposition from the side of Energy Companies, the Dutch government forced the Energy Companies by law[5] to split activities of network management from energy production and distribution and to create separate companies for both before January 2011. This enables the privatization of energy production and supply while keeping the distribution and transmission networks in public hands. Since this law was passed in 2007, several public shareholders of regional energy companies (provinces and municipalities) have sold their shares to multinational energy companies like RWE and E-On, while new regional distribution network companies (grid operators) have been created (i.e. Enexis, Alliander).[6] Since then the initiative and key role in the development and implementation of 'smart grids' and, connected to that, the electrical car is especially taken up by the newly created public grid operators.

New consumer roles in electricity supply

Compared to water and sanitation, the electricity sector is the most dynamic urban network with respect to changing provider–consumer relations. After the introduction of competition between electricity providers, the sector continued to change long-standing consumer–provider relations, culminating in the development of decentralized smart grids and electrical cars. Since the 1990s, householders can become involved as investors, owners and (co)regulators of renewable energy by installing solar PV panels, micro CHP or even wind turbines and delivering excess electricity to the distribution grid. Enhancement of this co-provider role may become essential for significant deployment of smart grids. A smart grid is an electricity network characterized by the active management of both information and energy flows in order to control practices of distributed generation, storage, consumption and flexible electricity demand. These practices are happening both before and after the (smart) meter installed in households and they involve multiple actors and different temporal-spatial dynamics (EC, 2006). Smart grids are also believed to be needed for the development of the electric car and more specifically the infrastructure to load its batteries. Fine-tuning and timing of load capacity in the network is crucial for the electrical car project to succeed and so is consumer behaviour. Energy companies are actively installing smart meters to millions of Dutch households. In contrast to conventional meters, which display aggregate Kilo Watt hours only being read once a year, smart meters can display real-time and aggregated energy use, in various household devices, and can be read anywhere at any time via the internet. They are being advertised as convenience devices ('Control and monitor your home from anywhere'; 'Set your mind at ease with customisable security alerts'; 'Expandable to suit your needs')[7], but smart meters do have other roles to play: to accommodate demand side management, tariff differentiation, distributed generation, and loading capacity for electrical cars.

Seeing social practices as the interplay of materials, skills and meanings (Shove, 2010) one could argue that energy monitoring can become a social practice in itself. The introduction of smart meters is accompanied by the diffusion of new devices and interfaces. They enable consumers to monitor their own aggregate and device-specific electricity consumption and production, to compare these data with previous figures and to their historic consumption levels or those of their neighbours. Monitoring electricity consumption, production and storage within and beyond the household is therefore a typical emerging social practice involving new routines, devices and interpretations. As there is a huge variety of interfaces, accessible data sets and security protocols on the market, it is still uncertain whether and how consumers actually use and incorporate monitoring practices in their household chores, and whether they sustain these practices after an initial period of experienced novelty. There is a huge variety in what smart meters actually mean to users: they may be seen as a vehicle of convenience, as an intrusion from the utility sector into the private domain or as a symbol of commodification of what had been considered universal services. Others have defined metering as the method to facilitate the necessary monitoring of energy use; to internalize energy consumption levels before consumers can be motivated to resource saving behaviour (Vollink and Meertens, 2006). Smart meters enable a further step in monitoring as consumers gain access to real time data concerning energy efficiency, sources, prices etc. With the materialization of these information flows, the previously clear-cut divide between the (energy) system and the citizen–consumer's life-world becomes blurred and needs to be renegotiated. Apart from such 'vertical' information flows between householders and utilities, also 'horizontal' information flows will be travelling between citizen–consumers. Through detailed monitoring of energy consumption inside the household (self-monitoring), it becomes possible to trace energy use back to specific practices (e.g. heating, lighting, transport) and to specific persons. Disclosure in the context of horizontal information flows can be distinguished into positive forms of 'self-disclosure' and un-wanted forms of 'self-exposure'. Self-disclosure might yield new forms of solidarity and (energy) cooperation among citizen– consumers. But self-exposure, the disclosure of matters that people do not want to become visible for others, may lead to 'fencing-off' efforts (Naus *et al.* 2014).

The social practice of (smart) energy monitoring has now been taken up by front running consumers while others are either indifferent to it or opposing it all together. For the 'old-school' data loggers who have always been counting their KWhs by regular meter readings, and for the technological gadget lovers, a smart meter would probably be a welcome device. For some others however, the self-monitoring would be seen as an additional household chore. More to the forefront in the debate about smart metering is the issue of privacy around smart metering. Many worry about the more detailed information that is gained on energy use inside one's home (the detailed energy demand patterns reveal pretty much the daily chores of householders, when they are at home, when they shower, when they go to bed etc.), the bigger the chance that such information will be disclosed to others than to consumers themselves. Electricity users of the nearby future will have to make up their minds about the 'smart monitoring' of their domestic, sustainable energy production and consumption while not intruding on their privacy which also depends upon their role in management and control over distributed generation and metering. Citizen consumers are also challenged by the new possibilities of smart grids to reorganize their routines of mobility, showering, heating and lighting to make their lifestyles more sustainable. In short, future 'smart' consumer behaviour in relation to smart grids entails the strategic balancing of being energy customers, co-producer, citizen and consumer at the same time while making choices about economy, privacy and sustainability.

CROSS-SECTORAL LESSONS AND IMPLICATIONS FOR URBAN RETROFITTING

Since the 1980s, all three urban networks have departed from their position to consider consumers as 'connections' only. Consumers have gained the attention of providers in several ways: as a target group for adopting innovations and new services; as clients to offer competitive deals on the electricity market; as co-providers of (solar) electricity or as concerned citizens to involve in and pay for water projects in the South. Second, the socio-technical innovations that have been taken place in the three sectors have at least partly been motivated by environmental issues and not only rhetorically. Examples of such innovations are the experiments and larger-scale implementation of solar panels, wind energy, biomass and Combined Heat Power systems; household water systems, water saving devices, grey water treatment systems, vacuum toilets, composting toilets, urine separation toilets. Third and strikingly, most of these innovations involve a downscaling of key technologies and infrastructures providing the services, which means that the formerly distinct domains of central provision and localized consumption of network-bound services have become mixed up as was illustrated in Figure 6.1.

Consumers play many different roles in the three urban networks and these roles even further diverge with ongoing innovation and decentralization within those systems. Strikingly, the different consumers of water, electricity and wastewater services with the different roles assigned to them are in reality the very same domestic consumers who smoothly combine the use of all urban networks together within their household practices. From a consumer point of view, it is therefore obvious to compare, combine but also easy to get lost in the complicated institutional boundaries between systems of energy or water services provision. For instance in our focus groups with water consumers (Hegger, 2010) participants were using the terms Water Company and Water Board interchangeably and were comparing their service levels and communication styles with Energy Companies. The precise distinctions between electricity production, distribution or grid operators were not familiar to these consumers either. This process of blurring has been accelerated by boundary crossing activities of water, energy and wastewater sectors as well as new providers in their search for new markets. In some new-built residential areas, Energy Companies are now starting to deliver hot tap water to householders through a neighbourhood-scale Combined Heat Power system. As about half of domestic water consumption comprises water that is heated for diverse high-valued purposes (most notably bathing, showering), Water Companies fear that their role will be reduced to providing toilet flush water (Hegger et al. 2009). Apart from Energy Companies being involved in water supply, many other boundary crossings occur: Water Boards being involved in new decentralized sanitation providing biogas for energy production (project Waterschoon in Sneek); electricity network companies providing electric car mobility services;[8] Gas Companies applying micro-heat power installations in households (Hommelberg et al. 2007) and thereby turning domestic gas consumers into electricity providers.

After the unbundling and fragmentation of urban networks and the separation of vertical and horizontal roles and types of consumers, space has been created for intermediaries to take up roles formerly divided between consumers and providers of services (Marvin and Medd, 2004). Such new intermediary service providers that have entered the splintered utility markets are for instance providers of grey water treatment systems, or solar energy systems; domestic energy consultants, web-based services for energy tariffs and services comparison, and companies mediating electrical car demand and availability of loading stations. There is no sign that these developments will eventually end up in stable constellations of network provision and consumption as it was before liberalization and decentralization. Environmental innovation and liberalization both continue to be the key conditions in urban network system dynamics, and a further differentiation of provision and blurring of domains of consumption and provision can be expected.

The implications for research on systemic urban retrofitting networks are two-fold. First of all, the analysis above implies that there is a need to address consumers not just as energy consumers, or water consumers, or consumers of waste water services, nor just as 'recipients' of urban retrofitting projects. They are 'knowledgeable agents' combining the use of all urban network-bound services in a series of daily social practices and in various roles towards the different providers of services. Such research on social practices related to urban network-bound services rather than on consumption of single products can build on the work of Shove and Walker (2010), Reckwitz (2002) Schatzki (2009) and Spaargaren (2011) on social practices. More research however is needed, in particular into the spill-over effects between multiple urban network uses within domestic social practices. For instance, in what it means for consumers to use a smart meter in electricity consumption and how that would influence the use of and appreciation for 'smart' water meters, when both systems of water and electricity will be utilized in combination within the social practices of bathing or cooking.

The other implication is that the need for an integrated analysis of systemic urban retrofitting and urban networks dynamics has come to the fore. So far the dynamics in urban networks are studied in a number of dimensions: socially in terms of new consumer– provider relations, technically in terms of new generation, treatment, distribution and monitoring systems, and spatially in terms of differentiation in geographical scales of urban networks. Urban retrofitting has mainly been the domain of (human) geography and urban studies, focussing on existing buildings and the urban fabric at large. Somehow the urban networks of water, waste and energy are interwoven in this fabric, but mainly dealt with in technical or spatial terms. This chapter has shown that new consumer practices and roles towards providers of services emerge as a consequence of systemic dynamics in urban networks. The study of implications of urban retrofitting for consumer roles and practices might as well be relevant. Monstadt (2009) made a plea for the integration of so-far rather distinct bodies of literature dealing with urban infrastructure dynamics that may count for urban retrofitting as well: history of technology studies; urban studies and science and technology studies. New studies into the urban political ecology of retrofitting would indeed be needed to embrace the emerging complex relationships between socio-environmental, socio-technical and urban infrastructure development.

CONCLUSIONS

Contemporary environmental innovations in energy, water and waste water services can be seen as processes of differentiation in resources, providers, technologies and consumer roles. The study of waste water innovations, water supply services and the development of smart electricity grids in the Netherlands show that new consumer roles vary widely among the sectors. In water supply and sanitation, consumers remain captive consumers although they are increasingly being treated as customers and citizens, especially in case of water supply. In terms of electricity supply, consumers have now become customers of commercially delivered electricity services or co-providers of electricity through various means, or citizen–consumers who are concerned about the climate impact of their energy consumption. But consumers do not separately consume water, electricity or waste water services or would necessarily act differently in all these sectors, rather they (smoothly) combine their use of network-bound services in a range of social practices. If we would take the role of the consumers in retrofitting ser-iously, the dynamics in all urban networks and in urban retrofitting at large should therefore be discussed in relation to each other as well as to the domestic social practices in which these networks play a role. The combined perspectives of differentiation in urban networks and urban retrofitting on the one hand and consumer roles and social practices on the other would help in understanding the current socio-technical dynamics that are at stake in urban retrofitting today. The evolving research agenda into social practices around the usage of urban network-bound services is a promising route to better understand consumer involvement in urban retrofitting.

Notes

1   This chapter is a revised and updated version of Van Vliet, B.J.M. (2012) Sus-tainable Innovation in Network-Bound Systems: Implications for the Consumption of Water, Waste Water and Electricity Services. *Journal of Environmental Policy and Planning* 14(3): 263-278.

2   'Wijziging van de Waterleidingwet (eigendom waterleidingbedrijven)' Eerste Kamer der Staten-Generaal (2003), 28 339, 9 December 2003 (www.eerste kamer.nl/9324000/1/ j9vvgh5ihkk7kof/vgm1kje0bqtk/f=y.pdf).

3   From project meetings minutes with the marketing specialists of Dutch Water Companies in 2008 and 2009 (Hegger *et al.* 2009, 2010).

4   Available at www.uvw.nl/opkomst-waterschapsverkiezingen-bijna-verdubbeld/
5   Act of 23 November 2006 to amend the Electricity Act 1998 and Gas Act in relation to independent network management.
6   Companies that have not yet split their network management and production and distribution activities continued opposition against the Law and were successful in June 2010 when the Court of Justice determined in an appeal case that the Law was not in line with European Law (Court of Justice The Hague, cases 200.035.392/01/02/03, 22 June 2010).
7   Available at www.alertme.com (accessed 1 March 2012).
8   Grid operator, Enexis, has launched the 'Mobile Smart Grid' see: www.smart charging.nl/en/

References

Brand, R. (2013) Facilitating sustainable behavior through urban infrastructures: learning from Singapore? *International Journal of Urban Sustainable Development, 5*(2): 225–240.

Chappells, H. (2003) *Re-Conceptualizing Electricity and Water: Institutions, Infrastructures and the Construction of Demand.* Lancaster: Lancaster University.

Chappells, H. and Medd, W. (2008) What is fair? Tensions between sustainable and equitable domestic water consumption in England and Wales. *Local Environment, 13*(8): 725–741.

Cuijpers, Y. (2006) *Verwaterend Burgerschap: Technologisch Burgerschap Rondom een Wijkwatersysteem.* MSc thesis, Enschede, Twente University. Available from http://essay.utwente.nl/66540/.

Dijkgraaf, E.E.A. (1997) *Mogelijkheden tot Marktwerking in de Nederlandse Watersector.* Rotterdam: Ministerie van Economische Zaken/EUR.

EC (2006) *European Technology Platform Smart Grids: Vision and strategy for European Electricity Networks for the Future.* Brussels: European Commission.

Estache, A. (1995) *Decentralizing Infrastructure. Advantages and Limitations.* Washington, DC: The World Bank.

Geels, F.W. (2002) Technological transitions as evolutionary reconfiguration processes: A multi-level perspective and a case-study. *Research Policy, 31*(8–9): 1257–1274.

Graham, S. and Marvin, S. (1995) More than ducts and wires: Post-fordism, cities and utility networks. In Healy, P. (ed.) *Managing Cities: The New Urban Context,* London: Wiley, pp. 169–190.

Guy, S. and Marvin, S. (1998) Electricity in the marketplace: Reconfiguring the consumption of essential resources. *Local Environment, 3*(3): 313–331.

Guy, S., Marvin, S. and Moss, T. (eds) (2001) *Urban Infrastructure in Transition: Networks, Buildings, Plans.* London: Earthscan.

Hammons, T. J. (2008) Integrating renewable energy sources into European grids. *International Journal of Electrical Power and Energy Systems, 30*(8): 462–475.

Hegger, D. (2007) *Greening Sanitary Systems: An End-User Perspective,* PhD thesis, Wageningen University, Wageningen. Available fromhttp://edepot.wur.nl/28474.

Hegger, D.L.T., Van Vliet, J. and Van Vliet, B.J.M. (2007) Niche management and its contribution to regime change: The case of innovation in sanitation. *Technology Analysis and Strategic Management, 19*(6): 729–746.

Hegger, D.L.T., Van Vliet, B.J.M., Spaargaren, G. and Frijns, J.A. (2009) *Meer dan drinkwater alleen. Nieuwe relaties tussen drinkwaterbedrijf en consument.* Wageningen/Nieuwegein: WUR Environmental Policy/KWR Watercycle Research Institute.

Hegger, D.L.T., Spaargaren, G., Van Vliet, B.J.M. and Frijns, J. (2010) Consumer-inclusive innovation strategies for the Dutch water supply sector: Opportunities for more sustainable products and services. *NJAS – Wageningen Journal of Life Sciences*, 58(1–2): 49–56.

Hodson, M., S. Marvin, *et al.* (2012). Reshaping urban infrastructure. *Journal of Industrial Ecology* 16(6): 789–800.

Hommelberg, M.P.F., Roossien, B., Warmer, J.K. and Kok, F.J. (2007) *Aggregatie Van Micro-wkk's in een Virtuele Centrale. First Trial Smart Power System.* Openbare Eindrapportage. Petten: ECN.

Hughes, T.P. (1983) *Networks of Power: Electrification in Western Society, 1880–1930.* Baltimore, MD: Johns Hopkins University Press.

Juuti, P.S. and Katko, T.S. (eds) (2005) *Water, Time and European Cities, History Matters for the Future.* Tampere: EU Water Time Project.

Kemp, R., Asselt, M. v. and Rotmans, J. (2001) More evolution than revolution: Transition management in public policy. *Foresight,* 3(1): 15–31.

Kok, K., Karnouskos, *et al.* (2009) *Smart houses for a smart grid.* Paper presented at the 20th International Conference on Electricity Distribution, CIRED, June 8–11, 2009, Prague.

Lens, P., Zeeman, G. and Lettinga, G. (eds) (2001) *Decentralised Sanitation and Reuse: Concepts, Systems and Implementation.* London: IWA Publishing.

Marks, J.S. (2006) Taking the public seriously: The case of potable and non-potable reuse. *Desalination,* 187(1–3): 137–147.

Marvin, S. and Medd, W. (2004) Sustainable infrastructures by Proxy? Intermediation beyond the production – consumption nexus. In D. Southerton, H. Chappells and B.J.M. Van Vliet (eds), *Sustainable Consumption: The Implications of Changing Infrastructures of Provision.* Cheltenham: Edward Elgar, pp. 81–94.

Medd, W. and Marvin, S. (2008) Making water work: Intermediating between regional strategy and local practice. *Environment and Planning D: Society and Space,* 26, 280–299.

Melosi, M. (2000) *The Sanitary City. Urban Infrastructure in America from Colonial Times to the Present.* Baltimore, MD: Johns Hopkins University Press.

Monstadt, J. (2009) Conceptualizing the political ecology of urban infrastructures: Insights from technology and urban studies. *Environment and Planning A,* 41(8): 1924–1942.

Naus, J. and Van Vliet, B. (2012). Over Spoelen en Vermalen : bewonersonderzoek naar percepties en gebruikerservaringen van het project Waterschoon in Sneek. Wageningen: Wageningen University.

Naus, J., G. Spaargaren, Van Vliet, B. and van der Horst, H.M. (2014). Smart grids, information flows and emerging domestic energy practices. *Energy Policy* 68(5): 436–446.

Reckwitz, A. (2002) Toward a theory of social practices. *European Journal of Social Theory,* 5(2): 243–263.

Rioned (2005) *Toestand van de Riolering.* www.riool.net/riool/binary/retrieveFile instanceid=20&itemid=997&style=default (accessed 27 August 2010).

Rioned (2009) *Riool in Cijfers 2009–2010*. Ede: Stichting Rioned.

Sauter, R. and Watson, J. (2007) Strategies for the deployment of micro-generation: Implications for social acceptance. *Energy Policy*, 35(5): 2770–2779.

Schatzki, T. (2009) Time, space and the organization of social life. In E. Shove, F. Trentmann and R. Wilk (eds), *Time, Consumption and Everyday Life*. Oxford: Berg, pp. 35–48.

Shove, E. (2010) Beyond the ABC: Climate change policy and theories of social change. *Environment and Planning A*, 42(6): 1273–1285.

Shove, E. and Walker, G. (2010) Governing transitions in the sustainability of everyday life. *Research Policy*, 39(4): 471–476.

Southerton, D., Chappells, H. and Van Vliet, B.J.M. (eds) (2004) *Sustainable Consumption: The Implications of Changing Infrastructures of Provision*. Cheltenham: Elgar.

Spaargaren, G. and Van Vliet, B.J.M. (2000) Lifestyles, consumption and the environment: The ecological modernisation of domestic consumption, *Environmental Politics*, 9(1): 50–76.

Spaargaren, G. (2011) Theories of practices: Agency, technology, and culture. Exploring the relevance of practice theories for the governance of sustainable consumption practices in the new world-order. *Global Environmental Change* 21(3): 813–822.

Summerton, J. (1994) *Changing Large Technical Systems*. Boulder, CO: Westview Press.

Telkamp, P., Mels, A. and van den Bulk, J. (2008) Praktijkervaringen met vacuüm technologie voor toiletten. *H2O*, 2008(10): 50–52.

Van Vliet, B.J.M. (1995) *Waterbesparing: Over spoeling en verspilling: een vooronderzoek naar de ontwikkeling en verspreiding van diverse technologieën met als doel waterbesparing in huishoudens*. Wageningen: LU, Wetenschapswinkel.

Van Vliet, B.J.M. (2002) *Greening the Grid: The Ecological Modernisation of Network-bound Systems*. PhD thesis. Wageningen: Wageningen University. Available from http://edepot.wur.nl/165778.

Van Vliet, B.J.M. (2003) Differentiation and ecological modernization in water and electricity provision and consumption. *Innovation*, 16 (1): 29.

Van Vliet, B.J.M. (2006) The sustainable transformation of sanitation. In J.P. Voss, D. Bauknecht and R. Kemp (eds), *Reflexive Governance for Sustainable Development*. Cheltenham: Edward Elgar, pp. 337–354.

Van Vliet, B.J.M. and Stein, N. (2004) New consumer roles in waste water management, *Local Environment*, 9(4): 353–366.

Van Vliet, B.J.M., Chappells, H. and Shove, E. (2005) *Infrastructures of Consumption: Environmental Innovation in the Utility Industries* London: Earthscan.

Van Vliet, B.J.M., Spaargaren, G. and Oosterveer, P. (eds) (2010) *Social Perspectives on the Sanitation Challenge*. Dordrecht: Springer.

Van Vliet, B.J.M. (2012). Sustainable innovation in network-bound systems: Implications for the consumption of water, waste water and electricity services. *Journal of Environmental Policy and planning*, 14(3): 263–278.

VEWIN (2007) *Water in Zicht 2006*. Rijswijk: VEWIN.

VEWIN (2008) *Dutch Drinking Water Statistics 2008* Rijswijk: Vewin.

Vollink, T. and Meertens, R.M. (2006) Technological innovations and the promotion of energy conservation: The case of goal-setting and feedback. In A. Verbeek and A. Slob (eds) *User Behavior and Technology Development.* Dordrecht: Springer, pp. 139–148.

Wuestenhagen, R., Wolsink, M. and Burer, M.J. (2007) Social acceptance of renewable energy innovation: An introduction to the concept, *Energy Policy,* 35(5): 2683–2691.

Zeeman, G. (2009) Centralised or decentralised sanitation chains? In J.C.v. Dijk, J.Q.J.C. Verberk and A.A. van Woerden (eds) *Nieuwe uitdagingen; 61e vakantiecursus in drinkwatervoorziening, 28e vakantiecursus in riolering en afvalwaterbehandeling.* Delft: Water Management Academic Press.

Part II

Governing and organising urban retrofit

Chapter 7

Retrofitting global environmental politics?

Networking and climate action in the C40

Michele Acuto

INTRODUCTION

'The country is the sum of cities. If cities do not work, then countries cannot work' admitted UN Secretary General Ban Ki-moon at the Rio+20 Summit's 'city leadership' day in June 2012. Certainly, it is now widely accepted in both scholarship and policy practice that cities have a central stake in contemporary global environmental governance. International issues are increasingly paralleled, intertwined, where not originated, in urban processes. The 'city' has nowadays become an almost ever-present factor in public policy discourses. On their part, cities are gradually demonstrating how they hold strategic governance potential in developing innovative responses to environmental concerns. They now do not solely represent 'local' partners, but have shifted from 'policy-takers' to be 'policy-makers' (Schultze 2003) in their own right.

The well-established literature on the urban dimension of socio-technical transition to low-carbon futures (Hodson and Marvin 2012) has certainly paved the way for this shift in urban and environmental studies. However, one of the major limits of this scholarship has been the predominant focus on the metropolitan response to national policies and, to a much smaller extent, international negotiations, and the generally 'domesticized' nature of these analyses. Even in comparative case studies cities have been depicted as relatively passive in relation to the overarching architecture of global climate governance. The main issue in this strand of research, as in most urban studies, is the relative limitation of holistic views that could situate cities within the broader governance structures that connect global developments with localized matters. Even multi-level perspectives on socio-technical transitions have struggled to convey this. Technical and innovation elements are generally privileged and rare are the studies that convey a balanced sense of the *political* context of this urbanization of environmental issues. To date, an even greater silence lingers on the capacity of cities to 'retrofit' the governance structures in which local, national and international responses to climate change are framed. As I argue here, cities are instead increasingly involved in potentially transformative efforts to retrofit not only their built environments but also global environmental governance more in general.

Beginning with the larger efforts of ICLEI and UCLG and developing into a myriad of smaller organizations, several are the examples of city-based engagements that at least since the 1990s have progressively established an urban presence within the realm of global governance. City networks have grown exponentially in numbers and membership and have progressively carved a more extensive role in environmental governance. Organizations such as ICLEI have made extensive efforts in this direction since the 1990, as with the Cities for Climate Protection (CCP) Campaign launched by ICLEI with the aim of gathering a coalition of local governments sufficient to account for at least 10 per cent of the global GHGs emissions. In recent years the Climate Leadership Group (C40) has fast emerged amongst peers as one of the most dynamic and proactive city networks in contemporary global environmental governance. By relying on a multi-regional membership of 'global' cities, a growing interconnectedness with key international actors like the World Bank, and an effective emphasis on networking, the C40 is today engaged in a numerous socio-technical transition efforts across more than fifty major metropolises. Retrofitting, financing and climate policy measurement are central tenets of the Group's agency.

RESPONDING TO CLIMATE CHANGE: THE C40

The development of the C40 as networked structure in global governance dates back to the autumn of 2005. Under the initiative of then-mayor Ken Livingstone and his deputy Nicky Gavron, the Greater London Authority gathered a group of large metropolises at a two-day World Cities Leadership and Climate Summit. The meeting, convened in partnership with ICLEI and the British non-profit organization The Climate Group, focused on the urban governance of climate change by showcasing best planning and financing practices from the various cities involved. The key issue at stake, as put forward by Livingstone, was to tackle bureaucratic and political obstacles to effective delivery in urban-focused climate initiatives. By presenting its agency on this issue as both source and solution for environmental challenges, London argued for cities' 'practical action on the ground'.[1] This was not so much for a 'brand new' approach, but a more extensive interconnection of the already established capacity of cities to tackle climate change.

The idea was not that major cities in the world were lacking the ability to tackle climate change: rather, these metropolises were already pioneering best practices in this field and the drawback was instead to be found in their limitations in exchanging expertise and coordinating efforts. Forming a network established around the indispensable role of large cities as delivery ends of environmental policy seemed the winning strategy. Core to development of the C40 was a narrative that depicts cities as central agents in climate politics and the role of the Group as key catalyst for innovative sustainability initiatives. Archetypal of this present-day evolution, the 2005 conference was set up around sessions on public transport, energy supply, building retrofitting and waste management, discussing the specifics of traffic congestions or comparing heath wave responses. If largely implied but not stated in these early meetings, a progressive duality between the world of 'cities acting' and the quandaries of 'states talking' was to develop into a core theme of the C40.[2]

Major catalyst for the expansion of the network to 63 cities was the partnership with the Clinton Foundation's newly-formed Climate Initiative (CCI) in August 2006.[3] Originally linked to C40 as 'delivery partner', CCI has since become crucial in setting the C40's retrofitting agenda, with a role rooted in three core initiatives sketched in the 2006 partnership, ahead of what was later (2011) to become a merger between the two secretariats. First, CCI functioned as a pivot to create a consortium capable of pooling the purchasing power of these metropolises and liaise with the major Energy Service Companies (the so-called 'ESCOs' such as Honeywell or Siemens) thus facilitating the C40's structural expansion into the global market to lower the prices of energy saving products and sustainable technologies. Second, the CCI also focused on mobilizing experts and IT from the private sector to provide conjunct technical assistance to member cities. Third, CCI fostered the development of city-based technical networking such as the testing of emission impacts measurement tools as well as the establishment of internet-based communications systems amongst local governments. Besides negotiating the enlargement of the C40 membership, the CCI functioned as a medium between the Group's own policymaking enterprise and global financial means to implement it on the ground. This meant that the linkage with Foundation's Climate Initiative acted as a network multiplier allowing the C40 to go beyond the transnational municipal effort of its early days. Through the CCI's mediation, the C40 has encompassed several other governance scales in a growing series of public-private partnerships pinpointed on these cities' key positioning vis-à-vis climate change. The CCI has since then become progressively integrated into what can now be rightfully labelled as a 'hybrid' governing arrangement: if in the seven years since the original partnership the link between the Foundation's Climate Initiative and the Group's key executive as represented by the London headquarters has unfolded through a loose coordination of mutually-supported initiatives, the two merged in January 2011 into a common secretariat. The CCI has fast become a key stakeholder steering the Group's activity. Formalized by mid-2007 the shape of the C40 network is now headed by a steering committee of nine and an elected chairman represented by a member city mayor. Participation to the Group is voluntary, and the linkage among the metropolises is continuously 'activated' through a series of issue-based practitioners' workshops and *ad hoc* meetings that assure a constant decentralized cooperation amongst members. Biannual conferences (London 2005, New York 2007, Seoul 2009, São Paulo 2011 and Johannesburg 2014) provide regular occasions for general assembly, as well as a window for continual problematization of the key role of global cities in environmental governance.

RETROFIT IN THE C40 NETWORK

Despite a growing political recognition, it is in its technical dimension that the Group has perhaps achieved the most in terms of climate action.[4] Retrofit in the Group is varyingly understood. First, in its narrower sense, it is seen in terms of repurposing the built environment towards more efficient and climate-friendly performances. Second, it is also communicated in the broader sense of a 'retrofit agenda' geared not only towards technical and behavioural advancement but also to convey the 'global change' foundations of climate action in the C40. Which sense is communicated varies according to audience, with stronger degrees of technological determinism not just in the more technical conversations, but also in some of the showcase events and pilot overview at summits and workshop. In this sense, limited 'techno-logical fixes' do remain a commonplace problem of the C40, but also (and importantly) the starting points for the most incisive climate action by the network, evidencing both limits in reflexivity and accountability of the Group as well as its very positive implementation capacity. The Group has been thriving on the development of common planning strategies, shared metropolitan policies, transnational instruments and preferential connections amongst global cities and major international institutions.[5] If the political role of the C40 has demonstrated a capacity to partake in the global governance discourse, the more technical tackling of climate issues has had the merit of implementing real action on the ground and foster collective responses to share and similar problems at the urban level.

Since the New York Summit in 2007 the C40 has set out to organize a series of issue-based workshops to bring together not only executives from the Group's global cities, but more specifically planners and technical officers working specifically on retrofit projects. Beginning with a meeting in Stockholm in December later that year, and following with a mounting succession of fora on, for instance, airports and ports planning (Los Angeles and Rotterdam 2008), waste management (London 2010), energy efficiency (Berlin 2010) and infrastructure financing (Basel 2011), the C40 has generated a now well-established practice of assembling practitioners in order to showcase best practices and exchange scientific knowledge on strategic urban planning.

The influence of the C40 in redefining the traditional alignments of environmental governance is in this sense neither just a function of a pro-active 'city diplomacy' (Acuto 2013) with key international bodies for climate action, nor of its members' city-to-city cooperation as developed through summits and municipal 'embassies' across the network. Equally important, if not even more fundamental from a practical standpoint, the C40 has gathered substantial implementation on the ground through low-carbon retrofitting initiatives. Here, the C40 has been able to leverage its collective influence even more effectively than in the international diplo-macy arena. For example, many of the Group's economic obstacles have been overcome through a CCI-led system of procurement.[6] For example, the C40/CCI Energy Efficiency Building Retrofit Program (EEBRP) brings together the Group's largest cities; multinational energy service firms (ESCOs) and financial institutions, in order to develop financing consortia. The Program allows C40 cities to access a 'purchasing alliance' admin-istered by the CCI's EEBRP team, where the latter 'leverages the buying power of the C40 to achieve affordable pricing on – and thus faster adoption of – the latest energy efficient and clean energy products and tech-nologies'.[7] In practice, CCI can act as a mediator for the Group by negotiating linkages among manufacturers and global cities thanks to the pooled resources of these metropolises and the preferential connection opened for ESCOs in their retrofit market. Here a direct advantage of the Group versus more traditional city networks is that provided by membership and visibility of the C40. The Group can leverage a rather exclusive membership and the presence of world leading financial, cultural, trade and mobility hubs (what urban studies has for long named 'global' cities), therefore offering a formidable PR and implementation platform, underscored by notable city leaders like Mike Bloomberg, to non-govern-mental partners and ESCOs. The Purchasing Alliance lowers investment barriers for products and technologies with significant energy efficiency improvement or fuel switching potential. Building owners can access the Purchasing Alliance products directly using their own procurement methods or as part of a larger retrofit project through an ESCO or other provider. The Initiative allows the establishment of a financing process which allows the C40 to implement on the ground the policies showcased in the work-shops. However, neither CCI nor C40 play a significant role in the final stages, where the CCI negotiates a ceiling benchmark price (not a final price) and procurement can be adjusted to adhere to a client's existing regulations and processes, leaving much of the specific implementation to the owner and its (international) market constraints. As Mikael Román (2010) noted, while the procurement operates in this case as a *de facto* governance mechanism, as an implementation strategy it seems to fall short in several cases: it may alienate some member cities with specific technology needs pushing for internationalization of standardized products and this, as a consequence, creates a tension between local industry and the global competitiveness of an exclusively-Western pool of ESCOs. This, of course, flags the tricky politics of the network in the wider 'global urban' landscape, where the 'global' cities of the Group could potentially overshadow smaller and less visible centres, and where internal differentiation between drivers and peripheral, generally global south, metropolises also surface at a closer inspection (Bouteligier 2012).

Importantly, public-private enterprises like EEBRP are aimed at the establishment of common practices and preferential pathways amongst global cities, as well as between these and the private sector as key intermediary for the implementation of the Group's goals. As such, the C40 structure gains network power vis-à-vis other actors by establishing 'best practices' and standards that define the 'cutting edge' in climate governance, while also developing almost obligatory paths for members' city diplomacy on climate issues. So, if the logic of public-private hybridization has been one of overcoming budgetary and action limits, this has also recast the traditional political-economic dependences of these cities on their global market bases, these have not been denied in the process of hybridization via CCI, but rather re-organized and mobilized through a urban-centred transnational process. Much of the same can be said for the C40's connection with the World Bank – one of the main structural developments of the Group since June 2011.

RETROFITTING GOVERNANCE, FORGING NEW LEADERS

While the CCI linkage, especially since the merger, has provided some substantive economic support for the Group's long-term sustainability, the prompt to establish a more formal connection with the World Bank has emerged from the concerns surrounding the financing of green retrofit in many of the C40 members. Seen as 'a natural extension of the Bank's relation with each city' the partnership with the Bank is considered crucial in order to catalyse more private capital and to allow a quicker pay-out of the various climate-sensitive projects implemented at the strategic planning level by the Group.[8] In this sense much emphasis has thus far been put on developing a consistent approach to climate action planning strategies across the C40. In particular, the agreement is aimed towards establishing a common approach to measuring and reporting on city greenhouse gas emissions. Yet, this is not simply a planning concern: as the agreement underlines, standardized action is mainly needed to permit potential investors to identify opportunities across cities and thus to multiply the Group's financing by emphasizing the capacity of the C40 to be a catalyst of action.

To be certain, this linkage offers distinct implementation advantages, especially in terms of offering incentives to the less active C40 members and affiliate cities to take up more extensive actions. Moreover, the connection with technical experts at the Bank, and especially at the World Bank Institute, brings some considerable experience in leveraging 'climate financing' instruments with the private sector, thus allowing for further hybrid linkages between the CCI-C40 and not solely ESCOs but private providers more in general. As the Bank's linkage begins to unravel in this direction in both the initial rhetoric on this key linkage and its related plans for action, the two tracks of the C40 have once again appeared central: connecting the Bank's apparatus not solely to the political, but chiefly to the *technical* dimension of the Group's agency, facilitates a particularly multi-scalar reach. Furthermore, this link allows C40 and Bank to bypass the inefficiency of the approach of the UNFCCC negotiations by setting up direct connections between the transnational scale of both the Bank and the C40's city diplomacy, and the urban sphere represented in the latter's planning track. This push for scalar reach and 'trouble jumping' echoed in former World Bank President Robert Zoellick's words. In 2011 he underlined how the Bank's interest in setting up a direct linkage with the C40 was mainly prompted by a need to '*deepen* our partnership *directly* with cities' as these latter 'are the future of climate change' – a declaration that reinforces these cities' appointment as obligatory passage points for global environmental governance.[9]

The C40 has not solely focused in acquiring a strategic policymaking positioning, but also to demand some more direct stakes in the unfolding of the global response to challenges such as climate change. For instance, at a recent C40 roundtable with the OECD held in Chicago, former C40 Chair Mike Bloomberg called for cities to be granted access to funding provided by the Clean Development and the Joint-Implementation mechanisms under the Kyoto Protocol, arguing that 'cities around the world are increasingly demonstrating that they have the desire, the knowledge, and the capacity to make effective use of such assistance'.[10] Quite simply, the contention here is that if mayors are indeed already pro-active and innovative components of global governance, then it is nothing but fair to allow them a room for manoeuvre and an institutional access that can match diplomats and statesmen. In this context, whether city leaders act as 'partners or adversaries of states', their crucial role is undeniably becoming more widely recognized by 'a growing number of spheres of authority' (Rosenau 1995: 24). By internationalizing their roles beyond mere local management, and thus taking up positions once assumed to be the sole privilege of state diplomats, the mayors involved in international networks are increasingly out to demonstrate how central governments and international organizations are no longer 'the only problem-solving units' (Mathews 1997: 65) in world politics.

C40 cities have attempted to overcome the problem of action beyond informal pledges that has stalled negotiations on universal environmental frameworks. By reconverting existing ties and well-established planning practices the Group has fostered more climate-focused and concerted types city-to-city cooperation and urban redevelopment that, right from the second C40 Summit, have begun to offer tangible results. The C40's policy-making style, focused on sharing information on environmental policy and facilitating public-private partnerships, represents relative structural novelties with respect to the 'global deal' (Falkner *et al.* 2010) universal decision-making take and the 'global civil society' (Lipschutz 1992) activism that have populated global governance in the past decades. The C40 does not rely on the traditional regime-building emphasis typical of both the former's bargaining and the latter's advocacy. Rather than constructing a binding scheme encompassing cities in similarities, the C40 emphasizes the productivity of difference (and the learning potential coming from its display) and the incentives of inter-city competition.

The capacity of initiatives like the C40 to reshape the architecture of global governance and the politics of socio-technical transitions is also indicative of the emergence of city leaders as a transnational force beyond the top-down world of international negotiations, or the 'bottom-up' advocacy of civil society groups. The C40 has in fact put much emphasis on how mayors are tasked with managing most of the 'global' challenges international specialists are so accustomed to, on a daily basis. This is not solely a matter of rhetoric. Mayors like those of the C40 have effectively expanded their local management capacities to encompass a plethora of activities aimed at tackling global challenges both through more effective urban policymaking and through transnational networking. The recognition given by actors such as the World Bank to this increasing influence is not casual. Most metropolitan mayors, both in the West or in the Global South, can today display sets of powers that allow them some substantial retrofitting competence to tackle climate change. Yet recognizing this requires international scholars some unconventional peregrinations beyond the traditional purview of diplomacy. ARUP, another corporate consulting partner of the Group, has extensively documented this policy capacity both of its June 2011 and February 2014 joint reports with the C40 titled *Climate Action in Megacities*.[11] While recognizing that 'not all problems of global warming can be tackled at a city level' these reports have detailed the wide reach of mayoral powers across several sectors of activity, including transport, building retrofit, waste and water management, energy supply, outdoor lighting, planning and urban land use, and food supply. Considered in terms of service ownership and operation, the capacity to shape public policy demonstrated by the leaders of the sixty-three C40 cities surveyed by ARUP is decisively substantial, documenting how actions by key metropolises have nearly doubled between 2011 and 2014 (from 4,734 'climate actions' to 8,068), in an effort to try and tackle the environmental challenges they are nowadays confronted with. Yet, this pervasive influence is not free from those constraints that Hodson and

Marvin (2012: 437) highlighted at the national sphere: the governance and language of retrofitting in the C40 is also mobilized by relatively limited interests that do not result in 'radical transitions but, rather, work to reproduce the economic status quo'. Here, then, the successful model of the C40, based on market mechanisms and networking, also runs the risk of locking the Group (and by proxy the wider landscape of climate action in cities) into a still limited system both in terms of accountability, deployment capacity and scalability, while facing important membership dilemmas.

CONCLUSIONS

The emergence of the C40 testifies that cities have capacity to re-spatialize parts of global environmental governance as policymaking dynamics are uprooted and recast beyond the 'global deal' skeleton of climate politics into the implementation capacity of cities. In these processes municipal leaders have a key stake in creating alternative paths for socio-technical transitions. However, this innovative role is confronted by the challenges of effective city agency. In particular, the role played by resource limitations, especially in terms of budgetary constraints to the local level of policy-making, remains a crucial one as it perpetuates the need to engage the economic dimension of global affairs beyond the scalar allocations of international politics.

In particular, the role played by resource limitations, especially in terms of budgetary constraints to the local level of policymaking, remains a crucial one. This tends to perpetuate a need to engage the economic dimension of global affairs beyond the scalar allocations of international politics. Cities are often prompted (directly or by proxy) to conform to broader underpinnings of a constrictive system dominated by the 'compromise of liberal environmentalism' (Bernstein 2001), which inevitably super-imposes the global economy on the room for action left to global cities. This is however not just a strategic urban planning concern: even when considered as actors in world politics, cities showcase a substantial drive towards a 'marketisation' of their international agency. In this sense, as Okereke, Bulkeley and Schroeder (2009: 63) also argued, 'the general preference for market mechanisms' such as procurement, emissions trading, voluntary baseline coordination or best practices exchanges, in contrast with more managerial and governmental (top-down) methods, as the means of tackling climate change 'could very well be regarded as evidence of the dominance of a particular rationality of government and social order'. Hence, perhaps even more than their sovereign limitations, resource scarcity and need for more extensive financing have been pushing cities toward transnational networking and capital pooling, which have allowed them to set up public-private hybridizations like the CCI procurement scheme, which in turn allow these metropolises to overcome such contingencies. Conversely, this rational continuity promotes a twin process: on the one hand, wary of the impediments and dominance of a mostly neoliberal global governance, global cities shift the locus, rhetoric and object of global political agency towards alternative (urban and transnational) scales in order to bypass such structural constraints. On the other hand, equally conscious of the possibilities that a neoliberal system allows for 'individual' agency, these metropolises exert networked influence and gain room for (political) manoeuvre via planning and market instruments which in turn perpetuate the centrality of economic and technical dimensions of the system itself.

This trend, while capable of re-spatializing the governance of retrofitting, can also result in a 'suspension of politics' that, by removing the space of contestation, allowing for existing power structures to be in fact 'accepted as a given' (Harriss 2002: 11). While effective, new generation city networks like C40 still lack open space for fair political discussion, responsible positioning in the broader landscape of cities the world over, while also needing more explicit reflection on their structural impacts on global environmental governance. The Group does not seek to contest or ameliorate the shortcomings of such climate responses, but rather devises parallel (or alternative) governance schemes to bypass it. Quite similarly, the inevitability of the global marketplace, as structured through the systems of international financing and global commodity chains, are taken for granted as inescapable fixtures in the emergence of the C40 actor-network, whose strategic planning or city diplomacy solutions are sought via neoliberal terms. This is certainly prompted by the intertwining of the C40 dealings with the CCI, which pushes for a market-friendly (if not 'oriented') approach to governance due to its 'mission of applying the Foundation's business-oriented approach to the fight against climate change in practical, measurable, and significant ways'. The coordination of so many metropolitan (and private, if one takes into account CCI, ARUP and World Bank) interests has thus far been pinpointed on a 'common gain' mentality that has to date been presented with little question either from within or without C40 circles. Yet, this means in practice that the C40 approach to climate change, already representative of an aggregate of many local governments needs, is also extending to encompass business agendas that see a great deal of benefits in a largely neoliberal approach to environmental challenges – a trend that neither tighter ties to effective, innovative but still only privately accountable actors such as ARUP, nor a privileged access to the World Bank, are likely to displace.

Notes

1   GLA Mayor Press Release (4 October 2005): 'Mayor brings together major cities to take lead on climate change'. Available at www.london.gov.uk/media.

2 The expressions have often been reiterated, not least by the successive C40 Chairs David Miller of Toronto and Michael Bloomberg of New York, at the outset of each biannual Summit.

3 For the text of the agreement see: Clinton Foundation Press Release, 1 August 2006: 'President Clinton Launches Clinton Climate Initiative'. Available at www.clintonfoundation.org/news/news-media.

4 Recent cases of academic attention to the case can be traced, amongst others, in Pattberg (2010) and Bouteligier (2012).

5 See for example the BBC World Service special *The Climate Connection* (9 December 2010): 'Part Four The New Leaders' which has pointed at the C40 as a model of innovative climate leadership: 'From Toronto to Seoul, Karachi to Addis Ababa the C40 leaders have put aside their naturally competitive instincts to create real environmental benefits for their own citizens and to share them with other cities'. Available at www.bbc.co.uk/worldservice/science/2010/12/101201_climate_connection_prog_four_tx.shtml.

6 'Procurement' is meant here as the acquisition of appropriate goods and/or services at the best possible total ownership cost to meet the needs of the purchaser in terms of quality and quantity, time, and location.

7 Clinton Climate Initiative, 'CCI's Energy Efficiency Building Retrofit Program, EPC toolkit for higher education'. New York, April 2009, p. 2. Available at www.clintonfoundation.org/what-we-do/clinton-climate-initiative/resources/EEBRP.pdf; and CCI Building Retrofit Overview, available at www.clinton foundation.org/what-we-do/clinton-climate-initiative/cities/building-retrofit. The administration will now shift to the CCI-C40 joint secretariat.

8 A summary of Robert Zoellick's speech at C40 São Paulo Summit (1 June 2011) and of the partnership is available at http://go.worldbank.org/BVGELE3NQ0.

9 Ibid, emphasis added.

10 Opening remarks by former C40 Chair Michael Bloomberg, OECD Roundtable of Mayors and Ministers, Chicago, March 8, 2012. Available at www.oecd.org/site/0,3407,en_21571361_45068056_1_1_1_1_1,00.html

11 ARUP and C40, *Climate Action in Megacities*, versions 1.0 (launched as part of the C40 summit in Sao Paulo, Brazil, June 2011) and 2.0 (launched as part of the C40 summit in Johannesburg, South Africa, February 2014). Available at http://issuu.com/c40cities/docs/c40_climate_action_in_megacities

References

Acuto, M. (2013) 'World Politics by Other Means? London, City Diplomacy and the Olympics'. *The Hague Journal of Diplomacy* 8 (4): 287–311.

Bernstein, S.F. (2001) *The Compromise of Liberal Environmentalism*. New York: Columbia University Press.

Bouteligier, S. (2012) *Global Cities, Networks and Global Environmental Governance*. London: Routledge.

Falkner, R., Stephan H. and Vogler, J. (2010) 'International Climate Policy after Copenhagen: Towards a 'Building Blocks' Approach'. *Global Policy* 1 (3): 252–62.

Harriss, J. (2002) *Depoliticizing Development: The World Bank and Social Capital*. London: Anthem.

Hodson, M. and Marvin, S. (2012) 'Mediating Low-Carbon Transitions?' *European Planning Studies* 20 (2): 421–439.

Lipschutz, R. (1992) 'Reconstructing World Politics: The Emergence of Global Civil Society', *Millennium* 21 (3): 389–420.

Mathews, J. (1997) 'Power Shift'. *Foreign Affairs* 76 (1): 65–6.

Okereke, C., Bulkeley, H. and Schroeder, H. (2009) 'Conceptualizing Climate Governance Beyond the International Regime'. *Global Environmental Politics* 9 (1): 58–78.

Pattberg, P. (2010) 'The Role and Relevance of Networked Climate Governance'. In F. Biermann, P. Pattberg and F. Zelli, (eds) *Global Climate Governance Beyond 2012: Architecture, Agency and Adaptation.* Cambridge: Cambridge University Press, pp. 146–164.

Roman, M. (2010) 'Governing from the Middle: the C40 Cities Leadership Group'. *Corporate Governance: The International Journal of Business in Society,* 10 (1): 73–84.

Rosenau, J. (1995) 'Governance in the Twenty-First Century'. *Global Governance* 1 (1): 24.

Schultze, C.J. (2003) 'Cities and EU Governance: Policy-Takers or Policy-Makers?' *Regional and Federal Studies* 13 (1): 121–2.

Chapter 8

Grassroots innovations vs. green cluster initiatives

Reconciling two different approaches in housing energy retrofit programming

Philip J. Vergragt and Halina Szejnwald Brown

INTRODUCTION

This chapter is about local programs aiming for energy upgrades of residential housing stock. The need to substantially upgrade the existing residential housing stock in the US is enormous. Weatherization in this context refers to a rather superficial degree of insulation; while (deep) energy retrofits or energy upgrading refer to a more comprehensive improvement in housing energy performance, which would also include energy-efficient heating and cooling equipment.

Some believe that top-down policies, such as regulations, subsidies, and performance standards are the most effective approaches for accomplishing the necessary transition. An alternative perspective holds that such a transition could only occur if the homeowners are motivated to act, irrespective of the above incentives. In the latter perspective, grassroots action could play a significant role in inspiring homeowners and local communities to take action and to innovate. In this chapter we examine the role of grassroots innovations and other closely relative local initiatives in the efforts to implement housing retrofits and community development in Worcester, Massachusetts.

Upgrading the residential housing stock can be much more than energy retrofitting. This is especially true in the older post-industrial cities that continue to be weighed down by the collapse of the manufacturing sector, such as Worcester, in some cases stretching over the course of the twentieth century. Many older houses in such cities have problems of contamination with lead, both indoors and in the soil. Some homeowners are barely holding on to their properties since the onset of the Great Recession, much less being able to invest into upgrades.

Additionally, neighborhoods may be immersed in a host of other social problems, such as crime, unemployment or underemployment, drug abuse, waste management, and a general feeling of deterioration, which makes investments of secondary importance. In communities hosting these kinds of problems many grassroots groups may be active in a wide range of areas, from soil decontamination, youth programs, local empowerment and jobs creation, to community-based energy retrofitting. Government programs for energy efficiency upgrades are often not aligned with those activities in an integrating and integrative way because they have limited mandates, usually focused on just one of the many interrelated problems.

In this chapter we examine energy retrofitting of houses as part of a program for addressing such multiple interrelated problems. As a departure point we conceptualize housing stock and its energy performance as a complex socio-technical system; and a large scale retrofitting process as a socio-technical systemic transition. This chapter is a further elaboration of research presented in our earlier published papers (Vergragt and Brown, 2012; Brown and Vergragt, 2012a, 2012b) and represents an ongoing thinking process about how to address complex systemic problems, and how to facilitate socio-technical transitions. Our main focus here is to incorporate into the socio-technical transition narrative the considerations of power relations (Avelino and Rotmans, 2011), community development, grassroots activities covering a wide range of issues, and business initiatives that on the first blush may seem to be unrelated to the socio-technological system in question.

This approach is a contribution to the literature on socio-technical transitions, which often overlooks these social and economic processes (Geels and Schot, 2007). Our case study analysis suggests that the distinction between niches and regimes is hard to make in practice; that grassroots innovations are often interwoven with mainstream innovations; and that the choice of 'framing' of local innovation projects can have a profound effect on their ability to reinforce each other toward a common goal or, alternatively, compete with each other. Finally, we reflect on how inter-actions of different problem framings can lead to higher order learning and an overall reframing of the problem at hand.

In section two we present the conceptual framework, which contrasts grassroots innovations and socio-technical transitions with business-led regional development perspectives. In section three we describe the case study in Worcester, Massachusetts. In the last section we draw conclusions and develop recommendations on how to improve collaboration between grassroots innovations and business-led innovations.

CONCEPTUAL PERSPECTIVES

Experimentation in niches features prominently in socio-technical transition studies, using the multi-level perspective of niches, regimes, and landscapes. In that conceptual framework, large-scale transitions transforming incumbent regimes occur when landscape pressures coincide with the emergence of successful technological niche alternatives and with growing tensions in the incumbent regime. Together they lead to destabilizing the incumbent regime while offering attractive alternatives (Geels and Schot, 2007). The regime shift is not necessarily assured under the constellation of such favorable circumstances. For example, Smith has shown in the case like organic food and eco-housing that some elements of the emerging niche might be adopted by the incumbent regime, leaving out other, often more radical elements; thus basically adapting and stabilizing the incumbent regime but not transforming it (Smith, 2006, 2007). So the question of under what conditions niche experiments could successfully diffuse into the mainstream without losing their original transformative power is still wide open, even after more than a decade of transition research.

As the interest in niche innovation has grown over the past decade within the socio-technical transition research community, so has the sophistication of the conception of niche activities. It is now widely accepted that niche experimentation is not only about diffusion of a technological innovation (in the past often conceived as technology push). Increasing attention has been given to the role of community-level multi-stakeholder collaborative initiatives that involve a mix of top-down and bottom-up approaches as well as a mix of participants, including civil society organizations, the business community, non-governmental organizations, and various level of government agencies.

Seyfang and Smith have studied 'grassroots innovations' as a way to expand the concept of niche activities. Grassroots innovations exist in the 'social economy' of community activities and social enterprise, rather than in the market economy (Seyfang, 2009; Seyfang and Smith, 2007). Among their examples are: local currencies, local farmers' markets, non-traditional housing, local energy generation or food production, and others. The institutional forms of those initiatives are different from market institutions, including cooperatives, voluntary associations, informal community groups, and other social enterprises. They are driven by two motives – social and environmental needs, and ideology – and emphasize different social, ethical, and cultural rules and values. Social and environmental needs could for instance consist of access to affordable and sustainable housing; fresh and sustainable food, sustainable transportation services, etc. Ideology refers to '...alternative ways of doing things, counter to the hegemony of the regime... Some grassroots innovations develop practices based on reordered priorities and alternative values. Examples are, for instance, the new economics focusing on the quality of life rather than on economic growth per se' (Seyfang, 2009; Seyfang, op. cit.: 74).

In the case study featured in this chapter, grassroots innovations play a central role in the local niche experiments aimed at facilitating the systemic transition in the housing stock toward high energy efficiency. It involved multiple actors and agendas that came together under a broad umbrella of community development, the framing that neatly accommodated such problems as energy performance of housing, youth unemployment, lead contamination, and other urgent community needs related to environment, energy, social equity, health, and economic opportunity.

Our case study also describes another set of initiatives that played a significant role in the evolution of the story of housing retrofits: business-led regional economic development efforts. Championed by the local political and business establishment, its primary objective was to create a green technology hub in the Worcester area, including renewables, smart grid, and other cutting edge technologies. Through a combination of government incentives such as regulations, subsidies and tax breaks, and incentives to cluster business in the vicinity of several local institutions of research and higher education, it was hoped that new business developments and associated jobs would facilitate economic growth in the region. The underlying assumption was that economic growth would aid in solving many social problems in the community; and create resources, capability and know-how for various other programs, including housing retrofits. Its rationale drew on the theory that spatial proximity between firms and universities fosters innovation through positive externalities, which then spill over to the regional economy (McCauley, 2012; Porter *et al.* 2008). The theory is popular among business and policy makers, and it has been successful in explaining comparative advantages of regions like Silicon Valley (ICT), Chapel Hill in North Carolina, and the Boston area (medical technology and biotech).

The case study described in this chapter examines two ongoing initiatives in Worcester, Massachusetts, that aimed at facilitating economic and social development around green technologies and energy upgrades of the housing stock. One initiative followed the model of business-led regional development, driven by a vision of economic growth, while the other was a grassroots effort driven by a vision of community development. The two initiatives overlapped significantly in terms of institutional and individual participation, and tried to build on that overlap by creating a synergy through multi-stakeholder engagement. These were two distinctive framings of the retrofit problematic. These different framings could in principle lead to innovative solutions if proponents of each of the framings were willing to collaborate and *learn*. We use the latter term to denote higher order learning: when the participants change their problem definitions or interpretive frames (interpretive frames are mental models that help identify the most salient features of situations, make sense of our observations, and ultimately lead to create problem definitions).

In our earlier paper we drew on a wide body of literatures to develop a framework for identifying and studying such learning processes in socio-technical experiments (Brown and Vergragt, 2008). Higher order learning takes place when actors representing a range of interpretive frames, problem definitions and core competences engage in intense interactions around a technological innovation, an issue, a problem or an idea. In our earlier work on learning through collaboration in a multidimensional complex problem we showed that even when each actor retains their original core values and world view, fruitful learning on the level of evolution of problem definition and framing can occur. 'Worldview' denotes '...deeply held values with regard to the preferred social order, including such issues as justice, fairness, equality, freedom, private versus public good, and so on. Discourse at this level rarely occurs, is unlikely to produce changes, and is most dangerous for a collaborative project. This is because the views of this order are very stable within each participant group' (Brown and Vergragt, 2008 op. cit.: 115). It is thus comparable to ideology as defined above (Seyfang, op.cit).

In the case of Worcester, we found that during the first few years the inconsistency in framings led to lack of progress. Most recently, the creation of Worcester Green to Growth Council, and the National Grid Smart Grid pilot promises to create a shared reframing and produce considerable progress.

TECHNOLOGY CLUSTERS AND GRASSROOTS ENERGY INNOVATIONS IN WORCESTER, MASSACHUSETTS

The context: The city of Worcester

With 175,000 inhabitants, Worcester is the second largest city in Massachusetts (after Boston), located in Blackstone Valley in the central part of the state. Worcester claims to be the 'birthplace of American Industrial revolution'. The original industries were textiles, clothing and shoes, which were replaced by, first, metal industry, and later, envelope folding and corsetry industry. In the 19th century the classic New England triple-decker house was invented here as a form of affordable housing, which was generally, occupied by the owner and two tenant families. Today, in 2014, Worcester is highly diverse in income, ethnicity and culture. While it has a well-established white middle and upper middle class with long family pedigrees, its median household income is $35 000 (30 per cent lower than Massachusetts), with 18 per cent of households below the official poverty line (twice that of the state); 15 per cent of residents are foreign-born and 28 per cent report the language spoken at home being other than English. The economy in Worcester is quite diversified, including a thriving biotechnology and medical centers, construction and insurance, and higher education: eight colleges and universities, including Clark University, are located in Worcester. And yet, Worcester is still living in the shadow of the collapse of the traditional manufacturing economy, and struggles to redefine itself.

Worcester has a vibrant community life, which could be branded as an emerging sustainable economy. The success of the biotechnology cluster which evolved during the past 15 years through collaboration between academia, government and business, leads in some quarters to a call for Worcester becoming in the future a sustainable energy cluster. This debate includes the local Congressman, the City, leading Universities such as Clark and Worcester Polytechnic Institute, and local businesses, and is driven by a vision of 'green economy' and 'green jobs' (Stephens and McCauley (2012); Benzaken, 2011). Another emerging vision of revitalizing the Worcester economy takes a broader view of sustainability, beyond the green technology cluster, to include social development, the new economy(Simms and Boyle, 2010; Harris, 2013; Korten, 2010), and the solidarity economy (Miller, 2012) and community participation and visioning. This is exemplified by the Green Solidarity Economy conferences which are organized by the Worcester Solidarity and Green Economy Alliance (SAGE) since 2011, and by periodical 'Barnraisings': local groups working together on weatherizing one neighborhood building in a single day. Like the green energy cluster, this vision also embraces multi-stakeholder collaboration, but its boundaries are wider, including grassroots and social services organizations, and it draws on the well-established community engagement of Clark University.

Grassroots activism in Worcester in relation to housing energy upgrades

During the past five years, several initiatives have sprouted in Main South, on one of the poorest neighborhoods in Worcester, and the home of Clark University, and adjacent areas around housing retrofits and creation of green jobs. These were triggered by state-level and national policies of subsidies for such projects as well as Worcester being designated by the State as a 'Green Community' under the Massachusetts Green Communities Act of 2008. Grassroots organizations have been very visible initiators of many of them. These include: the Regional Environmental Council (REC), the Worcester Energy Barnraisers, the Worcester Roots project (and affiliate programs as Toxic Soil Busters and Youth in Charge), EMPOWER Energy Coop, Coop Power, Stone Soup, and the Worcester Community Action Council (WCAC). Two new groups included the Worcester chapter of the Sierra Club, and the Worcester Transitions (Benzaken, 2011), while in 2012 the former Worcester Lead Action Coalition renamed itself as the 'Worcester Green and Healthy Homes Coalition' (WGHHC).

Several of those groups have started or have been involved in various housing retrofit programs, and/or are active in mobilizing citizens to engage in free energy audits. For instance, in the summer 2010 Worcester Community Action Council created a special program for at-risk youth to teach weatherization skills and provide summer employment in that area. The Worcester SAGE (Solidarity and Green Economy) – a coalition of grassroots activists, entrepreneurs, students, and individuals from environmental organizations – also promotes housing retrofits, along with other social objectives, such as local ownership, community empowerment, and healthy, living-wage jobs that contribute to the sustainability of the environment (SAGE, 2014). Its original mission statement (when it was still called the Worcester Green Jobs Coalition) was to organize '...a local movement for green collar jobs for all. We work for resources to create sustainable jobs that are in sync with our community, culture and needs'.

Coop Power is a worker cooperative in the North East, with various local chapters, among them in Blackstone valley. Its mission is '....to move our communities toward locally owned and controlled, energy efficient, self-sustaining, ecologically sound economies that are respectful of natural systems and all living beings. Our vision is to build energy independence within our community by using a cooperative model to bring justice to the social and economic arrangements we take part in, and to create opportunities for the development and recovery of power by oppressed groups with attention to class, race, gender, criminal record and legal status (Coop Power, 2014a). Coop Power created the Coop Academy with teaching modules to introduce members to cooperative business development (Coop Academy 2014b).

A related cluster of activities is centred around 'Stone Soup', a local gathering place for the Main south social activists. The mission of Stone Soup is to build grassroots power by connecting and enriching groups and individuals in our communities who are working for social justice in Worcester, MA. Stone Soup is a volunteer-run organization that brings together various Worcester leadership development and organizing groups doing social, environmental and economic justice work in the city of Worcester MA. In March 2009 a fire destroyed most of the building but has since been rebuilt and refurbished with help from volunteer groups.

In December 2010, Stone Soup became the owner of the building, with help of the fire insurance settlement. Each member group contributes what they can in monthly dues to keep the building running. Stone Soup members make decisions about the shared space and collective projects in a general meeting once a month, and build community in monthly potlucks. In addition to office spaces for organizations and work space for artists, the building boasted two community meeting rooms, a band practice room, an arts and crafts area, a free resource and lending library, a community kitchen, and a computer/internet lab. The Stone Soup training program provides on the job vocational training with expertise of skilled instructors, site supervisors and carpenters. Participants gain weatherization experience and receive BPI, LEED RRP and OSHA certifications. Previously separated, Stone Soup has brought together important social justice organizations under one roof providing for increased collaboration and sharing of vital resources (Stone Soup, 2014).

The Worcester Green Energy cluster

In 2009 a joint effort by a congressman from that region, the municipality, and the leadership of two major institutions of higher education in Worcester – Clark University and Worcester Polytechnic Institute – created Institute for Energy and Sustainability (IES, 2014) to promote local economic growth through innovative green technologies: research and development as well as manufacturing and use. The initiative modeled itself on the successful development of biotechnology industry in Worcester a decade earlier. Initially, EIS reached out to the university community, local and regional businesses and technology innovators, the municipality and to many social organizations in the Worcester area. Partly, this was in search of catalysts for innovation and investment, and partly because the ongoing grassroots activities centred on housing upgrades and community developments, which seemed to be well aligned with its overarching goal of economic development. But beyond the superficial outreach events the Institute defined its mission narrowly: to convince the green technology business sector to locate in Worcester. Researchers from Clark argued at the time, rather unsuccessfully, that EIS might benefit from closer cooperation with the existing grassroots initiatives seeking both economic and community development; and that housing energy retrofit project, which requires community mobilization and multi-stakeholder participation may provide a useful broader framing for IES activities.

To date, IES's successes have been mixed. In March 2010 IES organized a successful corporate conference that attracted over 100 business leaders and demonstrated considerable interest from the private sector. National Grid, a major power utility, organized a 'summit' in September 2011 jointly with IES, in order to promote smart grid developments www.green2 growth.com/events). Recently IES promoted installation of the first electrical outlets for electric vehicles in Worcester. However, to date these initiatives have not led to the expected formation of a green-tech cluster. A major project proposal aimed at obtaining federally-funded grant for a regional sustainable community development planning project in 2012 was unsuccessful, partially because by rivalry between IES and Clark University about the content of the proposal, framing of the project, and project management.

In a recent paper McCauley concludes that the lack of success is partially due to the differences in framing between grassroots innovations, socio-technical transitions, and cluster innovations (McCauley, op.cit). In addition, he points at differences in the nature of green technology as compared to the earlier ICT and biotech cluster technologies. Innovations in the green energy sector tend to be slower, and the sector lacks a defining technology. It encompasses both high end technologies and low tech services. Given these differences, local efforts toward economic and social development through green technology might benefit from different framings and different alliances: deemphasize business investment and top down government interventions, and emphasize investments into community development and multi-stakeholder partnerships. The opportunity to do so was available in the form of Worcester Housing, Energy, and Community, as described in the next section.

WoHEC: The Worcester Housing, Energy, and Community group

One of the most focused collaborative and self-organizing initiatives built around the idea of upgrading the energy performance of homes is Worcester Housing Energy and Community (WoHEC; www.wohec.org). It came together in 2009 before IES was established, through the initiative of faculty members and researchers at Marsh Institute at Clark University as a way to engage diverse local stakeholders in a community project; the latter denoting multiple framings and objectives. In this case, the objectives were: to design and facilitate a large scale energy-retrofitting of residential houses to a level that would significantly reduce energy use for heating and cooling; create a wide range of jobs; employ local at-risk unemployed youths; enhance vocational training programs; improve the quality of life in the community; improve the market value of houses; and improve indoor air quality (including eliminating lead where necessary). In short, in this vision it would be a sustainable community development. The underlying idea of WoHEC was that framing the project as energy conservation and climate change alone would not mobilize a community facing a plethora of more urgent social and economic problems. The researchers also saw it as a challenging socio-technical experiment, as discussed in Section 2.

The group convened for the first time May 2009 at Clark University, bringing together the grassroots and social service organizations already active in the Main South area, Worcester Polytechnic Institute, Worcester State College; and the City of Worcester. Issues identified at the first meeting collectively represented many dimensions of community life and the missions of the organizations present at the table: funding sources for weatherization (many participants were involved in raising money for all kinds of projects, ranging from weatherization and deep- energy retrofits to creating a revolving loan fund for energy retrofits); the need for measuring the effects of energy retrofits; the need to create jobs, especially among unemployed youths; vocational and jobs training generally; opportunities for energy retrofits at foreclosed properties; and the need to motivate middle income home owners to retrofit their homes.

Notably, a significant number of the WoHEC participants, including the municipality, some major social development organizations, and the academics, were also part of the EIS broader community. That created a promising opportunity of greater financial and human capital, and of an expanded arena for creativity and innovation. Over the following four years, the WoHEC kept monthly meetings, supported by the efforts of Clark researchers, who served as conveners, facilitators, idea entrepreneurs, and monitors of the learning processes. WoHEC defined its mission as 'a shared interest in community development built around upgrading existing housing stock; through retrofits pursue multiple agendas; drawing on bottom-up developments and new funding opportunities and policy developments'. The group kept open boundaries, which allowed new individuals and organizations to enter. The meetings largely consisted of information exchange, coordination, building bridges, and leveraging the new links and knowledge to seek federal and state funding for energy and community development projects.

WoHEC thus has become a learning group whose members represent several (but not all) elements of the socio-technical residential housing system in Worcester, with all its complexity; but it also extends beyond that system, bringing into its deliberations sustainable community development. During discussions, participants increasingly evoked the systemic nature of the challenge of retrofitting houses, and use multiple framings to discuss strategies for pursuing it. It engaged with the issue of house retrofits from a wider perspective. Several members tried to find connections between the IES activities and WoHEC activities: to bridge the grassroots community development framing with the green technology incubator framing. But this bridging effort was largely implicit, unreflected and rarely made it to the larger agenda of either organization. Over time the fault lines would become more visible.

In 2011 the City received funding from the State of Massachusetts for community-based energy retrofit project under the Massachusetts Green Communities Act. This created an opportunity to implement WoHEC's vision of a retrofit project as community development as well and a multi-stakeholder coalition-based approach to designing the project. But it also created almost immediately a tension between this one, and a more traditional vision for the project. From the start, the City began to lean toward the more traditional approach that was typical of many early retrofit projects across the country: focusing on financing and information dissemi-nation to homeowners. The program chose the middle income families as its target group, offering subsidies toward project costs. It also hired an independent consultant to conduct an outreach and social marketing campaign in order to increase participation, and to create a one directional informational web page. So far, while keeping the lines of communication open with WoHEC and the grassroots organizations in Worcester, the City has not actively engaged these groups in planning or implementation.

In short, in spite of considerable cross-participation in IES and WoHEC, the City took an approach that was less that of a multi-stakeholder grassroots mobilization around a broad vision of community development, and more akin to that of a technology cluster incubator: government subsidies for specific technologies, and an outreach to a relevant target group.

The Green2Growth coalition as an emerging bridge

In 2011 National Grid, a major utility company in Massachusetts organized a 'summit' to discuss broad stakeholder participation for its intended 'smart grid' pilot project. 'Smart grid' is a technological innovation which consists of smart meters in homes, and other technological upgrades in the grid, that allow two-way communication between the utility and the customers at home. After an earlier bid which failed because of limited stakeholder involvement, National Grid was successful in its subsequent bid after the 2011 summit, and obtained a $44.4 million grant from the Massachusetts Department of Public Utilities to implement the Worcester Smart Energy Solutions Program Pilot. In 2013–14 new smart electricity meters were placed in 15,000 households in Worcester, about 20 per cent of the total. Customers were informed by mail and house visits, and have the opportunity to opt out of the program. The main incentives for customers are financial: differentiation in pricing enables customers to save money by energy conservation on peak days and times.

Since the successful summit of 2011, many local organizations and noted individuals wanted to continue their involvement in the National Grid smart pilot, which led to the creation of the Green to Growth Council (G2G). The Council is led by the City of Worcester and National Grid, and convenes bimonthly since 2012. The Council was at first dominated by the City, National Grid, and IES, with participation by several important social services organizations in Worcester. The grassroots participation in this business-led initiative was rather low, despite the highly promoted official statements of its community-based and community-oriented mission. In essence, National Grid used the concept of community to find constituency support for its planned piloting of the smart grid, fully aware that in its absence of homeowners' participation the project would not succeed.

The birth of the Council also significantly diminished WoHEC, whose members from the municipality and social service organizations in Worcester became also members of the Council, and no longer relied on WoHEC to provide a platform for information exchange and dialogue. For a while, it looked like the business-technology-driven approach to energy and sustainability in Worcester would prevail, and that the idea of combining housing retrofits with community development would fade away. But that is not what happened.

In October 2013 National Grid, in partnership with Clark University, opened the Sustainability Hub: a spacious office close to Clark University campus. The company's intention for the Hub was to serve as a venue for promoting the adoption of the smart grid technology. It has a meeting space and sleek presentations of smart grid technologies. The presentations are given by 'ambassadors', student volunteers that are trained and paid by National Grid. The space is provided by Clark University and refurbished through a grant from the Smart Grid pilot project. Grassroots groups, represented in WoHEC, were initially not very happy with this development. For one thing, they saw the Hub as the face of the technology-based business development similar to Institute of Energy and Sustainability. Secondly, the name 'sustainability hub' misrepresented its narrow mission of promoting the smart grid technology; it did not include other aspects of community sustainability that are related to lifestyles, alleviating social problems, and community development.

What happened over the subsequent months was illuminating, and is an illustration of higher order learning among groups with different world views through collaboration in a concrete joint project (Brown and Vergragt, 2008). Through a whole series of conversations among stakeholders, a mutual adjustment process took place between, on the one hand, the Sustainability Hub, National Grid, and Green2Growth Council, and on the other hand grassroots organizations convened by WoHEC. National Grid became much more open to framing the mission of Sustainability Hub beyond simply facilitating the diffusion of the smart grid and energy efficiency technologies, and toward a wider sustainability mission and community development. And the grassroots organizations changed their original reservations about collaborating with National Grid and the Sustainability Hub.

At the present time the Hub and its stakeholders are becoming more engaged in developing and promoting a series of programs intended for education and jobs creation in the green economy. Early in 2014 these developments are still in an initial stage, but they represent a new function for WoHEC; as well as a broadening of the original mission of the Sustainability Hub.

CONCLUSIONS

Our earlier analysis of the socio-technical system for residential housing stock showed that a systemic change in the housing stock socio-technical system requires a concurrent change in all its constitutive elements. We suggested that multi-stakeholder engagement, including both top down and bottom up action, may help facilitate the transition (Brown and Vergragt, 2012a; Vergragt and Brown, 2012).

In this chapter the recent developments in Worcester with respect to housing, energy, and community have allowed us to shed light on how such multi-stakeholder engagement may work in reality and what the barriers and opportunities are. The case study describes two streams of initiatives, with their different framings and objectives, which came together in a deeply interactive way in the Worcester locality: one represents a business-led approach to energy conservation and renewable energy by way of developing a technology cluster. The Institute of Energy and Sustainability represents this approach. The second is a grassroots initiative; a platform of many stakeholders and academics aiming to create a systemic approach to energy conservation in housing while at the same time advancing community development goals. WoHEC represents this approach.

The two streams maintained their separate existences and activities, grounded in different world views about social progress, without much overlap or hope for synergy. The creation of Green 2 Growth Council, a multi-stakeholder locally-focused initiative with a top-down narrow agenda of promoting the smart grid pilot for National Grid, added a new important dimension to this picture. While the business-led stream of activities easily found common interests with the Council, the grassroots stream found itself initially an outsider, partially eviscerated, as some of its members joined the Council, and unable to find sufficient shared agendas with the Council. This tension, which might have led to complete break of contact, has, however, over time (measured so far only in months) evolved in a promising direction: G2G has morphed into a broader stakeholder coalition, with a broader framing of its mission and some grassroots organizations found sufficient overlap with their interests to enter into a more productive collaboration.

These developments illustrate two theoretical points. First, higher order learning can indeed occur in a situation where groups with different world views, framings and problem definitions, collaborating in a concrete project. In this case, the creation of the Sustainability Hub led to an opportunity for grassroots groups, collaborating within WoHEC, and business groups, as represented by National Grid, to collaborate and develop new plans and activities jointly. The 'business framing' is still represented by the Institute for Energy and Sustainability, which is a partner in the Green2Growth Council, and which continues its activities to promote green business and green jobs, as well as renewable energy and energy conservation. So far the success of this 'cluster approach' has been modest. A separate business framing is the 'smart grid pilot', which is in essence a technological innovation looking for constituents support in order to be successfully implemented; this framing is mainly supported by National Grid and the City of Worcester, collaborating within the G2G coalition.

An alternative framing – community development through energy technology projects – is represented by the local grassroots organizations; it emphasizes bottom-up small-scale initiatives that create economic and social equity opportunities for the underserved members of the Worcester community. The Sustainability Hub created a concrete opportunity for these groups to collaborate, overcome biases, and learn from each other. Their shared framing of 'local social and ecological sustainability through collaboration of business, grassroots, municipality, social services sector, universities and advanced technologies' appears to be emerging.

It is not clear whether energy retrofits of the housing stock in Worcester will benefit from this collaboration. So far, progress in that domain has been slow and uneven in time and space. It may very well happen that this original rationale that brought together the grassroots community and other participants into WoHEC may not be in the principal result of the collaboration that is taking place at the time of this writing. It is quite likely that other community-energy advances will be made more prominent, at least initially, building on the vitality and intellectual and institutional resources of the emergent coalition. And that the retrofitting will follow. That is the nature of higher order learning: the outcome of the evolution of the problem framing cannot be fully predicted or guaranteed. Monitoring the Worcester case study through continuous research will no doubt generate new insights on that score.

The second theoretical outcome of this case analysis pertains to the multilevel perspective on socio-technical transitions. That theory conceives of systemic change as driven by a diffusion of new technologies and associated social arrangements from a niche into the mainstream. Under favorable circumstances the niche innovations successfully challenge and, through a co-evolution of several dimensions of the system, eventually replace the incumbent regime (Geels and Schot, 2007). This case study is not consistent with this rather simple conceptualization of systemic change. Both WoHEC and G2G can be considered as niche developments; one focused on diffusion of energy housing retrofits and the other on diffusion of smart grid. But the structure of these niches, and the participating actors, are much more complex than envisioned by the multilevel perspective. Both comprise actors representing both the incumbent regime and the challenger niche. At least in the case of smart grid, the new socio-technical system evolves through interaction of both regime and niche constituents.

The implications of these findings for research are the following. First, we propose that research on niche development and initial socio-technical transitions carefully maps not only the stakeholders and their involvement, but more specifically each of their problem definitions, framings, and even their world views (ideologies). Second, we propose that researchers follow the changes in problem definitions and framings of each of these groups over time; especially in relation to their collaborations and conflicts with respect to specific projects and activities they are engaged in. Third, we propose to adapt the language of the multi-level perspective into a direction where the distinctions between 'levels' are less prominent, and which allows more 'horizontal' interactions between stakeholders with different framings and even worldviews- irrespective if they 'belong' to either the socio-technical regime or an emerging niche.

We suggest that such careful mapping of urban energy retrofit programs by researchers could not only lead to increased conceptual and theoretical understanding of the socio-technical processes and transitions, but also would benefit the outcomes of energy retrofitting in terms of more successful projects and effective policy interventions.

References

Avelino, F. and Rotmans J. (2011) 'A dynamic conceptualization of power for sustainability research'. *Journal of Cleaner Production* 19: 796–804.

Benzaken, H. (2011) 'Developing a green economy in Worcester'. Massachusetts, A Master's research thesis, Worcester, MA: Clark University.

Brown H.S. and Vergragt P.J. (2008) 'Bounded socio-technical experiments as agents of systemic change: The case of a zero-energy residential building'. *Technological Forecasting and Social Change*, 75, 107–130.

Brown, H.S. and Vergragt P.J. (2012a) 'Grassroots innovations and socio-technical system change: Energy retrofitting of the residential housing stock'. Chapter 8 in G. Marletto (ed.) *Creating a Sustainable Economy. An Institutional and Evolutionary approach to Environmental Policy*. Oxford: Routledge, pp. 154–176.

Brown, H.S. and Vergragt, P.J. (2012b) *Grassroots Innovations: Local Socio-technical Experiments and Systemic Change: The Case of the Residential Housing Stock*. Paper presented at the SPRU workshop 'Grassroots Innovations', May 2012, Brighton, UK.

Coop Academy (2014b) http://cultivate.coop/wiki/Academy (accessed Feb 16, 2014).

Coop Power (2014a) www.cooppower.coop/blackstone-valley (accessed Feb 16, 2014).

Geels, F. and Schot J. (2007) 'Typology of sociotechnical transition pathways'. *Research Policy*, 36, 399–417.

Harris, J. (2013) 'The macroeconomics of development without throughput growth'. In M. Cohen, H. Brown and P.J. Vergragt, (eds) *Innovations in Sustainable Consumption: New Economics, Socio-technical Transitions, and Social Practices*. Northampton, MA: Edward Elgar, pp. 31–47.

IES (2014) http://energyandsustainability.com (accessed Feb 12, 2014).

Korten, D. (2010) *Agenda for a New Economy: From Phantom Wealth to Real Wealth*, San Francisco, CA: Berret-Koehler Publishers.

McCauley S.M. (2012) *Hidden in Plain Sight: The Promising but Impeded Vision of Community-based Green Regional Development*. Paper for the 3rd SCORAI workshop Challenging Consumerism: Toward Living Well Sustainably, University of British Columbia, March 8–10 2012.

Miller, E. (2012) 'Solidarity economy: Key concepts and issues'. In E. Kawano (ed.) *Solidarity Economy I: Building Alternatives for People and Planet; papers and reports from the 2009 U.S. Forum on the Solidarity Economy*, Amherst, MA: Center for Popular Economics. www.communityeconomies.org/site/assets/media/Ethan_Miller/Miller_Solidarity_Economy_Key_Issues_2010.pdf.

Porter, M.E., Kwek J.-H *et al.* (2008) 'The Australian renewable energy cluster, Microeconomics of Competitiveness'. Harvard Business School, www.isc.hbs.

edu/pdf/Student_Projects/Australian_Renewable_Energy_2008.pdf (accessed April 11, 2012).

SAGE (2014) 'Worcester solidarity and green economy alliance'. www.worcester sagealliance.org (accessed Feb 12, 2014).

Seyfang, G. and Smith A. (2007) 'Grassroots innovations for sustainable development: Towards a new research and policy agenda'. *Environmental Politics,* 16(4), 584–603.

Seyfang, G. (2009) 'The new economics of sustainable consumption: Seeds of change'. Basingstoke: Palgrave Macmillan.

Simms, A. and Boyle D. (2010) *The New Economics: A Bigger Picture* London: Earthscan.

Smith, A. (2006) 'Green niches in sustainable development: The case of organic food'. *Environment and Planning C: Government and Policy,* 24, 439–458.

Smith, A. (2007) 'Translating sustainabilities between green niches and socio-technical Regimes'. *Technology Analysis and Strategic Management* 19, 427–450.

Stephens, J.C. and McCauley S. (2012) 'A sustainable energy clustering initiative in Central Massachusetts, USA: The role of geographic proximity and regional economic development in socio-technical transitions'. Unpublished paper, Worcester, MA: Clark University.

Stone Soup (2014) www.stonesoupworcester.org/ (accessed Feb 16, 2014).

Vergragt, P.J. and Brown, H.S. (2012) 'The challenge of energy retrofitting the residential housing stock: Grassroots innovations and socio-technical system change in Worcester, MA'. *Technology Analysis and Strategic Management,* 24 (4), 407–420.

Chapter 9

Beyond the split incentive

Governing socio-technical relations in private rental housing retrofit

Ralph Horne, Tony Dalton and Susie Moloney

INTRODUCTION

Building use contributes to greenhouse emissions and there is significant potential for low-cost retrofitting assisting building users to reduce their emissions (UNEP 2007). In Australia, the location of the case presented in this chapter, residential and commercial buildings are responsible for 20 per cent of national energy consumption (DCCEE 2010). This building stock is heterogeneous which is evident in the diversity of building materials, internal design, technologies, typology, urban design, governance (including tenure) and occupation. This heterogeneity presents a challenge to policy makers who are seeking to encourage retrofitting through regulations, fiscal incentives and other interventions designed to inform, enable and encourage upgrades beyond 'normal' maintenance.

This chapter focuses on rental housing stock owned by private landlords, in a cool temperate climate zone where residents commonly use energy intensive mechanical cooling and heating to realise their comfort expectations.[1] Within the broader possibility of a transition to significantly improve energy performance, the private rental sector is presented as particularly problematic. In economic terms, this can be understood as a 'principal-agent' or 'split incentive' problem (Gabriel and Watson 2012; Rehdanz 2007). The landlord (the principal) is responsible for the building fabric condition, which is a significant factor in heating and cooling energy demand, while the tenant is responsible for the energy/water bills. In this context, what might prompt a landlord to retrofit a dwelling, which would make it easier for tenants to reduce their energy/water use?

In this chapter, we examine this question by exploring the way small-scale private landlords think about and go about maintaining and improving their rental dwellings. The private rental stock is largely indistinguishable from owner occupied stock within large suburban metropolitan cities. Further, the rental dwellings are owned by thousands of landlords, each typically owning one or two dwellings, who are in the market for a variety of reasons. It is indeed useful to think about the Australian private rental market as part of a broader 'splintered urbanism' (Graham and Marvin 2001). If this housing is to be included in a green retrofit transition, these private landlords and other actors will have to begin to improve the energy/water efficiency of the rental housing stock. By green retrofit, we mean technical interventions in dwellings aimed at reducing energy and/or water use, ranging from new appliances/technologies to major reconfigurations.

To understand how this might happen, we examine private rental housing 'landlordism' and retrofit as a socio-technical phenomenon. In using this term we note the emergent 'transitions' literature, in particular the multi-level perspective, and ideas of niches (e.g. Geels and Schot 2010). It is possible to think of housing repairs, maintenance and retrofit as a regime and 'green retrofit' as an emergent niche. At the same time, we argue, there is a need to recognize and understand the localized, dynamic and contingent heterogeneity of retrofit, and the social relations involved in the practices of retrofitting. As Watson (2012:1) argues; '...practices (and therefore what people do) are partly constituted by the socio-technical systems of which they are part; and those socio-technical systems are constituted and sustained by the continued performance of the practices which comprise them'.

In this context the idea of intermediaries represents the various ways in which landlords are inter-linked with those housing processes that they can use to improve their rental dwellings. Our approach responds to the recognised shortcoming of analyses that assume the possibility of central and consensually driven large-scale change. Instead it is important to recognise the likely obduracy of economic and social relations that produce markets, such as the private rental market, and the motivations and relations of actors involved. In the context of private rental markets this means that it is important to understand the way landlords might think about low energy and water efficient retrofitting of their properties in relation to: their tenants; their understanding of the current state of their properties; the availability of government incentives, and; relations with other actor groups that might be involved.

Amongst the growing literature on resource-efficient housing retrofitting, there is some discussion of the rental sector and the role of landlords and tenants (Phillips 2012, Vergragt and Brown 2012, Hens 2010, Gupta and Chandiwala 2010, Pullen 2010, Boardman et al. 2005). This case study adds to the literature by addressing the question: 'How do private landlords currently maintain their properties and how are they responding to climate change and related retrofit initiatives?'

Within this question, two ideas are examined: (a) the split incentive between landlords and tenants, and (b) intermediaries in the processes of retrofit. For this examination, primary research was conducted, centered upon metropolitan Melbourne in Victoria, Australia. To reveal the complexity of socio-technical relations, this research took two stages. The first involved 20 semi-structured interviews that 'drilled down' into the way landlords understood the physical conditions of their dwellings, how they managed maintenance and their approach to larger scale improvement of their dwellings. This approach, akin to ethnographic methods, reveals the 'lived experience' of landlords, with their ideas and relations emerging through open-ended discussion, guided by a line of questioning that is structured but also follows the issues landlords raise as they arise. Analysis of the interviews then informed the design of a survey of 866 landlords that explored the way they managed their dwellings. Together the interviews and the survey provided a means for examining 'landlording' practices.

Through this research we discovered the importance of real estate agents who manage properties on behalf of landlords. They can be considered to be intermediaries (Hodson and Marvin 2010) in that they mediate between production and consumption, (landlords and tenants). They influence priorities and visions for the different interests. To investigate these intermediary processes further, we undertook interviews with two real estate agent firms with large rent rolls, who respond to tenant requests and complaints about rental property conditions, liaise with and advise landlords about property management and manage relations with suppliers and tradespeople who provide repair, maintenance and upgrade services.

The chapter is presented in four further sections. The next section describes key features of private rental market system of housing provision, which is based on small-scale landlordism in housing which is indistinguishable from the broader housing stock. This is followed by a section that outlines policy and program settings and initiatives, which shape investment in the private rental market and other initiatives which potentially could focus attention on improved energy and water efficiency. We then focus on landlord and real estate agent roles in the private rental market based on the interviews and survey, followed by discussion of the key findings. Finally we present a concluding discussion of the findings and possibilities for a more strategic approach to retrofitting private rental housing.

CASE STUDY CONTEXT: PRIVATE RENTAL HOUSING

The Australian private rental market is made up of small-scale owners and tenants that are only lightly governed through landlord-tenant legislation that reinforces a balance of power that favours landlords. This is a situation where, 'The creation of intermediaries is necessary to constitute a space outside of the obduracy of both existing urban governance regimes and existing socio-technical regimes' (Hodson and Marvin 2010: 482). The context lies in the exploration of ways in which intermediaries can work at mediating different priorities through which green retrofit becomes commonplace.

Of Victoria's 2 million occupied dwellings, approximately 20 per cent are privately rented, with the majority (67 per cent) separate and semi-detached/row/terrace houses and townhouses (Class 1 buildings). Most of the remaining (31 per cent) properties are flats or apartments (ABS 2006). The predominance of Class 1 buildings offers potentially readily realisable greenhouse gas savings because of the ease of green retrofit options such as insulation, hot water systems, and/or more efficient heating systems. The housing stock in Victoria is in need of upgrading to improve water and energy efficiency. Indeed, some 9 per cent of Victorian dwellings did not contain insulation in 2008, and a further 18 per cent of households did not know if insulation was present (ABS 2008). For rental properties, there is more uncertainty about insulation (47 per cent) but, for those that did know, more properties are proportionally without insulation (14 per cent).

It is notable that dwellings in the private rental sector are no different to owner-occupied dwellings. Rental properties are in the same streets, are similar in design and have the same age profile as owner occupied housing. Further, dwellings of all types and ages can change tenure between private rental and owner occupied housing and vice versa. So, what can be said about the condition of private rental housing and energy bills of private rental dwellings compared to owner occupied housing? One major study examining the 'environmental sustainability' of private rental housing (Gabriel *et al.* 2010:2) raises the question of the split incentive in the private rental market but found that there is 'no clear evidence to support the assumption that private renters face higher energy bills than home owners due to split incentive problems. ...[we] speculate that Australia is well placed to encourage home improvements in [the] private rental sector'. However, these improvements have not happened and there is clearly a need to examine landlords and their property management practices more closely.

Landlords themselves are not a homogenous 'type' but instead constitute a diverse mix including those who are 'accidental' (i.e. entering landlordism through inheritance or moving house); informal investors (i.e. owner-occupiers subletting); and the remainder who invest in rental housing as a means for reducing tax and/or building equity through capital gains (Hulse *et al.* 2012:29). Another important feature of landlordism is that the system is dominated by 'petty landlordism' where only 3 percent of rental property investors own two or more rental properties (Berry 2000). Further, there is evidence that their reasons for investing or remaining as investors are not always clear. As Seelig *et al.* (2009) argue many landlords are 'arguably naïve about investing and its likely outcomes'.

There are two main ways in which landlords manage their rental prop-erties. Landlords can manage the properties themselves and deal directly with tenants. Alternatively they can place the property with a real estate agent who will manage the property for a fee, usually based on a percentage of the rental income. Amongst real estate agent firms there are some that specialise in providing this service and have developed large rent rolls. They employ staff who secure tenants, collect rents, manage repairs and conduct regular inspections. In recent years management of rental properties by real estate agents has been growing as a proportion and now forms approximately 80 per cent of private rental tenancies (Hulse *et al.* 2012: 32). These specialist property managers can of course be seen as intermediaries and could potentially develop a more explicit role in green retrofit.

Tenants who occupy private rental housing are not homogenous either. For many on moderate and high incomes rental housing provides choice of location and easy mobility through the housing system. For others, especially those on the bottom 40 per cent of the income distribution, there is little choice and high levels of housing related poverty. However, all tenants experience a leasing system that enables landlords to evict tenants without cause and with little notice. A network of NGOs provides tenancy advice and advocacy services for tenants. However, there is no mechanism by which tenants can require landlords to go beyond simple maintenance requirements and make significant improvements to a property.

POLICY CONTEXT: AFFORDABILITY AND RETROFITTING

In Australia, as in many other westernised owner-occupier dominated housing systems, there has been a sizeable growth in investment in the private rental sector resulting in private rental housing forming a stable proportion of all housing. This investment has been supported by the deregulation of the finance system and a federal government tax regime that encourages small-scale landlordism, especially by high and moderate-income earners. It is a policy setting which encourages investment but fails to create 'a secure and stable living environment for tenants' (Hulse *et al.* 2012: 7). The recent investment pattern has built on the tradition of small-scale ownership and continues a trend of single dwelling investors borrowing from finance institutions who are assuming future capital gains.

This form of tax-assisted wealth generation has supported the growth of private rental housing and has contributed to increases in house prices. Meanwhile, the system of regulation of the landlord/tenant relationship has continued and tenants remain relatively powerless. As a result, households are encouraged to make the shift from renting to owning. However, sustained housing demand presents limited choices for lower income earners, many of whom cannot afford large deposits and mortgages in an inflationary housing market. In sum, although the value and size of the private rental sector has increased, the nature of petty landlordism has persisted. Comparisons can be drawn here with the UK buy-to-let boom where the Association of Residential Letting Agents and a grouping of mortgage lenders acted strategically to plan growth in supply and change the institutional arrangements and governance of the private rental sector (Crook and Kemp 2011: 181).

Over the past decade various policies and programs have sought to encourage increasing energy and water efficiency of the Australian housing stock. The principal focus has been on new housing and was implemented through the rollout of a '5 star' minimum performance standard in 2005–6 which was lifted to '6 star' in 2010. This came out of long term and complex intergovernmental negotiations between the federal and state governments. In this context the federal government is responding to international obligations to reduce carbon emissions while the state has responsibility for built environment regulation. However, the planned federal government attempt to improve the energy efficiency of existing housing stock has foundered. A key proposal was to require mandatory disclosure of energy rating at point of sale or lease of all dwellings (Allen Consulting 2011). However, this has been delayed indefinitely due to lack of agreement between the federal and state governments. In contrast, it was implemented for commercial buildings through the use of the federal government corporation's legislation.

With mandatory disclosure stalled for residential properties, the main green retrofit policy action has been a mix of state and federal government incentives aimed at particular groups. On the demand side this has primarily been owner-occupiers and on the supply side the incentives have sought to stimulate industry capacity. All of this has been evident in the growth in the use of labelling programs, installation of solar PV panels; solar hot water services; ceiling insulation; domestic rainwater tanks; energy efficient lights; home inspection and energy and water use audits; energy and water use rating of domestic appliances such as refrigerators, washing machines and televisions. Some of these programs, varying across state jurisdictions, have led to the creation of renewable energy certificates (RECS) being traded in an embryonic carbon market. What has been conspicuous in all of these initiatives is the absence of a deliberate focus on how landlords might be encouraged to respond to the incentives.

LANDLORDS, LANDLORDING AND RETROFITTING

In the Australian context landlords choose between two approaches to managing their rental properties. They either reach an agreement with a real estate agent to manage the property for a percentage of the rental income or manage the property directly. The first group we call type A and they constitute about 80 per cent of landlords and the second type B who constitute 20 per cent. This distinction is general rather than exclusive –

there are exceptions of landlords who are in 'both' types. The decision of landlords about which approach they will take appears on the basis of our survey to relate to the demographic characteristics of landlords, economic position in the rental market, the type of property, the number of properties and attachment to the property. The differences are evident in Table 9.1 that contrasts the approach of Type A and B landlords to their role in the private rental market.

Landlord 'type' clearly affects repairs and maintenance, including retrofits, both in the dynamics of how often and how. 'Direct' landlords do more upgrades and do more themselves, getting to know their tenants in the process. On the other hand, Type A landlords let their agents do the work and tend to avoid their tenants. However, there is almost unanimous agreement on the importance of being considered to be a 'good landlord'. Above 80 per cent of respondents across both types responded that the 'condition of my rental property reflects directly on me' and 'I only let properties I would be happy to live in'. Indeed, a number of them have lived in the houses they spoke about in the interviews, and talk about the possibility that they will live in their rental dwelling again in the future.

The notion of being a 'good landlord' is more complex when it comes to retrofitting and upgrading properties. Generally, landlords overestimate the likely thermal and environmental performance of their rental properties. This feeds through into refusals for retrofits as many believe their properties are in better condition than they actually are. When it comes to sources of expertise and advice, there is a clear split, with type A landlords relying heavily on agents and type B landlords who either seek no advice or rely on friends, family and the internet. Neither type A or B landlords could identify current retrofit assistance schemes, and showed little recognition when presented with lists of schemes. Rather than being a split incentive problem, it would appear that retrofitting is not important for type B, whereas type A landlords trust the advice they receive from agents on most matters, with a notable exception – energy/water efficiency (Figure 9.1).

Table 9.1 Landlords who use agents and those who do not

Type A – with Agents	Type B – no Agents
Higher rents	Lower rents
Higher income, younger investors	Longer ownership (41% > 10yrs)
Larger portfolios, more tertiary educated and management roles	Organise own upgrade work
Greater dominance of financial motivations	Get to know tenants
Much less likely to do proactive maintenance	More likely to do upgrades
More have property covered by owners corporations (50% vs. 31%)	More likely to own freestanding properties

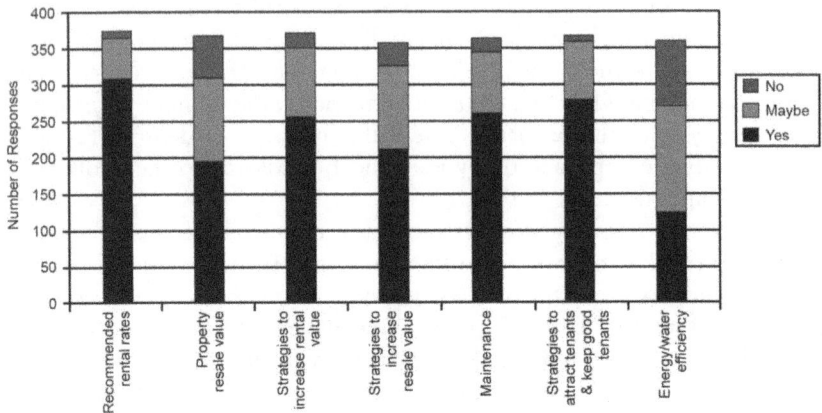

Figure 9.1 Level of trust Type A Landlords place in advice of agents

The use of agents by 80 per cent of landlords is associated with an apparent unwillingness to invest in retrofits. It is important to note that, unless requested, landlords are generally resistant to doing anything to properties with sitting tenants. Consideration of retrofits, including technology upgrades are typically prompted by reactions or small windows of opportunity – including, a mechanical failure in the existing heating system, a tenant leaving and/or a short period for repainting and potential retrofitting. At these times, amateur landlords have not generally planned for nor thought about green retrofit decision making. Hence, in the messy and splintered dynamics of landlording retrofit as a 'green niche' is ad hoc and unsystematic.

It is clear from the study that there is significant potential to develop the role of real estate agents in facilitating and co-coordinating sustainable retrofits as part of their management role. This accords with another study in Australia, where home investors expressed a preference for real estate agents taking a more proactive role in raising awareness about energy and water retrofit options; providing new tenants with green rental guides and; assisting landlords and tenants undertake efficiency measures (Gabriel and Watson 2012:318). Our research involving real estate agents who manage large rent rolls indicates that current property management systems are not set up to be pro-active but rather are concerned with responding to maintenance issues in rental properties as they arise. There are certainly key moments in the property management process where opportunities for intervention can take place, particularly where major renovations or appliance replacements are needed. In the case of the latter, one agent highlighted the important role that tradespeople play in deciding which new appliance will be chosen. Generally appliances are replaced with similar ones:

> It's just deemed replace with what is. If tradespeople go and do anything above and beyond that costs more money, owners tend to feel that there's something behind why they didn't just replace it with the existing one and that they wanted more money out of them....

The same interviewee was also confident of the influential powers of real estate property managers, saying 'you can pretty much get anything from a landlord, it's just the way in which you ask, or the way in which you direct it'. Seemingly, the relationship between the real estate agent/ property manager and the landlord as well as the between the real estate agent and trades people may be important factors in shaping retrofit. When a maintenance or appliance issue is raised by a tenant with a property manager, they generally advise the landlord about actions that need to be taken. Often, this advice will be based on the past experience of the property manager and/or the advice they receive from tradespeople. A clear opportunity arises to promote green retrofit through, for example, interventions in training, education, incentives and practice settings for both property managers and tradespeople when they choosing/fit/advise on energy and water efficient options. Put simply, if both the property manager and tradesperson involved understand the options available and the upfront and ongoing cost implications, and they see opportunities to further their position rather than facing risks associated with doing anything out of the ordinary, the case for green retrofit to uptake can be more easily 'sold' to the landlord.

When asked about how real estate agents respond to government funded initiatives such as rebate schemes (insulation, water efficient shower heads, etc), one real estate agent acknowledged that they were not very proactive and said they would only respond where a tenant or landlord made a request.

> Tenants pay for water usage, which is a good thing because they're conscious of it, and they will have contacted us, or have arranged for the shower head to be installed themselves, and then we have a few green landlords. But not many. Not many green landlords I can assure you...

> ...Where they (the landlord) has wanted those things done, I've even had one landlord that's suggested to the tenant that she would contribute to their electricity if they went through a green electricity provider... she was that adamant that she wanted them to only connect with that company. And what we said to the owner was 'We can ask them but we really can't force them to do it.

When asked how real estate agents might play a role in promoting government funded initiatives, ideas included; a privileged role for agents in a streamlined rebate process; a system of standardised green retrofit charging/provision; and a trade licensing requirement to upgrade/retrofit appropriately. These of course involve significant changes to policy and practice settings and/or government funded initiatives. When pressed on the agents' taking unilateral action, the responses were more circumspect:

> I guess it would need to be a decision made as a group, as in our company, that this is the path that we do want to go down and we want to make sure that every landlord has the opportunity to put one (i.e. low flow showerhead) in for instance. How are we going to get that across to them so that it is very clear....that last thing we want to do is have 5,000 landlords all ring us within two days going 'What's this letter?

In our research we did locate a real estate firm who has implemented a more systematic approach to 'green' upgrades, offering a 'free service' for landlords involving a checklist based property assessment and assistance with retrofitting technologies and trades and support for claiming rebates. The outcome was that a quarter of the landlords on the agent's rent roll made some improvements typically involving a low-flow showerhead exchange. This agent also sought to encourage broader industry uptake through the professional association, the Real Estate Institute of Victoria. However, broader acceptance failed for a number of reasons, including a lack of training for staff in an area where there is high staff turnover; a distrust of third party providers among managing agents hampering partnerships with retrofit services; and the familiar complexity and transaction costs associated with accessing rebates and other so-called 'support' measures.

Another programme, led by a non-government organisation (NGO), targeted low income homes without insulation. This proved to be a difficult trailblazing project, with general dis-interest among agents, suspicion amongst tenants, and a broad spectrum of landlord responses. Even when landlords, agents and tenants wanted to be involved it could take a very long time to obtain consent – particularly from agents. The project was highly labour-intensive, with the NGO relying on voluntary labour and rebates to cover costs. The retrofit pilot highlights a role for active intermediaries and for more stability and simplicity. Policy measures such as rebates and incentives designed to enable retrofits provided significant transaction difficulties for scheme participants.

DISCUSSION

This study presents a picture of private rental retrofit, held together by complex webs of relationships and decision processes involving landlords, tenants, tradespeople, agents, government policy and program makers, and NGOs. As in many other jurisdictions across the westernised world, there are a range of government funded grants for retrofitting and education. These grants are provided to a range of organisations including social service organisations, NGO's and local government, who are responsible for co-coordinating retrofit schemes in their particular regions. Beyond these ad hoc schemes however, there is little evidence of any systematic attempts to improve existing rental stock, or to purposefully steer 'upscaling' of retrofit. In this case study, decisions about which appliance to replace or retrofit to adopt are largely reactive. A least cost, lowest risk imperative is at play, although it is not explicit in the rationale of the majority of landlords, rather, it plays out in the management of retrofit and replacement decisions, over which (a) agents and (b) tradespeople have significant influence.

Returning to the question: 'How do private landlords currently maintain their properties and how are they responding to climate change and related retrofit initiatives?' Clearly, landlords in the Australian rental market are heterogeneous in terms of their reasons for owning and renting residential properties. However, one overriding characteristic is that they are over-whelmingly small scale in the way they own and rent properties. The way they go about managing their properties is to increasingly engage the services of real estate agents. Further, it is clear from our survey and inter-views that those landlords who relate to their properties through the mediation of real estate agents adopt different positions from landlords who directly manage their properties. The findings from our interviews and survey highlight significant issues and challenges for systematic eco-retrof-itting including: the diverse motivations amongst landlords; the different relationships between landlords and managing agents; and the potentially powerful gatekeeping role that these agents play in facilitating transfor-mations in physical-material conditions of rental housing.

If we consider the sociotechnical transitions framing of Geels and Schot (2010) there is little evidence of a retrofit niche in the rental sector in Melbourne – there is no identifiable 'protected space'. It is possible that pressures will build up on the regime due to emerging factors such as energy prices and growing environmental concerns. We speculate that with appro-priate interventions this may result in regime reconfigurations (e.g. Berkhout et al. 2003; Smith et al. 2005), more than through the development of niche(s).

In any event, private rental retrofit in Australia is a loose-knit and unor-ganized practice and, as Hodson and Marvin (2010:482) note 'an ad hoc and reactive alignment of social interests will not achieve the priorities encompassed in a vision'. In our view, because of their trusted position as gatekeepers, the role of agents is key to the development of systemic retrofitting activity.

This in-depth study shows that the alleged split incentive, while a factor, is not the primary issue inhibiting the retrofit of private rental properties. In the same way that many pro-environmental behaviour change programs are constrained by their reliance on rational choice models to encourage individuals to make voluntary 'sustainable' or 'green' choices, relying on agents to encourage retrofitting amongst landlords is unlikely to be successful on its own. The complexities in governing urban retrofit transitions require a more multi-faceted approach.

The private rental sector is not significantly different to other sectors when it comes to rates of retrofit. Rental housing stock is similar to owner-occupied homes and energy use is also similar. Landlords are also invariably homeowners themselves, and we found evidence that the majority of them tend to treat their rental properties in a similar manner to those they live in. In other words, a sense of what is 'right' in terms of property condition and upgrades is as important as who benefits in financial terms from any particular investment.

While more could be said on issues associated with body corporates or the explicit role of other city actors by examining landlording practices we found a lack of planning or conspicuous decision making and, despite the imperative to be a 'good landlord', improving or retrofitting properties is not a high priority. Instead agents are currently associated with maintenance rather than facilitating retrofits in a system that is splintered and under-professionalised. Our research suggests that the growing use of agents (as active intermediaries) alongside accompanying interventions may present an opportunity for a systematic rental retrofit scheme.

This raises questions of how purposive upscaling of retrofit in the private rented sector might be achieved. Given that proactive retrofitting by landlords is limited and largely depends on the relationship the landlord has with their rental property (e.g. whether they are likely to live in it themselves), and the role of intermediaries such as agents, it is unsurprising that the existing range of rational market-based policy and program interventions have had limited impact. The apparent range of maintenance approaches, diversity of landlord types and diffuse nature of the residential landlord sector suggests that no single type of voluntary intervention will be effective in bringing about large scale improvements to environmental performance of the rental housing stock. A portfolio of interventions will be required and will likely start from the sorts of policy instruments adopted elsewhere including regulatory and control mechanisms, economic/market based instruments, fiscal instruments and incentives and support, information and voluntary actions (Urge-Vorsatz *et al.* 2007: 460).

However, along with employing the necessary policy instruments, a key implication in improving the environmental performance of the rental housing sector, is the necessity to achieve effective coordination and cooperation between the different agencies and actors involved. Currently the management of rental properties is dominated by real estate agents acting on behalf of property owners. As intermediaries, real estate agents have the potential to play a key role as a coordinating body through the choice of skilled contractor employed to undertake property management, developing a trusted relationship with landlords and liaising with government agencies involved in funding retrofit initiatives and schemes. Agents have the potential to influence the process, however, they do not typically have any immediate, direct financial incentive to promote improvements in the environmental performance of rental housing, or any history of professional or social practice relating to green retrofit.

CONCLUSION

Green retrofit requires a shared vision and coordinated sets of actions if it is to emerge as a ubiquitous socio-technical phenomenon. It is useful here to recall the conditions Hodson and Marvin (2010:483) indicate as important in translating vision into action. While they cite seven such conditions, in this case study, all are absent: finance is insecure; there is no shared 'retrofit agent'; no systemic learning; insufficiently aligned social interests and; no evidence of systematic multiagency relationships or shared knowledge. This indicates multiple areas where interventions may be focussed.

The findings suggest long term sources of funding are the starting point for governing beyond the split incentive. Instead of funding short term interventions, Federal government could look to the $1 billion or so per year in rental assistance to channel purposive retrofit policies, and state governments could look to mandatory disclosure, and to the Rental Bonds system to improve urban retrofits.

A redesign of retrofit programs to promote the green retrofit of private rental housing would need to take account of the role of key intermediaries and their lived experience in the socio-technical relations of housing retrofit. One form this could take is suggested by this study, involving a clear role for estate agents/property managers. This would in turn require several issues to be addressed through policy settings. Firstly, the property managers currently have a poor understanding of options to improve environmental performance among agents. They are not (yet) enlisted as green retrofit advisors or experts, and instead occupy a low status position amongst the estate agency profession. Secondly, there is currently a lack of financial or other incentives for them to act as facilitators – to offset the perceived risks, time and resources required to organise and/or advise on green retrofit. Thirdly, landlords harbour considerable scepticism towards agents and their tradespersons – the research suggests that landlord distrust may be mitigated if an agent's motivations for suggesting particular measures or actions were obvious to the landlord. For example, we speculate that a landlord may be more receptive to an agent's suggestion to install ceiling insulation if they understood that the agent would receive a commission for signing them up to the insulation rebate scheme, and the savings and benefits to both landlord and tenant were well understood. Policy measures designed to encourage advisory or 'green brokering' roles for agents as intermediaries would need to address these limits to agents' participation.

Given that there is a diversity of agent types within a diverse private rental system, it follows that the flexibility to allow local experiments is required within a long-term overarching policy commitment and programs. While this policy approach does not in itself guarantee outcomes, it does at least respond to the current over-reliance upon notions of 'split incentives', rational-economic individual based mechanisms and it creates a role for agents as intermediaries in upscaling green retrofits.

Note

1   The research on which this article is based was funded by the Victorian Government in Australia. The authors would like to thank Anna Strempel at the Centre for Design, RMIT University for research assistance throughout the project. The authors also thank colleagues at the Department of Sustainability and Environment and Emeritus Professor Mike Berry for their input into the project design. Last but not least, sincere thanks also go to all of the landlord's agents and other stakeholders who participated in the interviews and survey.

References

ABS (2006) Census of Population and Housing.(CD-ROM).

ABS (2008) Environmental Issues: Energy Use and Conservation. (4602.0.55.001).

Allen Consulting (2011) *Mandatory Disclosure of Residential Building Energy, Greenhouse and Water Performance: Consultation Regulation Impact Statement*, fourth draft report to the National Framework for Energy Efficiency Building Implementation Committee. Australian Building Codes Board, Available from www.abcb.gov.au/ (accessed 25/8/2012).

Berkhout, F., Smith, A. and Stirling, A. (2003) *Socio-Technological Regimes and Transition Contexts*, Working Paper Series, Brighton SPRU, University of Sussex.

Berry, M. (2000) 'Investment in rental housing in Australia: Small landlords and Institutional investors', *Housing Studies,* 15(5): 661–681.

Boardman, B., Darby, S., Killip, G., Hinnells, M., Jardine, N., Palmer, J. and Sinden, G. (2005) *40% house*. Oxford: Environmental Change Institute, University of Oxford.

Crook, T. and Kemp, P.A. (2011) 'Transforming private landlords: Housing, markets and public policy'. Wiley-Blackwell, Chichester.

DCCEE (2010) *Report of the Prime Ministers task force on energy efficiency*, Department of Climate Change and Energy Efficiency, Commonwealth of Australia, Canberra.

Gabriel, M., Watson, P., Ong, R., Wood, G. and Wulff, M. (2010) 'The environmental sustainability of Australia's private rental housing stock'. AHURI Final Report No. 159. Australian Housing and Urban Research Institute, Melbourne.

Gabriel, M. and Watson, P. (2012) 'Supporting sustainable home improvement in the private rental sector: The view of investors'. *Urban Policy and Research*, 30(3): 309–325.

Geels, F.W. and Schot, J. (2010) 'Part 1: The dynamics of socio-technical transitions: A socio-technical perspective'. In Grin J. Rotmans J. Schot J (eds). *Transitions to Sustainable Development: New Directions in the Study of Long Term Transformative Change*, Routledge, London, p.11–104.

Graham, S. and Marvin, S. (2001) *Splintering Urbanism: Networked infrastructures, Technological Mobilities and the Urban Condition*, Routledge, UK.

Gupta, R. and Chandiwala, S. (2010) 'Understanding occupants: Feedback techniques for large scale low-carbon domestic refurbishments'. *Building Research and Information*, 38(5): 530–48.

Hens, H. (2010) 'Energy efficient retrofit of an end of the row house: Confronting predictions with long-term measurements'. *Energy and Buildings*, 42(10): 1939–1947.

Hodson M. and Marvin S. (2010) 'Can cities shape socio-technical transitions and how would we know if they were?' *Research Policy*, 39: 477–485.

Hulse, K., Burke, T., Ralston, L. and Stone, W. (2012) *The Australian private rental sector: Changes and challenges*, Positioning Paper No. 149, Australian Housing and Urban Research Centre, Swinburne Research Centre, Australia.

Phillips, Y. (2012) 'Landlords versus tenants: Information asymmetry and mismatched preferences for home energy efficiency'. *Energy Policy*, 45: 112–21.

Pullen, S. (2010) 'An analysis of energy consumption in an Adelaide suburb with different retrofitting and redevelopment scenarios'. *Urban Policy and Research*, 28(2): 161–180.

Rehdanz, K. (2007) 'Determinants of residential space heating expenditures in Germany'. *Energy Economics*, 29(20): 167–182.

Seelig, T., Thompson, A., Burke, T., Pinnegar, S., McNelis, S. and Morris, A. (2009) 'Understanding what motivates households to become and remain investors in the private rental market'. Final Report No. 130, Australian Housing and Urban Research Institute, Melbourne.

UNEP (2007) *Buildings and Climate Change – Status, Challenges and Opportunities*, United Nations Environment Program, Geneva.

Urge-Vorsatz, D., Koeppel, S. and Mirasgedis S. (2007) 'Appraisal of policy instruments for reducing buildings' CO_2 emissions'. *Building Research and Information* 35(4): 458–477.

Vergragt, P.J. and Brown, H.S. (2012) 'The challenge of energy retrofitting the residential housing stock: Grassroots innovations and socio-technical system change in Worcester, MA'. *Technology Analysis and Strategic Management* 24(4): 407–20.

Watson, M. (2012) 'How theories of practice can inform transition to a decarbonized transport system'. *Journal of Transport Geography*. Available online at http://dx.doi.org/10.1016/j.jtrangeo.2012.04.002 (accessed 25/8/2012).

Chapter 10

NGOs as intermediaries for pro-poor urban electrification

Bipasha Baruah

INTRODUCTION

Access to electricity is still only available to two-thirds of the world's population. Worldwide, 2.4 billion people rely on traditional biomass for cooking and 1.6 billion people do not have access to electricity (UN-Energy, 2005). While electrification is not a sufficient condition for economic development, it is socially desirable, and in both developed and developing countries, it has been strongly correlated with wealth (Ferguson *et al.* 2000). A growing body of literature analyzes how access to electricity benefits rural and urban communities in developing countries (Barnes, 1997; Ghanadan, 2004; Pasternak, 2000). Electricity provides a wide range of economic and social benefits, such as greater potential for education due to better lighting, savings in time and effort spent gathering traditional fuels, potential for improved access to information and digital connectivity, scope for greater productivity and improved health services, and improved indoor air quality (Waddams Price, 2000; World Energy Assessment, 2000). In recent years, researchers have more specifically identified the benefits of electricity as they relate to the Millennium Development Goals for eradicating poverty and hunger; achieving universal primary education; promoting gender equality; reducing child mortality; improving maternal health; combating HIV/AIDS, malaria and other diseases; and ensuring environmental sustainability (Flavin and Hull Aeck, 2006; Ha and Porcano, 2005).

This chapter discusses the experiences of two NGOs in India – the Self-Employed Women's Association (SEWA) and *Saath* – that have participated in a multiple-stakeholder pro-poor electrification programme that has electrified nearly 100,000 homes in the city of Ahmedabad and is currently being replicated in other smaller cities in Gujarat and the neighboring state of Rajasthan. The author draws upon academic literature on urban infrastructure provision, governance and politics in cities of the Global South to construct theoretical anchors and a framework of analysis for findings. She employs a pricing survey carried out by *Saath*, project reports prepared by NGOs and international aid agencies, internal and external evaluations of the project, and interviews with staff from the NGOs and the electricity utility in order to analyze the project in terms of its impacts upon access, tariffs, quality of service, tenure security, and its role in empowering women through the formation and maintenance of community-based organizations (CBOs). The author also identifies policy inputs that are required to scale up and optimize NGO participation in the design and implementation of pro-poor electrification activities, and in the energy reform process in general.

Electricity reform and the urban poor

In the last few decades, many countries around the world have reformed their electricity sectors. This has been justified in developing countries by the unsatisfactory performance of state-regulated and controlled power regimes. While different countries have chosen different models of reform, the overall direction tends to focus on commercialization of state-owned facilities (or outright privatization), deregulation and competition as key elements, often within the context of larger macroeconomic restructuring that has involved other service sectors such as water, transport and telecommunications. In countries like India and South Africa, for example, electricity sectors were at the forefront of newly liberalizing economies. The rationale behind reforms in services like electricity is that efficiency, commercial pricing, and greater involvement by the private sector will reduce pressure on national and local government budgets and create a profitable sector, which in turn will finance necessary investments for improvements in service and access (Bacon and Besant-Jones, 2001; Kessides, 2004).

In many countries, including India, this marketised vision of electricity provision represents a dramatic shift in policies that had guided the sector previously, serving to unravel public-service models of state-led development, in which electricity and water, among other services, were part of broader goals of nation building and explicit policy mechanisms for redistribution. These changes also involve subjective shifts in the vision and promises of development, influencing people's expectations, relations with the state, and understanding of national identity and citizenship (Ghanadan, 2010). Many infrastructures built earlier within the context of public or private monopolies and aspirations toward 'universal services for all' now operate according to imperatives of profit maximization and the prioritization of privileged users and markets. This 'splintering' of infrastructures can involve the construction of new 'premium' spaces or networks such as high-speed train lines, electronically tolled highways, skywalk city streets, privatized streets, or broadband communications networks, which bypass or become removed from the legacies of the inherited infrastructures (Graham and Marvin, 2001). More subtly, it may encompass the withdrawal of essential services from poorer or less profitable groups or spaces, as efforts concentrate on addressing the more profitable market segments. It may also be associated with tendencies to privilege selected premium infrastructures whilst reducing essential public involvement and maintenance from the wider inheritances of infrastructure converging entire, cities, regions, or nations (Graham, 2000). Thus, despite profound inequalities in water, sanitation and electricity service provision, India and Nigeria, for example, have the fastest growing mobile phone use in South Asia and sub-Saharan Africa respectively. Authors like Gandy (2005) have written about the 'concrete divide' between the rapid spread of new telecommunications technologies throughout cities in the context of widening inequalities in social and environmental conditions. There is growing evidence around the world that neo-liberal reform has been designed to mainly address macroeconomic concerns and to satisfy donor conditionalities without sufficient consideration for social justice and equity issues (see, for example, Dubash, 2002; Wamukonya, 2003a).

In the post-reform era, electricity delivery in most countries and contexts involve three key stakeholders: the government; the electricity company (either a private company or a commercialized state electricity board); and the consumers. The role of government is to safeguard public health and safety, which in turn implies overseeing the safety, quality and cost of electricity supply, authorizing tariffs – possibly even allowing for cross-subsidies for low-income consumers. Since land ownership and tenure falls under the government's purview, it also has the power to authorize right-of-way for utility infrastructure such as distribution lines and transformers. The role of the electricity utility is generally limited to providing infrastructure in the form of meters and wiring, billing and payment collection for the service, and maintaining the quality of the service provided in accordance with the rules that govern electricity supply. Consumers typically have no role in electricity delivery other than to expect that they will receive electricity reliably and safely as long as they pay their bills regularly. In India, most people are far removed from the policy processes that govern electricity reform and have virtually no ability to influence the process or to articulate their concerns. With the notable exception of the Pune-based organization, *Prayas*, very few public-interest or advocacy organizations have raised alternative perspectives on energy issues or played a watchdog role in electricity reform (Prayas, 2007). Consequently, electricity reform has taken place largely out of public view in India and in most other countries of the Global South.

Such reforms have not met the needs of the vast majority of the world's informal settlements, where most transactions are informal and not regulated by the government. Consequently, in many developing countries, increasing access to electricity – especially for rural customers who are off the grid and the urban poor who are grossly underserviced – is an urgent need. In the urban context, slum upgradation efforts tend to prioritize water (and even sanitation, which was previously often neglected) over electricity because these services are more essential for sustaining life and good health. Unlike water, for which there is no substitute, electricity can, albeit dangerously, be substituted with paraffin, coal and other energy sources. Electricity is also quite easy to steal and illegal electricity supplies are almost universally available in slums. Slum dwellers are willing to risk physical danger and possible prosecution to steal power themselves or to enter into agreements with illegal service providers. This is true in other contexts of expensive or limited access, where the poor have no choice but to find alternatives to utility suppliers by illegally tapping into 'formal' or 'legal' supplies. In Rio de Janeiro, informal or illegal connections made to water and electricity infrastructures are called *gatos* [cats]. They are often the only means by which urban poor communities can gain access to the city mains since regularization of settlements can be extremely slow and may not entail infrastructure provision (Fabricius, 2008). Therefore, for many of the world's urbanites – especially those in the burgeoning informal settlements which dominate many cities in the Global South – achieving an electricity, water or communication service is the result of a constant process of improvisation (McFarlane, 2010). Graham (2010) writes that for such urbanites, infrastructure networks are far from being black boxes that almost miraculously and invisibly bring electricity, internet connections, water, or food to any point or space. Instead, they are highly political assemblages or artifacts and practices within which continuous efforts at agency, or resistance, may – just may – allow services to be improvised, often beyond the bounds of markets and strict legality (10). That the urban poor value and need access to water and electricity is borne out by the fact that they pay for it almost globally at a higher per unit cost than people in legally served areas (McDonald, 2009a; USAID, 2004).

Since many governments barely even acknowledge that slums exist in their cities, slum dwellers typically have no legal entitlements to basic services. Informal and illegal systems grow in response to unmet demands for basic services such as water and electricity. Because the majority of the unserved populations reside in rural areas and in urban informal settlements, their load demands and incomes are low, and connection costs are frequently unaffordable. For example, low-income households in South Africa account for probably no more than 5 percent of national electricity consumption, with relatively little per capita demand growth on the horizon (McDonald, 2009a, 16). Private electricity companies (and state-owned commercialized utilities) are expected to operate on a cost effective and profitable basis. Even if governments expect and stipulate that private companies also provide services to economically weaker groups, electrifying such communities is often not financially attractive for the private sector for a number of reasons.

The narrow streets and alleys typical of slums raise the costs of serving such areas. The challenges of obtaining right-of-way documents to serve largely illegally settled areas also deter electricity companies from attempting to serve slums. Additionally, there may be physical risks for utility staff – particularly if they are seeking payment – in entering slums. Because their incomes are low or erratic and access to savings and financial services tends to be limited, poor households are also unable to, or unaccustomed to, making large lump-sum payments for connection. Competing illegal suppliers often succeed where legal providers fail, even when they charge more per unit cost, because they are familiar with slum communities and can package their services in ways that poor households find more affordable, such as monthly charges per appliance or flexible payment terms for connection and reconnection. Since illegal suppliers typically steal power from legal power lines and do not assume the cost of production and transmission of electricity to the locations they serve, they are able to offer much more flexible terms of payment. Within the private sector there is also an assumed culture of non-payment in informal settlements. The theft or 'non-technical' losses associated with slum communities represent only 3 to 5 percent of global revenue from electricity (USAID, 2004). Non-payment has been demonstrated to be far more rampant and significant in government agencies, large farms, corporations and middle-class homes (Wamukonya, 2003a). Nevertheless, all of these real and assumed deterrents severely limit private providers' interest in undertaking slum electrification efforts.

In the water supply sector, some private companies have acknowledged significant barriers to market expansion in the Global South (Bakker, 2007). Water supplies are currently being remunicipalised in many countries that had previously been part of the privatization bandwagon. In South Africa, for example, Suez was sent back to Paris after its much-protested mismanagement of municipal water from 2001 to 2006. Also in South Africa, in April 2008 a major constitutional lawsuit in the Johannesburg High Court resulted in a doubling of free water to 50 litres per person per day and the prohibition of prepayment water meters (Bond and Dugard, 2008).Since water and electricity service provision operate on similar terms, public statements made by senior executives of water firms about high risk and low profitability in supplying the poor (see, for example, Robbins, 2003) as well as well-publicized cancellations of water supply concession contracts in Argentina, Bolivia, Indonesia and the Philippines, to name a few other countries, have certainly also served as deterrents to private-sector driven pro-poor electrification efforts.

It is possible to argue that the informal or illegal arrangements that currently exist in urban informal settlements are a relatively painless way for better-off sections of society to subsidize the energy needs of the impoverished. Such arguments would, however, ignore compelling reasons for the urban poor to have access to legal electricity. First, illegal electricity supplies are notoriously unreliable and unsafe. Providers can and do cut off supplies at whim for days on end. Slum residents in Ahmedabad, India, where research for this chapter was conducted, complained that the illegal service provider cut off their electricity completely for four or five days a month, and sporadically at least once a day for several hours. Additionally, the voltage fluctuated uncontrollably during the day and was almost always very low at night. Despite the poor unreliable service, they were also cut off if they failed to pay their monthly 'dues' on time. The use of flammable energy alternatives when power is cut off (or unavailable to begin with) as well as faulty wiring and paraffin poisoning have caused devastating fires, destroyed homes, killed, injured and displaced tens of thousands of poor people in cities around the world (McDonald, 2009; SEA, 2006). Second, although the terms of payment of illegal suppliers may be better suited for the low and volatile incomes of the urban poor, per unit costs are much higher than those charged by legal suppliers. Finally, illegal supplies do not in any way strengthen or validate the urban poor's entitlements to secure land tenure. Formal land titles and sale deeds are still not available to the vast majority of slum dwellers. User charge documents such as water and electricity bills are perceived to be empowering by slum communities because they represent a *de facto* form of tenure security. People who have lived on the margins of society all their lives are eager to embrace all such symbols of 'official' recognition because they strengthen their right of residence in their homes and communities and provide a certain level of protection from eviction.

There is clearly a need for innovative approaches to provide affordable legal electricity to slum communities. Researchers working in other regional contexts in the Global South – Tanzania, South Africa, Kenya and Uganda, for example – have written specifically and explicitly about the need for NGOs, universities and other civil society engagement in electricity reform by providing adequate means of participation and oversight to create checks and balances between financial and development goals (Ghanadan, 2009; McDonald, 2009b). As with multiple-stakeholder initiatives for water and sanitation, certain civil society organizations are suitably placed to work in partnership with government agencies, electricity companies, urban poor communities and donor agencies to design and implement pro-poor slum electrification programmes. The rest of the chapter shares results and lessons from one such programme in urban India.

The Ujala Yojana slum electrification project

With a population of over 5 million in 2006, Ahmedabad is the largest city in the western state of Gujarat and the seventh largest metropolis in India. The Self-Employed Women's Association (SEWA) was founded in Ahmedabad in 1972 to organize women in the informal sector for better working conditions and social security provisions. *Saath* is a smaller NGO based in Ahmedabad with a mandate to improve access to health, education, infrastructure services, and livelihoods options for the urban poor. This chapter does not seek to provide detailed documentation of the two NGOs' activities and accomplishments other than those that relate to slum electrification. There are many excellent resources that document SEWA's history and organizing philosophy (see, for example, Bhatt, 2006; Chen, 2008).

A survey conducted by the Ahmedabad Municipal Corporation (AMC) in the mid-1990s revealed that 42 percent of the city's population, or approximately 1.2 million people, live in slums that lack the most basic amenities (Kundu and Mahadevia, 2002). An earlier study conducted by SEWA had revealed that 97 percent of its urban membership lived in slums (Rose, 1992). The Gujarat Mahila SEWA Housing Trust (MHT) was established in 1994 as a SEWA sister organization with the overall objective of improving the housing and infrastructure conditions of poor women in the informal sector. Since 1997, MHT and *Saath* have participated in implementing a Slum Networking Project (SNP) in Ahmedabad aimed at transforming the physical environment of slums as well as improving the social and economic lives of slum dwellers. Also known as the *Parivartan* [meaning 'transformation' in Hindi and Gujarati] project, it aims to provide a package of basic infrastructure services, including household connections for water supply, individual toilets, storm water drainage, solid waste disposal, paved roads, street lights and landscaping. MHT and *Saath* have worked to achieve these objectives through a partnership involving slum communities and their representatives, the community-based organizations (CBOs), the Ahmedabad Municipal Corporation (AMC), and international organizations like the World Bank and USAID. By the summer of 2006, the SNP had reached 35,500 slum dwellers in Ahmedabad with its services. It was awarded the prestigious Dubai International Award for Best Practices to Improve the Living Environment in the same year. Baruah (2007a) provides more detailed information about this project.

In 2001, building upon the successes in the SNP, MHT and *Saath* forged a partnership with the Ahmedabad Electricity Company (AEC), a commercialized public utility, on a slum electrification pilot project. The major objectives of the project were to ensure availability of safe and legal electricity supply to slum communities; to minimize process time for new connections and to organize and operate an efficient bill recovery system; to eliminate unauthorized use of electricity by regularizing connections and minimizing techno-commercial losses; to involve slum dwellers in the supply and payment of dues through representative CBOs; and to develop strategies for scaling up the programme at local, state and national levels. By 2008, close to 100,000 homes had been electrified in Gujarat and the programme is being replicated within Gujarat and in the neighbouring state of Rajasthan.

Successful features, weaknesses and broader policy implications

Building upon established trust in partnership approach: The successful implementation of a large multiple-stakeholder water and sanitation-focused Slum Networking Project (SNP) in many Ahmedabad slums seems to have enhanced trust between the slum communities, the municipality and the NGOs. The NGOs' primary responsibility in the SNP was to motivate and mobilize the slum communities to participate in the upgradation process. The NGOs facilitated the formation of registered CBOs to represent residents' interests. The NGOs were also largely responsible for the implementation of the SNP's community development programmes, including community health services, adult literacy and child care. Baruah (2007a) documents how the NGOs built relationships with slum communities through repeat visits and exposure and dialogue programs of all stakeholders. The successful delivery of water and sanitation infrastructure in a large number of city slums through the SNP made the motivation and mobilization for the electrification programme relatively easy to accomplish. The sequencing of the slum electrification programme was critical to its success. Since most slum dwellers understandably prioritized access to water and sewerage over legal electricity, these basic services were provided first. A full 90 percent of residents in SNP slums expressed a demand for legal electricity after receiving water and sanitation services (Bhatt, 2007). Although full legal tenure – in the form of land titles [*pattas*] – were not offered to any of the slums that were included in the SNP, the ten-year guarantee of non-eviction awarded by the municipality to SNP slums also played a big role in motivating slum residents to invest in legal electricity connections. In the early years of commercialization of the electricity sector in Ahmedabad, the AEC showed very little interest in serving slum communities with legal electricity. The operations of the AEC were at that time regulated by the 1991 Electricity Laws Act, which stipulated that the Government of Gujarat would bail the AEC out of 50 percent of revenue losses in its operations (ibid.). This Act, which initially ushered in commercialization and privatization of the electricity sector, was eventually amended again to require the Government of Gujarat to pick up only 30 percent of AEC's revenue losses (ibid.). After the amendment, the AEC became motivated to find new customers and also to reduce losses due to theft. Middle- and upper-income residential communities in Ahmedabad are already fully electrified. Slum communities with densely packed homes – served almost exclusively by illegal electricity supplies – presented tremendous opportunities for AEC to scale up its operations to meet the dual objectives of reducing theft losses and increasing revenue. As elsewhere, the commercialization of electricity in India is situated within a broader paradigm of policy reform since the early 1990s that is focused on market liberalization. The commercialization of utilities and the introduction of competitive markets are believed to lead to efficiency gains that can benefit the sector (Hunt, 2002).

Assessment of ability to pay

A primary concern (and a major source of conflict) in slum electrification programmes is the degree to which the household connection fees should be subsidized. It has become accepted practice in slum upgradation programmes – although not without controversy – to require the recipient household to pay part of the connection cost. This is based on the argument that the improvement would be valued more highly if the recipient household had to make an investment (Black, 2008). On the other hand, it is also widely acknowledged that large lump-sum payments can be very onerous, and often impossible, for poor households to manage. Most slum households were able to manage fees best when they could pay smaller sums of money over longer periods of time (McDonald, 2009a; USAID, 2004). Before the pilot project, there was a general assumption within the AEC that slum residents would be unwilling and/or unable to pay for legal electricity connections. A survey was conducted by *Saath* in 500 households in 5 city slums to estimate slum dwellers' ability to pay. The electricity consumption in legally connected households in slums was typically about 36 kWh per month, which at prevalent tariffs would cost Rs.108 (US $2.70) per month. Based on conversations with slum dwellers about rates charged by middlemen, it was estimated that the same level of consumption would cost Rs.216 (US $5.40) per month for an illegal connection – illegal providers typically charge Rs.50 (US$1.25) per 'power point' (light bulb connection), resulting in a payment of Rs.200–300 (US$5–$7.50) per month for a household with 4 to 6 connections. This amounts to 10–15 percent of monthly income for a household earning Rs.25, 000 (US $625) a year. The survey assumed that to finance the initial connection costs, the customer would take a loan from a moneylender at a very high interest rate payable over a 3-year period. These costs were integrated into the survey to arrive at the monthly repayment schedule. Therefore, the total monthly cost to the customer is the monthly loan repayment plus the average monthly charge for electricity consumption. Although there were wide variations in the ability to pay among the 500 households surveyed, some informative findings emerged from the analysis of this data (see table 10.1).

The precipitous drop in ability to pay as the connection fee increases beyond Rs.2,000 (US $50) indicates a clear guideline for pricing – penetration of legal electricity into slums would be low if initial connection costs exceed Rs.2,000 unless there are subsidies to cover higher amounts. Ahluwalia (2000) estimated that 50 percent of all households in India (81 million households) are unable to afford commercial rates for electricity.

Table 10.1 Ability to pay for legal electricity services

Connection fee in Rupees	Monthly instalment payment for connection	Monthly electricity bill	Total monthly cost	Percentage of households able to pay
Rs.1,000	Rs.60	Rs.108	Rs.168	98
Rs.1,500	Rs.91	Rs.108	Rs.199	88
Rs.2,000	Rs.121	Rs.108	Rs.229	84
Rs.2,500	Rs.151	Rs.108	Rs.259	28
Rs.3,000	Rs.181	Rs.108	Rs.289	6

These findings emphasize that if low-income households are to be provided with electricity at affordable rates, there should be no illusions about the continued need for subsidization and for public funding even in a commercialized and restructured sector (Barnes and Halpern, 2000; Dubash, 2002).

Suitable tariffs

The establishment of appropriate pricing guidelines for initial connection fees, which were demonstrated quite clearly in the *Saath*-administered survey, were complicated by a claim by AEC – based mostly on anecdotal information – that 40 percent of slum households were willing and able to pay up to Rs.8,000 (US $200) in initial connection costs. The NGOs played a crucial role in negotiating pricing policy. The AEC had initially worked out variable pricing from Rs.3,500 (US $87.50) to Rs.10,000 (US $250) for different households in slums depending on the distance from the electricity mains. The NGOs convinced AEC to adopt a uniform pricing policy for all households included in the pilot project. The costs for connecting an individual household and installing internal wiring was split between the household which contributed Rs.3,350 (US $83.75) and USAID and AEC, who each contributed Rs.2,200 (US $55) per household (see table 10.2). A total of 820 households in 4 slums were provided with legal electricity at this price – Rs. 7,750 (US $193.75) – in the pilot project.

Table 10.2 Connection fees: who pays what?

Payee	Amount in Rupees
Recipient Household	Rs.3,350
AEC	Rs.2,200
USAID	Rs.2,200
Total Connection Fee	Rs.7,750

Average revenue losses to AEC in these 4 slums were reduced from 27 percent to 4 percent after the pilot project (MHT, 2006). Average electricity consumption in these slums rose by 200 percent per day (ibid.). AEC reports that total non-technical losses in slum areas that have been legally electrified are 5 percent whereas they are as high as 30 percent in areas with widely prevalent illegal connections. Following the successful implementation of the pilot project, AEC decided that it would charge a lower uniform price of Rs.5, 200 (US $130) – inclusive of all subsidies – for all new service connections. NGO advocacy in pricing policies for low-income consumers has also indirectly benefited middle-class customers in the state of Gujarat. As AEC became more convinced about the profitability of slum electrification, one-time connection fees were further reduced to Rs.2, 300 (US $57.50) for all new connections. The NGOs are currently working on electrification projects in rural and urban areas of Gujarat in collaboration with private-sector electricity companies and commercialized state electricity boards who have all adopted Rs.2, 300 as the standard charge for new connections.

Facilitating billing policy change

AEC issues bimonthly (every two months) bills to mainstream consumers. Because of their low and volatile incomes, most slum residents are unable to pay larger bills for longer periods of time. Most expressed a clear preference for monthly bills. MHT intervened on behalf of slum residents and appealed to AEC to issue monthly bills to low-income consumers. AEC responded to this recommendation by revamping its management information system (MIS) software to facilitate the issuance of monthly bills. At MHT's request, the AEC also set up a special Slum Electrification Cell on its premises to specifically serve economically weaker sections of society and to facilitate the scaling up of the slum electrification programme. While most urban poor households have found monthly bills affordable thus far, in the future it may be necessary to further refine billing policy to make fortnightly or even weekly bills possible. There have been no reports thus far of households that have been cut off from their electricity supply as a result of non-payment, which also seems to suggest that monthly payments are affordable. Given the volatility of incomes in urban poor households, non-payment may become an issue in the future. Innovative humane solutions will be required to ensure that families do not lose access to legal electricity due to temporary inability to pay. Several researchers have called for less aggressive cost recovery in electricity provision or to an outright end to electricity cut-offs for non-payment of bills by low-income households. Writing about South Africa, McDonald (2009b) states that cut-offs make a mockery of post-apartheid constitutional rights and entitlements to basic services since they serve 'only to discipline and cajole potential low-income defaulters into payment in the interests of minimizing rates and tariff increases for the middle class and industry' (2009b: 442). The issue of non-payment can also become highly politicized. Public and private utilities have used non-payment as a justification for cutting supplies to cover for failures in repair and maintenance, as well as for rerouting supplies (ibid.). The pressure felt by many cities to recreate themselves as 'world' cities or as tourist destinations leads to changing land values and can motivate municipalities to demolish infrastructure in poor communities (McFarlane, 2010). The countervailing influence of a vigilant civil society is critical in such environments.

Writing about water supply, Bakker (2007) emphasizes that full privatization is inconsistent with constitutional guarantees of rights and entitlements to basic services unless it is coupled with a universality requirement (laws prohibiting disconnections of residential consumers), and with a strong regulatory framework for price control and quality standards. Privatized or commercialized electricity supply can and should also model itself along the same lines even though the right to electricity is much less explicit and more inferred than the right to water, which in enshrined in the Constitutions of many countries, including India.

Access to microfinance

In order to enable as many households as possible to benefit from the slum electrification programme, SEWA Bank facilitated access to electrification loans. The maximum amount offered as an electrification loan is Rs.4, 000 (US $100). To borrow this amount, an account holder must deposit at least Rs.500 (US $12.50) into the account. Like other housing loans, interest rate on the loan was 17 percent and borrowers were required to pay Rs.200 (US $5) every month. The loans are designed to be repaid within 21 months through daily, weekly, fortnightly, monthly or bimonthly instalments.

In order to take an entrepreneurship loan from SEWA Bank, a woman must become a member of SEWA. However, SEWA Bank did not require membership from households that borrowed for electrification purposes. Many women from households participating in the electrification project did eventually become SEWA members because they learned more about the benefits of membership over the course of the project. MHT acknowledges that slum upgradation and electrification projects have served as very effective vehicles for expanding SEWA's membership base within urban poor communities (Bhatt, 2007).

Establishing a legal framework for slum electrification

The issue of land tenure looms large in slum electrification programmes. India's Electricity Act prohibits the electrification of illegally occupied lands. To uphold his law, the AEC followed very strict norms for legal electrification. The consumer was required to provide what are called 7/12 records [documents demonstrating legal ownership of land] as well as other proofs of residence such as tariff bills, ration and election cards. Of course, the vast majority of slum dwellers are unable to provide such documentation. MHT and *Saath* lobbied the AEC to find creative ways to meet the requirements of the Electricity Act. They facilitated negotiations between AMC and AEC to find an alternative solution and managed to bring them to a consensus decision after six months. It was decided that a No Objection Certificate (NOC) issued by the AMC stating that the beneficiaries of the SNP would not be evicted by the AMC for a period of 10 years would be used as the support document in lieu of other proofs of ownership and residence. Since such letters could only be provided for slums that had received the SNP infrastructure, the AEC introduced an indemnity bond to specifically undertake electrification in non-SNP slums at a later stage in the project. The indemnity bond basically required slum residents to sign an agreement stating that they would not pursue legal proceedings against AEC if they were evicted from their homes or relocated in the future by the AMC. The combination of NOCs and indemnity bonds provided an adequate legal framework for the provision of legal electricity to slums. The challenges faced by the NGOs in addressing the right-of-way issue in Ahmedabad does point to a need to amend the Electricity Act to allow for the legal electrification of informal settlements in other states in India.

The findings from this research echo those from other contexts (see, for example, Gulyani and Bassett, 2008) that suggest that the 'infrastructure first' versus 'tenure first' debate in the literature on slum upgrading is not helpful in practice in improving the lives of the urban poor, especially when analyzed within the constraints of their lived realities. In their review of slum upgradation projects in sub-Saharan Africa, Gulyani and Bassett (2007) emphasize that efforts to regularize land titles to confer *de jure* security of tenure have not been encouraging. By contrast, infrastructure investment efforts have conferred *de facto* security of tenure and also ameliorated living conditions. Over time project-based learning and micro-level innovations have also helped improve upgrading performance. The same authors stress that to create broader and sustainable benefits, upgradation efforts need to be scaled up, preferably through a programmatic approach that is channeled through government, links slums to citywide systems, and combines a community-demand and participation approach with supply-side constraints and rules of access. These findings also hold water in the urban Indian context.

Role of CBOs in slum electrification project

MHT and *Saath* regrouped the CBOs that had already been formed as part of the SNP for the slum electrification project. The NGOs and the AEC worked with the CBO to identify a member – usually a woman – who was trained to read the individual household meters. AEC then pays the CBO Rs.10 (US $0.25) per meter read for each billing cycle. The meters are read fortnightly and customers receive monthly bills. The CBO's efforts in collecting electricity dues are complemented by the efforts of Bank *sathis* [friends] who are employed by SEWA Bank to conduct outreach activities in slum communities. Bank *sathis* typically come from slum communities and possess basic literacy and accounting abilities. They offer door-to-door financial services in slum communities. They have also been extremely effective at securing loan repayments. Bank *sathis* do not receive salaries but they earn commissions based on the volume of business they generate and the repayments they secure. SEWA Bank currently employs more than 75 bank *sathis*. MHT helped identify nearly 27 bank *sathis* in areas served by the SNP and *Ujala Yojana* projects. CBOs assumed the following other responsibilities in the slum electrification project: creating awareness and motivating slum dwellers to access legal electrification; conducting home visits and community meetings to facilitate the same; submitting applications to AEC on behalf of slum residents; and acting as watch dogs against electricity pilferage in slums.

While there are some obvious benefits to be derived from CBO involvement, some caution may also be merited in naively romanticizing community participation. Activism in support of collective, community-based forms of resource management can fetishise communities as coherent, relatively equitable social structures, despite the fact that inequitable power relations and resource allocation exist within even highly impoverished communities (Baruah, 2007a; McCarthy, 2005). There is no doubt that the CBOs that participated in this project carried out their duties in a well-organized and efficient manner. However, a closer look at the composition and dynamics of the groups revealed a few problematic trends. One of the most obvious characteristics of CBOs in all participating communities was the over-representation of women who were related to men in politically powerful positions within the slums. It was more the norm than the exception in almost each case for CBOs to be headed by wives of locally prominent men such as political organizers, moneylenders and chit fund managers. More marginalized groups like female-headed households were conspicuous in their non-involvement in the CBOs in almost every community included in the research. The poorest and most vulnerable households in slums frequently did not participate in slum upgradation activities (Baruah, 2007a). This is also true of their participation in CBOs. More incentives must be built into the process of organizing CBOs to ensure that they do not just represent the voices of the relatively better-off members of slum communities. Nebulous terms like 'community participation' can, in practice, be exclusive and regressive or inclusive and progressive, depending on how they are conceptualized and operationalised. In multiple-stakeholder projects that bring together 'partners' with very different core philosophies, motivations, working styles, strengths and constraints, urban poor communities and their representative CBOs can easily be co-opted to perform a very limited range of policing and collecting agency services as a proxy for 'participation'. Indeed, there is growing concern that civil society engagement in infrastructure provision, through NGO participation, for example, may become just another mechanism for corporatizing and commodifying delivery of basic services, by paying lip service to feel-good terms like 'participation' (Hall *et al.* 2005) while continuing to reflect and reproduce urban inequality (McFarlane, 2010).

Strengthening women's entitlements to land and housing

Land tax documents and water bills for households that participated in the SNP were issued in the name of the female household head. MHT and *Saath* also advocated for electricity bills to be issued in the names of the female household heads. A wide range of legal, cultural, economic, political and ideological factors influence women's marginalization in property ownership in South Asian countries (Baruah, 2007b). Such complexities seem to reinforce that urban land tenure in India is best understood as a multifaceted social and political process rather than as a system of laws and rules since it more closely resembles a continuum with many intermediate positions than a dichotomy of what is legal or illegal, formal or informal. A similar analogy can be made for women's property rights in urban areas where concretizing a woman's right of residence in her home may similarly serve as an intermediary position *en route* to the final destination of the right of independent or joint ownership. While the right of ownership can be established only through the execution of a sale deed on secure land, the right of residence can be strengthened through a variety of mechanisms. Since land ownership in its standard form is still not available to an overwhelming majority of slum populations and the concept of joint titles to urban land and housing is just beginning to gain currency, organizations like MHT and *Saath* attempt to empower women with whatever means available. It is usually more of a matter of 'putting women's names' on legal and quasi-legal documents such as promissory notes, electricity bills, and house and land tax. The best slum dwellers are assured of by way of tenure security at the moment is a ten-year guarantee of non-eviction. The NGOs work within this framework while advocating for the appropriate policy instruments and legislation at the state and national level. Enhancing women's ability to secure independent or joint titles to urban land and housing is certainly a worthy long-term goal for organizations like SEWA but documents like water and electricity bills also represent a realistic and effective strategy to enable large numbers of women to strengthen their entitlements to landed resources in urban areas. The two strategies do not have to be mutually exclusive.

Sensitization of other stakeholders and knowledge sharing

The NGOs played a very strategic role in sensitizing the other stakeholders to the ground realities of the lives of the urban poor. For example, MHT convinced AEC not to cut off access to the illegal supplies of electricity in slums until they had laid the cables to install the legal supplies. Through forums such as workshops and seminars organized by MHT and *Saath,* slum residents were able to share the difficulties they faced because of the lack of regular access to electricity. Most revolved around challenges in working at home after sunset, problems children faced with studying and doing their home work, and difficulties in performing household chores. Because the participating slum households already had established relationships with the NGOs, they participated actively in such forums. The NGOs used an informal question-and-answer format to facilitate such sessions, which also made participating in them less intimidating for participating slum families and the CBOs. As a result of such efforts, the partners in the slum electrification programme have worked proactively to ensure that a maximum number of legal electricity connections are provided in the slums of Ahmedabad.

After completion of the pilot project, MHT also organized a series of workshops aimed at sharing the philosophy, process and results of the *Ujala Yojana* with municipalities, electricity providers and NGOs from other cities in Gujarat and Rajasthan. As evidenced by replication of the programme in new cities, these workshops are effective vehicles for demonstrating the feasibility of multiple-stakeholder electrification projects and sharing learning about them.

Hybrid public-private and multiple-stakeholder models in basic service provision are emerging in other parts of the world. For example, Gilbert (2007) describes how the water company in Bogota, Colombia remains in public hands but has increasingly commercialized and subcontracted various functions to the private sector. These models may not be replicable everywhere but they do demonstrate that commercial practices can be combined with relative efficiency, political autonomy and a commitment to cross-subsidies to create systems that work well for different socio-economic groups. Such cases challenge both neoliberal and anti-liberal thinking because they demonstrate the ability to successfully combine public and private practices.

'Working in the dark': NGOs as intermediaries

Through their combined efforts, MHT and *Saath* have succeeded in making a contribution to slum electrification that few other NGOs in India can lay claim to. Their experience suggests that NGOs can play a very effective role in slum electrification as intermediaries between CBOs, municipalities and utilities. They can assist in developing innovative ways of addressing land tenure issues; devising equitable ways of paying for electricity; improving business processes, including metering, billing, collections and rate-making; dealing with non-payment and theft; and developing information and reporting systems by providing feedback to utilities and municipalities. However, it is important to understand that the NGO role in slum electrification is time-consuming, labour-intensive and expensive. Scaling up and optimizing NGO participation in pro-poor electrification activities requires strong state involvement in securing financial resources and developing a policy framework for NGOs to participate in the design and implementation of partnership projects and in the oversight of the electricity reform process in general.

MHT and *Saath* staff identified the absence of policy guidance and financial resources as the biggest impediment for NGO participation in pro-poor electrification projects. In an interview in 2007, Bijal Bhatt, the Coordinator of MHT, emphasized that without a recognized role and legal framework to guide their actions, NGOs are forced to 'work in the dark' in electrification projects. The profitability of slum electrification motivated AEC to progressively reduce connection fees for slum households after the completion of the pilot project. However, AEC completely ignored the pricing guidelines of the survey conducted by *Saath* in setting the unconscionably high connection fees in the pilot project. The lack of a recognized role for NGO participation made it easy for the utility to reject *Saath*'s findings and recommendations. Experiences in other countries corroborate that there is much ambivalence about the role of civil society organizations in electricity reform (Wood, 2005). This ambivalence exists despite the fact that grassroots protests, civil society campaigns and policy critiques are raising concerns about equity and the impact of service changes on the poor, participation in and legitimacy of the reform processes, and the effectiveness of market-based approaches in several countries in the Global South (Bayliss and Hall, 2000; Prayas, 2007; Veriava and Ngwane, 2004, Wamukonya, 2003b). While many private or commercialized utilities welcomed initial NGO involvement in clearing municipal barriers and building community trust, some were uncomfortable with NGOs playing an intermediary role for the indefinite future. In the interview cited previously, Bhatt mentioned that AEC had recently expressed a desire to 'go it alone' in the future. The fact that there were no administrative or capacity building funds available to the NGOs to participate in this project – both MHT and *Saath* had to absorb their own project–related costs – only serves to entrench the perception that the role NGOs play in slum electrification is not particularly valuable. Because the AEC staff did not fully appreciate MHT's role in the slum electrification programme, they were also very unwilling to share credit for the success of the project. During interviews conducted as part of this assessment, many AEC staff openly wondered why it was necessary to involve NGOs at all. The AEC did not share any technical information about electrification with the NGOs nor did it seek to build NGO staff capacity in any way while implementing the project. The need for state and national level policies on the role of NGOs in electricity reform is urgent.

MHT and *Saath* played an indispensable role in the development and implementation of the slum electrification project. While it is unfortunate that they have to 'justify' their long-term involvement in the electrification of urban poor communities, it may be incumbent upon them to make their contributions to the success of the project more visible to the different partners and to the development community at large. Collecting, maintaining and analyzing quantitative and qualitative data on a regular basis about key factors such as improved and effective cost recovery, savings to electricity utilities and municipalities due to NGO involvement, income generation for women, etc. will be crucial for 'legitimizing' and creating a long-term policy role for NGO participation in electrification of urban poor communities. Collaborating with academics and other development professionals to publish findings from such projects in peer-reviewed journals and other key development publications will also strengthen and validate NGO efforts.

CONCLUSIONS

Eighty two percent of urban India was electrified in 2000 versus only 33 percent of rural India (Dubash, 2002). The low rate of access in rural areas is due in part to the high per capita costs of remote rural infrastructural development, one of the reasons why countries like South Africa have said they will focus on off-grid, solar electricity in these areas. While endorsing the role that NGOs can play in electricity reform, it is also important to highlight currently neglected issues that multiple-stakeholder electrification projects must engage with in order to be considered truly socially, econom- ically and environmentally accountable. These include: rural electrification, which one can argue has unintentionally become the worst casualty of the reform process; formal sector job losses and associated social costs that result from downsizing public sector electricity utilities; and environmental considerations – most notably the counterintuitive biases towards fossil fuel-based technologies (nearly 80 percent of current energy generation in India) that electricity reform has, perhaps unintentionally, encouraged. While acknowledging that power sector reform was perhaps inevitable in India, it is also important to debate whether privatization and commercial- ization are the only possible solutions. Are there alternatives, beyond the ones discussed in this chapter, which could ensure an efficient sector that also meets poverty alleviation goals and environmental concerns? Since even so-called progressive strategies for basic service provision, like the ones discussed in this chapter, seem so deeply entrenched in the material and moral inequalities of neoliberal reform, future restructuring is inevitable and necessary.

References

Ahluwalia S. 2000, 'Power tariff reform in India', *Economic and Political Weekly*, 35(38), 3407–3419.

Altvater, E. 2009, 'Postneoliberalism or postcapitalism', *Development Dialogue*, 51(1), 73–88.

Bacon, R.W. and Besant-Jones, J. 2001, 'Global electric power reform, privatization and liberalization of the electric power industry in developing countries', *Annual Review of Energy and the Environment*, 26, 331–359.

Bakker, K. 2007, 'The "Commons" versus the "Commodity": Alter-globalization, anti-privatization and the human right to water in the global south', in *Antipode*, 39(3), 430–455.

Barnes, D.F. 1997, 'Tackling the rural energy problem in developing countries', in *Finance and Development*, 34, 11–15.

Barnes, D.F. and Halpern, J. 2000, 'The role of energy subsidies', in *Energy Services for the World's Poor* (ed.) Energy Sector Management Assistance Programme (World Bank, Washington DC), pp 60–66.

Baruah, B. 2007a, 'Assessment of Public-Private-NGO Partnerships: Water and sanitation services in slums', in *Natural Resources Forum*, 31, 226–237.

Baruah, B. 2007b, 'Gendered realities: Exploring property ownership and tenancy relationships in Urban India', in *World Development*, 35, 2096–2109.

Bayliss, K. and Hall, D. 2000, *Privatisation of water and energy in Africa* (Public Services International Research Unit, University of Greenwich, London).

Bhatt, B. 2007, 'Personal communication', July 31.

Bhatt, E. 2006, *We Are Poor but So Many: The Story of Self-Employed Women in India* (Oxford University Press, New Delhi).

Black, M. 2008, *The Last Taboo: Opening the Door on the Global Sanitation Crisis* (Earthscan, London).

Bond, P. and Dugard, J. 2008, 'The case of Johannesburg water: What really happened at the pre-paid "Parish pump"', in *Law, Democracy and Development*, 12(1), 1–28.

Chen, M. 2008, 'A spreading banyan tree: The self-employed women's association, India', in *From Clients to Citizens: Communities Changing the Course of Their Own Development*, (ed.) A. Mathie and G. Cunningham (Intermediate Technology Publications, Warwickshire, UK), pp. 181–206.

Dubash, N.K. 2002, *Power Politics: Equity and Environment in Electricity Reform* (World Resources Institute, Washington DC).

Fabricius, 2008, 'Resisting representation: The informal geographies of Rio de Janeiro', in *Harvard Design Magazine*, 28(1–8) 5.

Ferguson, R., Wilkinson, W. and Hill, R. 2000, 'Electricity use and economic development', in *Energy Policy*, 28, 923–934.

Flavin, C. and Hull Aeck, M. 2006, *Energy for Development: The potential role for renewable energy in meeting Millennium Development Goals* (Worldwatch Institute, Washington DC).

Gandy, M. 2005, 'Cyborg urbanization: Complexity and monstrosity in the contemporary city', in *International Journal of Urban and Regional Research*, 29(1), 26–49.

Ghanadan, R. 2004, 'Electricity reform in developing and transition countries: A reappraisal', in *Energy*, 31(6/7), 815–844.

Ghanadan, R. 2009, 'Connected geographies and struggles over access: Electricity commercialization in Tanzania', in *Electric Capitalism: Recolonizing Africa on the Power Grid* (ed.) D.A. McDonald (Earthscan, London) pp. 400–436.

Gilbert, A. 2007, 'Water for all: How to combine public management with commercial practice to the benefit of the poor?' in *Urban Studies*, 44(8), 1574.

Graham, S. 2000, 'Constructing premium networked spaces: Reflection on infrastructure networks and contemporary urban development' in *International Journal of Urban and Regional Research*, 24(1), 183–200.

Graham, S. and Marvin, S. 2001, *Splintering Urbanism: Networked Infrastructure, Technological Mobilities and the Urban Condition* (Routledge, London).

Graham, S. 2010, 'When infrastructures fail', in *Disrupted Cities: When Infrastructure Fails* (ed.) S. Graham (Routledge: New York and London) pp 1–26.

Gulyani S. and Bassett, E.M. 2007, 'Retrieving the baby from the bathwater: slum upgrading in Sub-Saharan Africa', in *Environment and Planning C: Government and Policy*, 25(4), 486–515.

Gulyani, S. and Bassett, E.M. 2008, 'Revisiting... retrieving the baby from the bathwater: Slum upgrading in Sub-Saharan Africa', in *Environment and Planning C: Government and Policy*, 26, 858–860.

Ha, P. and Porcaro, J. 2005, 'Energy and the millennium development goals: The impact of rural energy services on development', in *Journal of International Affairs*, 58(2), 193–209.

Hall, D. Lethbridge, J. and Lobina, E. 2005, *Public-Public Partnerships in Health and Essential Services* (Municipal Services Project, Cape Town).

Hunt, S, 2002, *Making Competition Work in Electricity* (Wiley, New York).

Kessides, I. 2004, *Reforming Infrastructure: Privatization, Regulation and Competition* (World Bank and Oxford University Press, Washington DC and Oxford).

Kundu, A. and Mahadevia, D. 2002, *Poverty and Vulnerability in a Globalizing Metropolis: Ahmedabad* (Manak Publications, New Delhi).

McCarthy, J, 2005, 'Commons as counter-hegemonic projects', in *Capitalism Nature Socialism*, 16(1), 9–24.

McDonald, D.A. 2009a, 'Electric capitalism: Conceptualizing electricity and capital accumulation in (South) Africa', in *Electric Capitalism: Recolonizing Africa on the Power Grid* (ed.) D.A. McDonald (Earthscan, London) pp. 1–49.

McDonald, DA, 2009b, 'Conclusion: Alternative electricity paths for southern Africa', in *Electric Capitalism: Recolonizing Africa on the Power Grid* Ed DA McDonald (Earthscan, London) pp 437–453.

McFarlane, C. 2010, 'Infrastructure, interruption, and inequality: Urban life in the global South', in *Disrupted Cities: When Infrastructure Fails* (ed.) S. Graham (Routledge: New York and London) pp. 131–144.

MHT, 2006, *My Home, My Workplace* (SEWA Mahila Housing Trust, Ahmedabad, India).

Pasternak, A.D. 2000, *Global energy futures and human development: A framework for analysis* (US Department of Energy, Washington DC).

Prayas, 2007, 'Need for Collective, Proactive and Vigilant Actions by Consumer Groups' *Money Life* (Accessed online on 29 December 2009 at www.pray aspune.org/peg/energy_home.php).

Robbins, P. 2003, 'Transnational corporations and the discourse of water privatization', in *Journal of International Development*, 15, 1073–1082.

Rose, K. 1992, *Where Women are Leaders: The SEWA Movement in India* (Zed Books, London and New Jersey).

SEA, 2006, *State of Energy in South African Cities: Setting a Baseline* (Sustainable Energy Africa, Cape Town).

UN-Energy, 2005, *The Energy Challenge for Achieving the Millennium Development Goals* (United Nations, New York).

USAID, 2004, *Innovative Approaches to Slum Electrification* (USAID, Washington DC).

Veriava, A. and Ngwane, T. 2004, 'Strategies and tactics: Movements in the neoliberal transition', in *Development update 5: Mobilizing for change. The rise of the new social movements in South Africa* (eds) D. McKinley, P. Naidoo (Interfund, Johannesburg), pp. 129–145.

Waddams Price, C. 2000, 'Better energy services, better energy sectors – and links with the poor', in *Energy Services for the World's Poor* (ed.) Energy sector management assistance programme (World Bank, Washington DC) pp 26–32.

Wamukonya N. 2003a, 'Power sector reform in developing countries: mismatched agendas' *Energy Policy*, 31(12), 1273–1289.

Wamukonya, N. 2003b, *Electricity Reform: Social and Environmental Challenges* (United Nations Environmental Programme, Roskilde, Denmark).

Wood, D. 2005, 'Taking power: Social and political dynamics of the energy sector', paper presented at the *New Frontiers of Social Policy* conference, Arusha, Tanzania, December 12–15; available online at www.siteresources.world bank.org/Resources/takingpower.pdf

World Energy Assessment, 2000, *World Energy Assessment: Energy and the Challenge of Sustainability* (United Nations, New York).

Chapter 11

From consumers to customers

Regularizing electricity networks in São Paulo's favelas

Andrés Luque-Ayala

INTRODUCTION

An estimated 20 per cent of the population of São Paulo, Brazil, lives in favelas, informal neighbourhoods established through illegal occupation. São Paulo's favelas and tenements (*cortiços*) are the main spaces of inequality in the city, with nearly 69 per cent of households earning only up to one minimum wage, legally defined as approximately US$300 per month, or less (UN Habitat, 2010). Since the early 2000s the State of São Paulo and the different municipalities that compose the Greater São Paulo Metropolitan Region have taken significant steps to address issues of inequality in the city, by providing a variety of improvements in infrastructural and living conditions in favelas (Cities Alliance, 2004; UN Habitat, 2010; Fernandes, 2011). A key expression of these efforts is an increase in formal electricity coverage. Favelas, traditionally served by a mix of formal and informal – or illegal – electricity connections, have become the focus of electricity regularization programmes. Such initiatives, implemented by private electricity providers often working in partnership with local governments, respond to mandatory requirements established by federal legislation. They exemplify a form of urban retrofit with positive social repercussions (through increased resource access) that also provides opportunities for increased urban sustainability by lowering the city's resource consumption (through a focus on efficiency). Materially, such initiatives involve deploying the city's electricity grid into areas historically characterised by informal and limited service provision. Socially, it means the recognition of the right to connection to the city's utility networks, and through this an acknowledgement of settlement rights.

This chapter argues that, despite its apparent technical nature, the sustainable urban retrofit associated with electricity provision in São Paulo's favelas is largely political in nature, characterised by its concern with an expansion of energy markets and, through this, the advancement of neoliberal understandings of the city. Such retrofit occurs through a socio-material reconfiguration of the urban electricity grid achieved via two interlinked rationalities. First, a reconfiguration of energy consumers into customers, or more explicitly, the transformation of those accessing electricity in an informal, unmetered and unregulated manner into metered and regulated customers with monthly responsibilities for the payment of electricity services. Second, a reconfiguration of notions of sustainability into 'ability to pay', achieved via an intervention in consumer practices towards an increase in energy conservation and a reduction in electricity use.

The analysis starts with an acknowledgement of the inherently political nature of urban infrastructures (Graham and Marvin, 2001), and of the specificity of infrastructure in cities in the global South (Bakker, 2003; McFarlane and Rutherford, 2008). The chapter contributes to a geographical debate around urban infrastructures, by examining specific processes of subjectification – or the creation of specific forms of environmental subjectivity– in the context of resource use (Dowling, 2010; Leffers and Ballamingie, 2013) and through interventions in social practices (Shove, 2004; Shove et al. 2012). The analysis draws on Foucault's governmentality (Foucault, 2009; Walters, 2012), focusing specifically on the way governing occurs through the mobilisation of particular forms of subjectivity (Raco and Imrie, 2000; Dean, 2010) and, in the case of neoliberal governmentalities, the promotion of a calculative subject willing to measure its experience in terms of financial gains, losses, costs and benefits (Rankin, 2001; Barnett et al. 2008; Miller and Rose, 2008). Drawing on the work of Bulkeley et al. (2015), this governmentality approach is complemented with theoretical contributions developed by scholars working on the interface between practice theory and infrastructures of consumption (Chappells and Shove, 2004; Van Vliet et al. 2005; Spaargaren, 2011). This means a discussion around ways of 'conducting conducts' (Foucault, 2009), framed by a recognition that retrofitting towards more 'sustainable' service provision must be based not only on new technologies but also on different consumption routines and practices. Such approach opens the possibility for new environmental and resource subjectivities working alongside new types of interactions between utilities and users (Van Vliet et al. 2005; Shove and Walker, 2007).

The resulting analysis suggests that successful urban sustainability retrofits, beyond being solely technological interventions, are political interventions that rely on specific understandings of the subject. In this case this involves the promotion of both an environmentally conscious or an energy aware individual, a move that, is inevitably entangled in the expansion of specific political rationalities. In the case of electricity access in São Paulo, a neoliberal rationality embodied in the expansion of energy markets is brought about in the context of social objectives review of through government regulation. This rationality is enacted through the promotion of demand practices in line with energy efficiency principles, which results in low energy bills that facilitate the creation of a new electricity market around low-income population.

Empirically, the chapter draws on project visits and interviews with members of staff of the private energy utility companies working in the São Paulo Metropolitan Region: AES Eletropaulo, Elektro Eletricidade e Servicos SA and EDP Bandeirantes. This was complemented with secondary sources obtained through a desktop review of how the organizations involved in the electricity retrofit describe their projects. The empirical material was collected in 2011 in the context of a broader research aimed at examining local energy governance in the São Paulo Metropolitan Region. The chapter's focus is on the way subjects are imagined and energy practices are fostered, and, as a result, the emphasis lies on the perspective of utility companies rather than users.

Retrofitting electricity infrastructure in São Paulo: Reverting the exclusionary trend of a 'splintered' network

Retrofitting the city for sustainability in the global South is both a social and technical effort, starting with increasing resource access and infrastructural connectivity. The way in which networked infrastructures, such as electricity, water, sewerage and telecommunications, shape both the spatial and political dynamics of the city is well documented. In the western world, between 1880 and 1960, access to electricity networks was instrumental for the emergence of the modern ideal of universal access and urban cohesion (Hughes, 1983; Nye, 1999). This modern ideal was not to last long, however, as the privatisation and liberalisation of utilities characteristic of the 1980s and 1990s resulted in processes of 'urban splintering', signalling the collapse of the idea of the integrated networked city (Graham and Marvin, 2001). The splintering urbanism thesis developed by Graham and Marvin points to the significant role of infrastructure in configuring issues of access, justice and equality in the city. Its application in non-OECD countries reveals additional layers of complexity. In cities of the global South, where the realisation of a modern infrastructural ideal has been highly uneven (Coutard, 2008), infrastructure throughout the twentieth century has been described as 'splintered' rather than 'splintering' (Kooy and Bakker, 2008: 1843).

Cities like São Paulo – are testament to a mode of service provision historically concentrated on the wealthy (Gandy, 2006; McFarlane, 2008). Rather than being based on a single unified network, infrastructure in cities of the global South is often characterised by a multiplicity of – formal and informal – provision mechanisms, configuring the city as a set of 'archipelagos' that make up 'spatially separated but linked 'islands' of networked supply' (Bakker, 2003: 337). In cities where a significant portion of the population lies outside the network itself (Gandy, 2006; Kooy and Bakker, 2008), the 'archipelagos' metaphor points to the social inequalities embedded within connection and disconnection (Swyngedouw, 2004), and to existing tensions between connectivity and issues of affordability, quality and reliability (Franceys, 2005; Furlong, 2012). In the context of overlapping formal/regulated and informal/unregulated strategies for service provision, electricity networks and interventions in cities of the global South often generate further fragmentation by exclusively linking social agendas supporting the disadvantaged with the formalised spaces of the city. Such interventions disregard those sectors of the population in greater need and who are often living in informal/unregulated conditions (Jaglin, 2008: 1897).

The urban electricity retrofit of São Paulo reverts the exclusionary trends described above, by prioritizing investments in urban infrastructure in the unregulated areas of the city. Electricity coverage in São Paulo is nearly 100 per cent. However, this is provided by a combination of formal supply and informal connections. By 2006 only 70 per cent of the residents of the city's favelas and tenements were formally connected to the electricity grid, a relatively low figure when compared to 97.3 per cent living outside favelas and tenements (USAID, 2009). Informal connections are seen as illegal by both the state and private utility providers, and underpinning a deep sense of exclusion within those who use them (Mimmi and Ecer, 2010). They are undersized for the amount of energy they are required to deliver and present constant voltage variations that result in supply interruptions and damaged domestic appliances. They are also characterised by the use of improvised substandard equipment and an absence of safety standards leading to fires and health hazards. Whilst this limited connectivity is an expression of the broader social justice challenges that characterise the city, it also has implications for issues of resource consumption and sustainability. The unmetered and unregulated nature of informal connections leads to high consumption patterns.

Since the 1990s, both federal and state governments in Brazil have taken significant steps towards the reduction of urban inequality via slum upgrading and the regularization of favelas (UN Habitat, 2010). As part of these attempts to regularise favelas, the federal government, through the Electricity Act of 2002, mandated the electricity sector – deregulated in 1996 – to achieve 100 per cent electricity coverage. Until the 1st decade of the 2000s the electricity sector avoided a solid engagement with favelas, as this was seen as engaging with 'a segment of customers considered to have little or no return value on investment in the near to mid-term, primarily because most were already informally (illegally) connected to the electricity system but were not paying for their usage' (USAID, 2009: 11). Since 2006, formal electricity access figures indicate that the formal electrification of favelas has made rapid progress in recent years (UN Habitat, 2010). Such progress has been achieved with the additional support of federal legislation on energy conservation developed by ANEEL, Brazil's national electricity regulator. These federal mandates require electricity utilities to invest 1 per cent of their annual net income in R&D and energy efficiency initiatives (*Lei 9.991, de 24 de Julho de 2000*). The investment is highly regulated, covering energy efficiency (50 per cent of the funds) and research and development (20 per cent of the funds), amongst other areas. Since 2010, the pro-poor policies established by President Lula have required 60 per cent of the energy efficiency funds to be invested amongst low-income customers (*Lei 12.212, de 1 de Dezembro de 2010*).

It is within this context that electricity distributors in São Paulo have developed programs to regularize energy networks in their respective geographic areas of responsibility. These have been largely modelled after an 'integrated' (social and technical) approach to slum electrification piloted in 2006 by AES Eletropaulo, the largest electricity distribution company within the São Paulo Metropolitan Region, with the support of USAID and the International Copper Association (USAID, 2009). Whilst each utility company is autonomous on how to develop such programs, they all share a technical intervention through the installation of electricity meters in dwellings, the use of anti-theft cables (to avoid further illegal connections), and the redeployment of the neighbourhood grid via transformers and other equipment for electricity distribution. These programs also place a strong emphasis in lowering consumption levels as a means to increase payment capacity. In this way, the development of particular types of users, ones who consume less electricity and thus have the ability to pay for it, becomes a constituting element of the electricity retrofit.

Governing retrofits: The role of configuring subjectivities

The transformation of urban energy infrastructures – for reasons as varied as resource access, sustainability, energy efficiency and the need to manage demand in the context of limited supply – inevitably requires significant amounts of governing: conducting the conduct of others towards the achievement of a predetermined set of goals (Foucault, 2009). The agents involved in such governing efforts are not limited to the formal institutions of the state, but include a plethora of other actors, private and public, human and non-human. In procuring the required financial resources for the retrofit and securing physical access to the (often informal and unregulated) areas of the city where the retrofit is required, governing energy infrastructures is revealed as a complex exercise in power and an attempt in realising authority. Governing is understood here as the art of achieving the 'right disposition of things' (Foucault, 2009: 98). It means 'to act on the actions of subjects who retain the capacity to act otherwise' (Li, 2007: 17). In the urban retrofit, the achievement of the right disposition of things is only possible if the objectives of the subjects of government and those of the governor are aligned (Dean, 2010).

Given its emphasis on the interface between the rationalities underpinning action, the techniques that make it possible and the subjectivities that are constructed in the process, a governmentality framework provides useful entry points for evaluating São Paulo's urban electricity retrofit. In the past, various scholars have used governmentality to uncover how processes of subjectification play a key role in the constitution of electricity networks in cities. Bulkeley *et al.* (2015) have pointed out how governing smart grid development – achieving its defining nature around 'active network management' – relies on acknowledging domestic practices and advancing a transformation of how users engage with electricity. Similarly, Giavedoni has uncovered how specific governmental technologies aimed at securing energy services for the poor (e.g. social tariffs) operate not only as a form of energy governance but also as an intervention that consolidates a neoliberal rationality through the creation of 'deprived subjects' and the roll out of strategies that regulate behaviour and consumption (Giavedoni, 2011).

As an analytical approach, governmentality is 'concerned with thought as it becomes linked to and is embedded in technical means for the shaping and reshaping of conduct' (Dean, 2010: 27). It examines the role that shaping subjectivities plays in the activity of governing. This means unpacking the mechanisms by which the objectives of the governed are aligned with those of the governor – and by doing so, revealing how it is possible to govern through freedom (Rose, 1999; Dean, 2010). In the case of neoliberal regimes, governmentality analyses have revealed how such regimes 'actively create the conditions within which entrepreneurial and competitive conduct is possible' whilst establishing techniques that enable a form of economic freedom that is practised as personal autonomy (Barry *et al.* 1996: 10). Governing, thus, occurs 'without governing *society*, [but] through regulated choices made by discrete and autonomous actors' (Rose, 1996: 328, original emphasis). New forms of rationality are fostered in subjects, with individuals and organizations required to measure their experience in terms of costs and benefits, financial gains and losses and productivity maximization (Rose, 1999). The economic and moral dimensions of actors merge, aiming for the production of 'prudent subjects' whose morality is entangled with a rational assessment of costs and benefits (Barnett, *et al.* 2008: 629; see also Lockwood and Davidson, 2010). Subject formation is undertaken not only by the state, but also by a multiplicity of other actors (Rose, 1999; Barnett *et al.* 2008). Dean refers to this configuration of identities as a technique of citizenship: 'a strategy or technique for the transformation of subjectivity from powerlessness to active citizenship' (2010: 83). Here citizenship and freedom come together, as citizenship is not an entitlement, but a manifestation of 'free' individual choice (Rankin, 2001; Leffers and Ballamingie, 2013).

Neoliberal governmentalities see citizenship developed not only in relation to the state and the public sphere, but also to other actors and spaces, particularly in relation to spaces of consumption. The power of the citizen is activated in public and private domains, including corporate and semi-public practices beyond the dwelling such as working and shopping (Rose, 1999: 166). It has been argued that this establishment of neoliberal rationalities through subjectification imposes limits on the possibilities for pursuing agendas outside such rationales. This has been illustrated by Rankin (2001: 27) in her study of women and microcredit in Nepal, where 'the market has become an end in itself and microcredit has been identified as the governmental technology most suited to the objective of building [rural] financial markets'. Here a multiplicity of interests intersect beyond those of state actors, such as the aim of private interests to position and sell their products through techniques of identity and identification, targeting and developing communities for marketing, fostering specific lifestyles and narratives, and developing ethical implications associated to conducting one's life in a particular manner (Rose, 1999).

Retrofitting consumption practices in the city

Whilst traditional approaches to (formal) electricity infrastructures see users as the passive receivers of a service, a re-consideration of the role of users opens up possibilities for them to become active players in the 'co-management' of demand *between* consumers and providers' (Van Vliet *et al.* 2005: 3, original emphasis). Here users of electricity are no longer 'anonymous captive users', but rather a new type of 'energy subject' (Van Vliet, 2004: 79). Combining governmentality with a practice theory approach, Bulkeley *et al.* (2015) argue that transforming the electricity network depends on the reconfiguration of everyday practice and the creation of new forms of electricity conducts in the subjects of intervention. They draw on previous work around infrastructures of consumption which points to a new understanding of the relationship between consumer (demand) and provider (supply) in energy, water and other urban systems (Chappells and Shove, 2004; Van Vliet *et al.* 2005; Spaargaren, 2011). When used to evaluate environmental innovation in urban infrastructures, such approaches recognize that the relationship between consumer and provider is mediated by technology, and that existing technological systems shape both demand patterns and consumption practices. As a result, new modes of 'sustainable' provision must be based not only on new technologies but also on different routines and practices, opening the possibility for new types of interaction between utilities and users. The recognition of how both institutions and infrastructures create and structure patterns of demand points to the relevance of such analysis of the co-evolution of technology and consumption practice (Van Vliet *et al.* 2005). Consumers are considered to be the sensitive fingertips of the system, and hence play a key role in its functioning (Southerton *et al.* 2004; Van Vliet *et al.* 2005). Drawing on practice theory, this approach to infrastructure requires an understanding of the processes of transformation towards greater (or lesser) sustainability via an analysis of the forms of know-how, routines and expectations embedded within sociotechnical regimes. It calls for a better understanding of the 'patterns of demand inscribed in what remain largely technological templates for the future' (Shove and Walker, 2010: 471). This leads to a recognition that any transformation – or, for that matter, retrofit – towards more sustainable regimes is likely to require a new set of expectations, new understandings of everyday life, and 'different forms of consumption and practice' (Shove and Walker, 2010: 471).

It is in this sense that a transition towards sustainability must depend on social innovation rather than on technical or institutional innovation. However, this implies calling society's status quo into question, as new conventions, regimes of resource consumption, routines and know-how are envisioned. As a result, transitions are not smooth processes, but rather involve contestation and fracture (Shove, 2010). Yet, practice theory and the literature on infrastructures of consumption provide limited access points for an understanding of the rationalities and logics that inform different forms of consumption. This constrains the possibility of meaningfully engaging with the politics associated with the urban retrofit efforts. This possibility is opened by Bulkeley *et al.* whose combination of practice theory and governmentality highlights both 'the unruly, emergent nature of practice' and the extent to which such practice 'may just as likely emerge from the social and private world as from interventions designed to act on practice in line with particular governmental projects' (2015: 125).

Targeting urban inequality: The regularization of electricity in São Paulo's favelas

In 2006 the U.S. Agency for International Development (USAID) in partnership with AES Eletropaulo launched a program to test integrated solutions in urban energy with the twin purpose of slum electrification and electricity loss reduction. The explicit objective of the program was 'to convert formerly 'free' electricity consumers into satisfied and paying customers in a manner that was financially viable for the distribution company' (USAID, 2009: 1). The program was designed in three phases. The first of these involved 'pre-regularization' activities, including the establishment of contact with community leaders and the development of community campaigns aimed at preparing 'the population for the upcoming changes'. This initial phase mapped customers whilst developing educational activities. The second phase, known as 'regularization', involved, for the first time, the installation of electricity meters in all households, alongside new electricity distribution equipment at the neighbourhood level. The third and final phase, 'post-regularization', focused on additional community campaigns and one-to-one work with the new customers to improve energy efficiency.

This involved deploying a team of community facilitators to explain new customers how to read their electricity bill, discuss with them the link between consumption level and financial charge, and jointly examine the household's electricity consumption (usage and equipment) in order to identify possible reasons for above average consumption. Resulting from this interaction, community facilitators would provide a set of recommendations to customers on how to reduce consumption. Very often these recommendations suggested avoiding unnecesary high powered equipment for certain domestic uses, using instead more efficient and appropriate power equipment that achieves the desired function via a lower electricity consumption (e.g. avoiding the use of electric showers for kitchen functions such as making coffee, or the use of kitchen fridges for air cooling at home). Project literature highlights how 'the upgrades of the distribution system and service infrastructure made it more difficult to steal electricity and provided safer, better quality, more reliable and efficient electricity service within the area' (USAID, 2009: 1).

The pilot project, implemented in the favela of Paraisópolis, is considered a success by the institutions involved. It is hailed as responsible for two key results: a 40 per cent reduction in electricity consumption and a reduction in non-payment from 98 per cent to 32 per cent within the pilot area. The investment generated a payback for the utility company of less than 1.4 years, with an additional benefit associated with 'the transformation of non-paying or illegal electricity consumers into paying customers' (USAID, 2009: 1). The pilot sits within a broader initiative called *Program for the Transformation of Consumers into Clients*, created by AES Eletropaulo in 2004, and provided a template for other private utility companies to follow. Between 2004 and 2011 AES Eletropaulo connected 437,000 clients, and over 1,750,000 people. The final user is not charged directly for the regularization of the electricity network, and the costs are assumed by the private utility company. Surveys with beneficiary population develop by AES Eletropaulo claim an approval rate between 83 and 98 per cent. The main reasons cited by beneficiaries are the elimination of fire risks resulting from low-quality electricity connections, the provision of stable electricity connections that do not damage white goods, reliability in electricity provision and access to a registered address in the form of a utility bill (AES Eletropaulo, 2011).

The model implemented by AES Eletropaulo draws inspiration from business models referred to as 'the bottom of the pyramid', specifically developed to target the poorest socio-economic groups of society, particularly in developing countries (Prahalad and Hart, 2002; London and Hart, 2004; Hart, 2005). These models operate within neoliberal rationalities and advocate for an understanding of the poor not as victims, but as a profit opportunity developed through low profit margins in tandem with large sales volume and capital efficiency. The emphasis is on 'creating buying power, shaping aspirations, improving access and tailoring local solutions', configuring the poor as 'a very profitable market' (Prahalad and Hart 2002: 5–6). As an approach to the informal spaces of the city, it is not far from de Soto's *Mystery of Capital* (2000), where the slum is rich in dormant assets to be unlocked through their capital incorporation into formal economies. Both 'the bottom of the pyramid' as well as de Soto's transformation of the slum's dead urban assets into liquid capital have been termed by critical urban scholars as a form of 'poverty capitalism', characterised by 'the conversion of poverty into capital' whilst drawing the 'new frontiers of capital accumulation' (Roy, 2011: 228–229).

The role of energy efficiency: reconfiguring sustainability as 'ability to pay'

In the case of São Paulo's electricity retrofit, the transformation of consumers into clients relies on two specific interventions: the installation of electricity meters and the introduction of energy efficiency measures aimed at transforming consumption practices. First, a material intervention in the form of meters constitutes a new subject within the electricity network, now easily identifiable, calculative, accountable and with the responsibility to pay for its metered consumption. This material intervention governs the relationship between consumer and utility operator. Yet, the meter does not establish the frontier of activity of the utility company, since the utility company also attempts to change demand practices (Guy and Marvin, 1996). Meters and technical interventions at the neighbourhood level are supplemented by a domestic program for energy efficiency. This includes the substitution of incandescent light bulbs, the retrofit of household energy installations aiming at the identification and reduction of leakages, and, for some of the new clients, the substitution of old and low efficiency fridges and the substitution of electric showers for solar water heaters or electric showers of lower wattage – see Figures 11.1 and 11.2. There is also innovation and experimentation with energy efficiency products, such as the use of heat recovery shower mats aimed at pre-heating showering water.

The energy efficiency program also targets user practices. Indeed, their transformation is one of the pillars of the electricity regularisation initiative. With the installation of electricity meters thousands of low-income families face, for the first time a requirement to pay for their electricity consumption. Initial bills tend to be large, as the historic combination of unmetered and unpaid electricity generated high consumption demand patterns. The nature of the built environment within favelas contributes to this high demand, with many dwellings having few or no windows thus requiring permanent electric lighting and cooling systems. The use of electric showers, the most popular form of heating water for showering in Brazil (Andrade de Souza, 2009), adds to this elevated consumption. In

Figure 11.1 Solar hot water system donated by utility company

Figure 11.2 Retrofitted domestic electricity networks

addition, allegedly as a result of the large availability of credit for the purchase of electric goods in Brazil (Oliven and Pinheiro-Machado, 2012), favela inhabitants make extensive use of a variety of electric goods such as white appliances, large screen televisions, DVDs and stereos, further increasing electricity demand.

Energy companies see the combined issue of energy affordability and high consumption habits as the main hurdle in the roll out of the electricity regularisation programs in the city. The need to transform practices of consumption in order to align service provision with the overall payment capacity of the specific market is seen as an imperative towards the development of this new market. Notions of sustainability adopt new meanings within the space of consumption, with 'ability to pay' becoming a form of sustainability. As illustrated by a Community Program Manager of an electricity distribution company, the key challenge with the low-income markets 'is to find a solution for those families to reduce their consumption over time in a sustainable way... we want to significantly reduce the energy consumption of that population, without necessarily affecting their comfort... to talk about sustainability, to find a solution so that people have the capacity to consume our services' (Anonymised interview, 2011b). Fostering in these new energy subjects a form of consumption in line with their payment capacity enables the consumption of commercial energy services. As the Community Program Manager further explains, 'it does not make any sense for us to bring these services to the people if they do not manage to pay for them. And the way I have to help them in achieving such capacity for payment is to help them to reduce their consumption, so that they have the conditions to have regular access to energy'.

In response to this challenge, utility companies have implemented educational programmes and awareness raising activities on energy consumption. In parallel, payments for electricity are introduced in a phased manner allowing for gradual adjustment. Users receive an electricity bill from the moment the meter is connected, although for the first months they are not required to pay the full cost. The first electricity bills operate as a record of the level of consumption, and as a warning on the costs associated to such consumption. Teams of community support officers carry out door-to-door visits helping users monitor their consumption, working with customers on the identification of the reasons behind high electricity usage and promoting changes in consumption practices – see Figure 11.3. Drawing on business models around 'the bottom of the pyramid', a reduction in consumption enables a lower expenditure in electricity services for each consumer, something that is highly valued by utility companies: '...if we allow users to spend too much energy, they will not have enough money to pay the bill... For us it is interesting if they consume less and pay the bill rather than consuming a lot and not being able to pay. ... Lots of people do not have the means to pay USD$45 per month as a bill. Now, to pay USD$14 per month,

Figure 11.3 Community facilitator discussing energy issues with a user
Image copyright AES Eletropaulo

practically over 95 per cent of the families have the means to pay regularly. That is our objective' (Anonymised interview, 2011b). This approach lowers profit margins for the utility company, but is balanced by large sales volume and capital efficiency.

Whilst a combination of market rationalities and social objectives characterise this electricity retrofit, its social dimensions go beyond strategies for changing consumption practice. Favelas are often characterised by low institutional presence alongside a variety of illegal activities and parallel (non-formal) authorities that restrict access and mobility for those who do not live in them. Within this context, a wide variety of social strategies and the mobilisation of additional community benefits are used by electricity companies to secure the physical access of its staff members to the favela, ensuring that their work is carried out without local resistance or disruption. This requires negotiations with local leaders during the 'pre-regularization' phase towards obtaining permission for access. This initial phase often involves the donation of non-energy related goods and services such as a community centre, sports facilities, playgrounds, training and educational programmes. Non-governmental organizations with experience in community programmes often play an important intermediary role, brokering the relationship between the community and the utility company. Formal energy provision by the private sector, perceived as a public good, also occurs through public sector mediation: the initial access to the favela is often carried out alongside representatives of the municipal government, which benefits from a renewed presence in those spaces of the city where local government has historically been absent. As explained by the Energy Efficiency Manager of a private energy provider, municipal authorities facilitate contact with 'community leaders and the population, to aid in the integration of those new consumers with the electricity provider. [This intervention] also helps the mayor's office, because it is taking the municipality to areas where before they would not have so much access. So there is a gain for both sides' (Anonymised interview, 2011a).

Besides a safer energy network which reduces the risk of fires and accidents, utility companies point to an additional social benefit: a renewed recognition of rights and citizenship. Along with the installation of electricity meters, both the municipality and the utility company find a need for implementing street names, installing street signage and developing a formal address registration system – see Figure 11.4. For dwellers in informal settlements a registered address is an important asset that facilitates access to a variety of social services, including postal deliveries, credit and others, arguably contributing to social inclusion. Marketing material prepared by AES Eletropaulo highlights these benefits, stating that the regularization of electricity 'encourages the exercise of citizenship, since [beneficiaries] will officially have a proof of address' (AES Eletropaulo, 2011: 10; translated from Portuguese). This claim to social benefits beyond electricity access is illustrated by a Community Program Manager at a utility company, whom, by imagining a dialogue between a favela inhabitant and a credit provider, emphasises a newly generated visibility that reaffirms a form of citizenship which, in his words, is achieved through energy payment:

> People [in favelas] do not have a fixed address. As soon as you install a meter, and they have an address with [the utility company], then they have a fixed address, they can ask for credit... 'I exist'. You can say where you live. 'I live in X street'; 'Can you give me a document to prove that you live there?' 'No, I don't have'. Now they can! They pay energy, and therefore they have that document. That is part of that inclusion. ...You're going to pay for energy, but thanks to you paying energy you're going to have citizenship, greater security, a series of benefits, that I am putting in place for you.
>
> (Anonymised interview, 2011b)

Following the same logic of de Soto's *Mistery of Capital* (2000) – and its reproduction of capital through tenure security via property titles – citizenship is realised through the ability to operate within markets. The energy bill is seen as a document that recognises and provides proof of residence, enabling further access to other financial and social services. What is interesting here is how a renewed recognition of citizenship is achieved through an engagement with networked infrastructures, particularly the energy grid. The space from where such recognition occurs is also worthy of attention: an expansion of energy markets under the leadership of the private sector. In the case of favelas, access to formal energy means more than an upgrade in service provision. Yet, this attempt to create customers out of consumers is not exempt from conflict and challenge. Transforming consumption practices is not always a straightforward process. In narrating the experience of these electricity retrofit efforts, the Brazilian media reports persistent user complaints around excessive electricity charges in favelas. Users blame what they see as faulty electricity meters. They voice their financial struggles, as they are requested to pay the accumulated utility charges of months and sometimes years, or face disconnection. Utility companies respond to these complaints by pointing out that the meter readings are accurate, and the high bills are the result of a sustained high consumption (Balza, 2011; Vieira, 2009). Brazilian academics have argued that the electricity payments brought about by the retrofit efforts have limited the ability of low-income population to adjust to challenging economic conditions, by making it more difficult to develop micro-enterprises at home – a common practice within favela's economic life (Mestre, 2013). Research conducted in 2013 in the favela Heliopolis, arguably the largest in the city, illustrates the extent to which illegal connections remain after the electricity retrofit, by documenting cases where users tamper with the newly installed electricity meters in order to avoid payment.

Figure 11.4 Plaques indicating street names

In dealing with this, utility companies avoid confrontation by promptly replacing those meters and staying away from the enforcement of fines (Mestre, 2013). The retrofit indeed brings efficiency and through a form of this sustainability, but it is a contested space that is transforming electricity access for the poor in both positive and negative ways.

CONCLUSION

In the urban infrastructure literature, the shift in the primary concern of electricity utility companies from supply to demand has traditionally been seen as an attempt to achieve broader network balance, operating as a co-management mechanism that reduces peak loads and fosters both environmental innovation and energy efficiency (Van Vliet *et al.* 2005). It accounts for a significant change, as 'electricity ceases to be taken for granted and greater attention is directed to the... energy system' (Guy and Marvin, 1996: 153). Yet, the case of São Paulo provides an example of a transformation in consumption practices where the primary objective is not exclusively the co-management of the grid through systemic transformation, but the creation of new electricity subjects operating under specific political rationalities: a low-income consumer that, with limited access to financial means but operating as the engine of an emerging neoliberal economic model centred around the poor, can regularly pay for electricity services.

The process of transforming existing informal and illegal electricity networks and unmetered consumers into formal networks and metered customers, referred by the organizations involved as a 'transformation of consumers into customers' (USAID, 2009), relies on a wide range of social interventions. These are both energy and non-energy related, and have broad political implications ranging from issues of state presence to the recognition of citizenship. In São Paulo, where what is at stake is a process of incorporation of a partially connected and informal archipelago to the formal (connected and regularised) network, the retrofit efforts attempt to transform not only material networks but also consumption practices. Electricity demand practices take a renewed role, not necessarily as the primary mechanism to achieve sustainability or connectivity, but as the prerequisite for a new mode of energy circulation through markets, and thus, for maintaining long term connectivity within a new economic model. The regularization of electricity networks in the city's favelas, mandated by national legislation but implemented by the private sector, is mediated through market logics seeking to expand energy markets and facilitate the – now regulated – circulation of energy in the city.

In these conditions, notions of affordability, sustainability, energy efficiency and a change in consumption practices are mobilised as the key elements of this retrofit, playing an important role in the creation of a new market and in securing revenues for the incumbent utility providers. It is precisely the interaction between utility and user, through payment capacities enabled by energy efficiency, that permits the existence of the network: a rebundling that responds to both social and market objectives. Practices of demand are thus fully connected to the network – becoming an integral part of it, but also connected to a broader political economy. Energy interventions open up spaces where a specific type of urban politics is addressed: they engage with a social agenda, where the emphasis lies on issues of poverty alleviation, social justice and the poor's ability to pay for essential services, but through a clear logic of market expansion and the need to remove obstacles in the circulation of energy through markets. The mobilisation of a change in practices does not only respond to notions of sustainability or resource efficiency, but primarily to notions of affordability towards securing the development of new markets. Whilst in this case market based logics and ecological objectives appear to support each other, a multipliticity of tensions and contradictions are generated in the process. The connection between market and ecological objectives rests on a desired change in practice which is contingent and resisted. Notions of sustainability are mobilised with new meanings (ability to pay), and are subservient to market development logics. The same applies to social objectives, which are mobilised only in as much they serve a market rationale. Infrastructure comes to matter politically by shedding light on specific forms through which citizenship is recognised, yet still opening opportunities to move towards more or less inequality beyond and above energy connection and disconnection.

The combination of governmentality and practice theory leads to un-covering the mechanisms behind the governing of social practice: the governing of energy use requires intervening in social practices and the creation of new forms of conduct. This involves new forms of 'self-government' and their alignment with specific rationalities, such as climate change, energy efficiency, or, in the case of São Paulo, neoliberal ration-alities that operate through market expansion. The key contribution of governmentality to an understanding of consumption practices lies precisely in the acknowledgment of the link between a change in practice and the political nature of the embedded rationalities within such change.

References

AES Eletropaulo. (2011). *Programa de Transformação de Consumidores em Clientes.* [Online] August 2011. Available from: www.consumomaisinteligente.com.br/wpcontent/themes/aes/img/AES_book_0508_3.pdf. [Accessed 10 April 2014].

Andrade De Souza, A. (2009). *Brazil solar water heating (SHW) market overview.* [Online] December 2009. Available from: http://toolkits.reeep.org/file_upload/8917_tmpphp1UJrFL.pdf. [Accessed 10 April 2014].

Anonymised Interview (2011a). *Interview with Energy Efficiency Manager / Energy Utility Provider on 29th November 2011.* São Paulo. [Recording in possession of author].

Anonymised Interview (2011b). *Interview with Community Program Manager/ Energy Utility Provider on 11th October 2011*. São Paulo. [Recording in possession of author].

Bakker, K. (2003). Archipelagos and networks: Urbanization and water privatization in the South. *Geographical Journal*. 169(4): 328–341.

Balza, G. (2011). Comunidade pobre de SP se revolta com contas de luz e dá calote coletivo na Eletropaulo. *UOL Noticias* [Online]. 30th July. Available from: http://noticias.uol.com.br/cotidiano/ultimas-noticias/2011/07/30/comunidade-pobre-de-spse-revolta-com-contas-de-luz-e-da-calote-coletivo-na-eletropaulo.htm [Accessed 10th April 2014].

Barnett, C., Clarke, N., Cloke, P. and Malpass, A. (2008). The elusive subjects of neo-liberalism. *Cultural Studies*. 22(5): 624–653.

Barry, A., Osborne, T. and Rose, N. (eds) (1996). *Foucault and political reason: Liberalism, neo-liberalism, and rationalities of government*. Chicago, IL: University of Chicago Press.

Bulkeley, H., Powells and G. Bell, S. (2015). Smart grids and the governing of energy use: Reconfiguring practices? In Y. Strengers and C. Maller (eds). *Beyond Behaviour Change*. London: Routledge.

Chappells, H. and Shove, E. (2004). Infrastructures, crises and the orchestration of demand. In D. Southerton, H. Chappells and B.J.M. Van Vliet (eds). *Sustainable consumption: the implications of changing infrastructures of provision*. Cheltenham: Edward Elgar Publishing.

Cities Alliance. (2004). *Integrating the poor: Urban upgrading and land tenure regularisation in the City of São Paulo*. São Paulo: Cities Alliance and World Bank.

Cities Alliance. (2009). *Social Housing in São Paulo: Challenges and New Management Tools*. Washington DC and São Paulo: World Bank/Prefeitura de São Paulo.

Coutard, O. (2008). Placing splintering urbanism: Introduction. *Geoforum*. 39(6): 1815–1820.

De Soto, H. (2000). *The mystery of capital: Why captitalism triumphs in the West and fails everywhere else*. New York: Basic Books.

Dean, M. (2010). *Governmentality: Power and Rule in Modern Society*. London: Sage Publications Ltd.

Dowling, R. (2010). Geographies of identity: Climate change, governmentality and activism. *Progress in Human Geography*. 34(4): 488–495.

Fernandes, E. (2011). Regularization of informal settlements in Latin America. *Policy Focus Report*. Cambridge, MA: Lincoln Institute of Land Policy.

Foucault, M. (2009). *Security, Territory, Population: Lectures at the College de France 1977–1978*. London: Picador.

Franceys, R. (2005). Charging to enter the water shop? The costs of urban water connections for the poor. *Water Supply*. 5(6): 209–216.

Furlong, K. (2012). Mediating the gap between custom, cost-recovery, and 'networks': An example from Colombia. In *From networked to post-networked urbanism: new infrastructure configurations and urban transitions* (LATTS Conference). Autin, France, 17–20 July 2012.

Gandy, M. (2006). Planning, anti-planning and the infrastructure crisis facing Metropolitan Lagos. *Urban Studies*. 43(2): 371–396.

Giavedoni, J.G. (2011). Gobierno, pobreza y energía: La construcción del sujeto carenciado en la tarifa social de la Empresa Provincial de la Energía de Santa Fe. *Entramados y Perspectivas: Revista de la Carrera de Sociología.* 1(1): 37–59.

Graham, S. and Marvin, S. (2001). *Splintering Urbanism: Networked Infrastructures, Technological Mobilities and the Urban Condition.* London: Routledge.

Guy, S. and Marvin, S. (1996). Disconnected policy: The shaping of local energy management. *Environment and Planning C.* 14(1): 145–158.

Hart, S.L. (2005). *Capitalism at the crossroads: The unlimited business opportunities in solving the world's most difficult problems.* Upper Saddle River, NJ: Pearson Education.

Hughes, T.P. (1983). *Networks of Power: Electrification in Western society, 1880–1930.* Baltimore, MD: Johns Hopkins University Press.

Jaglin, S. (2008). 'Differentiating networked services in Cape Town: Echoes of splintering urbanism?' *Geoforum* 39(6): 1897–1906.

Kooy, M. and Bakker, K. (2008). Splintered networks: The colonial and contemporary waters of Jakarta. *Geoforum.* 39(6): 1843–1858.

Leffers, D. and Ballamingie, P. (2013). Governmentality, environmental subjectivity, and urban intensification. *Local environment* 18(2): 134–151.

Li, T.M. (2007). *The will to improve: Governmentality, Development, and the Practice of Politics.* Durham, NC: Duke University Press.

Lockwood, M. and Davidson, J. (2010). Environmental governance and the hybrid regime of Australian natural resource management. *Geoforum.* 41(3): 388–398.

London, T. and Hart, S.L. (2004). Reinventing strategies for emerging markets: Beyond the transnational model. *Journal of International Business Studies.* 35(5): 350–370.

McFarlane, C. (2008). Governing the contaminated city: Infrastructure and sanitation in colonial and post-colonial Bombay. *International Journal of Urban and Regional Research* 32(2): 415–435.

McFarlane, C. and Rutherford, J. (2008). Political Infrastructures: Governing and experiencing the fabric of the city. *International Journal of Urban and Regional Research* 32(2): 363–374.

Mestre, A.P. (2013). Novos usos do território e o consumo de energia elétrica na cidade de São Paulo. XIII Simposio Nacional de Geografia Urbana, Rio de Janeiro (UERJ, 18–22 November), [unpublished]. Available at: www.simpurb2013.com.br/wp-content/uploads/2013/11/1316_GT04_Ana.pdf [Accessed 1 February 2015].

Miller, P. and Rose, N. (2008). *Governing the present.* Cambridge: Polity.

Mimmi, L.M. and Ecer, S. (2010). An econometric study of illegal electricity connections in the urban favelas of Belo Horizonte, Brazil. *Energy Policy.* 38(9): 5081–5097.

Nye, D.E. (1999). *Consuming power: A social history of American energies.* Cambridge, MA: MIT Press.

Oliven, R.G. and Pinheiro-Machado, R. (2012). From 'Country of the Future' to Emergent Country: Popular Consumption in Brazil. *Consumer Culture in Latin America.* J. Sinclair and A.C. Pertierra (eds). New York: Palgrave Macmillan.

Prahalad, C. and Hart, S. (2002). The fortune at the bottom of the pyramid. *Strategy+Business* 26(First Quarter): 54–67.

Raco, M. and Imrie, R. (2000). Governmentality and rights and responsibilities in urban policy. *Environment and Planning A.* 32(12): 2187–2204.

Rankin, K.N. (2001). Governing development: Neoliberalism, microcredit, and rational economic woman. *Economy and Society.* 30(1): 18–37.

Rose, N. (1996). The death of the social? Re-figuring the territory of government. *Economy and Society* 25(3): 327–356.

Rose, N. (1999). *Powers of freedom: Reframing political thought.* Cambridge: Cambridge University Press.

Roy, A. (2011). Slumdog cities: Rethinking subaltern urbanism. *International Journal of Urban and Regional Research.* 35(2): 223–238.

Shove, E. (2004). *Comfort, cleanliness and convenience: The social organization of normality.* Oxford: Berg.

Shove, E. (2010). Social theory and climate change: Questions often, sometimes and not yet asked. *Theory, Culture and Society.* 27(2–3): 277.

Shove, E., Pantzar, M., Watson, M. (2012). *The dynamics of Social Practice: Everyday Life and How it Changes.* London: Sage Publications Limited.

Shove, E. and Walker, G. (2007). Caution! Transitions ahead: Politics, practice and transition management. *Environment and Planning A.* 39 (4): 763–770.

Shove, E. and Walker, G. (2010). Governing transitions in the sustainability of everyday life. *Research Policy* 39(4): 471–476.

Southerton, D., Vliet Van, B.J.M. and Chappells, H. (2004). Introduction: Consumption, infrastructures and environmental sustainability. In Southerton, H. Chappells and B.J.M. Van Vliet (eds). *Sustainable consumption: The implications of changing infrastructures of provision.* Cheltenham: Edward Elgar Publishing.

Spaargaren, G. (2011). Theories of practices: Agency, technology, and culture: Exploring the relevance of practice theories for the governance of sustainable consumption practices in the new world-order. *Global Environmental Change.* 21(3): 813–822.

Swyngedouw, E. (2004). *Social Power and the Urbanization of Water: Flows of Power.* Oxford: University Press Oxford.

UN HABITAT. (2010). *São Paulo: A Tale of Two Cities.* Nairobi: UN-Habitat/SEADE Fundação Sistema Estadual de Análise de Dados.

USAID. (2009). *Transforming electricity consumers into customers: Case study of a slum electrification and loss reduction project in São Paulo, Brazil.* Washington D.C.: United States Agency for International Development.

Van Vliet, B.J.M. (2004). *Shifting Scales of Infrastructure Provision. Sustainable Consumption: The Implications of Changing Infrastructures of Provision.* D. Southerton, H. Chappells and B.J.M. Van Vliet. Cheltenham: Edward Elgar Publishing.

Van Vliet, B.J.M., Chappells, H. Shove, E. (2005). *Infrastructures of consumption: environmental innovation in the utility industries.* London: Earthscan/James & James.

Viera, M. (2009). *Com mais segurança, favelas agora começam a receber contas.* O Estadao de S. Paulo [Online]. 20th April. Available at: www.estadao.com.br/noticias/impresso,com-mais-seguranca-favelas-agoracomecam-a-receber-contas, 357554,0.htm [Accessed 10th April 2014].

Walters, W. (2012). *Governmentality: Critical Encounters.* New York, NY: Routledge.

Part III

Experimenting with and learning from retrofit

Chapter 12

Placing low carbon transitions
Learning to retrofit in living laboratories

James Evans

INTRODUCTION

> The laboratory is the place where things that are uncommon and
> unproven are tested: a learning process by definition.
> (Paolo Soleri, 2002, Chapter 5)

In 2010 the European Regional Development Fund (ERDF) awarded
Salford University a grant to build a brand new 1930s terraced house inside
their old physics laboratory, with the goal of developing and testing energy
saving technology. Intended to be an accurate replica of the dominant type
of 'hard to heat' housing stock in the UK, the house was constructed by
local builders inside a fully controllable Heating Ventilation and Air Conditioning chamber that allows temperature, precipitation and even rain to be
precisely controlled (Figure 12.1). A series of homely touches compound the
innate weirdness of building a fully functioning house in a hermetically
sealed shed; a Lowry picture hangs on the living room wall while a bottle
of red wine idles on a work surface in the corner of the kitchen. These
human touches hint at the purpose of the Salford Energy House, which is
to simulate 'real' life in a living laboratory, right down to the rhythms of
fridge doors opening and shutting, pizzas going in the oven and toilets
flushing.

Living laboratories like the Salford Energy House represent an increasingly popular strategy to expedite low carbon retrofit. A form of
'experimental governance', whereby urban stakeholders experiment with
new technologies and forms of development to address the challenges of
climate change (Bulkeley and Castán-Broto, 2012; Evans, 2011), living
laboratories are distinctive because they are designed to permit formal
experiments, whereby interventions can be made, monitored and learnt
from (Evans and Karvonen, 2011). Built from scratch in a sealed chamber,
the Salford Energy House is an extreme example; monitoring equipment is
hardwired into the house, while the faux atmosphere is produced by a huge

Figure 12.1 The Salford Energy House

air conditioning unit. But living labs for low carbon research are emerging all over the world. Examples abound, from individual buildings like the Queens Building for energy research in Leicester, to the European Network of Living Labs, which encompasses over 300 cities. Living labs are often characterised by an emphasis on ICT, which simultaneously enables users to innovate and the performance of those innovations to be monitored. That said, the spectrum of places labelling themselves as living labs runs from projects that have done little more than roll out free high speed wireless internet in an existing urban neighbourhood to places that have been constructed from scratch with little or no ICT component.

These places, and they are very much places, hold a strong appeal for politicians, funding bodies, university vice chancellors, companies and the public alike. Their emphasis on partnership, learning and innovation places them in the vanguard of the low carbon knowledge economy – promising a reality to match the political rhetoric. The laboratory moniker confers pseudo-scientific legitimacy upon what goes on in such places and the knowledge that is subsequently produced. This is important in terms of the potential to scale up; no one is interested in retrofitting a single terraced house, but the rigour of the controlled experiment promises knowledge that will be relevant to every terraced house. It is exactly this relevance that is conferred by the living part of the living lab equation. In reality retrofit either does or does not take place through what Shove and Walker (2010; 476) term the 'ongoing transformation' of practices; practices that structure peoples' everyday existence. Demonstrating solutions through their reification and subsequent exhibition as real places that can be seen and touched provides a powerful tonic for the public and politicians alike.

Adopting a register more akin to the Human Genome Project, living labs position themselves as the places where the DNA of the sustainable city is being discovered; anticipatory beacons of the low carbon future from whence a broader scale low carbon transition will emanate. As Hodson and Marvin note (2009a), the twin goals of economic growth and carbon reduction are increasingly intertwined with technical and social infrastructure transitions, which require new and effective forms of urban knowledge to be interactively produced, communicated and appropriated. As a new form of research infrastructure living labs do just this (ESFRI, 2011). The following chapter explores the practices through which living laboratories are established and how those involved perceive their role, in order to better grasp how they might contribute to the retrofit agenda and the wider low carbon transition of which it forms part.

Living labs for retrofit

> There are 26 million homes in the UK, and only 21 million minutes from now to 2050. So if we are going to make all our homes energy efficient by 2050, we need to fix up one house every 50 seconds, for the next 40 years.
>
> (Chris Huhne, Former Secretary of State for Energy and Climate Change)

Because living labs emphasise real world transformation, they offer a powerful salve for well intended but alarmist statements like the one above. Talking about the future prosperity of Europe, the European Union have suggested that cities 'must become real implementation fields creating platforms for change where universities, public bodies and those from private and third sectors must operate together in a new and creative mood' (Committee of the Regions, 2011). Turning cities into 'real implementation fields' is precisely what living labs do, designating a city, or more commonly a part of it, as a laboratory within which physical interventions can be made and monitored. Definitions have proliferated almost as rapidly as the concept has spread (Schliwa, 2013), but in some important sense living labs constitute what transition scholars term 'niches', or places which have the ability to host experiments and generate innovations that may then spread. Niches form incubation rooms where unique combinations of expertise and resources are available that provide the seeds for change, for example protecting radical innovations that may be commercially unviable at first from wider economic forces. The Multi-Level Perspective model of technological transition suggests niches break-out to effect regime change as they become more economically competitive than the incumbent technologies, prompting wider transition. A distinction is made in the literature between 'fit and conform' experiments that simply reproduce regime inertia and 'stretch and transform' experiments that prompt change, although in practice the former are far more common as niche experiments become captured by dominant actors and interests (Smith and Raven, 2012).

In stark contrast to the scientific laboratory, which is designed to fix non-experimental variables, the real world is a messy and multivariate place. Rather than fixing non-experimental variables, living laboratories seek to create environments in which every variable can be monitored, more akin to field-based branches of scientific knowledge. 360 degree data collection allows causal links to be identified between interventions and outcomes, and the institutional and spatial characteristics of living labs reflect this goal, being designed to host physical interventions and equipment to monitor them. They tend to be clearly defined geographical and/or institutional spaces with the capacity to collect large amounts of data that can be analysed to identify causal links between experimental interventions and outcomes (Evans and Karvonen, 2011).

Transition management is a model of governance that relies on a cycle of problem structuring, visioning, experimentation, policy development, implementation and adaptation (Kemp *et al.* 2007) to drive change; a continuous feedback loop of experimentation that allows novelty to emerge (Castán-Broto and Bulkeley, 2013). Seen in this way, the ability of niches to stretch and transform depends upon pushing the rules of experimentation (Coenen *et al.* 2010). This observation draws attention to the way in which experiments are framed in niches so as to enable the emergence of novelty. Talking about this process in the biological sciences, Rheinberger (1997; 134) states that surprises are 'made to happen through the inner workings of the experimental machinery for making the future', as the hypothetical basis of the experimental test opens up more than one possible outcome. Experimental logic controls variables to allow the emergence of underdetermined 'epistemic things' that were previously unknown in such a way that allows the experimenter to be open to surprises but at the same time to 'control the surprising event as a basis for learning' (Gross, 2010; 29).

Research infrastructures like living labs play an important role in allowing cities and universities to position themselves as leaders in low carbon innovation and major players in regional economic development (König and Evans, 2013; Trencher *et al.* 2013). On paper, then, it is easy to see why living labs are springing up all over the world, but what happens in practice? The existing literature on low carbon experiments suggests that often incremental learning through developing, testing and introducing new technologies and services does not occur in any meaningful way, as technology is simply dropped into places, tested and then removed without any meaningful stakeholder participation (Hodson and Marvin, 2009b). These more critical accounts underpin a broader concern that the Multi-Level Perspective model over-simplifies the exact processes by which niche experiments influence the wider world. For example, economic competitiveness itself is determined by a series of broader social and political factors, from institutional learning and regulatory change to political and public opinion which the Multi-Level Perspective approach does not fully account for (Coenen and Truffer, 2012; Lawhon and Murphy, 2012). As Brown and Vergragt (2008, 110) argue, 'little systemic study has been done on defining the learning processes in experiments, monitoring them, assessing their societal impacts, or examining the conditions under which learning does (or does not) occur, and by what mechanisms'.

While they vary wildly in scale and focus, living labs constitute key nodes within learning networks that offer a window onto the changing role of scientific knowledge production in low carbon transitions (Monaghan, 2012). Recent research has emphasized the need to understand the capacity and capability of specific places to undertake systemic transformations of infrastructure through reconfiguring existing urban stakeholders (Hodson *et al.* 2013). The concept of urban intermediaries captures the work of actors like consultants and NGOs who operate in between the more conventional groups to facilitate infrastructure transitions (Guy *et al.* 2010). In this sense, living labs act as intermediary spaces that enable experimental reconfigurations of people and things to literally take place, exhibiting both alternative futures and underlying styles of development. In relation to retrofit and the broader backdrop of low carbon transition, living labs raise a number of questions. How do these partnerships come together to stage experiments? Are they simply test-beds or does learning occur, and, related to this, how do the partners involved see pathways of change, whereby solutions becomes scaled up? Put simply, does anything new and exciting happen, or are living labs simply an iteration of business-as-usual public private partnerships?

This chapter presents an analysis of six living labs based in the UK and USA that focus on retrofitting urban environments. The cases are drawn from a broader population of projects that are knowledge-driven and operational. Some of these projects are included in recent heroic global surveys of urban partnerships for sustainability; for example Castán-Broto and Bulkeleys' (2013) survey of urban sustainability partnerships and Trencher *et al*'s. (2013) survey of university-driven partnerships for sustainability. The selection here is not intended to be exhaustive of all types of living labs, but to focus on a range of types that differ in terms of longevity, focus and scale to highlight commonalities. In doing so it fills the gap between case specific accounts and global surveys to enable the comparative exploration of how place-based learning drives broader transition. Table 12.1 lists the cases and their key characteristics, with the final column distinguishing between those living labs that were built from scratch and those that were installed in existing urban landscapes.

The Queen's Building houses the Institute for Energy and Sustainability at De Montford University in Leicester and was designed by architects Short Ford Associates to act as an object for study as well as to house standard teaching and research functions. The building won various awards in the mid 1990s for its innovative environmental design; with distinctive towers providing natural daylight and ventilation (see Figure 12.2). The Salford Energy House described in the opening paragraphs is similarly located on university premises, but differs in that it is not a working building. Arcosanti differs in being an auto-constructed settlement, founded in the late 1960s by Italian architect Paolo Soleri, which puts the concepts of what he called 'arcology' in to practice. Seeking to enact ecological principles through cosmic architecture, Arcosanti is a self-styled 'urban laboratory' (see Figure 12.3) that comprises a series of dome shaped buildings and closed loop food and water systems. Although developing little since the early 1990s it has recently become a popular destination for Asian town planners.

Turning to the three cases that have been installed in existing landscapes, North Desert Village is an area of suburban housing in Mesa City that became the property of Arizona State University. A team of sociologists and ecologists subsequently used part of the site to test out different landscaping types, ranging from classic grass lawns to indigenous xeric desert-scapes.

Table 12.1 Living labs for retrofit

Living Lab	Scale	Open	Lead partner	Focus	Type
Queens Building (Leicester, UK)	Building	1993	De Montford University	Energy use	Built
Salford Energy House (Salford, UK)	Building	2010	Salford University	Energy consumption	Built
Arcosanti (Arizona, USA)	Village	1970	Cosanti Foundation	Building design, closed loop systems	Built
North Desert Village (Meza City, USA)	Neighbourhood	2005	Arizona State University	Landscape design	Installed
Elmer Avenue (Los Angeles, USA)	Neighbourhood	2010	Council for Watershed Health	Drainage and biodiversity	Installed
Oxford Road Corridor (Manchester, UK)	Urban sector	2010	Manchester City Council	Urban planning	Installed

Figure 12.2 Queens Building, Leicester

Environmental factors like infiltration, water consumption and biodiversity were measured alongside resident use and preferences over a period of a number of years. The Elmer Avenue project in northern Los Angeles brought residents and municipal authorities together to remodel and subsequently maintain green infrastructure in the form of bio swales (linear planted strips alongside the road – see Figure 12.4) and French drains to deal with storm water, increase biodiversity and enhance the aesthetic appeal of the street. By contrast, the Oxford Road Corridor in Manchester, UK, is a city centre project to enhance the urban realm along a key transport conduit that runs through the city's knowledge quarter.

Overall half of the lead partners are universities, with two NGOs and a city authority. Perhaps unsurprisingly universities tend to be lead partners where facilities are built from scratch, in contrast to those that are installed in existing landscapes that involve close partnerships with municipalities. The focus on energy consumption and landscape design reflects the scale of the installations, with buildings more concerned with the former and neigh-bourhoods with the latter, although as Trencher at al. (2013) note it is hard to separate elements out in broader sustainability projects. Between 2010 and 2013 site visits to each case and 16 interviews were conducted with

Figure 12.3 Arcosanti – the urban laboratory

those involved setting up, running and experimenting in these living labs, focusing on who is involved and why, how experiments are staged, and how learning and scaling are supposed to occur. These interviews and visits were complemented with secondary material produced by and about the labs. The remainder of the chapter considers these themes, before reflecting on the implications for learning, transition and retrofit.

Constituting the Lab

The cost of establishing large scale research infrastructure necessitates a partnership approach, and universities highlighted the opportunities presented by living labs to foster links with both multinational and local businesses. As one researcher stated, 'we have the labs for friendship from a business point of view', and partnering with business is seen as the main way in which living labs promote wider low carbon transition. The importance of encouraging local technology clusters as part of regional low carbon growth strategies was highlighted in all three of the UK cases. In two cases this involved subscribing to networks of UK businesses to find partners that were keen to engage with academics. Although open calls

Figure 12.4 Elmer Avenue Bioswale

were put out for any types of technology, most requests came from companies wanting to trial building management systems. From the point of view of partners, living labs provide clients with an experimental setup that they wouldn't otherwise be able to afford, 'harnessing the research and academic expertise in support of what the project partners are doing'. Beyond the financial commitment, there is a feeling that this kind of approach makes sense in relation to the challenges of sustainability; as an Elmer Avenue partner stated, 'it made sense to try lots of things in one place'; in this case ecologically appropriate landscaping, low energy street lighting and so forth. But while the integrated approach makes sense, sustainability requires a huge budget to transform buildings and install equipment in real urban settings.

Overridingly universities perceived living labs as vehicles to establish critical mass and profile in terms of energy research and its organisation. As a member of the Queens Building team noted, 'we use it as a platform to go and get money... because of the living lab they [the funders] could see that we knew what we were talking about'. Indeed, financial commitment was seen by some as a prerequisite to attract funding to 'do something new'. The potential to develop relationships that go beyond the labs was highlighted in four of the living labs, although they all noted the uncertainties surrounding how much interest there would be from private industry. Three factors were identified explaining their appeal to private partners: cheapness, legitimacy from working with a university, and the appeal of being able to solve generic problems.

The status of the experiments was seen as critical to the success of these places. On the one hand, the scientific credentials of the living labs were presented as fundamental to what they do; as one researcher stated, 'the authority is science, the things are real science'. Similarly, the head engineer at Salford identified replication and control as the most significant achievements of the laboratory. In terms of how to achieve scientific legitimacy in a 'living' context, scientists involved in the various cases highlighted the different measures used to control variables. IIn the case of the Salford Energy House it was the chamber in which the house was sealed that brought 'the science to the experiment', while in the Queens Building it was triangulation of multiple datasets including physical and psychological data. In the case of the Oxford Road Corridor, which occupies a real urban landscape, the ability to replicate experiments was pinpointed as the key to controlling variables. Ironically, a year on from the Energy House opening, the most pressing challenge facing the engineers has been how to automate human activities. While originally intended to be inhabited, the health and safety issues of living in a hermetically sealed chamber and the unpredictability of real human behaviour have meant their exclusion from the laboratory. Replacing humans with automated appliances was necessary to ensure replicability.

A number of practical issues complicate the rhetoric of these experiments. Negotiating the legal and institutional ramifications of allowing industrial partners to install experimental equipment was highlighted by four of the living labs investigated, including all of those located in buildings. Installations on university property had to follow time-consuming tendering procedures on a case by case basis to ensure accountability. Similarly, dealing with municipal services in an existing urban environment raised a whole series of cooperation issues. In the case of Elmer Avenue, water pipes had to be lowered, gas pipes had to be split and routed down under the pavement, requiring street services, water, power and sanitation departments to cooperate. In terms of installing monitoring equipment, especially for the living labs with a landscape component, it was often hard to get permission from the relevant home owners and agencies to install monitors. As one researcher stated, 'you're not just walking out to nature and dealing with it'.

Conversely, a number of the retrofitted experiments in real urban settings were facilitated by simplicity. The fact that there was only a single land owner involved to negotiate with, or a place had little existing infrastructure were both identified as enabling factors. For example, an Elmer Avenue manager confirmed, 'we wouldn't have been able to do this if they [the neighbourhood] had conventional storm drains. We could only try these things out because there was nothing here already'. In this instance the particularities of place enabled and shaped experimentation.

The cost and practical difficulties of establishing living labs meant that they were seen by some as calculated gambles. As one city planner said, 'there's a lot of risk involved. I'm certain over the years that we have quietly wasted, well not wasted, but an awful lot of money has gone down the drain trying to set pilot schemes up that weren't that successful. It's the price you pay for chasing an innovative approach, I suppose'. The risk associated with experimenting in real environments meant that trust had to be built over time, especially amongst traditionally conservative municipal engineers and estates managers. The aversion of publicly accountable partners to risk is entirely understandable, given that any dereliction of statutory duty can result in legal action. In examples where experimentation had been possible strong risk management to cover eventualities where a company might go bust, high levels of commitment from key partners and a change of mindset to focus on innovation served to mitigate risk.

The influence of living labs

Talking about the urban laboratory he founded in 1970, Italian architect Paolo Soleri states that 'Arcosanti is not a utopia but an urban laboratory *modestly nudging reality*' (2002, Chapter 6, emphasis original). But what impact do these places actually have? The overriding rationale given by those involved in the living labs studied was that they were primarily test sites for new technologies and designs. Often the research infrastructure was presented as an apparatus waiting for a user. So for example, North Desert Village was spoken of as 'more of [an] infrastructure long term monitoring experiment that the people can come to and use in any way they want'. The Salford Energy House explicitly positions itself as a data producing test facility that avoids analysis; as one member stated, they literally hand the data over to the companies and researchers that use the facility 'on a memory stick'. The approach in the Queen's Building complemented testing with some evaluation as well, positioning themselves as a kind of technology watchdog centre to provide independent information about different building management systems in what is a fast emerging market. The emphasis on testing was particularly strong in the built labs, with demand from business far outweighing that from academics. As one researcher stated, 'many of the technologies are not our own technologies anyway, they're not things we want to test… so really *we are testing to see what the problems of the real world are rather than testing particular systems*' (emphasis added). The goal here is clearly to understand implementation rather than create innovation.

On the one hand, then, living labs seem to be more about easing new technologies to market, but on the other, they start to question the distinction between experimenting (as the discovery of something new) and testing (as the trialing of a discovery). To a large extent, the power of living labs lay in their ability to materialise something new, and it is this quality that was identified by those involved as underpinning their ability to stimulate wider changes. Talking about the Oxford Road Corridor, one of the partnership directors noted that 'the city … see the corridor as being important because it is actually quite hard for them to make things happen. So actually having this area as a potential exemplar is a real benefit'. Another partner noted (humorously) that because the evidence from real world experiments could be presented to decision-makers as incontrovertibly valid in that place, it 'gives us a stick to beat people with'. Other comments highlighted the ontic importance of living labs, saying '[it] is based upon a physical heart, which could be attractive', a sentiment also reflected in the statement that 'it's all theory until you build it'. Thomas Gieryn (2006) coined the term truth spots for places like these that valorise the knowledge produced therein through their sheer physical existence. At their most bullish, partners suggested that the power of these places lay in their ability to demonstrate not only a particular configuration of things and people, but also a different mode of development.

A lexicon of exceptionalism supported claims that these labs were special or unique as research facilities. Herein lay another tension, between the living labs as generic analogues for any office building/terraced house/urban landscape, and their uniqueness as a site of knowledge production. There is a parallel schism here between the huge cost and vision of living labs and what is often a fairly unassuming reality. The North Desert Village manager prepared me to be disappointed, saying he doesn't usually take visitors to see it anymore as it is too scruffy and 'doesn't live up to people's expectations'. Even the Salford Energy House sits in an unassuming shed in a corner of the university campus, and once inside the visitor can't help but be disappointed at the lack of impressive control room or viewing area. The entire facility can be controlled remotely from a PC or tablet.

In terms of wider impacts, very few of the living labs actually traced where the knowledge they produced went, how it was subsequently used or what changes it engendered, and this included the academic as well as the non-academic knowledge that was produced. Anecdotally those managing each facility spoke about being mentioned in parliamentary debates (the Salford Energy House), or hosting a delegation of Chinese town planners (Arcosanti), but little hard data was available concerning the number of mentions or visitors, or the subsequent influence upon other places, organizations, companies or regulatory bodies. Such pathways to change constitute the black box of transition; the very mechanisms through which niches drive wider change. They seem as yet largely un-proscribed and understudied, despite constituting the processes through which wider change and upscaling occurs. A potentially fruitful avenue of research would involve mining grey literatures and funding evaluations produced by and for research infrastructures and test sites to trace the post-experimental journey of knowledge.

The living labs in actual urban landscapes talked about embedding scientific practice into policy through a live feedback process, but highlighted the lack of governance structures in place to support this, and the challenges to traditional institutional roles and boundaries posed by this kind of research infrastructure. In reflective mode, one researcher mused that there were:

> Two different types of knowledge; the first is the scientific knowledge gained ... The other set of knowledge is more practical in terms of what's it like to do the sort of experiment on people and all the stuff we have to worry about because it doesn't work out as planned ... So it's sort of knowledge about the process that was as valuable if not, more valuable than scientific knowledge gained.
>
> (Interview conducted 21/6/2012)

Scientists spoke of having to be advocates working with communities to develop buy-in for experiments, or in the case of the prefabricated living labs operate like sales people engaging with corporate partners to negotiate testing and intellectual property rights.

These challenges were highlighted as transcending living labs to apply to sustainability transitions more generally. As one manager noted, it is not just technical systems that do not yet exist but a whole set of social and organizational systems. Social learning was identified as a key output of living labs, whereby partners 'learnt how to learn', picking up the ethos of experimentation and monitoring. An Elmer Avenue stakeholder suggested that the most important lesson for the organizations involved was how something so successful in its local context could then fail to be rolled out more widely. The capacity of a governance system to stage an experiment does not necessarily include the ability to learn from them or upscale. Understanding how technological and social aspects interact was identified as critical in scaling up from the lab to the wider world. It is within the context of how cities learn to be sustainable that living labs have perhaps the most to offer (Campbell, 2009) – an element that is missing from current attempts to frame impact in energy research through numbers of patents, products or publications produced (Tecnalia, 2012).

CONCLUSIONS: RETROFIT, RESEARCH INFRASTRUCTURES AND LOW CARBON TRANSITIONS

Retrofitting is a complex undertaking, involving the systemic transformation of the socio-material environment. There are few precursors upon which to base action, stimulating the emergence of new research infrastructures spanning the public and corporate sectors that are explicitly designed to generate innovative solutions to socio-technical problems. This chapter has focused on living laboratories, which are self-designated spaces capable of hosting real world experiments in built design and sustainable technologies. Living laboratories represent a niche approach to learning that equips specific places to monitor various infrastructure interventions. As real world experiments it is assumed they will yield applicable knowledge that can be easily transferred to wider contexts. This chapter has outlined how and why such claims are constructed by a range of actors, and explored the implications that experimentation in the real world holds for a wider low carbon transition.

Establishing living labs is resource intensive, involving either large-scale experimental infrastructure (like the energy house and Arcosanti), or the negotiation of complex legal and administrative duties between partners to allow experiments to occur in real cities (for example Elmer Avenue and Oxford Road). But living labs provide that rare thing – a platform for universities, public bodies and those from private and third sectors to engage in collective experimentation, focusing on innovation-driven economic development, user-centric digital infrastructure, and packaged up in the familiar and unthreatening rhetoric of partnership. But while they represent a type of research infrastructure that has innovation and upscaling hardwired into it, the cases studied here had little idea where the knowledge went or what impact it had beyond largely anecdotal stories. Further, the focus on testing produced a view of knowledge as a discrete product, over-looking an important set of softer learning outcomes.

It is here that the governance of experiments blurs into experimental governance. As a kind of project-style experimental governance living labs appeal to universities, NGOs, commercial organizations and public bodies because it suggests a way to both be and be seen to be innovative. Govern-ing by experiment resonates with the wider fracturing of urban governance under neoliberal conditions, as places compete to attract investment and talent. Within this frame experimental governance can be criticized as an adaptive, reactive and largely piecemeal response to climate change, a fancy dress parade devoid of political content that does little more than conceal higher level failures to effect regulatory change. Alternately, it reflects the rising importance of places in taking action in the absence of national level change, predicated upon an associated generational and cultural shift in organizations towards more collaborative forms of project working, as they learn how to learn and renegotiate traditional roles and boundaries.

Perhaps the most important challenge that living labs highlight is the need to better understand the processes and pathways that connect place-based experiments to national-level change, whether it be through a diaspora of residents as in the case of Arcosanti or through hard data as in the case of the Energy House. As Hodson *et al.* argue (2013), this involves under-standing how the episodic nature of one-off projects are articulated within larger scale programmes, but the challenge is potentially broader than this, requiring researchers to trace the flows of things, people and ideas that accrete in and pass through these places. Just as cities shape transitions, so place structures experiments and their subsequent pathways to impact. These pathways vary perhaps more than is commonly recognized in the literature – from ministerial visits to Twitter trends.

Places like living labs hold relevance for the retrofit and transition agendas more widely because they are the stones that cause ripples through the broad-er pond. These ripples are variously conceived; in the policy literature they are the basis for the upscaling of solutions, while in the innovation literature they are how innovations diffuse through a system. In the multi-level perspective model they provide the mechanism through which a technological transition propagates through a regime. Although somewhat poetic, the notion of ripples is useful in directing attention to the various media through which influence and impact travel. Mainstream politics, public interest, product adoption, legal patenting, academic publication, funding priorities and pro-fessional networks are the water through which waves of change travel. The movement of ripples through these multifarious networks holds the key to understanding how transitions literally *take* place, in relation to both retrofit and the broader low carbon agenda of which it forms a part.

References

Brown, H. and Vergragt, P.J. (2008) Bounded Socio-technical experiments as agents of systemic change: the case of zero-energy residential building. *Technological Forecasting and Social Change* 75, 107–30.

Bulkeley, H. and Castán-Broto, V. (2012) Governing by experiment? Global Cities and the governing of Climate Change. *Transactions of the Institute of British Geographers* 38, 361–375.

Campbell, T. (2009) Learning cities, knowledge, capacity and competitiveness. *Habitat International* 33, 195–201.

Castán-Broto, V. and Bulkeley, H. (2013) Maintaining climate change experiments: Urban political ecology and the everyday reconfiguration of urban infrastructure, *International Journal of Urban and Regional Research* 37, 1934–1948.

Coenen, L., Raven, R. and Verbong, G. (2010) Local niche experimentation in energy transitions: A theoretical and empirical exploration of proximity advantages and disadvantages. *Technology in Society* 32, 295–302.

Coenen, L. and Truffer, B. (2012) Places and spaces of sustainability transitions: Geographical contributions to an emerging research and policy field. *European Planning Studies* 20, 367–374.

Committee of the Regions (2011) *The Role of Local and Regional Authorities in Achieving the Objectives of the Europe 2020.* European Union, Brussels.

ESFRI (European Strategy Forum on Research Infrastructures) (2011). *Strategy Report on Research Infrastructures.* European Union, Brussels.

Evans, J. (2011) Resilience, ecology and adaptation in the experimental city. *Transactions of the Institute of British Geographers* 36, 223–237.

Evans, J. and A. Karvonen (2011) Living laboratories for sustainability: Exploring the politics and epistemology of urban adaptation. In H. Bulkeley, V. Castán Broto, M. Hodson and S. Marvin (eds) *Cities and Low Carbon Transitions,* Routledge, London. 126–141.

Gieryn, T. (2006) City as truth spot. *Social Studies of Science* 36, 5–38.

Gross, M. (2010) *Ignorance and Surprise: Science, Society and Ecological Design.* MIT Press, London.

Guy, S., Marvin, S., Medd, W. and Moss, T. (eds) (2010) *Shaping Urban Infrastructures: Intermediaries and the Governance of Socio-technical Networks.* Earthscan, London.

Hodson, M. and Marvin, S. (2009a) Urban ecological security: a new urban paradigm? *International journal of Urban and Regional Research,* 33, 193–215.

Hodson, M. and Marvin, S. (2009b) Cities mediating technological transitions: Understanding visions, intermediation and consequences. *Technology Analysis and Strategic Management* 21, 515–34.

Hodson, M. and Marvin, S. and Bulkeley, H. (2013) The intermediary organisation of low carbon cities: A comparative analysis of transitions in Greater London and Greater Manchester. *Urban Studies* 50, 1403–1422.

Kemp, R., Rotmans, J. and Loorbach, D. (2007) Assessing the Dutch energy transition policy: how does it deal with managing dilemmas of managing transition? *Journal of Environment Policy and Planning* 9, 315–31.

König, A. and Evans, J. (2013) 'Experimenting for sustainable development? Living laboratories, social learning, and the role of the university'. In: König, A. (ed.)

Regenerative Sustainable Development of Universities and Cities: The Role of Living Laboratories. Edward Elgar, Cheltenham. 1–24.

Lawhon, M. and Murphy, J. (2012) Socio-technical regimes and sustainability transitions: Insights from political ecology. *Progress in Human Geography* 36, 354–378.

Monaghan, P. (2012) *Low Carbon Futures at a City-Scale: Understanding the Complex Relationship Between Learning, Partnerships and Infrastructure*. MSc. Thesis, De Montfort University, Leicester, September 2012.

Rheinberger, H-J. (1997) Experimental complexity in biology: Some epistemological and historical remarks. *Philosophy of Science* 64, 245–254.

Schliwa, G. (2013) Exploring Living Labs through Transition Management: Challenges and Opportunities for Sustainable Urban Transitions. MSc. Thesis, University of Lund, Sweden, September 2013.

Shove, E. and Walker, G. (2010) Governing transitions in the sustainability of everyday life. *Research Policy* 39, 471–476.

Smith, A. and Raven, R. (2012) What is protective space? Reconsidering niches in transitions to sustainability. *Research Policy* 41, 1025–1036.

Soleri, P. (2002) *What If? Collected Writings 1986–2000*. Berkeley Hill Books, Berkeley CA.

Tecnalia (2012) *Research Infrastructures on Energy Efficiency in Buildings: Enhancing the Scientific and Socio-Economic Impacts of Research Infrastructures*. Available at: www.energiaenedificacion.com/wp-content/uploads/2012/03/RIEEB_Brochure_20120319.pdf accessed 28/08/2012.

Trencher, G., Yarime, M., McCormick, K., Doll, C. and Kraines, S. (2013) Beyond the third mission: Exploring the emerging university function of co-creation for sustainability. *Science and Public Policy*. Available at: http://dx.doi.org/10.1093/scipol/sct044.

Chapter 13

Demonstrating retrofitting
Perspectives from Australian local government

Robyn Dowling, Pauline McGuirk and Harriet Bulkeley

INTRODUCTION

Cities are critical to transitions to low carbon futures, not only because of the large and growing global urban population but also because global resource consumption is concentrated in cities (Gossop, 2011: 208; Hodson, Marvin, Robinson and Swilling, 2012; Monstadt, 2007). Ensuring that new urban spaces, such as new housing or new city precincts, are low or zero carbon is central to these transitions (Hodson and Marvin, 2010). Yet, equally important to reducing urban carbon consumption is the retrofitting of existing urban planning frameworks and imaginaries, infrastructure, built form and patterns of daily life (Eames et al. 2013; Pincetl, 2012). Retrofitting involves the modification of what already exists in cities: altering the ways in which existing buildings are heated and cooled, diverting households, businesses and organisations toward renewable sources of energy rather than fossil fuels, encouraging the take up of energy efficient appliances, altering urban infrastructures of energy and transport provision toward renewable sources.

Retrofitting is both a social and a technological challenge. Technologically, it involves the installation of a diverse range of new or upgraded zero or low carbon technologies in the existing urban fabric. These include, often in combination, new forms of building insulation to minimise heat transfer between the inside and outside of buildings, more efficient lighting and heating (e.g. heat pump rather than electric hot water systems) and micro-generation of energy supply. Retrofitting technologies can be applied at a number of scales. These include individual buildings, clusters of buildings, precincts, entire local authority areas, or supra-urban systems of energy infrastructure. In the Australian case, for example, where 60 per cent of carbon emissions are generated by energy use and 75 per cent of electricity generation is coal-fired (Australian Government, 2011), micro (i.e. individual building) installation of solar PV is the most common retrofitting technology. Retrofitting is also a social process in which technologies are adopted, accommodated and altered by urban actors. The behaviours and choices of individuals have a potentially profound impact on the effectiveness of technologies. For example, a recent Cambridge study suggested that attention to behaviour change can double the energy savings of retrofitting (Markusson, Ishii and Stephens, 2011).

Surprisingly, given the importance of retrofitting to the achievement of low carbon cities, and the voluminous literature on urban carbon governance (Bulkeley and Castán Broto, 2013; Rice, 2010; While, Jonas and Gibbs, 2010), explicit focus on enabling retrofitting through governance is rare. There is some analysis of programs that encourage retrofitting at household or building scales (see Deakin, Campbell and Reid, 2012; Ghosh and Head, 2009; Kelly, 2009; Sunikka-Blank, Chen, Britnell and Dantsiou, 2012; Willand et al. 2012), but little consideration of what institutions and mechanisms might best enhance cities' capacities to adopt retrofitting technologies and behaviours. This chapter hence provides a theoretical framework for understanding the governance of urban retrofitting as well as empirical answers to the question of the character of retrofitting governance.[1] Specifically, we develop and implement a framework for understanding the governance of urban retrofitting that considers the assemblage of institutions, materials, agencies and mechanisms that might enable the transformation of cities. This framework is outlined in the first section. The second section presents a more detailed examination of retrofit governance at the 'sub' urban scale, using an audit of local scale retrofitting initiatives in Australia's largest city – Sydney – to develop a typology of means or techniques through which retrofitting is governed. Developing our argument that an understanding of governing retrofit requires attention to the mechanisms and techniques through which conduct is 'conducted', in the final empirical section we outline two cases in which retrofitting is pursued through demonstration. We ask how and by whom they are enabled (and simultaneously, what are the constraints they negotiate), what the mechanisms through which they become productive are, and what their relationship to the existing carbon governance regime is. We also focus on the 'demonstration' or 'showcase' elements of these projects to critically interrogate the multifaceted learning processes embedded within them. We conclude with an analysis of the limitations of retrofitting governance as currently practised and reflections on the purchase of demonstration as a governmental technique at citywide scales.

Governing urban retrofit

Our purpose in this section is to provide the conceptual tools to understand how and by whom retrofitting is governed in the city. We start with the notion that retrofitting is a socio-technical process. By this we mean that retrofitting not only requires the application of technologies, but also the adoption and accommodation of these technologies across diverse sites and spheres. Conceived in this manner, retrofitting raises questions not only of technological performance and individual behaviour, but also of the means through which the co-production of socio-technical systems is fostered and directed. Coupled with the diversity of sites (e.g. buildings, infrastructure systems) and actors (e.g. businesses, individuals, NGOs) through which retrofitting occurs, we hence turn to three dimensions of urban carbon governance to frame an understanding of retrofit.

First, we consider governance as multi-scalar: institutions governing carbon in the city encompass and exceed the urban scale, folding into and through each other in complex ways (Betsill and Bulkeley, 2006). There is therefore no one scalar centre of governance as such, but rather the governing of retrofit takes place through shifting scalar constellations. Actions of transnational networks have shaped urban responses to climate change, for example, as have national scale policies. The diverse initiatives of local authorities are also critical: urban authorities have driven emissions reduction and low carbon transitions through a diverse array of action (Betsill and Bulkeley, 2007; Hoffmann, 2011). Thus our analysis is alert to multi-scale responses to the retrofitting challenge.

Second, urban carbon governance is carried out by both state and non-state institutions. Governing is a dispersed form of rule that cuts across conventional public/private spheres (McGuirk and Dowling, 2009; Schroeder and Lovell, 2011). Governing occurs through an assemblage or alignment of diverse actors, interests and institutions as well as materials and artifacts that enable programmatic aims to be achieved (Li, 2007). In the case of retrofitting, recent work has suggested that considerable effort is required to assemble institutions capable and willing to implement retrofitting, and that the motivations of these institutions are often divergent (Deakin, et al. 2012; Schiellerup and Gwilliam, 2009). Extending this idea, we suggest that one task of retrofitting governance is to orchestrate a supportive policy framework and suite of related interventions through which builders, energy retailers, appliance and car manufacturers, infrastructure providers and householders may consider and embrace the possibilities for retrofitting. In simple terms this means that retrofitting technologies need to be taken up by, and are also mediated by, two central groups of stakeholders: those responsible for building the city (builders, developers, landlords, homeowners, governments) and also those that inhabit these spaces (residents, building tenants, workers, organisations, members of the public etc.). In our empirical analysis we are hence alert to this 'dispersed nature of rule' (Ekers and Loftus, 2008: 703) being enacted in the governance of retrofit.

Third, building upon insights that have been highly productive for understanding urban responses to climate change, governance is enacted through the 'conduct of conduct' (in relation to climate governance see Keskitalo, Juhola and Westerhoff, 2012). By this it is meant that shaping how an issue is framed, its objects or materials aligned and, crucially, its subjects and their practices enrolled are central to governing (Paterson and Stripple, 2010; Whitehead, 2009). In relation to retrofitting the two key targets of this 'conduct of conduct' are the stakeholder groups identified above: those shaping urban infrastructures and built environments and those who inhabit them. The first relates to the systems of provision that shape cities; entities responsible for generating the provision of retrofitting materials and technologies, supporting the development of markets, technologies, business models, skills, expertise and so on. Retrofitting, therefore, requires changes in conduct within the 'systems of provision' that shape urban socio-technical systems. The second target relates to the adoption and accommodation of these new and upgraded technologies into the routines and cultures of daily life (Glad, 2012); the adoption of new behaviours and shifts in behavioural norms or hegemonies. This in turn means that the governing of behaviour change is critical in retrofitting just as it is in diverse other fields of low carbon transitions (Hargreaves, 2011). Here, the governance challenge for retrofitting is to encourage individual householders, workers and organisations not only to retrofit their respective spaces materially (dwellings, commercial buildings, vehicles), but also to accommodate and embrace retrofitting technologies into daily practices and behaviour of residents, organisations, workers, and travellers.

Within the general context of scholarship that elaborates and questions behaviour change interventions across diverse policy realms (Jones, Pykett, and Whitehead, 2013), mechanisms to encourage the adoption of low carbon routines and habits generally are the subject of considerable research. Diverse techniques like social marketing, smart meters, public accountability measures like carbon diets, are instigated and monitored by diverse groups, including NGOs, governments and the private sector. Such mechanisms intersect with retrofitting directly and indirectly. Directly the challenge is to encourage individual householders, workers and organisation not only to retrofit their respective spaces materially (dwellings, commercial buildings, vehicles), but also to accommodate and embrace retrofitting technologies into the conduct of daily home and work lives. It is also the case, as suggested in the phrase 'co-production of technology', that technological objects (hybrid cars, smart meters) shape behaviour as well. The urban governance of retrofitting therefore requires attention to both structures of provision (builders, developers, landlords, homeowners, energy providers etc) and to practices of consumption (residents, organisations, workers, travellers etc), which takes us into the domain of behaviour change.

In contemporary analyses of behaviour change initiatives, attention has recently turned to mechanisms through which deeper engagement with subjects of governance may be facilitated, which is also our focus here. One strand of analysis emphasises various forms of deep learning processes that, it is argued, have greater potential to instigate change. These include: (i) 'social learning', a 'combined act of discovery and analysis, of understanding and giving meaning, and of tinkering in the development of routines' (Glad 2012: 280); (ii) higher order learning in which heterogeneous groups come together to exchange and perhaps transform framing of an issue (Vergragt and Brown 2007): and (iii) explicitly deliberative processes involving structured sharing of knowledge and practice (Hobson and Niemeyer 2011). Across these diverse perspectives is a belief that the sharing of knowledge, information and experience can change individuals' perceptions and practices (Cheng *et al.* 2011: 90). A second strand of analysis emphasises the materiality of engagement, in particular Marres' work (2009) on socio-material modes of involvement constituted through eco-homes and other forms of green living experiments. Materials, it is argued, play a critical role in transitions to a low carbon future and, more specifically we argue, in orchestrating retrofit.

Both material and pedagogic strands come together in the notion of demonstration. Initially connected to technology analysis in the sense of 'exhibiting a technological device in action' (Rosenthal 2005: 346) or promoting or selling a technology (Markusson *et al.* 2011: 294), demonstration embeds an impetus for learning through a material mode. Through demonstrations, an artefact is shown to multiple audiences. Demonstration's reliance on techniques of exhibition highlights its materiality. Exhibitions, according to Whitehead (2009), can be seen as 'demonstrating perfection' (ibid.: 74) representing in a holistic way how things could and should work. As part of a broader set of pedagogies, exhibits use moral and economic persuasion in conjunction with new forms of knowledge. Thus, in Whitehead's case study of the governance of atmospheric pollution in Victorian Britain, exhibitions materially recreated the smoke-free home and, in so doing, built new knowledge and social networks around a technology (see also Markusson *et al.* 2011). Socio-material engagements as facilitated through demonstration are governmental in that they bring both practical technologies to a wider audience and in the process 'allow the people to know and thence to regulate themselves' (ibid.: 72), through facilitating an experience of a different reality. As a pedagogy of climate governance, demonstration hence provides a revealing window on the techniques of governing urban retrofitting that we pursue in this chapter.

In what follows we use the framework developed above to capture the multi-scalar, multi institutional and multi-mechanism dimensions of governing retrofit. Whilst principally interested in local-scale governance, we see this as constituted by actors at local and non-local scales. We are also alert to the importance of context in shaping governance limits and possibilities, and attend specifically to the broader Australian context in the next section. We conceive of governance as occurring through both state and non-state actors, as well as partnerships. And finally, we are interested in the mechanisms and techniques of governance as a means through which conduct is 'conducted', with a particular focus on demonstration. These conceptual tools, as the analysis will show, bring to the fore both the potentials and pitfalls of governing retrofit.

Governing retrofit at the local scale in the Australian city: The case of Sydney

As we have discussed elsewhere (Dowling, McGuirk and Bulkeley, 2014), retrofit is governed at multiple scales in Australia, principally state, national and local. State and national government involvement in governing retrofit has two key characteristics. First, and specifically in relation to the socio-technical nature of retrofit, is the relative lack of engagement with the social practices of energy consumption. By far the majority of policies are targeted at the installation of more energy efficient technologies and renewable energy sources: for example, providing rebates to install solar PV, grants to retrofit buildings, information programs to promote purchase of environmental offsets for fleet vehicles. With rare exceptions, such as mandatory environmental standards for residential renovations, engagement with the use and integration of retrofitted technologies into patterns and practices of daily life is not constructed as being within the remit of state or federal government. Second is the indirect nature of much of this involvement: with few exceptions outside the regulation of the energy sector and government itself, policies engage soft measures to enable or encourage retrofitting rather than hard measures to mandate it. Moreover, these are overwhelmingly policies that require multi-institutional cooperation across states or partnerships with local governments and community organisations. The state and federal approach to retrofitting Australian cities can be succinctly summarised as 'governing at a distance'.

Local scale retrofitting governance in Australia is certainly imagined within and conditioned by these federal and state scales, as suggested by the plethora of grants available. Yet local governance with some independence from state and federal parameters is also feasible and, indeed, is evident within Australian cities. Thus in 2011/2012 we carried out a survey of carbon abatement initiatives across the domains of energy infrastructure, buildings and transport being undertaken at the local scale across all eight of Australia's state and territory capital cities (Sydney, Brisbane, Canberra, Darwin, Adelaide, Melbourne, Hobart and Perth). Importantly, this survey encompassed not just explicit carbon abatement strategies, but also interventions and initiatives that indirectly targeted carbon abatement – such as environmental education programs that incorporate reductions in energy use. Given our resources, it was not possible to survey each local jurisdiction in the capital cities. Instead, a sample of approximately a third of local government areas in these cities was surveyed, encompassing a theoretically informed selection of small and large, CBD, inner and mid city, and outer suburban jurisdictions. The audit started with websites of local governments, known not-for-private and community organisations, and documented private sector interventions, and then snowballed out from these to identify less visible interventions. This approach resulted in the identification of 896 initiatives related to buildings, transport and energy infrastructure, of which one-third had a retrofitting component. Then, using a framework developed by Castán Broto and Bulkeley (2013), we classified these according to who initiated/participated, the focus of the initiative, the mechanisms through which it was undertaken, its target audiences and its funding. We draw from the Sydney initiatives documented in the audit to capture and characterise retrofitting governance at the local scale.

Of the 278 initiatives identified in Sydney, 103 had a retrofitting component (see Table 13.1). Mirroring the state and national policy context, these initiatives can generally be described as intentional but small-scale retrofitting interventions, with an absence of holistic visions for retrofitting the city. Turning first to the institutions of retrofitting governance, we found that most were initiated by local government (79 per cent), principally acting alone (44 per cent), though occasionally using funding from other sources. The rest were initiated by a diverse group, of which the private and non-government sectors were the most active, with minimal direct federal and state government involvement as instigators of initiatives. The retrofitting of transport (e.g. the conversion of existing vehicles to alternative fuels) is marked by its relative absence (just two initiatives); with most local retrofitting governance instead focusing on residential, commercial or public buildings. Thus most prevalent in terms of a material focus was retrofitting energy provision at the building scale, typified by installing devices that enable individual buildings to be powered from renewable or low carbon sources. Technologically, there was an overwhelming focus on micro-generation in the form of the installation of solar PV, and on energy efficiency through the conversion of lighting, heating and cooling to more energy efficient forms (LED, gas, solar). Compared to state and federal policies, these initiatives have an equal focus on the initiating organisation and residential buildings/households (43 and 44 per cent respectively) and are less likely to address retrofitting by businesses or of business premises. Initiatives were much more likely to use enabling mechanisms such as the provision of advice, audits and information, suggesting again the predominance of governing at a distance.

The techniques through which governing retrofit is pursued are the focus of the rest of this chapter. For these purposes, we classify each Sydney-based retrofitting initiative captured in our audit in terms of a four-fold typology (Table 13.2). The categories of the typology are not mutually exclusive: though all initiatives fall into one of these categories; some fit into two or more. We describe and analyse these techniques in what follows.

Table 13.1 Characteristics of local retrofitting initiatives in Sydney, 2012

	Energy Infrastructure		Buildings		Transport		Total %
	#	% of 24	#	% of 77	#	% of 2	% of 103
Total initiatives	24	100.00	77	100.00	2	100.00	100
TARGET AUDIENCE							
Own organisation/ personnel	23	95.8	19	24.7	2	100	**42.7**
Residential building/ household/travellers	1	4.2	42	54.5	2	100	**43.7**
Business tenant	0	0	26	33.8	0	0	**25.2**
Landlords	n/a	n/a	3	3.9	n/a	n/a	**0**
Schools	0	0	1	1.3	n/a	n/a	**0**
FOCUS							
Technical	23	95.9	72	93.5	2	100.0	**94.1**
Social	5	20.8	52	67.5	0	0	**55.3**
MECHANISM							
Regulation	5	20.8	14	13.6	0	0	**18.4**
Market	1	4.2	23	22.3	0	0	**23.3**
Enabling	22	91.7	75	97.4	2	100	**96.1**
Provision	11	45.8	30	38.9	0	0.0	**39.8**
INSTITUTIONS – INITIATOR							
Local government	24	100	56	72.7	2	100	**79.6**
Private sector	0	0	9	11.7	0	0	**8.7**
NGO/community	0	0	11	14.3	0	0	**10.7**
Federal/state	0	0	7	9.1			
INSTITUTIONS – PARTNER							
None	15	62.5	29	37.6	1	50	**43.7**
Federal government	0	0	5	6.49	1	50	**0**
State government	0	0	16	20.78	0	0.0	**0.2**
Local government	7	29.1	29	37.6	0	0.0	**34.9**
NGO/community	0	0	11	14.3	0	0.0	**0.1**
Corporation	4	16.7	21	27.3	0	0.0	**24.2**

Source: Authors' survey, 2011/2012

Holistic retrofitting is a technique that tackles retrofitting in a coordinated and multidimensional manner. It pertains to large-scale programs to retrofit the energy infrastructure, travel patterns and building fabric of a particular geographical area (e.g. a local government area), most

Table 13.2 Techniques for locally governing urban retrofitting in Australia

Technique	Focus	Materials	Institutions	Mechanisms
Holistic	Built environment structure of provision	Micro-generation Solar PV Cycling infrastructure	Whole-of-government; large-scale partnerships	Multiple: demonstration, provision, regulation, grants, education
Self governance	Own institution: built form, employee activities	Solar PV, LED lighting, insulation	Single organisation; funding from national and state governments	Financial: subsidies, grants
Facilitative	Businesses, households, schools, other organisations	Lighting, heating and cooling systems	Local government as broker/enabler	Financial; Education; Ratings
Educative	Activities of households, businesses in utilising retrofit technologies	Lighting, Solar PV, insulation	Local government	Information provision; engagement; demonstration

often as part of a clearly articulated retrofitting vision. These are rare in urban Australia, and are thus far confined to the well-resourced CBDs of Sydney, or federally-funded programs like *Solar Cities* or *Smart Grid, Smart City*. Unlike the more narrowly-focused initiatives in the other elements of the typology, these initiatives focus on retrofitting the wider energy infrastructure in combination with retrofitting individual buildings. They do so through facilitation, direct intervention, as well as through widespread education and demonstration. Interestingly, the use of strong regulatory measures is rare even across these schemes with wide ambition. Australian cities have not, for example, restricted cars from their city centres nor have they mandated building energy performance for existing buildings.

The City of Sydney's Sydney 2030 program is illustrative here (see: www.sydney2030.com.au/). Following a comprehensive visioning and strategic planning process, the City (an area encompassing the CBD and immediate surrounds) developed a strategic plan that prioritised sustainability, in which initiatives targeting the retrofitting of diverse sectors (transport, energy, buildings) were introduced across the city. As befits the term holistic, the City of Sydney example involves a broad spectrum of governance mechanisms, as well as a multi-dimensional focus across residents, businesses, transport and infrastructure. These include a business-coordinated retrofitting of commercial buildings, a plan to move city buildings off the coal-fired state-wide electricity grid and onto a city-scale trigeneration system, the conversion of road space to cycling paths, as well as the conversion of council vehicle fleets, lighting and buildings to low or zero carbon energy sources. Such holistic governance, though politically and popularly contested, is underpinned by a strongly articulated vision matched by political and economic resources to bring the vision to fruition. It is also connected to the City of Sydney's economic strategy to be identified as 'green and global' (Acuto, 2012).

Retrofitting through *self-governance* in the form of retrofitting an organisation's own assets is our second mode of governance. This includes the retrofitting of public buildings like council offices, local-government-owned swimming pools, libraries, or the headquarters of non-government organisations. About 40 per cent of retrofitting interventions were of this type, suggesting that local authorities in Australia have a most pronounced capacity to act with respect to their own organisation. Self governance sees various adaptations to buildings made to reduce carbon footprints, including installation of insulation, or solar PV and changes in lighting. Beyond individual buildings this also includes the conversion of systems of street lighting to LED and the conversion of council car fleets to non-gasoline fuels. Specific examples are numerous and are found extensively within and beyond Sydney; buildings retrofitted in this way can be found in almost every Australian local government area. Funding via the federal and state grant programs outlined in the previous section is critical to self-governance. A number of inner city councils, for example, use various grant schemes to retrofit the lighting, heating and cooling systems of their swimming pools, parks and community centres. In this mode, local institutions are principally enacting an authority and capacity to govern the consumption of energy in their own buildings, though primarily through application of energy efficient or renewable technologies rather than a concerted focus on behaviour. Self-governance can, nonetheless, have an educative component, in that many of these buildings are also used to demonstrate low carbon living to a broader audience.

Closely related though different is retrofitting through facilitative techniques, in which local governments *facilitate* or *broker* the retrofitting activities of local businesses, organisations (e.g. schools) and households through a combination of education, provision and access to funding. Local governments (and sometimes non-government or private sector actors) facilitate access to grants, audits and bulk purchase schemes to enable households etc to decarbonise their buildings through retrofitting measures. Here, local agencies (government, non-government and commercial) use publicity and access to knowledge, programmes and other schemes to attempt to shape conduct so as to initiate retrofitting, primarily at the building scale. Local agencies connect businesses and households with the practicalities and materials of retrofitting. An example here is Auburn and

Parramatta's *Streamline Your Business* program in which the local authority provides a business with access to an on-site energy assessment and a tailored Energy Action Plan detailing how they can save energy, including through retrofitting technologies. A program with wider geographical reach is *CitySwitch*, a national local government-commercial tenant partnership that includes four local authorities in Sydney. The program explicitly works with commercial tenants in the geographical areas to provide information, tailored advice and implementation plans on reducing their carbon footprint, including a strong emphasis on retrofit. Local government involvement is essential: facilitating access to organisations, assisting in the hosting of events and administering associated grant programs.

Governing retrofit in an *educative* mode is by far the most common strategy both across our sample nationally and in Sydney. This emphasis no doubt stems from local governments' long term environmental education focus as well as the assumption that correcting the 'information deficit' is key to changing energy-related behaviour (Shove, 2010). Thus our audit captured myriad initiatives that aimed to inspire, inform and educate households and businesses about retrofitting their premises and to integrate retrofit technologies into their daily lives. A wide range of educative strategies is evident, with information provision through leaflets, websites and newsletters most prevalent. A number of organisations, for instance, use a commercially produced 'Sustainable Living Guide' in which households are informed about the carbon-reduction benefits of installing newer energy efficient appliances as well as insulation. Local governments also run workshops for residents to see retrofitting technologies in practice. For example, the *Treading Lightly* initiative, which operates collectively across several Sydney local governments, consists of 6-monthly blocks of weekly workshops primarily targeting local householders and focusing on domestic and household activities. The focus is on encouraging the update of technologies rather than their use. Information provision, toolkits, and workshops all facilitate, encourage, and inform rather than mandate. Thus governing retrofit in an educative mode shapes conduct indirectly and in this respect shares the focus of facilitating retrofit.

In sum, the retrofitting challenge is certainly being addressed at the local scale in Sydney, through a proliferation of initiatives and by a variety of actors. Governing retrofit in educative, holistic, facilitative and self-governing ways, these initiatives largely eschew direct intervention in favour of 'at-a-distance' techniques that render the issue and its solutions visible to a broad audience. Thus the potential of local scale retrofitting governance in Australia is yet to be fully realised. This is partly because of poor alignment between the technological and social dimensions of retrofitting. In short, where the system of provision is being directed towards retrofitting, the intended subjectivities and practices are scarcely taken into account and hence are likely to fail to materialise or at least to under perform. Likewise, interventions to create new subjects and practices (e.g. through education) are not supported by systems of provision in which these subjects could act. Demonstration, as we flagged earlier in this chapter, can potentially bring together technologies and materials, a claim that we investigate further in the next section.

Demonstrating retrofit

In terms of the above typology, demonstration is a subset of educative mechanisms. However, unlike the largely at-a-distance techniques that dominate educating for retrofit in our sample, demonstration has the capacity to act more directly, and with a simultaneous focus on social and technical aspects. Across the sample of Sydney interventions we charted, the demonstration of low carbon retrofitting technologies, creating life-like contexts and connecting technologies to their daily use, was spasmodic. These largely focused on the domestic sphere, such as the home of a sustainability pioneer regularly open to the public, purpose-built show homes for low carbon living, or 'demonstration homes' established in council-owned premises, demonstrating retrofitting *in situ*. There were also a number of demonstrations of retrofitting corporate and public spaces (i.e. demonstration connected to self governance) that take us beyond the increasingly well documented domestic-focused demonstrations. We briefly present two such cases here as a means of excavating the different means and purposes of demonstrating retrofit.

Our first example – Greening the Wharf (GTW) – entailed retrofitting one of Sydney's heritage-protected former wharves, which is the current home of the Sydney Theatre Company. After being used as a theatre for more than 20 years, in 2007 a comprehensive retrofitting program was initiated following an environmental audit and the appointment of high profile celebrity husband and wife climate activists Cate Blanchett and Andrew Upton as artistic directors. By the end of 2010 the wharf had been retrofitted with Australia's second largest rooftop solar array; a rainwater harvesting system; solar hot water and the installation of energy efficient appliances through the theatre, focusing on lighting and the public bathrooms; and integrated, interactive public displays detailing the retrofit, its effect and the possibility for wider adoption of its approach (see Figures 13.1 and 13.2). GTW is deliberately ambitious, encompassing 'infrastructure projects, company-wide behavioural change, environmentally responsible theatre production, community engagement and education' with the quantified goal being to reduce annual carbon emissions by 550 tonnes (greeningthewharf.com).

A distinctive, corporate-focused and multiscalar set of institutions were assembled in GTW, with minimal local government involvement. Primary funding of $1.2 million was provided as part of the Federal Government's

Figure 13.1 Greening the wharf solar rooftop PV

Green Precincts Program and the NSW Government, as owner of the wharf and landlord, carried out the retrofitting. Further philanthropic funding of more than $2 million was received from a small number of wealthy individuals and family foundations. This amalgam of public private partnerships, with philanthropy and celebrity, underpin the distinctive form that demonstration has taken here.

A second distinctive element of GTW is its positioning as demonstrating cutting edge technologies. The solar array, for example, is noted as the first commercial installation of this new type of PV cell. Likewise, the rainwater harvesting system is one of only a handful in the world. For GTW, an important goal was to 'demonstrate that complex infrastructural projects – such as the solar array and the rainwater harvesting system – can succeed at high profile heritage sites' (greeningthewharf.com). GTW encourages learning, though in a scientific register. Scientific knowledge is valorised, whether that be through hosting special talks of the Wentworth Group of Concerned Scientists,[2] telling the retrofit story through the evidence of numbers, and engaging audiences through data (Figure 13.2). Through smart metering, toolkits and guides, it involves data gathering and monitoring as part of the daily practice of running a theatre: checking production sourcing against sustainability criteria, being aware of and adjusting energy use in response to data gathered. The principal audience for the demonstration was professionals in the arts and heritage sectors. Nonetheless, theatre audiences are also engaged digitally through 'Green Screen' information kiosks that highlight energy efficiency information and through touch screens which invite theatre patrons to understand the technologies used in retrofitting the wharf and consider undertaking them in their own homes.

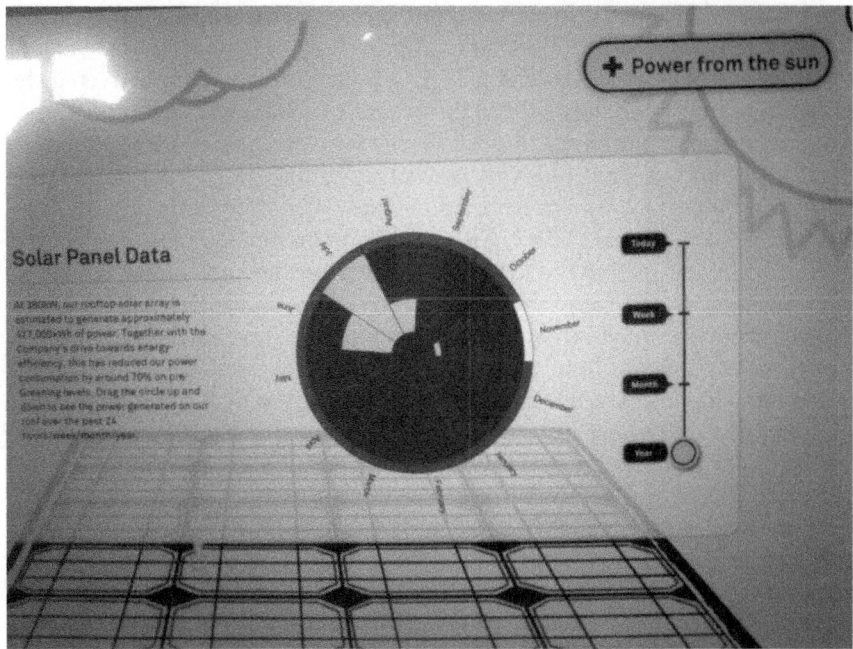

Figure 13.2 Greening the wharf 'green screen'

Our second example is also an iconic site in Sydney. Located approximately 100 kilometres west of the CBD, the Blue Mountains town of Katoomba is the geographical heart of a World Heritage site that attracts millions of tourists each year, as well as a burgeoning resident population, many of whom articulate a very strong 'green ethos'. Our retrofitting example is the Blue Mountains Sustainable Precinct, which consists of three non-contiguous buildings – the Echo Point Visitor Information Centre, Katoomba Civic Centre and Blue Mountains Cultural Centre – with the first two being retrofitted and the last being a redevelopment of an old site. Together, the buildings serve both resident and tourist populations, and are owned and managed by the local authority – Blue Mountains City Council. In 2010 the Civic Centre was upgraded with rainwater tanks, new windows and solar photovoltaic panels, and in 2012 the Echo Point Visitor Centre was retrofitted with a stormwater harvesting system and solar PV (see Figure 13.3 and photos at: www.environment.gov.au/topics/water/water-cities-and-towns/green-precincts-fund/blue-mountains-city-council/gallery-blue). Both projects were completed through part funding from the Federal Government's Green Precincts fund, and as such had a critical demonstration element, in particular to showcase working examples of innovative design in an environmentally sensitive context.

The Blue Mountains Sustainable Precinct was enacted by a set of state-based actors. Significant financial support was provided by the Federal Government. The Blue Mountains City Council initiated and delivered the project, and part-funded it through the use of local environmental levies. This amalgam of interests flowed through to the means through which demonstration occurred. With the exception of the solar PV on the Visitor Information Centre, the retrofitted technologies were largely invisible. Visitors to the Cultural Centre, for example, are reminded that many of the green features of the building (like the solar panels or the unique insulating wall cavities) would be invisible to them. The pedagogic elements of the project were confined to signage across the precinct, and can hence be described as having a light touch, being attuned to context, and decidedly non digital. Signage around Echo Point asks tourist to look differently at the buildings they may have just visited and suggests ways visitors could incorporate similar changes in their own spaces (Figure 13.4). Discussions of the project emphasise the capability of the Blue Mountains City Council to implement green strategies, suggesting that the project is demonstrating the capacity and authority of local government to act as much as the efficacy of retrofitting.

Figure 13.3 Echo Point information centre solar PV

Did you see what was on the roof?

Blue Mountains City Council has installed solar power (photovoltaic panels) for electricity usage at Echo Point. By using solar power we are protecting the environment and saving money.

Sunlight is converted into electricity by the photovoltaic panels. Solar power is the cleanest and most viable form of renewable energy available.

The 55 panels at Echo Point produce 10 kilowatts of power at their peak. They have a long life that will produce over 16,000kWh of electricity every year. This will reduce greenhouse emissions by over 17 tonnes every year.

Photovoltaics generate electric power by using solar cells to convert energy from the sun into electricity. They are made of semiconductors such as silicon. When light strikes the cell, energy from the sun is absorbed. This energy allows electrons to flow freely.

This flow of electrons is a current, and by placing metal contacts on the top and bottom of the photovoltaic cell, the current is drawn off for external use. Cells require protection from the environment and are usually packaged tightly behind a glass sheet. Cells are connected together to form solar panels.

Power generation varies throughout the day with the majority of power generated at the peak of the day. The solar panels work in all weather but work best on clear, cool days.

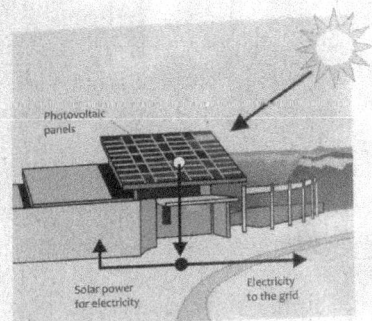

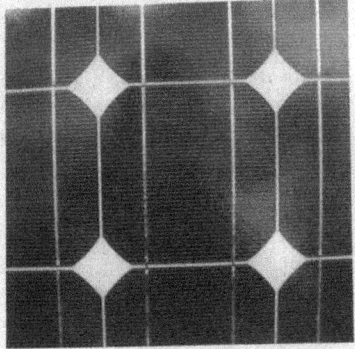

How you can help

At home, you can use energy more effectively through insulation, going solar, choosing heating and cooling carefully and by being energy smart with your appliances.

Environment Levy

Figure 13.4 Educating retrofit in the Blue Mountains sustainable precinct

These examples highlight the multiscalar, multi-actor constitution and the at-a distance nature of governance that is broadly characteristic of the way urban retrofits being governed in Australia's largest city. Governance interventions that pursue retrofitting through demonstration have the potential to bridge this constructed dualism of social and technical elements by exhibiting retrofitting technologies in a specific context for a specific audience. In so doing, they bring technologies into context, and with the assistance of pedagogical strategies like information provision, may induce retrofitting. The examples discussed here, however, illustrate the complex and fragile connections between a demonstrational intent and deeper learning as theoretically envisaged. In both cases, multiple registers and audiences of demonstrations were in evidence as the projects sought to address actors concerned with structures of provision and wider audiences as inhabitants and users of various spaces with retrofitting potential (heritage sites, residential spaces etc.). However, the ambitious reach of these projects diluted their outcomes as retrofitting demonstrations. Both the Sydney Theatre Company and Blue Mountains Council can be interpreted as attempting to demonstrate institutional authority and capacity to instigate change, with the consequence that direct educational engagement was a weaker element. Both projects were trying to reach domestic audiences through a commercial context. While this allowed an extended reach for the demonstration in terms of the considerable number of annual visitors to each site, it also necessitated a less direct engagement with various publics. In both sites visitors were not able to materially engage with retrofitting technologies in their habitual context. In this sense the technique of demonstration, as practiced in the cases examined here, struggles to overcome the distance between technology and practice, to engage with the socio-technical nature of retrofitting and to promote related learning across its diverse target audiences. In sum, these examples necessarily force us to develop a more complex understanding of demonstration as a governance technique, acknowledging the role that context plays in shaping audiences, purposes and mechanisms used.

CONCLUSION

In this chapter we have illustrated how the governance challenge of transitioning cities to low carbon futures through retrofitting is being addressed by multiple state and non-state institutions, and through diverse mechanisms. Focusing on just one Australian city, we have found a proliferation of initiatives, principally at the local scale, that aim to directly or indirectly (through incentives, education, etc.) retrofit diverse elements of cities. Beyond this proliferation, the landscape of governing urban retrofitting in Sydney is an uneven one. There is no citywide vision or program of retrofitting in Sydney, and the local initiatives we have documented here are piecemeal across multiple dimensions – geographical focus, technical focus, materiality of engagement.

Nonetheless these initiatives – in their educative, facilitative, self-governing and holistic forms – provide insights for thinking about retrofitting at the citywide scale. Initiatives that work through the self-governing, facilitative and educative modes of governance are likely to be incremental in their effect, through an accretion of multiple actions by multiple actors from individual households to place-based organisations, to organisations involved in the structures of provision operating citywide. They constitute an ecology of initiatives that collectively can contribute substantially to city-wide retrofitting (McGuirk, Bulkeley and Dowling 2014), notwithstanding the tendency to date for them to focus on a technical rather than a socio-technical conception of retrofitting. Holistic retrofitting, in addressing infrastructure and behaviour simultaneously, escapes this limitation. Such initiatives tend to arise through multi-level partnerships, and encouraging wide-reaching local government involvement in such partnerships may be a productive option for enhancing city-wide retrofitting that engages technological and social practice dimensions. The challenge of the diversity of means and modes through which retrofitting is being governed is one of coordination. The diverse modes of retrofitting governance identified here may reach their limits however when they encounter urban systems – notably infrastructural systems – that are integral to the capacity to retrofit, yet require coordinated, citywide action. The multiple purposes and practices of retrofitting governance revealed in this chapter, therefore, highlight its existing limitations as well as its potentials to be explored in further policy and theoretical work.

Notes

1 Portions of this chapter have been published as Dowling, R., McGuirk, P. and Bulkeley, H. (2014). 'Retrofitting cities: Local governance in Sydney, Australia', *Cities* 38: 1824. The research on which this chapter was based by funded by the Australian Research Council (DP110100081). We are grateful for research assistance provided by Nicola Vaughan.

2 The Wentworth Group is an independent group of leading Australian scientists concerned with intervening in debates and policy setting to secure the sustainability of Australia's land water and biosecurity.

References

Australian Government (2011). *Securing a Green Energy Future: The Australian Government's Climate Change Plan*. Canberra: Commonwealth of Australia.

Acuto, M. (2012). Ain't about politics? The wicked power-geometry of Sydney's greening governance. *International Journal of Urban and Regional Research, 36,* 381–399.

Betsill, M. and Bulkeley, H. (2006). Cities and the multilevel governance of global climate change. *Global Governance, 12,* 141–159.

Betsill, M. and Bulkeley, H. (2007). Looking back and thinking ahead: A decade of cities and climate change research. *Local Environment, 12,* 447–456.

Bulkeley, H. and Castán Broto, V. (2013). Government by experiment? Global cities and the governing of climate change. *Transactions of the Institute of British Geographers, 38,* 361–375.

Castán Broto, V. and Bulkeley, H. (2013). A survey of urban climate change experiments in 100 cities. *Global Environmental Change, 23,* 92–102.

Cheng, A., Danks, C. and Allred, S. (2011). The role of social and policy learning in changing forest governance: An examination of community-based forestry initiatives in the US. *Forest Policy and Economics 13,* 89–96.

Deakin, M., Campbell, F. and Reid, A. (2012). The mass-retrofitting of an energy efficient low carbon zone: Baselining the urban regeneration strategy, vision, masterplan and redevelopment scheme. *Energy Policy, 45,* 187–200.

Dowling, R., McGuirk, P. and Bulkeley, H. (2014). Retrofitting cities: Local governance in Sydney, Australia. *Cities, 38,* 18–24.

Eames, M., Hunt, M., Dixton, T. and Britnell, J. (2013) Retrofit city futures: Visions for urban sustainability. Report. University of Cardiff, Cardiff, Wales.

Ekers, M. and Loftus, A. (2008). The power of water: developing dialogues between Foucault and Gramsci. *Environment and Planning D: Society and Space 26,* 698–718.

Ghosh, S. and Head, L. (2009). Retrofitting the suburban garden: morphologies and some elements of sustainability potential of two Australian residential suburbs compared. *Australian Geographer, 40,* 319–346.

Glad, W. (2012). Housing renovation and energy systems: the need for social learning. *Building Research and Information, 40,* 274–289.

Gossop, C. (2011). Low carbon cities: an introduction to the special issue. *Cities, 28,* 495–497.

Hargreaves, T. (2011). Practice-ing behaviour change: applying social practice theory to pro-environmental behaviour change. *Journal of Consumer Culture, 11,* 79–99.

Hobson, K. and Nienmeyer, S. (2011). Public responses to climate change: the role of deliberation in building capacity for adaptive action. *Global Environmental Change 21*(3): 957–971.

Hodson, M. and Marvin, S. (2010). Can cities shape socio-technical transitions and how would we know if they were? *Research Policy, 39.*

Hodson, M., Marvin, S., Robinson, B. and Swilling, M. (2012). Reshaping urban infrastructure. *Journal of Industrial Ecology, 16,* 789–800.

Hoffmann, M.J. (2011). *Climate governance at the crossroads: Experimenting with a global response after Kyoto.* Oxford; New York: Oxford University Press.

Jones, R., Pykett, J. and Whitehead, M. (2013). Behaviour Change policies in the UK: An anthropological perspective. *Geoforum, 48,* 33–41.

Kelly, M.J. (2009). Retrofitting the existing UK building stock. *Building Research and Information, 37,* 196–200.

Keskitalo, E.C.H., Juhola, S. and Westerhoff, L. (2012). Climate change as governmentality: Technologies of government for adaptation in three European countries. *Journal of Environmental Planning and Management, 55,* 435–452.

Li, T. (2007). *The Will to Improve: Governmentality, Development, and the Practice of Politics.* London: Duke University Press.

Markusson, N., Ishii, A. and Stephens, J.C. (2011). The social and political complexities of learning in carbon capture and storage demonstration projects. *Global Environmental Change, 21*, 293–302.

McGuirk, P. and Dowling, R. (2009). Neoliberal privatisation? Remapping the public and the private in Sydney's masterplanned residential estates. *Political Geography, 28*, 170–185.

McGuirk, P., Bulkeley, H. and Dowling, R. (2014). Practices, programs and projects of urban carbon governance: perspectives from the Australian city. *Geoforum 52*, 137–47, 10.1016/j.geoforum.2014.01.007.

Monstadt, J. (2007). Urban governance and the transition of energy systems: institutional change and shifting energy and climate policies in Berlin. *International Journal of Urban and Regional Research, 31*, 326–343.

Paterson, M. and Stripple, J. (2010). My space: governing individual's carbon emissions. *Environment and Planning D: Society and Space, 28*, 341–362.

Pincetl, S. (2012). Nature, urban development and sustainability – What new elements are needed for a more comprehensive understanding? *Cities, 29, Supplement 2*, S32–S37.

Rice, J.L. (2010). Climate, carbon, and territory: greenhouse gas mitigation in Seattle, WA. *Annals of the Association of American Geographers, 100*, 929–937.

Rosenthal C, 2005, Making science and technology results public: a sociology of demos, in Latour B and Weibel P (eds), *Making Things Public. Atmospheres of Democracy*, Cambridge, MA: ZKM/MIT, pp. 346–348.

Schiellerup, P. and Gwilliam, J. (2009). Social production of desirable space: An exploration of the practice and role of property agents in the UK commercial property market. *Environment and Planning C: Government and Policy, 27*, 801–814.

Schroeder, H. and Lovell, H. (2011). The role of non-nation-state actors and side events in the international climate negotiations. *Climate Policy*, 1–15.

Shove, E. (2010). Beyond the ABC: Climate change policy and theories of social change. *Environment and Planning A, 42*, 1273–1285.

Sunikka-Blank, M., Chen, J., Britnell, J. and Dantsiou, D. (2012). Improving energy efficiency of social housing areas: A case study of a retrofit achieving an 'A' energy performance rating in the UK. *European Planning Studies, 20*, 131–145.

Sustainable Sydney 2030. Available from www.sydney2030.com.au/.

Vergragt, P.J. and Brown, H.S. (2007). Sustainable mobility: from technological innovation to societal learning. *Journal of Cleaner Production* 15(11–12): 1104–1115.

While, A., Jonas, A. and Gibbs, D. (2010). From sustainable development to carbon control: Eco-state restructuring and the politics of urban and regional development. *Transactions of the Institute of British Geographers, 35*, 76–93.

Whitehead, M. (2009). *State, science and the skies: Governmentalities of the British atmosphere.* Chichester: Wiley-Blackwell.

Willand, N., Moore, T., Hunter, S., Stanley, H. and Horne, R. (2012). *Drivers of Demand for Zero and Towards Zero Emissions Residential Retrofits*, Report for the Australian Sustainable Built Environment Council. Available from http://asbec.asn.au/files/120913%20Drivers%20of%20Demand%20for%20Zero%20and%20Towards%20Zero%20Emissions%20-%20Final%20Draft_0.pdf

Chapter 14

Partnerships for climate change in Maputo, Mozambique

Vanesa Castán Broto, Emily Boyd, Jonathon Ensor and Sirkku Juhola

INTRODUCTION

The notion of climate compatible development (Mitchell and Maxwell 2010) is promoted by the Climate Development Knowledge Network and associated organisations as a means to transcend the dichotomy between climate change mitigation and adaptation. This is particularly important in an urban context in which the emphasis on either mitigation or adaptation depends on the timescale adopted in planning and decision-making (Davoudi *et al.* 2009). While short-term plans tend to emphasise the management of increasing risks, policies looking at a longer timescale will have to consider the need to mitigate anthropogenic impacts in the resource base in the city and beyond.

When thinking about current climate change challenges in urban Africa, the key question is what kind of intervention will be appropriate for a particular context. Because of the heterogeneity of climate change impacts, vulnerability factors and the multiple possibilities to address them, climate change calls for solutions tailored to specific contexts (Simon 2010). In many cities in Africa, however, the absence of good forms of planning has led to a situation in which

> planning systems are relics of colonial days, and cities suffer from failed attempts by international aid and development agencies to address urban issues through development models based on assumptions that rarely hold in this part of the world.
>
> (Parnell *et al.* 2009: 233)

There is thus a need to rethink what kind of interventions are suitable in specific urban contexts such as the one studied in this chapter, Maputo, where the need to reconfigure infrastructure systems towards more sustainable ones, meets the need to provide universal and equitable services. This is both a material and a governance challenge, one which also involves systemic retrofitting thinking in the sense of building sustainability within a given spatial and historical context. It is thus 'a fundamental issue' of 'systemic retrofit' that

> requires bringing together not just those working at the levels of buildings, pipes and cables but policy-makers, utilities, business, communities, users and so on.
>
> (May *et al.* 2013: 7)

Feasibility is a condition for service provision, but a degree of institutional development to address current environmental challenges will also be needed.

What institutional mechanisms will thus, enable accomplishing retrofitting measures for climate compatible development in cities in the global south? Partnerships are most often valued by policy makers and delivery agencies as a flexible means to respond to uncertain and ever-changing challenges. Yet, there is a case for re-examining partnerships within a cooperative model of environmental governance, one in which both knowledge and values are negotiated through the constitution of the partnership. The objective of this chapter is, thus, to examine partnerships as a form of environmental governance to deliver climate compatible development. As institutions, partnerships invoke a 'self-reliant green city' model, underpinned by cooperative and collectivist values which highlight participation, shared ownership, mutualism and a strong concern for social equity (Eames *et al.* 2013). Thus, the chapter presents the notion of partnership in relation to the tradition of cooperative environmental governance and links the operation of partnerships with the context in which they emerge.[1]

After a theoretical review of the notion of partnership, the second part of the chapter examines the operation of partnerships in context. To do so we present a comparative analysis of three different forms of partnership, which emerge associated with different forms of service delivery crucial for achieving climate compatible development in the city of Maputo, Mozambique. From this analysis we conclude that: 1) partnerships open up spaces for the operation of multiple actors in climate compatible development at different scales; 2) actors, however, do not necessarily adopt predetermined roles and partnerships provide spaces for actors to act in unorthodox manner; 3) partnerships may also represent the displacement of responsibilities for climate protection and service delivery. Overall, the comparative analysis suggests that partnerships open up a variety of institutional models for the delivery of systemic retrofit projects.

Partnerships as forms of cooperative environmental governance

Public-private models of service delivery have emerged as a strong model of climate policy delivery within the city. A recent survey of hundreds of climate change initiatives in cities, for example, highlighted that nearly half of them are achieved through a form of partnership (Castán Broto and Bulkeley 2012). This overall enthusiasm for partnership has generated an urgency to deal critically with this concept, not only in terms of its practical applications, but also in relation to broader governance processes in which partnerships are embedded. This section examines the concept of partnership within broader environmental governance debates by situating it within a cooperative environmental governance paradigm. After looking at partnerships from this perspective, the review then focuses on different aspects of and approaches to partnerships and broader criticisms which have emerged as the approach has gained currency. The review concludes with a discussion of the relevance of partnerships in the context of climate change governance.

Meadowcroft (1998: 22) defined a cooperative management regime as 'a form of social regulation in which groups originating in different spheres of social life, and reflecting distinct perspectives and interests, participate in debate and negotiation to achieve a common understanding of a scientific problem, and then implement a collective plan for its resolution'. In his analysis he described cooperative environmental governance as a set of processes, which bring together a cross-section of actors with different interests but implicated in a similar environmental problem. These processes are oriented, in principle, towards developing forms of periodic consensus that enable all parties to jointly commit to collective solutions.

Cooperative environmental governance models come into view as alternatives to models that emphasise separate roles for actors belonging to different social spheres (government, business, civil society) in environmental policy (e.g. regulation, market-led innovations, activism). Overall, cooperative environmental governance emerges linked to the withdrawal of government following privatization and decentralization ideals and the inclusion of private-sector values in administrative structures (Glasbergen 1998; Meadowcroft 1998). In this sense, cooperative environmental governance agreements need to be understood not only as policy delivery mechanisms, but moreover, as processes whereby policy is made (Forsyth 2005a; Meadowcroft 1998). While encouraging mechanisms associated with pluralism, consensus building, flexibility and adaptability, cooperative governance becomes a strategy to extend authority beyond the traditional realms of the government.

An analysis of the terminology employed in cooperative environmental governance showed that this type of agreement is most often deployed in relation to ideas of partnership and collaboration (Plummer and Fitz-Gibbon 2004). Plummer and FitzGibbon (2004) reviewed several cases of cooperative governance agreements and identified two fundamental models (Figure 14.1). The government is a pivotal actor in both models, but each model is actually defined by the type of non-governmental partner who

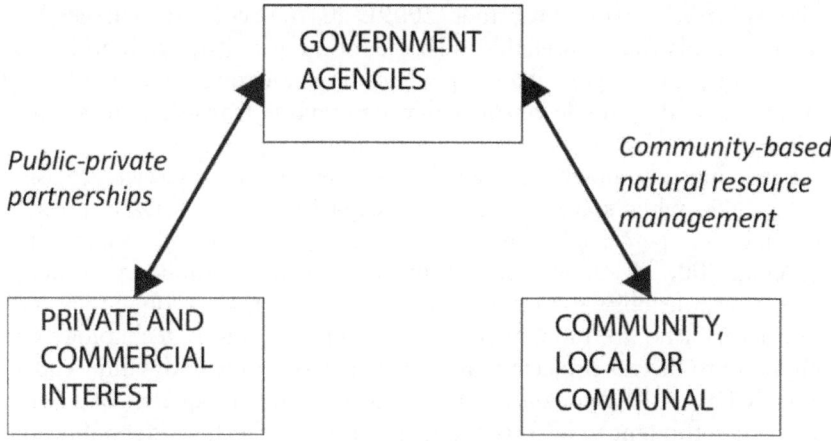

Figure 14.1 Cooperative environmental governance models (adapted from Plummer and Fitzgibbon, 2004)

intervenes in the agreement. In the first model, agreements are directed towards creating collaboration between government and business, which has generated public-private partnerships models popular in service delivery and infrastructure management. In the second model, agreements include cases in which the state devolves responsibilities to communities, following the growing enthusiasm in the past two decades towards community-based management of natural resources in development projects.

Yet, limiting cooperative environmental governance agreements to these two distinct models overlooks the heterogeneity of collaborative mechanisms found in practice. Flexibility and ambiguity are at the core of this evolving paradigm. In the context of climate change, in which the need to deliver better low carbon services while protecting communities from the increasing risks requires focusing on service provision agreements, the dominant model is that of partnership but partnerships emerge in a variety of settings and forms.

Partnerships for service provision

Within climate change governance, much emphasis has been directed either towards international agreements on national-level commitments or towards individual behaviour changes both for emissions reductions and the reduction of vulnerability. However, disenchantment with the possibilities of these strategies and evidence from the ground has led to the growing realization that advancements towards a low carbon, resilient society may rather emerge following a reconfiguration of service provision

(Bulkeley *et al.* 2011; Monstadt 2009). In this context, partnerships emerge as tools that can enable such reconfiguration, by facilitating new hybrid institutional agreements capable of implementing the technological innovations and systemic retrofits that can enable transitions to sustainability.

Partnerships are mostly associated with new models of service provision in which the public sector brings in the capacities of the private sector to overcome the perceived limitations of the public sector (Vining and Boardman 2008; Wettenhall 2003). In this model, the public sector maintains the responsibility to provide public services in association with private sector actors who are thought of as being able to bring in technology and capital and to deliver projects more efficiently – on time and within budget (Bovis 2010). This is not only expected to improve the quality of service, but also it is thought to be a tool to gain legitimacy both for the public and private sectors in providing a particular service in a more equitable and efficient manner (Ahmed and Ali 2006). This model has influenced infrastructure development and service provision projects bringing in private capital, particularly in developing countries. This understanding of public-private partnerships as a mechanism whereby the private sector can come into the rescue of the public sector, however, has limited purchase beyond forums dominated by neo-liberal and privatization ideals and is limited in its ability to explain the broad phenomenon of partnership and cooperative agreements for global environmental governance.

There is clear evidence of the diversity of partnership arrangements, not only because they serve many purposes, but also because they may entail diverse forms of cooperation to achieve common objectives (Hodge and Greve 2005; Wang 2000). In this vein, Brinkerhoff (2002; 21) defines partnership 'as a dynamic relationship among diverse actors, based on mutually agreed objectives, pursued through a shared understanding of the most rational division of labour based on the comparative advantages of each partner'. In this notion, partnership entails not just agreeing to deliver common action in relation to each partner's capacities, but rather the fulfilment of an agreed common goal, the sharing of both responsibilities and risks and the transfer of skills and know-how between partners (Kyvelou *et al.* 2011). To achieve this, Brinkerhoff (2002) argues, the partnership needs to achieve high levels of mutuality (in terms of recognizing and responding to the interests of each partners) and high levels of organizational identity (in terms of maintaining the original purpose for each of the organizations involved). In this way, partnership contrasts with other models of association between organizations in which mutuality and organizational identity are not maintained (Table 14.1).

Moreover, there is a need to re-asses the relevance of portraying partnerships as being only within the realm of the private business sector. As emphasized above, for example, there is a body of literature that emphasizes

Table 14.1 Characteristics of a working partnership (Adapted from Brinkerhoff 2002)

		Mutuality	
		Low	**High**
Organisational identity	**High**	Contracting	Partnership
	Low	Extension	Co-optation and gradual absorption

state-community forms of collaboration in partnerships for the management of natural resources. Although this literature focuses on the potential of these forms of agreement within the context of managing natural resources, the same argument can apply to the provision of services, especially in urban and peri-urban areas. While community-based resource management also emerges associated with a critique of state-centred policies and in the context of a general retreat of the state, it may also work as a powerful antidote to all-encompassing narratives of privatization, particularly when emphasizing locally based strategies of self regulation and governance. In the context of development, the literature highlights the need to establish long-term collaborations and social learning processes for the co-production of services (Jaglin *et al.* 2011). Romanticizing the role of communities in providing fair and egalitarian public services overlooks that, on the one hand, they may also operate under highly unequal and inefficient power and authority structures and, on the other, they may also provide mechanisms to reduce local independence and subsume local institutions under more powerful and centralized mechanisms of power. Thus, their effectiveness can only be evaluated in context and on a case-by-case basis.

Within the context of delivering climate change innovations and services, Forsyth (2007) has emphasized the need to reassess the nature of partnerships as deliberative. Building on the hypothesis of institutional diversity, Forsyth (2005b; 429) emphasizes the need to redefine partnerships 'as sites where norms of environmental concern and political accountability are formulated and replicated' beyond their dominant utilitarian definition as mechanisms for the provision of infrastructure and services. In this context, deliberate public-private partnerships are directed towards maximizing opportunities for public debate among a wide range of actors within the spheres of government, market and civil society and with an explicit focus on inclusiveness and establishing the relevance of the partnership goals to local needs. In emphasizing the notion of partnership as a deliberative process, rather than as an established mechanism for the achievement of prefigured goals, Forsyth argues that partnerships are not desirable because of the outputs they generate, but rather, because of their potential to generate a process of institutional development in which new norms emerge from the act of partnering between different actors.

THE RISKS OF WORKING IN PARTNERSHIP

The literature on partnerships has focused on the quasi-privatisation model of government-backed, private-provision of services, and thus, much of the critique of the notion of partnership is associated with the complications emerging from the association of government and private business. Some authors emphasise the difficulty to enrol private partners, by demonstrating the potential economic benefits or adjusting goals to short-term timescales (Koppenjan and Enserink 2009). Most authors, however, focus on the difficulties to bring about a working relationship between partners with regards to negotiating the terms of agreement, ensuring delivery and implementing a monitoring strategy (Osborne 2000; Rosenau 2000).

A deeper critique of the emergence of partnerships as a characteristic phenomenon of global environmental governance requires examining them theoretically within the cooperative environmental governance paradigm. The most fundamental critique, as expressed by Meadowcroft (1998: 33) is the extent to which cooperative and deliberative arrangements recognize that '…real world politics is not about negotiation among equals, but [about] power-centred interactions'. Regardless of the scale, any negotiation process is likely to be shaped by the power arrangements within which the negotiation emerges. As a deliberative mechanism, partnerships should be understood as opening spaces for unheard voices, which inherently may challenge established power arrangements (Forsyth 2005b). Yet, empirical evidence adds a note of caution about the extent to which less powerful actors are able to shape technological and environmental decisions (Forsyth 2005a). Here, the struggle in partnership building is less about the specific mechanisms whereby the partnership is made functional and more about the definition of what counts as knowledge. Partnership actors are defined as stakeholders, interested parties, who will act upon pre-defined interests. This may compromise their ability to represent concerned and vulnerable populations. In other cases, the knowledge brought into the partnership will also be predetermined by existing interests. In this way, rather than providing a forum for the voiceless, partnership processes may lead to the consolidation of existing ways of defining environmental problems in relation to pre-established solutions (e.g. privatization, capital investment, infrastructure development) and responding to the interest of dominant elites.

In conclusion, there is a need to approach partnerships as flexible tools, in which roles and responsibilities are not predetermined. In the context of climate change, such roles will have to be negotiated in relation to the emerging unresolved uncertainties and the multiplicity of values that shape decisions about the future. In that context, cooperative environmental governance agreements and partnerships link to adaptive institutions and networks, capable to respond to the on-going challenges of complex socio-ecological environments. The ambiguity and flexibility of partnerships can, indeed, be described as a strategy to deal with uncertainty (Fennell *et al.* 2008). Here we have argued that the central aspect of the establishment of the partnership is not the agreement of a common goal (and the ensuing solution) but rather, the collective negotiation of the terms of reference in which a common goal is defined and the knowledge and evidence base that supports such a decision. Given that, as explained above, partnerships are likely to emerge from within existing unequal power relations and are open for co-optation by powerful actors, the progressive potential of partnerships as deliberative and cooperative processes resides in their ability to open up spaces for contestation of established logics and the formulation of alternative and experimental solutions. Such progressive potential is examined within the case study of Maputo, Mozambique in the following sections.

PARTNERSHIPS FOR SUSTAINABLE SERVICE DELIVERY IN MAPUTO, MOZAMBIQUE

The capital of Mozambique, Maputo, is located in the South of the country covering an area of 300 Km². With a population of ca. 1.1 million people, the city belongs to the larger metropolitan area of Greater Maputo which, with a fluctuating population of 2 to 2.5 million inhabitants, is the most densely populated area in Mozambique.

Mozambique is highly vulnerable to natural disasters, in particular those of hydro-meteorological origin such as floods, drought and cyclones. Both increases in temperature and average precipitation due to climate change will exacerbate the already high incidence of extreme events in Mozambique. This will contribute to the uninterrupted sequence of drought and floods that Mozambique has suffered from. Since 1970, Mozambique has been hit by 34 cyclones or tropical depressions and major flood events. These events have had dramatic social and economic consequences. For example, in 2000 the most devastating floods in the history of Mozambique killed 700 people with damages estimated at 600 million dollars (Kundzewicz *et al.* 2001; McBean and Henstra 2003).

In the city of Maputo, the main hazards associated with climate change are likely to be temperature increases, extreme events related to precipitation and sea level rise. The rising sea level has already resulted in saline intrusion, which affects urban land and infrastructure. There are already noticeable coastal erosion problems, but further sea level rise will increase the risk of flooding in the lowest topographical areas (MMC *et al.* 2012). The potential impacts of extreme events in Maputo are likely to be associated with the deterioration of the already precarious infrastructure system, food insecurity and the increase of vector-borne diseases.

The impacts of climate change need to be understood in the context of vulnerability in the city of Maputo (Castán Broto *et al.* 2013). Approximately 54 per cent of Maputo City's residents live below the poverty line of

$1.50 per day and 70 per cent live in informal settlements and areas of dense unregulated growth which lack common infrastructure services such as water, sanitation, drainage and electricity (MMC *et al.* 2012). Government authorities link vulnerability to floods to a proliferation of unplanned human settlements during the last three decades, which has gradually expanded to topographically depressed and marshy areas characterised as having high flood risk. More than 60 per cent of the population has limited access to services such as energy, cooking fuel and sanitation (Alkire *et al.* 2011): access to services and infrastructure constitutes one of the main aspects of urban deprivation in Maputo. This is especially important in informal settlement areas in which sanitation and drainage is often very poor. For example, an ethnographic study (Home Space) of the informal settlements in Maputo found that 33 per cent of households have only a simple pit latrine, which can lead to serious health issues following flash floods (Sollien *et al.*). Furthermore, 68 per cent of respondents in the Home Space study were not saving money regularly in any form, although there was considerable investment in their homes, which makes coping and recovering from flood damage all the more difficult.

The capacity of the city to respond to extreme events related to climate change is limited by existing urban conditions. Not only the impacts will be more severe in deprived areas, but also, residents in such areas may have fewer opportunities to cope with the aftermath of these disasters. Moreover, the focus in developing formal strategies for land planning may clash with informal strategies to access land and resources adopted by residents in deprived areas. The urgency of the climate change challenge may lead to policies that overlook the complexity of arrangements whereby these citizens not only survive but also make and maintain the city.

In this context, partnerships as a form of environmental governance emerge in Maputo associated with two main dimensions: on the one hand, they mostly focus on the provision of services, often related to the development of infrastructure or the lack of thereof; on the other hand, they constitute a vehicle whereby a range of heterogeneous actors may intervene in actions for climate compatible development, sometimes playing unorthodox roles. The following sections provide three examples of such partnerships for disaster risk reduction, water provision and waste management.

Disaster risk reduction in Mozambique

The first example concerns the emerging strategies for disaster risk reduction in Mozambique. Since 2006, the national government has worked with UN-Habitat in the program 'Living with Floods' (Spaliviero *et al.* 2011). The objective of the program is to improve the ability to cope with floods in rural communities. In Maniquenique village, Gaza province, flooding from the Limpopo River is of great concern. Hence, as part of the project, an elevated school has been constructed which can act as a safe refuge for the local community during times of flood. This was built using labour from the local area and those taking part received on the job training, including being taught how to use the rainwater harvesting system, ensuring a safe supply of drinking water even during floods. A more recent development has been that of a participatory planning consultation in which a range of stakeholders, including the target community, central government officials, local authorities, technical experts, and the private sector, met to discuss disaster risk reduction. Through the creation of maps local knowledge was integrated with formal scientific knowledge, and both local problems and solutions were identified. These 'workshops' culminated in the drafting of local plans for priority interventions, although these plans have since been limited in their scope by funding restrictions.

In what sense does this program constitute a partnership? The objective of the 'Living with Floods' strategy, and the later participatory planning consultation, was to ensure that there was communication between a range of stakeholders acting at different scales. It was also important to ensure that awareness of the issue of increasing climate variability was better understood in local communities. This was achieved using a game in which the Limpopo River course is depicted on a board, along with simple instructions and recommendations for flood preparedness, land use management, and early warning systems. In this sense the initiative has established a forum of dialogue, which is deliberative, provisional, and ongoing: a dialogue that attempts to change existing practices towards the long-term collaboration between the different partners. However, citizens do not participate directly of this partnership because their organizational identity is not recognised. Instead, the partnership emerges at a higher scale, between UN-Habitat and the national government, both recognising each other's remits and competences and building on mutual support. The cooperation between the national government in Mozambique (especially through increasing collaboration with the National Institute for Disaster Management, the INGC) and UN-Habitat on Disaster Risks Management and Climate Change Adaptation has continued with different programs at the national and local scale.

However, participatory work remains confined to direct interventions in localised and predominantly rural settings such as Maniquenique. The dominant assessments of urban vulnerability to disaster focus on economic damages and hence ignore the importance of taking vulnerability as a starting point for climate change analysis, rather than as an end point. Maputo city is highly susceptible to flooding and landslides and so, the INGC, with the support of UN-Habitat, has identified priority measures for reducing damage from disasters such as coastal drainage improvement and land bank improvement (INGC 2011; MMC et al. 2012). However, for those living in impoverished neighbourhoods, lack of effective drainage infrastructure is the key problem that determines their vulnerability to disasters. The partnership favours the circulation of particular types of knowledge (e.g. scaling down understandings of climate change in the context of Maputo from a biophysical perspective) but not others, as there is still not a full appreciation of the conditions of vulnerability, which affect Maputo's citizens. Hence, while the partnership has undoubtedly favoured knowledge circulation and deliberation between the mutually recognised partners, it still lacks the capacity to incorporate the contextual knowledge required to respond effectively to disasters in Maputo. While the example of Maquenique points at the potential of participatory processes to open up the partnership to the needs of those whose service needs are met, it also suggests that when one of the relevant partners (in this case users and citizens) lacks collective identity (what we have called above 'organisational identity') and when the levels of mutuality are low, the participatory processes is a mere substitute for a true partnership, rather than contributing to reinforce it.

Small scale private water providers in Maputo

The second example of partnerships, that which involve small scale private water providers in Maputo, is situated in Maputo although it also builds upon national-wide policies for water provision. During the 1990s water provision went through a process of decentralisation in Mozambique which culminated in the creation of two management organisations. The first of these, FIPAG (Investment and Patrimony Fund for Water Supply), is in charge of investments for the expansion of water infrastructure and for the delegation of water provision to the private sector. The other, the CRA (Water Regulatory Board), is an independent regulatory agency. In 1999 the water supply in Maputo was leased for 15 years to AdeM (Aguas De Mocambique), a private company jointly owned by a Portuguese firm and local investors. However, due to service deficiencies and a highly uneven distribution of water supply infrastructure there has been a rapid proliferation of small-scale private water providers (SSPWPs) since 2000. Although these exist in a range of different forms, for example based on size or operational logic, the general model for water provision is based on (often interconnected) boreholes, pumps and a hose-pipe based private distribution system. It is estimated that there are currently 500 of these SSPWPs in Maputo supplying approximately 360,000 inhabitants. Although not officially recognised by the government until 2007, SSPWPs are now seen as beneficial to the city's population.

This situation led to the initiation of the Maputo Water Supply Project. The main objective of the Maputo Water Supply Project, which is financed by FIPAG, is to improve and regulate the water supply of SSPWPs in areas where there is no AdeM coverage. This is especially important in public health terms particularly when some form of chlorination may be necessary to ensure a continued supply of clean water. Furthermore, FIPAG are keen to construct twenty new independent networks in areas that currently have no water supply and delegate responsibility for their management to 5 small operators who have proven themselves capable of managing a water distribution system. As part of this process, there is a concern to ensure that there will be allocations of private water networks to the poorest in Maputo. The project has created an alternative to the standard model of public-private partnership for the provision of services adopted by AdeM, but establishing alternative forms of partnership which in certain contexts may be more suitable to meet the needs of the most deprived population sectors in Maputo and other Mozambican cities.

This project has particular relevance in Maputo as many residents rely on SSPWPs for water, especially in the poorer peri-urban areas. A study of one district consisting of 11 neighbourhoods found that 45 per cent of residents used SSPWPs for their water supply and only 13 per cent relied on AdeM (Matsinhe et al. 2008). It is particularly important to enhance water provision in Maputo because of the limited access to running water among the poorest sectors of the population (Alkire et al. 2011). Reliable access to water is essential in post-disaster contexts, and the flexible system advanced in these partnerships may provide alternatives to big infrastructure works, which may be directly affected by flooding and cyclones. Also, a decentralised water system may have implications for the long-term sustainability of the water supply because of its potential reliance on local resources and the reduced need to transport piped water. Recognition of SSPWPs in the form of supporting their activities through investment in decentralised infrastructures is a key aspect in the functioning of a working partnership for service provision.

Waste collection and recycling in Maputo

For the third example, we turn to a civil society-led initiative to improve waste management in Maputo. AMOR (or Assoçiacao Moçambicana de Reciclagem) is an organization established in Maputo, and in other cities such as Beira, Inhambane and Maxixe. The scheme adopted by AMOR follows the implementation of a network of 'eco-points' where citizens can sell their recyclable waste. AMOR is subsequently responsible for purchasing 'waste' from these usually male, informal waste collectors at each eco-point and sell this further in other markets. Waste is separated into bags according to the type and a price is calculated on weight.

AMOR has the overall aim of encouraging recycling within the city of Maputo in order to improve the concomitant problem of waste management with an escalating urban population. In addition to this, employment generation has become a central objective of their work. AMOR also helps informal waste collectors, 'catadores', to sustain the source of their livelihoods, helping them to set up bank accounts and acquire credit as a supplementary source of revenue. The President of AMOR, who also established PAGALATA (an organization further along this supply chain of recycled waste which brings the waste streams to other markets), claims that both the new direct and indirect jobs generated mean that the main beneficiaries of AMOR are informal waste collectors. According to AMOR, around 300 of 'catadores' currently sell waste items; with many more expected to follow the prospective creation of 12 more eco-points.

The city currently generates approximately 1,000 tons of waste per day (Karani *et al.* 2008). Extreme events such as the floods in 2000 put in evidence the inadequacy of existing sanitation and waste management infrastructures. Particularly in Maputo, nitrate contamination is alarmingly in excess of World Health Organisation standards, perhaps in reflection of the uncontrolled dumping sites. Despite traditionally being associated with the public sector, waste disposal has experienced a shift towards private service providers following the lack of funding and the subsequent implementation of a waste tax (Kruks-Wisner 2006). Household waste recurrently ends up being dumped in urban areas, along the beaches of Maputo or in the open landfills (Karani *et al.* 2008). The increasing role of non-public actors, including an NGO (AMOR) and informal waste collectors emerges as a response to the insufficient waste disposal services provided by the government. What is interesting here is the need for AMOR to recognise informal waste collectors as key actors in waste collection and develop a mutual relationship whereby they establish a long-term partnership. While AMOR provides the infrastructure for waste collectors to channel the flows of waste, it also relies on them to maintain this stream and the associated waste markets.

Understanding the operation of partnerships in Maputo

The initiatives above have not emerged out of a concern with systemic retrofit but rather, as a response to the lack of basic services in Maputo and the need to respond to heightened risks. The examples above suggest that partnership is already a common strategy to develop environmental governance arrangements for climate compatible development. Thus, partnerships could be approached strategically as institutional mechanisms for systemic retrofit interventions in service provision. In this sense, the three examples also show the increasing heterogeneity not only in terms of the different types of partnership which emerge, but also in relation to the non-orthodox actors that may intervene in the partnership (Table 14.2).

The examples suggest that the characteristics of the partnership depend on the context and on the nature of the issue involved. One important aspect is how a particular urban issue has been addressed through history and how feasible is to change the dynamics of existing institutional arrangements. For example, disaster risk reduction has traditionally seen as the preserve of government intervention, even though recent years have seen an increasing interest on community-based risk management. While there is a clear interest in opening up risk management to the voices of citizens or local residents through, for example, participatory processes, the partnership-defined in terms of the establishment of an ongoing and relatively long-term deliberative process based upon mutuality between

Table 14.2 Comparative assessment of the three case studies

Partnerships	Disaster Risk Reduction	Small Scale Private Water Providers in Maputo	Waste collection and recycling in Maputo
Main actors involved	UN-Habitat National Government Institutions (INGC and others)	FIPAG (Investment and Patrimony Fund for Water Supply) and small scale water providers	AMOR (Civil society) and catadores (informal waste collectors)
Role of the state	Supporting implementation	Financing infrastructure investment	Limited or absent
Link across scales	National and International scales	National and local scales	Local and neighbourhood scales
Development of dialogue structures	Confined to national level assessment of disaster risk	Partnership responds to the needs of small providers which supply directly deprived areas	AMOR and the catadores have develop a relationship of mutual dependence
Relevance for systemic retrofit in an urban context	The city challenges the capacity of the partnership to incorporate local priorities	Small scale partnerships for water provision can reach deprived areas better than the more standard model of water provision implemented at the national level	The model contributes to improve public health, providing livelihoods at the local level and ensuring the continuity of the system by providing markets for different waste streams
Establishment of new institutions	No	Small water providers	Collection centres as key institution
Citizens' involvement	They are consulted through participatory process but they are not part of the partnership	Small water providers may be able to respond to citizen's needs	'Catadores' emerge within the local population, and respond directly to existing waste collection needs

actors involved and the maintenance of organisational identity is only maintained in organisations supported by formal institutions at the national and international level. This limits the circulation of ideas and the capacity of the partnership to deliver a service- in this case protection against risk- directly to citizens. This is particularly apparent within an unbounded and dynamic urban context, where communities are not easily identified and broader processes of negotiation may be required to develop collaborative approaches to environmental management. In recent years INGC has starting working with the local municipality in Maputo to improve their risk management strategies in Maputo (Dávila *et al.* 2008).

The other two examples emphasise how partnerships can reach citizen's needs for service provision by enabling flexible arrangements in which different actors adopt unorthodox roles. The case of small water providers in Maputo highlights the enormous contrast between standard public-private partnership models of water provision and decentralised ones. The AdeM model continues centralised models of water provision but relying on private capital to maintain and service the network. As emphasis concentrates on supplying profitable (or at least non-loss) areas, this model leads to a network that provides services to only a select part of the city. SSPWPs providers, in contrast, may be able to manage reduced profits at localised scales, and hence, provide an opportunity to improve the supply of deprived areas, conditional to having governmental support in the development of infrastructure. Government's recognition of the role of these providers – which may be more difficult to identify and classify than the type of corporation which is thought to intervene in public-private partnerships – is crucial to develop the mutual relationship that should maintain the partnership in the long term. This is a model of decentralised service provision through local operators.

The main difference with the case of waste management is that SSPWPs can establish themselves as an organisation, while in the case of 'catadores', the informal waste providers, the maintenance of organisational identity depends on the recognition of the role that they play within the partnership. AMOR's emphasis on supporting their livelihoods through the formalisation of certain aspects of their practice (e.g. by helping those opening bank accounts) signifies an attempt to establish the terms of the mutual relationship that support the partnership. On the other hand, AMOR's intervention is perhaps favoured by the lack of formal institutions regulating the waste collection service. Regardless of the extent to which existing structures should be formalised (which may not necessarily be beneficial for 'catadores' who operate informally) the partnership appears to work because a) the recognition of each other's role in the partnership, and hence, preservation of identity within the partnership; and b) the establishment of a relationship of mutuality. Overall, in spite of the heterogeneity of partnership arrangements and unorthodox roles played by those intervening in them, they emerge associated with a long-term engagement which develops into formal and informal institutions allowing for the exchange of knowledge and resources, which eventually should lead to the establishment of mutual relations in which the roles of each partner are recognised.

CONCLUSION: PARTNERSHIPS, CLIMATE CHANGE AND SYSTEMIC RETROFITTING

Actions for delivering climate compatible development emerge in a context of uncertainty and multi-scalar interaction. Commentators tend to emphasise the need to deliver adaptive governance mechanisms, which are flexible enough to navigate the complex spatial and temporal contexts in which climate compatible development is delivered and can bridge the views and perceptions of the multiple actors affected and intervening in these processes. Systemic retrofit thinking thus needs to address not just how to reconfigure existing systems of service provision but also, how this will be achieved in the complex and changing context of climate change governance. What partnerships, as a form of cooperative environmental governance, can contribute to this question is their potential to open up spaces for the operation of multiple actors in climate compatible development at different scales. Delivering partnerships in context, however, requires understanding that actors do not necessarily adopt a predetermined role. Indeed, partnerships provide spaces for actors to act in unorthodox manner.

However, for all their potential, the comparative analysis in this chapter raises notes of caution in regards to partnerships and their proliferation to address climate change concerns. In the first example the public sector leads but has limited capacity to respond directly to the needs of citizens in partnerships that address environmental risks. In the other examples in which local and civil society actors take the initiative to fill a governmental vacuum. While this supports the argument that partnerships have a great potential to enrol citizens and civil society actors in climate compatible development, they also signify a displacement of responsibilities for public services and support arguments about the retreat of the state in cities in the global south. In Mozambique, recent reforms have led to an increase of power in local municipalities, which may be able to fill this vacuum and play a vital role both in supporting and leading partnerships for climate compatible development both recognising the important role than non-governmental actors may play, but also ensuring equitable mechanisms for universal service provision.

Future work should focus on the extent to which partnerships can be co-opted by powerful actors or contested by those who do not intervene in it- an essential aspect to understand to what extent partnership arrangements can not only deliver services, but can also do so in a socially inclusive manner. Ultimately, partnerships for systemic retrofit should be understood within a collectivist and cooperative vision of environmental and resource governance, in which achieving well-being for all citizens in an equitable manner takes precedence over the interests of specific organisations or particular sectors.

Note

1   The research in this chapter was funded by the Climate Development Knowledge Network. The Climate and Development Knowledge Network ('CDKN') is a project funded by the UK Department for International Development and the Netherlands Directorate-General for International Cooperation (DGIS) and is led and administered by PricewaterhouseCoopers LLP. Management of the delivery of CDKN is undertaken by PricewaterhouseCoopers LLP, and an alliance of organisations including Fundación Futuro Latinoamericano, INTRAC, LEAD International, the Overseas Development Institute, and South-SouthNorth. **Disclaimer** This document is an output from a project funded by the UK Department for International Development (DFID) and the Netherlands Directorate-General for International Cooperation (DGIS) for the benefit of developing countries. However, the views expressed and information contained in it are not necessarily those of or endorsed by DFID, DGIS or the entities managing the delivery of the Climate and Development Knowledge Network, which can accept no responsibility or liability for such views, completeness or accuracy of the information or for any reliance placed on them.

References

Ahmed, S.A. and Ali, S.M. (2006), 'People as partners: Facilitating people's participation in public-private partnerships for solid waste management', *Habitat International,* 30 (4), 781–96.

Alkire, S., *et al.* (2011), 'Mozambique country briefing', Oxford: Poverty and Human Development Initiative (OPHI) Multidimensional Poverty Index Country Briefing Series. Available at: www.ophi.org.uk/policy/multidimensional-poverty-index/mpi-country-briefings/.

Bovis, C. (2010), 'Public-private partnerships in the 21st century', *ERA Forum, Scripta Iuris Europaei,* 11 (3), 379–98.

Brinkerhoff, J.M. (2002), 'Government-nonprofit partnership: A defining framework', *Public Administration and Development,* 22 (1), 19–30.

Bulkeley, H., Castán Broto, V., Hodson, M. and Marvin, S. (2011), *Cities and Low Carbon Transitions* (London: Routledge).

Castán Broto, V. and Bulkeley, H. (2012), 'A survey of urban climate change experiments in 100 global cities', *Global Environmental Change.*

Castán Broto, V., Oballa, B. and Junior, P. (2013), 'Governing climate change for a just city: Challenges and lessons from Maputo, Mozambique', *Local Environment,* 18 (6), 678–704.

Dávila, J, Kyrou, E., Nuñex, T. and Sumich, J. (2008), 'Urbanisation and municipal development in Mozambique: Urban poverty and rural–urban linkages', *University College London, London.*

Davoudi, S., Crawford, J. and Mehmood, A. (2009), *Planning for Climate Change: Strategies for Mitigation and Adaptation for Spatial Planners* (London: Earthscan).

Eames, M., Dixon, T., May, T. and Hunt, M. (2013), 'City futures: Exploring urban retrofit and sustainable transitions', *Building Research and Information*, 41 (5), 504–16.

Fennell, D., Plummer, R. and Marschke, M. (2008), 'Is adaptive co-management ethical?', *Journal of Environmental Management*, 88 (1), 62–75.

Forsyth, T. (2005a), 'Enhancing climate technology transfer through greater public-private cooperation: Lessons from Thailand and the Philippines', *Natural Resources Forum*, 29 (2), 165–76.

Forsyth, T. (2005b), 'Building deliberative public-private partnerships for waste management in Asia', *Geoforum*, 36 (4), 429–39.

Forsyth, T. (2007), 'Promoting the 'Development Dividend' of climate technology transfer: Can cross-sector partnerships help?', *World Development*, 35 (10), 1684–98.

Glasbergen, P. (1998), *Co-operative environmental governance: Public-private agreements as a policy strategy* (Dordrecht, London: Kluwer Academic Publishers).

Hodge, G.A. and Greve, C. (2005), *The Challenge of Public-Private Partnerships: Learning From International Experience* (Cheltenham: Edward Elgar).

INGC (2011), 'Preparing cities – INGC Phase II', (Maputo).

Jaglin, S., Repussard, C. and Belbeoc'h, A. (2011), 'Decentralisation and governance of drinking water services in small West African towns and villages (Benin, Mali, Senegal): The arduous process of building local governments', *Canadian Journal of Development Studies-Revue Canadienne D Etudes Du Developpement*, 32 (2), 119–38.

Karani, P., Jewasikiewitz, S.M. and Da Costa, J. (2008), 'A comparative analysis of waste management and sustainable development in South Africa and Mozambique: Implications for development financing and the role of knowledge management', in Toma V. Golush (ed.) *Waste Management Research Trends*, 321–377.

Koppenjan, J.F.M. and Enserink, B. (2009), 'Public-private partnerships in urban infrastructures: Reconciling private sector participation and sustainability', *Public Administration Review*, 69 (2), 284–96.

Kruks-Wisner, G. (2006), 'After the flood: Crisis, voice and innovation in Maputo's solid waste management sector', Thesis, Cambridge, MA: Massachusetts Institute of Technology, Dept. of Urban Studies and Planning. Available at: http://hdl.handle.net/1721.1/37672.

Kundzewicz, Z.W., et al. (2001), 'Floods and droughts: Coping with variability and climate change', (Bonn: International Conference on Freshwater).

Kyvelou, S., Marava, N. and Kokkoni, G. (2011), 'Perspectives of local public-private partnerships towards urban sustainability in Greece', *International Journal of Sustainable Development*, 14 (1–2), 95–111.

Matsinhe, Nelson P., et al. (2008), 'Regulation of formal and informal water service providers in peri-urban areas of Maputo, Mozambique', *Physics and Chemistry of the Earth, Parts A/B/C*, 33 (8), 841–49.

May, T., et al. (2013), 'Achieving 'systemic'urban retrofit: A framework for action', in William Swan and Philip Brown (eds), *Retrofitting the Built Environment* (Chichester: Wiley), 7–19.

McBean, G. and Henstra, D. (2003), 'Climate change, natural hazards and cities'., *Research Paper Series n. 31* (Toronto: Institute for Catastrophic Loss Reduction (ICLR)).

Meadowcroft, J. (1998), 'Co-operative management regimes: A way forward?', in Pieter Glasbergen (ed.), *Co-operative Environmental Governance: Public-Private Agreements as a Policy Strategy* (London: Kluwer Academic Publishers).

Mitchell, T. and Maxwell, S (2010), 'Defining climate compatible development', *CDKN ODI Policy Brief* (London: Climate and Development Knowledge Network).

MMC, UN-Habitat, and Agriconsulting (2012), 'Availação detalhada dos impactos resultantes dos eventos das mudanças climáticas no Município de Maputo', (Nairobi: UN-Habitat).

Monstadt, J. (2009), 'Conceptualizing the political ecology of urban infrastructures: Insights from technology and urban studies', *Environment and Planning A,* 41 (8), 1924–42.

Osborne, S. (2000), *The Challenge of Public-Private Partnerships: Learning From International Experience* (London: Routledge).

Parnell, S., Pieterse, E. and Watson, V. (2009), 'Planning for cities in the global South: An African research agenda for sustainable human settlements', *Progress in Planning,* 72 (233–241).

Plummer, R. and FitzGibbon, J. (2004), 'Some observations on the terminology in co-operative environmental management', *Journal of Environmental Management,* 70 (1), 63–72.

Rosenau, P. V. (2000), *Public-Private Policy Partnerships* (MIT Press).

Simon, D. (2010), 'The challenges of global environmental change for urban Africa', *Urban Forum,* 21, 235–48.

Sollien, S.E. Andersen, A.B. da C. and Jenkins, P. (n.d.), 'HomeSpace Maputo: Meanings and perceptions of the built environment in a rapidly expanding African City', (Homespace project).

Spaliviero, M., *et al.* (2011), 'Participatory approach for integrated basin planning with focus on disaster risk reduction: The case of the Limpopo River', *Water,* 3 (3), 737–63.

Vining, A. R. and Boardman, A. E. (2008), 'Public-private partnerships in Canada: Theory and evidence', *Canadian Public Administration* 51 (1), 9–44.

Wang, Y (2000), 'Public-private partnerships in the social sector', (Manila: Asian Development Bank).

Wettenhall, R. (2003), 'The rhetoric and reality of public-private partnerships', *Public Organization Review,* 3 (1), 77–107.

Chapter 15

Retrofit transitions and the creative dynamics of squat tech

Jana Wendler and James Evans

INTRODUCTION

In the context of urban sustainability much attention is currently given to experiments: purposive interventions in the city in which alternative technologies, infrastructures and social arrangements are created and tested in an 'explicit attempt to innovate, learn or gain experience' (Bulkeley and Castán Broto, 2013: 363; Evans, 2011). Most of these interventions centre on unique solutions to infrastructure and built environment challenges, with a focus on energy efficiency, water and waste reduction. In the transition literature, these experiments are usually conceptualised as a type of niche, or shielded environment from which innovations can diffuse into the mainstream regime (Seyfang and Smith, 2007; Vergragt and Brown, 2012). Increasingly, however, there is an acknowledgement that such solutions are not restricted to formal 'labs' and innovation hubs. Grassroots innovation combines such technological experimentation with social dynamics, as local groups and communities respond to immediate social or environmental needs and problems (Seyfang and Smith, 2007). These phenomena foreground actors that are generally regarded as marginal in the mainstream transition perspective, and suggest that experiments may be valuable beyond a narrow focus on innovation diffusion as alternative sites of learning and inspiration.

Squatters are one social group who find themselves outside of formal experimentation. Yet they have always employed experimental techniques to deal with urgent problems of living in abandoned spaces and with dysfunctional infrastructures. Newly built squat structures also deviate from standard forms of urban construction and design, as they are subject to the constraints of uncertain occupation rights and few resources. They are examples of what may be termed 'squat tech' solutions – a notion that describes not only the context of their creation but a distinctive process of building and making, characterised by intricate relationships between social and physical structures, people and materials, skills and creativity. The idea of squat tech resonates with the urban retrofit agenda, although the squatters

would probably not describe their practice in these terms. Their constructions and fixes are examples of low-cost and low-resource technologies that
are employed to improve existing buildings, often with a strong focus on
sustainability and underlying notions of self-sufficiency and resilient living.

Investigating how squat tech is created offers potentially valuable
insights into how bottom-up forms of sustainable retrofit based on local
resources and approaches break with existing paradigms of infrastructure
provision. In this sense, they offer an alternative to the more formal modes
of steering environmental change that have tended to rely on a two-pronged
approach of offering market incentives and providing information to
encourage pro-environmental behaviour. While undoubtedly part of the
solution, both have been criticised 'largely because they do not challenge the
status quo and overlook the routines of everyday life' (Maller, Horne and
Dalton 2012: 257). The idea that simply providing more information about
why and how to go green will result in more green behaviour has been
undermined by the persistent gap between people's everyday actions and
their stated values. Similarly, market incentives to invest in loft insulation,
for example, have little impact unless they fit in with people's life, such as
when moving house. Weaving everyday routines and low carbon infrastructures together, squat tech offers broader insights into these less formal
and experimental aspects of retrofit.

The following chapter develops the notion of squat tech based on a case
study from recent field work. Starting with a short discussion of the term and
its practical and academic context, it then focuses on a particular project, the
building of a compost toilet in an eco-squat in Barcelona. The description
highlights the social and material dynamics of the construction process with
an emphasis on competence, material agency and learning. Finally, these
dynamics are linked to notions of creativity and innovation to consider the
relevance of grassroots experimentation to the wider retrofit agenda.

Squat tech in context

> A great aspect of squatting old buildings is the mixture of archaeology
> and innovation needed to make a space usable. Somewhere between
> low tech and no tech is squat tech. Squat tech is assessing available
> resources, appreciating that most of them are broken or in disrepair,
> and dismantling existing items in order to use their parts for more
> urgent functions. In this case, through an interesting process of old
> community knowledge, archaeology, and squat tech innovation, we
> managed to get one of the water mines to feed into a spring in the
> gardens near the house...
>
> (Cordingley, 2004: 56)

This description of reconnecting the water supply to a squatted building – the same building from which the case study is drawn – outlines the notion of squat tech that this chapter explores. It starts by referring to a need: as the former hospital of Can Masdeu, on the outskirts of Barcelona, was abandoned for over 50 years, there was no functioning water supply when squatters initially occupied it in 2001. To make it liveable, getting the water system to work was an urgent necessity. The next step involved taking stock of the available resources and repurposing materials for the new job. In squat building, the resources are largely limited to what can be found on-site or sourced for free through recycling, salvaging or exchange. Absence of funds as well as an ethic of non-consumption means that buying materials and parts is not usually an option. Finally, the description refers to the different kinds of knowledge and practices that were required to reconnect the mountain springs to the garden and house (where they still provide the water now). The contributors to a squat tech project bring different forms of knowledge and expertise with them, but as the problems and resource base are never standardised, this knowledge needs to be combined and adapted in a process of creative innovation. The three aspects of need, resources and knowledge are of course shorthand for more complex processes, but they provide an entry point for engaging with the dynamics of squat tech as a form of innovative grassroots retrofit.

The combination of elements outlined above indicates a process of creation in which material and social dimensions interact. In the current literature, there is an interest in such processes from an assemblage perspective (see Dovey, 2011; Farías, 2011; McFarlane, 2011a). This view considers a space or structure not as a static entity, but as the contingent outcome of the relations and interactions of diverse elements within. This focus on 'the fluid attributes of urban materiality' (Edensor, 2011: 239) allows an understanding of urban structures as the result of an ongoing process of becoming. Assemblage thinking also contains a view of agency as collective and distributed: divorced from intentionality, it emerges from the interaction of its constituent elements and their capacities to affect each other (DeLanda, 2006). This recognises an active role for the non-human world and emphasises 'the agency of the *materials themselves*' (McFarlane, 2011a: 215, emphasis in the original). Consequently, we need to consider urban constructions, including squat tech retrofit, as sociomaterial as well as fluid, and engage with the dynamics that bring them into being. This view comes with methodological implications. For any structure or space, we cannot know in advance which actors and relationships we will encounter. Assemblage thinking denies the possibility of any preconceived structural explanation, and commits our research to open exploration and in-depth inquiry (Farías, 2011), with a focus on grounded empirical work. It also suggests greater 'attention to micro-spatialities [...] and the ways that an assemblage of small-scale adaptations can produce synergistic emergent effects at higher levels' (Dovey, 2011: 348). The question of how individual experiments exert influence beyond themselves is of critical importance to understanding how sustainability transitions do or do not occur. Using an assemblage approach, which invites us to look at the details of a construction process, can help us understand the broader urban relevance of squat tech.

Improvised, spontaneous and home-made solutions to infrastructure and construction problems are not unique to squats. They are common features of many other forms of building and creating, in particular the Do-It-Yourself (DIY) movement (see Davidson and Leather, 2000; Watson and Shove, 2008), and housing practices in slums and informal settlements (see McFarlane, 2011b; Roy, 2005). In their in-depth study, Watson and Shove (2008: 72) describe DIY as a process 'in which the relation between tools, materials and competence is plainly significant' and that is 'typically transformative, both of those who do DIY and of the physical objects and structures on which they work'. In taking a relational approach this description echoes the diverse sociomaterial components of squat tech. Within the DIY assemblage, the authors regard competence as the central element. Described as the interaction between skills and resources for the accomplishment of a particular project, competence is 'embedded in and distributed between tools and materials and many other sources including people, DIY manuals and the internet' (ibid.: 79). Understanding the dynamics of DIY, then, requires an appreciation of how this competence assemblage is formed in particular situations – a question that is equally relevant for squat tech projects. The key point here is how competence emerges when a diverse set of knowledge and skills meet an array of different and unique materials in a situation of real life needs and pressures.

Materials are given a central role in this assemblage of competence in DIY projects. As described by Watson and Shove (2008), materials and tools are frequently employed in overcoming limitations that currently hinder the practitioner at fulfilling his or her project: a new tool will make new jobs and further progress possible. But the consumption practices surrounding materials are not always as straight forward. DIY projects rarely go exactly as anticipated as they involve the complex coordination of plans, tools and expertise in response to often surprising problems. Materials also help to create and shape projects, as available tools and materials determine what jobs a practitioner might consider feasible – a process that Ingold (2006) describes as the revealing of a tool within a narrative of construction. The active role of materials is developed further by the literature on informal urbanism. Slum-dwellers operate under much greater need when creating their home-made solutions (compare a loft-conversion to building a shack as family shelter) and buying materials or tools for a job are not usually an option, but the material practices within their construction processes are no less rich. Studies of post-disaster settlements show the importance of freely available materials and recycling in informal construction (Lizarralde and Davidson, 2006; McFarlane, 2011b). While availability will shape the constructions, this cannot be equated with a lack of choice: the houses often reveal 'vibrant colours, façade decoration, and careful choice of textures' (Lizarralde and Davidson, 2006: 7) illustrating the aesthetic considerations and skills of the builder. Resource constraints mean that informal building is an incremental and often iterative process, and the builders make use of this evolution to adjust buildings to changing social requirements (McFarlane, 2011b). The materiality of both DIY and informal construction is revealed as complex, and addressing retrofit from a squat tech perspective requires an equally careful engagement with materials.

As indicated before, the material dimension is part of a more complex assemblage of competence that also includes knowledge and skills. The vibrancy of informal constructions points to a builder who manages to assemble diverse and improbable materials, presenting the observer 'with a sense of the labour and craft that has been put into this house' (McFarlane, 2011b: 35). The skills needed for this kind of construction develop slowly. Going back to DIY practices, Watson and Shove (2008) show how learning not only takes place through formal channels (such as being taught or reading manuals), but also develops from the physical engagement with tools and materials, and the successful completion of tasks. Acquiring a skill then is never a straight-forward process of repetition or copying – its essence, Ingold (2006: 79) describes, '[lies] in the improvisational ability of the practitioners'; in their aptitude to respond to the quirks and irregularities of the material. Improvisation becomes even more central for the creation of competence when the context and materials are challenging and unusual, as in the case of slum and informal construction. It is a 'process of creatively tinkering with urban space' which involves 'learning different uses and relations of materials over time' (McFarlane, 2011b: 39). Possibilities are explored in different contexts, building up an assemblage of competence in incremental steps. This is a kind of learning through dwelling – an incremental and embodied acquaintance with the sociomaterial dynamics of an environment through a lived immersion within it.

The next section applies these notions of competence, material agency and improvised learning to explore the sociomaterial assemblage of squat tech, using the example of the construction of a compost toilet in the eco-squat of Can Masdeu in Barcelona. It should be noted that this is not an attempt to romanticise the notion of informal urbanism, or to depoliticise issues around property and the right to the city. The aim instead is to highlight alternative ways of urban problem solving that hold relevance for the retrofit and wider sustainability agendas.

Can Masdeu's Letrina Seca

The eco-squat of Can Masdeu, located in the Collserola Park on the outskirts of Barcelona, is an example of an experimental space in which ideas for alternative urban living are created, lived and shared, and in which squat tech solutions inform much of the repair and building work. The former hospital was first occupied by squatters as part of the Rising Tide climate campaign in 2001 and is now home to around 25 permanent residents who live as a communal group with shared responsibilities and consensus-based decision-making. Can Masdeu have also become an internationally known site of ecological and social experimentation? The interest is reflected in the busy twice-weekly open days with workshop sessions, communal gardening and guided tours of the grounds. A key feature of these tours is the detailed explanation of the many self-built structures that surround the main building. The compost toilet is one such notable feature of the public part of the house. It is a small wooden construction which seems at once shambolic and carefully crafted, with a mix of natural wood colours and bright wall parts that upon closer inspection turn out to be old doors. On the side, a set of beautiful steps complete with a railing and outdoor sink lead up to the door. A hand-drawn sign on the roof identifies the structure as a *letrina seca* (dry toilet). Compost toilets are the only option for toilet facilities in Can Masdeu, as the buildings are not connected to the sewer system. This particular one, the newest of three, was built to improve facilities in the public part of the building, which on its weekly social centre days hosts up to 200 people. The project was coordin-ated by Mia, a German carpenter journeywoman who was a long-term guest in the squat and agreed to tell me about its construction.

As indicated earlier, squat tech constructions are shaped by materials that can be found on-site or sourced freely through local networks, and they rely on a range of skills and knowledge. This was also the case here. Materials for the walls and roof – various boards and planks, the coloured doors, old signs, windows – came from the extensive storage area of the squat. A dark shed full of things sometimes unrecognisable to an outsider, it contains materials and objects that the residents have accumulated over time: acquired from recycling points and junk yards, from exchanges with other communities, from local structures that have been dismantled. Other materials, such as the steel core boards that form the basic shell above the brick foundation, were picked up from construction site dumps, using a network of contacts established by the squatters. These boards are not reused in conventional building when the wood shows signs of damage, even though the steel core retains its strength. The steps leading up to the toilet were made of locally found wood. The expertise for employing these diverse materials came together in the working group that carried out the construction. Mia's involvement began during a visit to the house, when the

Figure 15.1 The compost toilet of Can Masdeu (Photo: Jana Wendler)

residents discussed the need to build another public toilet. Because of her training as a carpenter, her experience of building compost toilets in both Spain and Germany and some mutual acquaintances, she was asked to take on the project. She then assembled a team for the construction, consisting of two of her friends, a guest to the house, and a permanent resident. Each of the participants contributed her or his knowledge – some as carpenters, another with experience in various DIY building projects and glass work. The existing toilets served as models, with added ideas (such as the brick base) and adaptations (such as external air pipes) picked up from their experiences elsewhere.

These materials and knowledge came to be assembled in such a way that the squat tech toilet is now one of the most photographed structures in the house, a reference point on the tours, as well as a functioning toilet that is in daily use by the residents. Understanding how this happened can give a clue as to how experimental interventions become successful retrofit projects that solve infrastructural deficiencies. The literature highlighted the role of material agency in shaping informal constructions, and this is reflected in the recycling practices of the Can Masdeu community and the specific construction processes of the compost toilet. Recycling is central to the material practice of squat living, and in Can Masdeu this spans everything from the tiles on the floor of the bakery to the jam jars that serve as glasses and mugs. The residents tend to talk with pride about this practice, but they also acknowledge that it can be a difficult and tedious process. Materials require adapting and disassembling, resources might run out without a chance of replacement, and work flows become far more complicated and unpredictable. Talking about her experience with recycling materials for the toilet, project coordinator Mia explains:

> To recycle [nails and screws] can be the most annoying thing that can happen to you. In the lower part we screwed everything in place, and you really have to switch the drill head every five minutes because you have a different kind of screw. So you're sitting in front of this box of recycled screws, and that's great, we did also use a lot of them [...] but at some point like – pfft.
>
> (Interview, March 2012)

There are different ways in which the squatters respond to these constraints. In some cases, the material difficulties are mediated by the social aspects of squat building work. The toilet builders were able to use recycled scaffolding boards because they had enough people in the group to share the work of cutting steel cores to resize them. Similarly, much of the initial sourcing of recycled material depends on the capacity of the group to search for and pick up these materials, often with only the help of bicycle trailers. These time investments reflect a commitment to what residents call 'creative leisure time': a rejection of a simple dichotomy of work and leisure in favour of an integrated, slower approach to life that enables low-consumption practices and self-reliance. This casts squat tech practices as embedded in particular social environments. In other cases, the material constraints of salvaging and recycling directly shape the way the building progresses. Having gotten fed up with the recycled screws, the group decided to use classical timber joints for the internal connections, and after finding sheets of glass, they added a window. Such material diversions have a clear impact on how the final structures are perceived. The wide assortment of materials used for the toilet creates borders and transitions between colours and textures, giving it a unique aesthetic and a richness of detail that transcends its function. The beautifully crafted timber joints add a dimension of craft accomplishment, emphasising the skills of the builders. But none of these are decisions taken in advance; they are organic responses to material requirements. The materials have a say in the creation of the constructions, eliciting a response from the builders that bring particular community values to the building process: ecological consciousness, creative leisure time, and openness to playful and colourful aesthetics. The assemblage of the toilet and other structures gives a material expression to these themes.

These socio-material interactions give a clue towards the quirkily distinctive creativity of the toilet and other squat tech solutions that visitors are fascinated by. But the solutions are not only a creative diversion or opportunity to practice a skill for the residents: they are serious responses to infrastructural problems that are tied to the habitability and long-term sustainability of the squat. This requires a negotiation of knowledge in order to direct the material dynamics towards a functioning outcome. In the case of the toilet, there was a diverse set of skills, experiences and competences within the group, supplemented by the existing compost toilets on the site and materials such as the *Einfälle statt Abfälle* (Ideas not Waste) manual, a publication focused on recycled DIY constructions. These disparate elements do not always align naturally, however. Describing the work process during the toilet construction, Mia explains:

Yeah it can be stressful [to work in a group like this]. ... You always have to clean everything up to protect your tools. That's something you also need to get into everyone's head, that you can't just go over a concrete-covered board with a hand chainsaw, because then the blade gets messed up and then you have to buy a new blade. ... It would then probably be cheaper to buy new wood, or ready-made wood. You always have to organise yourself, which is the problem when working in groups. Especially when half of the people don't yet know how it works. That's why we turned some of it into a workshop, like how to make the timber joints. Three of us prepared it, and then did the workshop and others joined in.

The description indicates that assembling competence from these various sources is a slow and complicated process. The ability to work together and to successfully move forward with the construction involves not only matching skills and tools to particular requirements, but an active negotiation of different work approaches and levels of knowledge through social and material interactions. Good organisation would matter in any work group, but the sets of expertise here are more diverse than in most cases. Practices that would be second nature to a professional or even dedicated DIYer (such as protecting tools) need to be agreed upon. Some contributors had to learn skills (like how to make timber joints), which the group adapted to by turning parts of the process into a workshop led by the trained carpenters. There are also problematic characteristics of recycled materials which require the right response (not sawing through boards covered in concrete). These negotiations and moments of learning take place not on an abstract or planning level: they are grounded in the specific material dynamics of the project (the concrete, the screws, the lack of replacement blades), where conditions have to be assessed and responses worked out continually. While knowledge sharing would be desirable in any case, the specific material context both demands and facilitates a negotiation of knowledge and practices which leads to the formation of competence. This underlines squat tech solutions as sociomaterial assemblages. They are not simply an assortment of materials and knowledge put together, but the emergent and dynamic outcome of their interaction: a 'mutually constitutive symbiosis rather than just parts that are related' (McFarlane, 2011a: 208).

Creativity and innovation

It is in this assemblage that the squat tech toilet and other solutions assume their role as both functioning infrastructure and examples of squat creativity – in short, as grassroots experiments. The competencies needed for their creation rely on incremental and ongoing embodied processes: selecting and becoming acquainted with the materials, developing working responses to their peculiarities, adapting decisions as the trajectory of the building changes. Hence, the toilet and many other structures in Can Masdeu are improvised. They are not the outcomes of instantaneous creative acts, nor are they based on a singular vision of how a problem should be solved, or how a building should be constructed or 'retrofitted'. There is no one final combination of elements that the craftsperson envisages and then pursues. They are incremental assemblages of materials and competence, which also includes their subsequent use. The assemblages are never finished but continue to evolve in response to particular practices (such as the addition of curtains and sketches on how to use the toilet), while also shaping these practices through their own maintenance requirements (such as regularly checking the chambers and cleaning the urine separator). In both its creation and use, the toilet as one such assemblage is improvised and constantly evolving.

This has consequences for how we understand creativity and innovation in the context of squat tech solutions. In their work on creativity, Ingold and Hallam (2007: 3) distinguish between creativity as innovation and creativity as improvisation. Where the former focuses on radically novel results that break away from established norms, the latter considers creativity as a generative, relational process of 'adjustment and response to the conditions of a world-in-formation'. For the discussion above, this processual reading of creativity makes sense. The toilet, along with other DIY solutions in Can Masdeu, is playful, unique and quirky in its aesthetics and details – but it was never designed or planned in that way. Its creativity lies not in the novelty of using of old doors and windows, and a mix of screws and timber joints, but in the process that made them come together in an assemblage. What takes place here is an ongoing shift in perception, an education of attention that allows materials and people to be brought into new relationships. Creative construction 'takes place by seeing not just materials but possibilities' (McFarlane, 2011b: 36). When the toilet builders found old doors in the material storage, Mia picked them for the walls: 'That was my work. I wanted it to be a bit colourful'. Her perception of the doors shifted when she realised their capacity to be colourful solid boards as well as doors with a specific function. This allowed her to place them into new relationships with other materials, making it part of a wall. Much of the creativity of the toilet resides in that process, but there is room for personal expression, too. Some of the timber joints that replaced the screws were shaped into hearts, and one became a place to store toilet paper. In neither case, creativity is reduced to a deliberate design.

Ingold and Hallam (2007) suggest this improvisational reading of creativity in opposition to a focus on innovation. But this case study also hints at a way to rethink innovation itself as a process of improvisation rather than as novelty in results. Like its creativity, the innovation aspect of the toilet is not a claim of novelty – which in any case would be questionable as DIY compost toilets are not new and, as one of the builders described: 'every compost toilet is essentially a copy of others'. Instead, it is innovative in its particular assemblage of elements – of screws, doors, carpenters, experiences, workshops, and the way this arrangement gives rise to a functioning, ecologically sustainable toilet in a particular setting. Rather than reducing innovation to examples of radical novelty, a relational approach also makes sense here. Barry (2001: 211) hints at this by describing inventiveness as situated 'not [in] the novelty of artefacts and devices in themselves, but [in] the novelty of the arrangements'. Squat tech solutions are innovative and valuable in the search for alternative retrofit methods, but not because of the particular solutions they create. Instead, they indicate

Figure 15.2 Heart-shaped timber joint (Photo: Jana Wendler)

how conceiving of infrastructural solutions as a process of incremental, sociomaterial learning opens up opportunities for responses that are grounded in local characteristics: materials as well as social dynamics, values and approaches.

Conclusion: learning and experiments

This chapter has explored the concept of squat tech as a way of problem solving in situations of infrastructural need and resource constraints. Squat tech should be understood as a socio-material assemblage, in which material agency, social setting and different knowledge become aligned to respond to a particular need. This alignment is a gradual, messy process, grounded in particular material conditions and the formation of different clusters of competence. Charting the way a compost toilet was created in one squat shows how recycled materials shape and sometimes challenge the building progress, and how the negotiation of knowledge is always contingent and based on specific material questions. The construction that emerged from this process is both a functioning toilet and a public demonstration: it is an infrastructural innovation as well as an example of squat creativity. Both of these qualities stem from the same improvisational dynamics of the construction process: the incremental learning and adaptive responses that mark out the negotiations of each step – made more unpredictable by the use of unusual materials and the diversity of knowledge involved. This provides a perspective on creativity and innovation as independent of any particular outcomes. Instead of ascribing radical novelty to prior design, a structure can be creative and innovative through the way it came into being.

Focusing on the conditions and dynamics of assembling squat tech solutions holds some interesting implications for the wider debates surrounding retrofit experiments and sustainability transitions. Squat tech constructions are a kind of retrofit experiment that introduces particular dynamics (rather than specific solutions) into the picture. Their experimentality is based on a combination of function and exposition: they are innovative in their process of making, their creativity attracts attention, and, like the compost toilet on the tour of Can Masdeu, they can become public demonstration objects. They are also experiments that are lived and therefore continuously tested, highlighting the importance of long-term practices to the functioning of the solution. Although squatters are freer to experiment with ideas, materials and arrangements in the absence (or rather, disavowal) of rules and regulations than residents in more traditional settings, there is much to be learnt from the inspirational solutions of squat communities. While not endorsing potentially dangerous domestic alterations, squat tech experiments exemplify a kind of retrofit that addresses what Shove and Walker (2010: 476) term the 'ongoing transformation' of practices.

Most importantly perhaps, squat tech experiments provide focal points for learning. Learning takes place not only within the project itself, but through numerous informal channels and encounters. Because squats are often embedded in wider networks of alternative communities and attract visitors (some more formally than others), there is an ongoing exchange of inspiration and knowledge, of mutual help and personal connections, and of active copying. But with a greater interest in alternative urban living and low-resource construction and retrofit, the squat tech examples have much wider potential. There are many alternative projects that actively invite people in to show their solutions and ways of living, not as a way to gain recognition but because of a belief that their approaches can be applied in many situations. If housing is a cultural asset that is 'embedded in the fabric of everyday lifestyles, communities, and livelihoods' (Ravetz, 2008: 4463), then squat tech experiments 'exhibit' not only alternative forms of infrastructure but also the alternative social arrangements and belief systems required for their functioning. Different perspectives on time, work ethics and social negotiation all matter as the example of the toilet shows. Some developments in this direction are visible in more mainstream settings, such as communal energy or waste water systems for sustainable dwellings, or the circulation of DIY know-how through social networks. But a deeper understanding of the interaction between social and material dimensions is required to better understand communal retrofit practices (Karvonen, 2013).

Upon this reading the commonplace view of squats as separate from mainstream society is somewhat misleading, as the people that learn from these projects are scattered across the world, often moving in and out of alternative spaces. In this sense, squat tech shines a light on what Bulkeley and Castán Broto (2013) call the art of experimentation more generally, whereby technical interventions in infrastructure provision are simultaneously social experiments that establish different relations between people. Squat tech experiments invite people to think differently about climate change because they alter their collective relations to the resource flows upon which they depend. Exploring experiments in this way opens up a more nuanced understanding of how they influence wider society through a complex set of socio-material and cultural dynamics that resists the simple evolutionary explanations of much transition thinking. In some sense then, there is no such thing as a failed experiment: they always leave traces. Our job is to follow them.

References

Barry, A. (2001). *Political Machines: Governing a Technological Society*. London: Athlone Press.

Bulkeley, H. and Castán Broto, V. (2013). Government by experiment? Global cities and the governing of climate change. *Transactions of the Institute of British Geographers*, *38*(3), 361–375.

Cordingley, L. (2004). Can Masdeu: Rise of the Rurbano Revolution. In B. Bloom and A. Bromberg (eds), *Belltown Paradise/Making Their Own Plans* (pp. 53–68). Chicago, IL: University of Chicago Press.

Davidson, M. and Leather, P. (2000). Choice or necessity? A review of the role of DIY in tackling housing repair and maintenance. *Construction Management and Economics*, *18*(7), 747–756.

DeLanda, M. (2006). *A New Philosophy of Society: Assemblage Theory and Social Complexity*. London: Continuum.

Dovey, K. (2011). Uprooting critical urbanism. *City: Analysis of Urban Trends, Culture, Theory, Policy, Action*, *15*(3–4), 347–354.

Edensor, T. (2011). Entangled agencies, material networks and repair in a building assemblage : The mutable stone of St Ann's Church, Manchester. *Transactions of the Institute of British Geographers*, *36*(2), 238–252.

Evans, J.P. (2011). Resilience, ecology and adaptation in the experimental city. *Transactions of the Institute of British Geographers*, *36*(2), 223–237.

Farías, I. (2011). The politics of urban assemblages. *City: Analysis of urban trends, culture, theory, policy, action*, *15*(3–4), 365–374.

Ingold, T. (2006). Walking the Plank: Meditations of a Process of Skill. In J.R. Dakers (ed.), *Defining Technological Literacy: Towards an Epistemological Framework* (pp. 65–80). New York: Palgrave Macmillan.

Ingold, T., and Hallam, E. (2007). Creativity and Cultural Improvisation: An Introduction. In E. Hallam and T. Ingold (eds), *Creativity and Cultural Improvisation* (pp. 1–24). Oxford, New York: Berg.

Karvonen, A. (2013). Towards systemic domestic retrofit: A social practices approach. *Building Research and Information*, 41(5), 563–574.

Lizarralde, G., and Davidson, C. (2006). Learning From The Poor. In *i-Rec Conference Proceedings: Post-disaster Reconstruction: Meeting the Stakeholders' Interest*. Florence.

Maller, C., Horne, R. and Dalton, T. (2012). Green renovations: Intersections of daily routines, housing aspirations and narratives of environmental sustainability. *Housing, Theory and Society*, 29(3), 255–275.

McFarlane, C. (2011a). Assemblage and critical urbanism. *City: Analysis of Urban Trends, Culture, Theory, Policy, Action*, 15(2), 204–224.

McFarlane, C. (2011b). *Learning the City: Knowledge and Translocal Assemblage*. Oxford: Wiley Blackwell.

Ravetz, J. (2008). State of the stock – What do we know about existing buildings and their future prospects? *Energy Policy*, 36(12), 4462–4470.

Roy, A. (2005). Urban informality: Toward an epistemology of planning. *Journal of the American Planning Association*, 71(2), 147–158.

Seyfang, G. and Smith, A. (2007). Grassroots innovations for sustainable development: Towards a new research and policy agenda. *Environmental Politics*, 16(4), 584–603.

Shove, E. and Walker, G. (2010). Governing transitions in the sustainability of everyday life. *Research Policy*, 39(4), 471–476.

Vergragt, P.J. and Brown, H.S. (2012). The challenge of energy retrofitting the residential housing stock: Grassroots innovations and socio-technical system change in Worcester, MA. *Technology Analysis and Strategic Management*, 24(4), 407–420.

Watson, M. and Shove, E. (2008). Product, competence, project and practice: DIY and the dynamics of craft consumption. *Journal of Consumer Culture*, 8(1), 69–89.

Chapter 16

Conclusion

Mike Hodson and Simon Marvin

Retrofitting cities is a deeply social and political concern. The contributions to this book have illustrated that the retrofitting of cities encompasses a wide range of perspectives, activities and social interests. From contestations as to what is to be retrofitted, why, how and by whom the chapters in this book have also shown that it is the mutual shaping of the material and the social in an urban context that what we need to be sensitive to in order to achieve systemic change. As well as how retrofit remakes the city it is important to understand how the urban context is mobilised in retrofit strategies. This mobilisation has multiple dimensions: through governance arrangements, the historically generated resources that are drawn upon, what economic, ecological, social and political problems retrofitting the city is intended to address, how the city is conceived in relation to retrofit and the frameworks of assessment and evaluation that are constructed to know whether city retrofit is having its intended effects or otherwise. This means that addressing the concern we set out at the start of this book – how cities develop the knowledge and capability to systemically reengineer their built environment and urban infrastructure in response to climate change and resource constraints – is less than straightforward.

First, it is apparent that, although cities and those who claim to speak on their behalf may be facing what seem often to be the same economic, ecological and social problems, these actually often manifest themselves variably between and within urban contexts. Not only do they manifest differently but they are also interpreted variably depending on the social interests perceiving the pressures and framing retrofit responses. The chapters in the book demonstrate this vividly – whether it is the professional forms of knowledge dominant in Ben Sim's account of seismic retrofitting of urban infrastructure, urban policy knowledge prevalent in accounts of retrofit in Cardiff, Greater Manchester (De Laurentis *et al.*) and Australian cities (Dowling *et al.*), through the promotion of urban growth coalitions via the networked cities of the C40 (Acuto) and also the absent forms of knowledge and expertise that contribute to the limited retrofitting of well-established district heating technologies in the UK (Webb). Retrofit problems and responses are also co-constructed by consumers as well as producers (Van Vleit), through both top-down and/or bottom-up forms of knowledge (Vergragt and Brown; Wendler and Evans), embodied in new intermediary organisations (Baruah), new forms of partnership and governance arrangements (Castán-Broto *et al.*), grassroots innovations (Wendler and Evans), relationships between landlords and residents (Horne *et al.*), consumer practices and changing conceptions of users (Luque-Ayala).

Second, from these different settings and the ways in which pressures for retrofit are received, interpreted and responded to, responses have a variety of elements that incorporate not only a range of social interests but which prioritise certain technologies that often aim to address issues such as increasing renewable and decentralised energy, promoting carbon reduction, and enhancing water savings and waste reduction. Yet, the scales at which this is undertaken are many, from the construction of a global network of powerful world cities in the C40 (Acuto) to the role of the consumer (Van Vleit) and from the green infrastructure of Los Angeles (Pincetl) to the living laboratory (Evans), the favelas of Sao Paulo (Luque-Ayala), district heat networks in UK cities (Webb) and slum electrification in urban India (Baruah).

Third, retrofit is configured according to different interests and forms of knowledge to construct an understanding of particular contextual problems. Technological artefacts and possibilities are integrated with existing spaces and new conceptions of spaces to configure responses to problems to which retrofit is seen as the response. Part of this configuration is not only spatial but temporal. Retrofit problems and/or responses are conceived of, for example, to address carbon reductions to 2020 and 2022 (De Laurentis *et al.*), as part of visions to 2030 (Dowling *et al.*), but also through ongoing improvisation (Baruah) and other temporal orientations or backwards, 'prior to 1971' (Sims) and beyond.

In summary then the issue of whether retrofit is a managed and purposive process is thus not straightforward. In many of the chapters, though there are attempt to manage retrofit there are also various examples of unfolding and unintended consequences and attempts to experiment and improvise (Wendler and Evans). This is not surprising given the heterogeneity of what constitutes city retrofit: the different infrastructures, different types of built environment, the variety of urban contexts – from world cities, to cities of the global south, small cities and towns and to neighbourhood, household and consumer levels and less pre-defined spatial arrangements – and their various configurations. But it also means that as well as the transformative element that is inherent to processes of retrofit it is important to recognise that complex processes of urbanisation create lock-ins and path dependencies and that the transformative potential of retrofit must always be understood in terms of its dynamic with the obduracy of existing urban socio-technical systems.

Key themes

The strength of the chapters collected in this book is in the light that they not only shed on the variety of retrofit responses but also in providing the basis for comparative exploration of retrofitting in and at city-scale. Four key themes emerge.

Retrofit is a concept with significant interpretative flexibility and multiple framings

Discussion of retrofit is commonly viewed primarily as a technical and economic feasibility issue and often focuses on a building or group of buildings. By re-thinking the relationship between retrofit and cities the contributors to this volume explicitly or implicitly go beyond techno-economic analysis, to extending the very conception of retrofit. There are competing and alternative framings of retrofit. Ben Sim's chapter, for example, focused on seismic retrofit of Californian bridges, while Michele Acuto's addressed efforts to retrofit global environmental governance as well as built environments and the role of cities within this. Stephanie Pincetl examined biogenic infrastructure, its purpose and transformative potential in mitigating negative environmental impacts and the messiness of its implementation through the case of the Million Trees initiative in Los Angeles. Each of these and other examples are discursively constructed by different coalitions of interest with various motivations.

Retrofit is about existing context as well as changing context

Discussion of retrofit often emphasises a language of transformation and reconfiguration. What the chapters in this book show is the importance of existing context in conditioning retrofit – in constraining and enabling. In many ways the multiple framings of retrofit can be linked to struggles between how contexts are organised and how coalitions of interests seek to re-organise them, shaped by politics. In Andrés Luque-Ayala's chapter, for example, the reader gets a sense of a pre-existing configuration of favelas, informal electricity supply, consumption and inequality and exclusion. It is the reconfiguration of this existing context and its values and politics that is important. The vision is one of governmental efforts to retrofit this configuration and to regularise and formalise electricity supply through configuring consumers as customers. It does this through the elements of a retrofit that involves metering, use of anti-theft cables, lowering consumption, but creating a group of users (clients, customers) who have the ability to pay and so on through creating new routines and practices. This example, along with others in this collection, shows that retrofit is a largely political and governing endeavour that involves struggles between existing and aspirational spatial socio-technical configurations.

Struggles over retrofitting context are struggles to constitute capacity

The chapters in this book have shown not only the centrality of governing to framing the retrofit agenda and setting out the problems to which retrofit is the answer but also the messy processes of undertaking or implementing retrofit in action. Given the technical, buildings, infrastructural, policy, financial (Webb) and other forms of specialist expertise that need aligning the challenge for retrofit is one of constituting capacity. Existing municipal and local authority departments are often organised in specialised divisions of labour that do not always coordinate in ways that retrofit responses require. Furthermore, given the shifts from government towards governance that have taken place in recent decades in many contexts this means that capacity is often distributed across agencies and private bodies and so not only is capacity distributed but requires significant efforts to coordinate it. This can be seen in various examples (De Laurentis *et al.*; Baruah; Dowling *et al.*; Evans). The benefits but also the difficulties of bringing together top-down approaches to retrofit with bottom-up forms of capacity were set out in Philip Vergragt and Halina Szejnwald Brown's chapter. These questions of capacity and how it is organised are likely to become more pressing rather than less so, particularly not only in an era where modernist ways of organising governing have been challenged but where, certainly in many western contexts, the ideology of austerity has gained traction. Whether coordination becomes effective or not is a challenge for governing retrofit and how it is organised.

Governing retrofit involves experiments at scale and with new forms of organisation

Forms of governing and organisation and the politics of how they shape retrofit is perhaps the key insight that this book makes. Many of the chapters highlight the ways in which social interests are organised to include and exclude and to inform the discursive construction and the material consequences of retrofit. The organisation of retrofit as the domain of world cities, their mayors and corporate actors is organised through the networked governance of the C40, the promotion of an obviousness and exclusivity (both in terms of interests and the cities involved) of the retrofit agenda (Acuto). By contrast, social interests including community action groups and grassroots activists demonstrate localised organising of grassroots innovations in Worcester, Massachusetts but also the organisational challenges of connecting such interests and agendas with more top-down responses (Vegragt and Brown). Andrés Luque-Ayala's chapter highlighted the important role for public-private partnerships in market expansion and reconfiguring consumers as customers. Bipasha Baruah detailed the ways in which intermediary organisational form sought to shape the marketised large-scale provision of electricity in urban India; and Vanesa Castán-Broto and colleagues set out the role of partnership in climate change planning in Maputo. In more micro interactions, Ralph Horne and colleagues highlighted the missing context of a shared vision between landlords and renters and the need not only for a shared vision but also more active forms of intermediation in building systematic retrofit in the rented housing sector. This highlights the possibilities, with the right organisational context, for more co-production of retrofit responses where, as Bas Van Vleit points out, a collection of networked services are integrated with roles and practices where new relationships develop beyond that of the passive or captive consumer.

Future policy and research

In short, retrofitting at city scale is a heterogeneous endeavour, as the chapters in the book have demonstrated. As a process of remaking the city, or parts of it, these responses are experimental. They can also be understood processually – as processes of making and remaking the city. This is important as it tells us that there are many processes of urban transition but also many ways of understanding urban transition. Work on urban approaches to retrofit allows us to see making and remaking through governing by experiment as involving both a processual analysis of configurations and reconfigurations, their constitution through inclusion, exclusion and negotiation.

Clearly, given this plurality of responses there is both a research and policy need to understand the range of different retrofit approaches that contribute to making and remaking the city. This means:

- First, developing a better understanding of the range of approaches to retrofitting the city through research that presents an overview of different retrofit experiments; from this there would be significant value in typologies of approaches to retrofitting the city being constructed that provide an analytical overview of the field.
- Second, working to build rich case studies of the processes of making and remaking the city through retrofit are necessary. The range of case studies would exemplify the different typology approaches to retrofitting the city in some detail. They would set out not only the elements and processes of constituting retrofit experiments but also the governing coalitions doing so and the politics and governing of this.
- Third, methodologically this requires the development of research frameworks for doing so. One can see from the chapters in this volume, but also other work on retrofitting the city that, in keeping with the heterogeneity of retrofit, there are a variety of approaches to researching

retrofitting the city. So, for example, there is engagement with literatures around socio-technical niches, living laboratories, urban and regional governance, actor-network theory, an assemblage approach, a governmentality approach and so on. This is understandable to some extent given not only the wide range of retrofit responses but also that retrofitting the city is in many ways built on novel action and the uncharted development of efforts to develop new socio-technical configurations and new ways of governing. There is an exploratory element to researching retrofitting the city. That said, as this book has demonstrated, it is important to think not only of the re-making of the city but also to keep the context of transition *from* as well as transition *to* close to hand as well. Whilst there is a productive side to this variety, it would also be helpful for a methodological overview of approaches to retrofitting the city to be developed.

There is richness to the variety of approaches that contribute to retrofitting the city in terms of their configurations and processes and organisation of governing. There is also variety in terms of the purposes of retrofitting the city and how these are negotiated. An important element of the retrofitting the city agenda that is undeveloped is what this multiplicity of approaches adds up to. In amongst the experiments and demonstrations, the assemblages and coalitions of interests, the different organisational forms, the learning by doing, changing consumption practices, and top-down and bottom-up approaches is the question: what effects do these interventions have? This is a question which relates to individual retrofit experiments but also one which has a wider resonance in terms of what the totality of retrofit approaches add up to. What sort of cities are being re-made and on what basis? This requires that research and policy develop meta-frameworks for understanding the effects of retrofit interventions in ways which take account of the multiple problems they seek to address, the retrofit responses and strategies that are constructed, the variety of governance actors and forms of organisation and the different ways in which these elements are configured. Clearly, this is a long-term agenda. This book contributes to this by setting out a range of approaches to retrofitting the city, the complexity and challenges of this agenda, but also through sketching out aspects of what needs to be done in the future.

Index